THE RIGHT OF THE CHILD TO A CLEAN ENVIRONMENT

Programme on International Rights of the Child
Series Editor: Geraldine Van Bueren

Titles in the Series:

Children's Rights and Traditional Values
Edited by Gillian Douglas and Leslie Sebba

Cultural Pluralism and the Rights of the Child
Michael Freeman

Of Innocence and Autonomy
Children, Sex and Human Rights
Eric Heinze

The Human Right to Education
Douglas Hodgson

The Child and the European Convention on Human Rights
Ursula Kilkelly

Legal Secrets, Cultural and Scientific Truths
Katherine O'Donovan

Childhood Abused
Protecting Children against Torture, Cruel, Inhuman and Degrading Treatment and Punishment
Edited by Geraldine Van Bueren

The Right of the Child to a Clean Environment
Edited by Agata Fijalkowski and Malgosia Fitzmaurice

The Right of the Child to a Clean Environment

Edited by
AGATA FIJALKOWSKI
T.M.C. Asser Institute
for Private and Public International Law,
The Hague, The Netherlands
MALGOSIA FITZMAURICE
Queen Mary and Westfield College,
University of London

Routledge
Taylor & Francis Group
LONDON AND NEW YORK

First published 2000 by Dartmouth Publishing Company and Ashgate Publishing

Reissued 2018 by Routledge
2 Park Square, Milton Park, Abingdon, Oxon OX14 4RN
711 Third Avenue, New York, NY 10017, USA

Routledge is an imprint of the Taylor & Francis Group, an informa business

A Library of Congress record exists under LC control number: 99055600

ISBN 13: 978-1-138-70791-7 (hbk)
ISBN 13: 978-1-138-70789-4 (pbk)
ISBN 13: 978-1-315-20131-3 (ebk)

Contents

List of contributors

General editor of the series:
Geraldine Van Bueren, Director of the Programme on International Rights of the Child, Faculty of Laws, Queen Mary and Westfield College, London, United Kingdom.

Editors:
Agata Fijalkowski and **Malgosia Fitzmaurice**

List of contributors:
Soledad Aguilar, Lawyer, Catholic University of Argentina.
Michael Anderson, Director of Studies, The British Institute of International and Comparative Law, London, United Kingdom.
Maria Louise Bistrup, Programme Co-ordinator, Childwatch International, Oslo, Norway.
Sylvia Bluck, Legal Consultant, The British Council, United Kingdom.
Holly Cullen, Senior Lecturer in Law, University of Durham, Durham, United Kingdom.
Maria G. Doglioli, Lawyer, University of Buenos Aires, Argentina.
Olufemi Elias, Legal Officer, United Nations Compensation Commission, Geneva, Switzerland.
Agata Fijalkowski, Editor, T.M.C. Asser Institute for Private and Public International Law, The Hague, The Netherlands.
Malgosia Fitzmaurice, Chair of Public International Law, Faculty of Laws, Queen Mary and Westfield College, London, United Kingdom.
Maaike Jansen, Consultant for UNICEF and UNEP, Regional Office for North America, New York, United States.
Marcos Oliva-Day, Co-Founder of the Fundación Patagonia Natural, Province of Santa Cruz, Patagonia, Argentina; Public Prosecutor, Court of First Instance, Puerto Deseado, Province of Santa Cruz, Patagonia, Argentina.
Harry Post, Professor of Law, University of Exeter, Exeter, United Kingdom (until 9/99, Associate Professor, Institute of Public International Law, Utrecht University, Utrecht, The Netherlands), Adjunct Professor, Department of Political Science, University of Victoria, Canada.
Veronic Wright, Director of Legal Office, Ministry of Justice, The Gambia.

Foreword

The *Right of the Child to a Clean Environment* is dedicated to a topic which has for a long time lacked in the academic world the attention it deserves. The editors have to be congratulated to have to put together this volume. The various contributions put focus on important problems in the area of environmental protection and human rights. The much-discussed problem of environmental rights has mostly been appraised from a general point of view. However, recent events such as the *Minors Oposa* case (decided by the Supreme Court of the Philippines) and the *Lopez Ostra* case (decided by the European Court of Human Rights) highlighted the problem of environmental rights of the child. Until now there has been a distinct lack of a study dealing with all the issues involved. The present book addresses in a coherent and comprehensive manner these issues by describing and analysing developments at the national, European and international level.

In the introductory remarks the reader will find an interesting and useful analysis of the issues concerning a human right to a clean environment. The contributions to this volume show in-depth research and admirable understanding to the issues involved. They assess the right of a child to a clean environment from the points of view of theory and practice, which makes the book an indispensible reading for both practitioners and theorists. The value of the book is greatly enhanced by bringing to the attention of the reader legislation from all parts of the world, thus enabling to make a comparative studies of the issues involved.

Thus, both as a theorist and a practitioner, and a participant in many United Nations projects and initiatives in the field of the environmental protection, I strongly recommend this study as a very interesting and useful contribution in the ongoing discussions on the topic. I am convinced that this volume will be most valuable for understanding the problems arising in the field of environmental protection of the child.

Professor Gerhard Loibl
Institute of International Law and International Relations, University of Vienna, Austria; Director for International Affairs, the Federal Ministry for Environment, Youth and Family Affairs, Austria

Acknowledgements

The Editors would like to thank Professor Geraldine Van Bueren, the General Editor of the series, for suggesting the timely and stimulating idea for the workshop, which resulted in this book. The Editors would also like to thank the authors for the timely submissions of their essays and for their cooperation. The Editors are grateful to the various governments and institutions which responded to the questionnaire. Further appreciation goes to the Faculty of Laws, Queen Mary and Westfield College, University of London, for invaluable assistance in organising the workshop on 'The Right of the Child to a Clean Environment', and in particular, to Mrs Julie Herd.

Series preface

The concept of international children's rights has come of age, and the Programme on International Rights of the Child Series is the first series of volumes dedicated to exploring specific aspects of international children's rights. The series comprises both sole authored and edited volumes, and single disciplinary and multi-disciplinary monographs, all considering issues which are at the rapidly expanding boundaries of international children's rights.

Geraldine Van Bueren
Series Editor
Programme on International Rights of the Child
Queen Mary and Westfield College
University of London

Introductory remarks

AGATA FIJALKOWSKI
MALGOSIA FITZMAURICE

The Right of the Child to a Clean Environment originated in the framework of The Programme on the International Rights of the Child, under the Directorship of Professor Geraldine Van Bueren. On 20 November 1997, the workshop on 'The Right of a Child to a Clean Environment' was organised at Queen Mary and Westfield College, University of London. The workshop was preceded by an extensive survey of the right of a child to a clean environment at the international and national level conducted in 1996 to 1997 by Agata Fijalkowski and Malgosia Fitzmaurice. The results of the field research thus far can be found in the Annexes I and II.

This book consists of the extended versions of some of the papers which were presented at the workshop, as well as additional contributions to the book. The workshop participants included Michael Anderson and Sylvia Bluck, Harry Post, Marcos Oliva-Day, Holly Cullen, Marie Louise Bistrup, Agata Fijalkowski, and Olufemi Elias. The additional contributors to the book are Maria G. Doglioli and Soledad Aguilar, Veronic Wright, and Maaike Jansen. The book comprises essays on general issues, selected case studies and Annexes.

The introduction is divided into three parts. In the first and second parts a general overview of the problems related to the relationship between human rights and a clean environment is presented, of which the right of a child to a clean environment constitutes an important part. In the second part the main points that are raised in the submissions are summarised.

1. Human Right to a Clean Environment – General Considerations

The most comprehensive study on the topic of the relationship between human rights and the environment has been published in 1996, *Human Approaches to Environmental Protection.*[1] In this study Anderson aptly states that several pertinent issues can be singled out. He asks, for example, 'how are environmental rights, defined, justified, and applied;

[1] *Human Rights Approaches to Environmental Protection*, (ed.) by Alan Boyle and Michael Anderson (Oxford: Clarendon Press, 1996).

and what are the advantages and disadvantages of approaching environmental issues through a rights framework?'[2] Indeed, this relationship is far from clear. Fitzmaurice observes that the outset of the whole problem of linking the environment with the issue of human rights is vague and controversial.[3] Despite the obvious doctrinal differences concerning such a right, it can be said that it may exist in several different forms, namely as a substantive right, as a procedural right or a constitutional right. Despite the doctrinal attitudes, the difficulty in determining the existence of a human right to a clean environment and its significance is not only doctrinal but also practical; its existence may imply that it can be claimed.[4] However, even if we assume that there is such a right, we do not know whether it is a 'right to an environment', or to a 'decent', 'healthy', or 'safe' environment.[5]

There are three main schools of thought relating to the relationship between human rights in general and an environmental human right. The first school strongly supports the view that there are no human rights without an environmental right.[6] In short, the above-mentioned school takes the stand that a right concerning the environment is absolutely fundamental to the existence of other human rights. In contrast, Handl disagrees with this view, and states rather that a 'generic international environmental entitlement, both as an already existing and emerging human rights concept, is a highly questionable proposition'.[7] Handl further observes that the so-called right to environment (with all the modifications, such as the right to a 'clean', or to a 'safe' environment) would be difficult to conceptualise as an inalienable right. He considers the constant changes concerning environmental protection measures as being subject to the reordering of socio-economic priorities, and to the adjustment to meet public policy objectives, i.e., ensuring the continued 'development' or 'saving jobs'. On a more practical level, Handl does not find much evidence where states have accepted the existence of a generic environmental right, which necessitates the claiming of an environmental entitlement in an indirect manner. Finally, he correctly points out that

---

2 *Ibid.*, p. 1.

3 M. Fitzmaurice, 'The Contribution of Environmental Law to the Development of Modern International Law', in *Theory of International Law at the Threshold of the 21st Century: Essays in Honour of Krzysztof Skubiszewski*, (ed.) by Jerzy Makarczyk (The Hague: Kluwer Law International, 1997), pp. 909–914, 922–925.

4 P. Cullet, 'Definition of an Environmental Right in a Human Rights Context', 13 *Netherlands Quarterly of Human Rights* (1995), pp. 25–40.

5 R. Desagne, 'Integrating Environmental Values into the European Convention on Human Rights', 89 *American Journal of International Law*, (1995), pp. 263–294.

6 *Environmental Protection*, (ed.) by A.A. Cancado Trinidade and *Human Rights in the Twenty-first Century*, (ed.) by Kathleen E. Mahoney and Paul Mahoney (Dordrecht: Martinus Nijhoff, 1993).

7 G. Handl, 'Human Rights and Protection of the Environment: A Mildly "Revisionist" Point of View', in A.A. Cancado Trinidade, (eds.) *Human Rights, Sustainable Development and the Environment* (San Jose, 1992), pp. 120–121.

environmental entitlements differ according to the area where they arise, i.e., whether they relate to the North and the South. There is also the most moderate group, which admits the existence of some environmental right, but derives its existence from other human rights.[8]

Another difficult consideration lies with the categorisation of the environmental right as being either a group right,[9] an individual right,[10] or third generation rights.[11] Third generation rights are primarily viewed as being collective in nature, with regard both to their objects and their subjects. Within this category of environmental rights belong also the right to development, the right to peace, the right to co-ownership of the common heritage of mankind and the right to communicate. Human rights experts consider these collective rights as immensely vague, some arguing, in fact, that they are so vast that they encompass anything and anybody. This approach to human rights is sometimes referred to as 'globalist', 'third worldist', or 'nationalist'.[12] Specialists of human rights attempt to find a link between human rights in general and environmental law, though it must be pointed out that these theories are not always self-explanatory. The much needed connection can found in the Preamble of the Universal Declaration of Human Rights, which refers to 'the inherent dignity and inalienable rights of all members of the human family'. The right to environment, according to this theory, derives from this dignity.[13] Another important approach bases the environmental right on the right to life and the right to health.

Another of the problems relating to an environmental human right is that the contents of this right are not specified.[14] There are many questions which remain unanswered, such as, is it a procedural right; is it a right enforceable through legal proceedings; is it merely a policy statement?[15] Some of the most prominent environmental lawyers are of the view that procedural rights have the most important role to play in the protection of

---

8 S. Weber, 'Environmental Information and the European Convention on Human Rights', 12 *Human Rights Journal* (1991), pp. 177–185. See also Sylvia Schikoff, 'Right to Clean Environment' (text unpublished, 1994).

9 For example, see M. Simon, 'The Integration and Interdependence of Culture and the Environment', in *Human Rights in the Twenty-first Century*, op. cit. n. 6, at pp. 521–528.

10 M. Kamminga, 'Mensrechten en milieubescherminng – en nuttige combinatie' ('Human Rights and Environmetal Protection – a Good Match'), *Nederlandse Tijdschrift voor Mensenrechten*, NIJCM Bulletin 18 (1993), p. 99.

11 P. Alston, 'A Third Generation of Solidarity Rights: Progressive Development of Obfuscation of International Human Rights Law', 29 *NILR*, (1982), p.309.

12 M. Galenkamp, 'Individualism versus Collectivism: The Concept of Collective Rights', Ph.D. dissertation, Erasmus University, Rotterdam (1993), p. 35.

13 A. Kiss, 'Concept and Possible Implications of the Right to Environment', in *Human Rights in the Twenty-first Century*, op. cit. n. 6, p. 55.

14 *International Law and the Environment*, ed. by Patricia Birnie and Alan E. Boyle (Oxford: Clarendon Press, 1992), p. 197.

15 Alston, op. cit. n. 11, pp. 307–322.

16 Birnie and Boyle, op. cit. n. 14, p. 196.

environmental rights, 'the existence of individual procedural rights helps shape domestic environmental policy and facilitates the resolution of transboundary conflicts through equal access to the same private law procedures'.[16] Fitzmaurice finds most convincing the view that human rights and environmental rights represent different but overlapping issues.[17] The reasoning is based on a premise that although both fields share the same objectives, it would be artificial to link them forcibly together, since not all violations of human rights have an environmental context, likewise forcing all environmental issues into the framework of human rights may damage fundamentally their concept. Only this approach seems to take into account the possibility of these two fields coming into conflict. According to these views environmental problems may be asserted through existing human rights (such as the right to life); secondly, a set of environmental rights is proposed, based upon the existing right to information; and thirdly, a specific right to environment could be formulated and added to the current catalogue of human rights.[18] This link is not entirely new. As early as 1972, the Stockholm Declaration on Human Environment stated that 'man has the fundamental right to freedom, equality and adequate conditions of life, in an environment of quality that permits a life of dignity and well-being'.[19] In comparison, the Rio Declaration UNCED 1992, in Principle I, provides only that 'human beings are in the centre of concerns for sustainable development, entitled to a healthy and productive life in harmony with nature'.[20] It is understood that the main source for this formulation was the tension between the protection of the environment and the right to economic development which reflected the conflict between the North and the South – the theme of the entire conference.[21]

Recently, however, human rights and the environment have received more attention. In 1994, the Draft Declaration of Principles on Human Rights and Environment was passed. The same year the United Nations Special Rapporteur, Madame Fatma Zohra Ksentini, issued her final Report on Human Rights and the Environment to the Sub-Commission on Prevention of Discrimination and Protection of Minorities. (For details see Annex III). The two events are assessed as 'remarkable progress in the

17 See *supra* n. 3, p. 912.
18 D. Shelton, 'Human Rights, Environmental Rights, and the Right to Environment', 103 *Stanford Journal of International Law* (1991), pp. 104–105.
19 Declaration of the United Nations Conference on Human Environment, U.N. Doc. A/Conf./48.14, Rev.1.
20 Rio Declaration (1992).
21 D. Shelton, 'What Happened in Rio to Human Rights?', 3 *Yearbook of International Environmental Law* (1992), p. 93.
22 A. F. Aguila and Neil A. Popovic, 'Lawmaking in the United Nations: The UN Study on Human Rights and the Environment', 3 *RECEIL* (1994), p. 197.

field of human rights and the environment'.[22] The Draft Declaration treats environmental rights as a comprehensive package, which presents them not as a new type of right, but rather, describes existing rights contained in the Draft Declaration as consisting of substantive rights and procedural rights. These substantive rights include the right(s) for present and future generations to: safe food and water; a safe and healthy working environment and living environment; housing in an ecologically sound environment; and the right of indigenous peoples to control their environment. The procedural rights include the right(s) to: environmental information; participation in environmental decision-making; and to environmental and human rights education.

The presentation of the environmental rights as a package deal is considered an invaluable and novel feature. In her report,[23] Ksentini addresses the relationship between human rights and the environment, using examples from the link between indigenous peoples and the environment, protection of environment during armed conflict and the question of the environment and international peace and security. She also addresses the position of the most vulnerable groups: children, disabled, environmental refugees. Ksentini stresses the very significant point that development must evolve together with environmental protection. Cameron and Mackenzie rightly point out that the Ksentini Report reflects interdependence between procedural and substantive rights.[24]

The human right to a clean environment may be distinguished between both the international and national levels. Over fifty constitutions now include the right to a clean environment. The formulations of the right to a clean environment are slightly different. For example, they impose the duty on a state to preserve and protect the environment (the Netherlands, Panama, Romania); or they declare the duty to be the responsibility of the state and of the citizens (Albania, Ethiopia, Sweden); or of the citizens (Algeria, Russian Federation) or declare that the individual has a substantive right to the clean environment (Burkina Faso) or provide for an individual right together with the individual, or collective duty of the citizens to safeguard the environment (Korea, Spain) or provide for a combination of state and citizen duties to an individual right (Chile, Colombia, Vietnam).[25]

---

23 Commission on Human Rights, Sub-Commission and Prevention of Discrimination and Protection of Minorities, 46th Session, Final Report of Further Developments in Fields with which the Sub-Commission has been Concerned, Human Rights and the Environment, E/CN.4/Sub.2/1994/9, 6 July 1994.

24 J. Cameron and R. Mackenzie, 'Access to Environmental Justice and Procedural Rights in International Institutions', in Boyle and Anderson, op. cit. n. 1, p. 133.

25 P. Sands, *Principles of International Environmental Law* (Manchester: Manchester University Press, 1995), p. 224.

Mobilising existing civil and political rights and economic, social and cultural rights, as enshrined in the 1966 UN Covenants, crosses over national and international levels. As mentioned above, several authors are of the view that human rights which already have been protected under existing international instruments and domestic constitutions may be utilised *vis-à-vis* the protection of environmental rights.[26] Civil and political rights, such as the right to life, and legal redress, are 'necessary preconditions' for mobilising environmental issues, and naming effective, claims to environmental protection'.[27] Economic, social and cultural rights, or the so-called 'second generation rights', lay the groundwork for standards for human well-being. The right to health may be useful in protecting the human right to a clean environment; equally important is the right to education, which forms a very important part of shaping human awareness about the necessity of environmental protection.

On an international level, only two regional human rights treaties expressly recognise environmental rights. Under Article 24 of the 1981 African Charter 'all peoples shall have the right to a general satisfactory environment favourable to their development'. The 1988 San Salvador Protocol to the 1969 American Charter of Human Rights, provides that '1) everyone shall have the right to live in an healthy environment and to have access to basic public services. 2) The state parties shall promote the protection, preservation and improvement of the environment' (Art.11). According to Sands, the San Salvador Protocol distinguishes between the rights of individuals 'to live in a healthy environment' and the positive obligation of states to protect, preserve, and improve the environment. Further, the same author claims that the failure of a state to carry out that obligation can give rise to an enforceable right of action.[28]

There are two international conventions, the 1989 Convention on the Rights of the Child and the 1989 Convention Concerning Indigenous and Tribal Peoples in Independent Countries, which refer explicitly to environmental matters. In the first of these documents (see *supra* and Annex III), Article 29E requires 'the development for the respect for the natural environment'. The second document calls for adoption of special measures to protect and to preserve the environment of indigenous and tribal peoples (Arts. 4, para. 1; Art. 7, para. 4). The latter convention also requires that the rights of the peoples to natural resources of their lands must be especially safeguarded (Art. 15, para. 1).

26 For example, see J.G. Merrills, 'Environmental Protection and Human Rights: Conceptual Aspects', R. Churchill, 'Environmental Rights in Existing Human Rights Treaties', and A. Harding, 'Practical Human Rights, NGOs and the Environment in Malaysia' in Boyle and Anderson, op. cit. n. 1, pp. 25–42, 89–108, and 227–244, respectively.

27 Boyle and Anderson, op. cit. n. 1. p. 5.

28 Sands, op. cit. n. 25, p. 225.

In general, the right to a clean environment can be divided into substantive rights and procedural rights. There are many proponents of the view that procedural right is more effective since it guarantees participation in decision-making on the one hand, and *locus standi* before national courts and tribunals, on the other hand. There are many examples of environmental litigation on both levels.[29]

At this juncture, we shall now turn to two landmark cases: the *Minors Oposa* case and the *Lopez Ostra* case. The *Minors Oposa* case is based on a substantive procedural right to a clean environment contained in Article II, Section 16, of the Philippines Constitution which provides 'the state shall protect and advance the right of the people to a balanced and healthful ecology in accord with the rhythm and harmony of nature'. In the Court's judgment, fundamental and significant pronouncements on the issue of intergenerational equity and responsibility were made. The concept of intergenerational equity is treated very often as part and parcel of human rights. There are several fundamental principles contained in this concept, originally presented in the framework of environmental law by Brown-Weiss.[30] The concept of intergenerational equity, as developed by Brown-Weiss, treats human beings as a part of nature. Degradation of nature has a direct effect on human beings. All generations are inherently linked to each other: present, past and future. There are no generations which are more favoured or cherished; all of them are in a position of equality. The basis of the concept is to view human community as a partnership among generations. Intergenerational equity is based on three fundamental principles. The first one is 'conservation of options', which requires each generation to observe the diversity of natural and cultural base. Future generations should be entitled to a degree of diversity comparable to that enjoyed by previous generations. The second principle is that of 'conservation of quality', the gist of which is that the next generation should enjoy the same quality of the planet as the previous generation. Finally, the third principle is that of 'conservation of access', which professes that each generation should provide its members with equitable right of access to the legacy of past generations and should conserve the access for future generations.[31] The proper summation of the complex system of intergenerational rights is found in statement that has to 'pass the planet in no worse condition than

---

29 See *Environmental Rights: Law, Litigation and Access to Justice*, ed. by S. Deimann and B. Dyssli (London: Cameron May, 1995).

30 E. Brown-Weiss, 'In Fairness to Future Generations: International Law, Common Patrimony and Intergenerational Equity', *United Nations University* (1989), and E. Brown-Weiss, 'Our Rights and Obligations to Future Generations for the Environment', 84 *American Journal International Law* (1990), p. 198.

31 *Ibid.*, 'Our Rights and Obligations to Future Generations for the Environment', p. 202.

it received it and to provide equitable access to its resources and benefits'.[32]

According to Brown-Weiss, intergenerational rights are group rights, or 'generational rights', i.e., the rights which generations may enforce against each other. Brown-Weiss construes the whole system in order to implement these rights. First of all, she proposes the appointment of an ombudsman for future generations. Other organs would be a Planetary Rights Commission to hear complaints, and the Commission for the Future of the Planet to assess the effect of present actions on future generations. She also foresees the creation of certain funds and trusts for maintaining the planet and for compensating future generations for the costs which are imposed on them.

Brown-Weiss's theory was the subject of fierce criticism. One author goes as far as to claim that if we intervene to conserve the environment to protect future generations, we are doomed to disaster. D'Amato's main criticism is based on the so-called 'Parfit Paradox', in combination with the theory of chaos. He presents a dual argument: firstly, future generations cannot have any rights because they will consist of individuals who at the moment do not exist; and, secondly, there can be no rationale behind actions and interference taken by us at the present time in terms of the effect they will have on future generations, as we do not know, what will be the requirements, or physical or psychological make-up, of these generations as a result of our input. The same author, further assesses the whole concept as anthropocentric, thus not taking into account to a sufficient degree the rights of animals.[33]

Brown-Weiss defends her approach by pointing out that intergenerational equity is a group right, thus the position of an individual is not important in the shaping of the rights of future generations. As to other criticisms, Brown-Weiss emphasises that the concept of intergenerational rights does place human beings together with other living creatures, thus not isolating them or doubting the importance of non-human creations.[34]

Other criticism derives from the human rights context. According to these critics, Brown-Weiss wrongly conceptualised human rights in relation to intergenerational equity. She extends human rights concepts (which according to this author underlines her theory), across time, 'while at the same time embracing a generic human right to a decent

32 *Ibid.*

33 Anthony D'Amato, 'Do We Owe a Duty to Future Generations to Preserve the Global Environment', 84 *AJIL* (1990), pp. 192–194.

34 Brown-Weiss op. cit. n. 30, 'Our Rights and Obligations to Future Generations for the Environment', p. 204.

environment'.[35] The same author expresses doubts as to whether the human rights context is a proper forum in which to discuss intergenerational equity, since it is unclear if environmental rights exist at all. He further argues for the possibility of the existence of such rights since they operate 'across space and time on behalf of broadly defined social and economic goods'.[36] He sees as a valid point of criticism, however, the problem relating to the needs of future generations: we do not know what future generations would be like, even less so what will be the condition of our planet in some distant future.

This justified criticism did not, however, constitute an obstacle for the Philippines Supreme Court to base in part the judgment in the *Minors Oposa* case on the concept of intergenerational equity. The plaintiffs in this case were a number of minors and Philippine Ecological Network, Inc., a non-profit organisation. The claim was tried at several instances before the courts in the Philippines. The original claim, which was filed as a tax payers' class action, was to have all existing Timber Licence Agreements cancelled.[37] Having their claim dismissed at first instance, the plaintiffs petitioned the Supreme Court to reverse the ruling. The Supreme Court reversed the ruling and the claim returned to a lower court.

The Supreme Court based its judgment on two grounds: the human right to a clean environment as enshrined in the Constitution of the Philippines and the concept of intergenerational equity. Since this case has broken new ground in environmental litigation, it merits broader discussion.

The petitioners based their claim, *inter alia*, on Section 16, Article II of the 1987 Constitution which recognises the right of people to a balanced and healthful ecology,[38] the concept of the generational genocide in criminal law and the concept of man's inalienable right to self-preservation and self-perpetuation embodied in natural law. The respondents argument was focused on the proposition that the petitioners did not succeed in alleging in their complaint a violation of any specific legal right for which relief is guaranteed by law; and that logging is a political not a legal question and should be dealt with by the executive or legislative branches not by the courts of law.

---

35 G. P. Supanich, 'The Legal Basis of Intergenerational Responsibility: An Alternative View–The Sense of Intergenerational Identity', 2 *Yearbook of International Environmental Law* (YIEL), (1992), p. 96.

36 *Ibid.*, at p. 97.

37 *Minors Oposa et al. v. Secretary of the Environment and Natural Resources Fulgencio Factoran*, 30 July 1993, reprinted in: 33 *ILM* (1994), p. 173; see also Alfred Rest, 'Implementing Principles of Intergenerational Equity and Responsibility', 24 *Environmental Policy and Law* (EPL) (1994), pp. 314–320; Antonio G.M. La Viña, 'The Right to a Sound Environment in the Philippines: The Significance of the *Minors Oposa Case*', 3 *RECIEL* (1995), p. 246.

38 'The State shall protect and advance the right of the people to a balanced and healthful ecology in accord with the rhythm of nature.'

The Court agreed with the arguments submitted by the petitioners; and that timber licensing agreements are contracts which cannot be impaired under the Constitution of the Philippines. The Court referred as well to Article II, Section 15 of the Constitution, which obliges the state to 'protect and promote the right to health of the people and instill health consciousness among them'. The Court relied on the Exec. Order No. 192 (1987), the Administrative Code, and the Philippines Environmental Policy, which introduce the general policy of environmental protection.

The position of *parens patrie* is also the position of South Africa as a result of its ratification of the Convention on the Rights of the Child.[39] The substance of the provisions of the Philippines Constitution are reflected in Sections 24 and 27 of the South African Constitution and in the jurisdictional powers of the courts. This approach is equally applicable to the industrial and urban environment. The judgment of the Philippines Supreme Court begs the question which other rights in the economic and social sphere 'exist from the inception of mankind'.[40] Poverty, like the lack of healthy ecology, also concerns nothing less than self-preservation and self-perpetuation, as the child and infant mortality rates for South Africa indicate. In situations of rapid change new juridical situations have to be found to 'see justice transformed into a true instrument of community expression'.[41]

The Court made a ground-breaking pronouncement as to the right to a clean environment and intergenerational equity as possible causes of action and as to *locus standi*. It stated that:

> [w]hile a right to a balanced and healthful ecology is to be found under the Declaration of Principles and State Policies and not under the Bill of Rights, it does not follow that it is less important than any other civil and political rights enumerated in the latter. Such a right belongs to a different category of rights altogether for it concerns self-preservation and self-perpetuation – aptly fittingly stressed by the petitioners – the advancement of which may even be said to predate all governments and constitutions. As a matter of fact, these basic rights need not even be written in the Constitution for they are assumed to exist from the inception of humankind. If they are explicitly mentioned in the fundamental charter, it is because of the well founded fear of its framers that unless rights to a balanced and healthful ecology and to health are mandated as state policies by the Constitution itself, thereby highlighting their continuing importance and imposing upon the state a solemn obligation to preserve and

39 See Geraldine Van Bueren, 'Alleviating Poverty through the Constitutional Court' (publication forthcoming, 1999).

40 *Ibid.*

41 *Ibid.*

> protect and advance the second, the day would not be too far when all else would be lost not only for the present generation, but also for those to come – generations which stand to inherit nothing but parched earth incapable of sustaining life ... The right to a balanced and healthful ecology carries with it the correlative right to refrain from impairing the environment.[42]

Equally important was the part of the judgment of the Court which dealt with the *locus standi* of the petitioners in this case.

> Petitioners instituted [the case] as a class suit ... The subject matter of the complaint is of common and general interest not just to several, but to all citizens of the Philippines. Consequently, since the parties are so numerous, it becomes impracticable, if not totally impossible, to bring all of them before the court ... This case, however, has a special and novel element. Petitioners minors assert that they represent their generation as well as generations yet unborn. We find no difficulty in ruling that they can, for themselves, for others of their generations, file a class suit. Their personality to sue on behalf of the succeeding generations can only be based on the concept of intergenerational responsibility insofar as the right to balanced and healthful ecology is concerned. Such a right ... considers the "rhythm and harmony of nature". Nature means the world created in its entirety ... Needless to say, every generation has a responsibility to the next to preserve that rhythm and harmony for the full enjoyment of a balanced and healthful ecology. Put a little differently, the minors' assertion of their right constitutes, at the same time, the performance of their obligation to ensure the protection of that right for the generations to come.[43]

The Supreme Court as well stated that licensing agreements are not contracts within the scope of the constitutional prohibition and that they are merely licences which can be withdrawn in cases when public interest or welfare are involved. Even if licensing agreements were contracts, the non-impairment clause cannot be invoked because there is no law involved.[44]

Judge Feliciano offered a second concurring opinion. First of all, he put in doubt the cause of action of the petitioners in that he did not identify a specific right on which to base their claim. The constitutional right to a balanced and healthful ecology was found by Justice Feliciano too general and not self-executing to be a sufficient cause of action. The same applies to all other laws cited by the petitioners.

He also disputed the petitioners *locus standi* on the basis of their lack of legal interest and points out that the Court's understanding of the 'class'

---

42 *Minors Oposa case*, op.cit. n. 37, pp. 187–188.
43 *Ibid*., p. 185.
44 La Viña, op. cit. n. 37, p. 248.

is too broad. Importantly, Judge Feliciano considered cancellation of timber licensing agreements a political not a legal question. Thus, he cautioned the courts not be propelled 'into the uncharted ocean of social and economic policy making'.[45]

Although the Supreme Court's decision was of ground-breaking character, it did not result in cancellation of any timber licensing agreements, and it took the judiciary three years to decide on a procedural issue. The Supreme Court, as a matter of due process, ordered that all TLA holders must be impleaded as indispensible parties, which means that evidence had to be shown against each TLA holder who numbered in the thousands. 'One can only surmise how much this will cost and how much time it will take.'[46]

Also, the decision did not prevent further depletion of the Philippines forests. Annual deforestation continues at the rate of 100,000 hectares. According to La Viña, while the case was pending 300,000 hectares of forest were lost.[47]

At the international law level, Judge Weeramantry, in his Dissenting Opinion, pointed out that the *Nuclear Test II* case[48] raised the issue of intergenerational equity (this issue has been pleaded by Professor Lauterpacht on behalf of New Zealand) as an important and rapidly developing principle of international law.[49] In relation to intergenerational equity, Judge Weeramantry saw the International Court of Justice as being the trustee of intergenerational rights to the same degree as a domestic court is a trustee of the interests of an infant unable to speak for itself, and he took the view that Court should not ignore the concept, which has found its way into the *corpus* of international law, just because of the lack of a precedent on which it may rest.

The *Lopez Ostra* case was decided by the European Court of Human Rights. It was not the first case with an environmental aspect before this court, nonetheless, in this case the court made far-reaching pronouncements in relation to ecology issues in the context of human rights.

The 1950 European Convention on the Protection of Human Rights and Fundamental Freedoms (ECHR) does not contain any specific right to a clean environment. Thus far any environmental questions which were considered by the Court were viewed in relation to other provisions of the

45 Judge Feliciano Concurring Opinion, p.205.

46 La Viña, *op. cit.* n. 37, p. 250.

47 *Ibid.*

48 *Request for an Examination of the Situation in accordance with paragraph 63 of the Court's Judgment of 20 December 1974, in the Nuclear Test case (New Zealand v. France)*, (hereafter *Nuclear Test II* case) Order of the International Court of Justice of 22 September 1995.

49 *Nuclear Test II case*, Dissenting Opinion of Judge Weeramantry at p. 17.

Convention, such as Article: 8 (right to privacy);[50] Article 3 (prohibition of torture and degrading treatment);[51] Article 2 (right to life);[52] and Article 5 (right to liberty and security as a person);[53] Article 11 (right to freedom and peaceful assembly);[54] and 6 (right of tribunal).[55] Furthermore, Article 1 of the First Protocol[56] was considered.

---

50 Article 8:1. 'Everyone has the right to respect for his private and family life. His home and correspondence. 2. There shall be no interference by a public authority with the exercise of this right except such as in accordance with the law and is necessary in a democratic society in the interest of security, public safety or the economic well-being of the country, for the prevention of disorder or crime, for the protection of health or morals, or for protection of the rights and freedoms of others.'

51 Article 3: 'No one shall be subjected to torture or to inhuman or degrading treatment or punishment'.

52 Article 2:1. 'Everyone's life shall be protected by law. No one shall be deprived of his life intentionally save in the execution of a sentence of a court following his conviction of a crime for which this penalty is provided by law. 2. Deprivation of life shall not be regarded as inflicted in contravention of this Article when it results from the use of force which is no more than absolutely necessary; a. in defence of any person from unlawful violence; b. in order to effect a lawful arrest or to prevent the escape of a person lawfully detained; c. in action lawfully taken for the purpose of quelling a riot or insurrection.

53 Article 5:1. 'Everyone has right to liberty and security of person. No one shall be deprived of his liberty save in the following cases and in accordance with a procedure prescribed by law: a. the lawful detention of a person after conviction be a competent court; b. the lawful arrest or detention of a person for non-compliance with the lawful order to secure the fulfilment of any obligation prescribed by law; c. the lawful arrest or detention of a person effected for the purpose of bringing him before the competent legal authority on reasonable suspicion of having committed an offence or when it is reasonably considered necessary to prevent his committing an offence or fleeing after having done so; d. the detention of a minor by lawful order for the purpose of education supervision or his lawful detention for the purpose of bringing him before the competent legal authority; e. the lawful detention of persons for the prevention of spreading infectious diseases, of persons of unsound mind, alcoholics or drug addicts or vagrants; f. the lawful arrest or detention of a person to prevent his effecting an unauthorized entry into the country or of a person against whom action is being taken with a view to deportation or extradition; 2. Everyone who is arrested within provisions of paragraph 1(c) of this Article shall be informed promptly, in language which he understands, of the reasons of his arrest and of any charge against him; 3. Everyone charged with a criminal offence has the following minimum rights: a to be informed promptly, in a language which he understands and in detail, of the nature and cause of the accusation against him; b. to have adequate time and facilities for the preparation of his defence; c. to defend himself in person or through legal assistance of his own choosing or, if he has no sufficient means to pay for legal assistance, to be given it free when the interests of justice so require; d. to examine or have examined witnesses on his behalf under the same conditions as witnesses against him.'

54 Article 11:1. 'Everyone has the right to freedom and peaceful assembly and to freedom of association with others, including the right to form and join trade unions for the protection of his interests; 2. No restrictions shall be placed on the exercise of these rights other than such as are prescribed by law and are necessary in a democratic society in the interests of national security or public safety, for the prevention of disorder or crime, for the protection of health or morals or the protection of the right of freedom of others. This Article shall not prevent the imposition of lawful restrictions on the exercise of these rights by members of the armed forces, of the police or of the administration of the State.'

55 Article 6: 'In the determination of his civil rights and obligations or of any criminal charge against him, everyone is entitled to a fair and public hearing within reasonable time by an independent and impartial tribunal established by law. Judgment shall be pronounced publicly but the press and public may be excluded from all or part of the trial in the interest of morals, public order or national security in a democratic society, where the interests of juveniles or the protection of the private life of the parties so require, or to the extent strictly necessary in the opinion of the court in special circumstances when publicity would prejudice the interests of justice. 2. Everyone charged with a criminal offence shall be presumed to be innocent until proved guilty according to law. 3. Everyone charged with a criminal offence had the following minimum rights; a. to be informed promptly, in a language which he understands and in detail, of the nature and cause of the accusation against him; b. to have adequate time and facilities for the preparation of his defence; c. to defend himself in person or through legal assistance of his own choosing or, if he has no sufficient means to pay for legal assistance, to be given it free when the interests of justice so require; d. to examine or have examined witnesses against him and to obtain the attendance and examination of witnesses on his behalf under the same conditions as witnesses against him.'

56 Article 1 of the First Protocol: 'Every natural or legal person is entitled to the peaceful enjoyment of his possessions. No one shall be deprived of his possessions except in the public interest and subject to the conditions provided for by law and by general principles of international law. The preceding provisions shall not, however, in any way impair the right of a State to enforce such laws as it deems necessary to control the use of property in accordance with the general interest or to secure the payment of taxes or other contributions or penalties'.

The first decision of an environmental nature appears to be that of the European Commission in case *X and Y v. Federal Republic of Germany*. The application was submitted by the members of an environmental organisation which owned 2.5 acres of land for the nature conservation. They complained that the adjacent area was used for military purposes. The Commission, however, rejected the application as incompatible *rationae materiae* with the Convention. It stated that 'no right to nature preservation is as such included among the rights and freedoms guaranteed by the Convention and in particular by Arts. 2, 3 or 5 as invoked by the Applicant'.[57] In 1981, the case X *v. Federal Republic of Germany*, the Commission, rejected the claim as 'manifestly ill-founded'.[58]

In the UK, there were many cases which concerned noise from airports, such as *Arrondelle v. United Kingdom*. In that case, the applicant complained about noise from Gatwick airport. He based his claim on Article 8 of the ECHR and on Article 1 of the First Protocol. The Commission admitted the case while recognising for the first time that environmental issues (noise) are connected with human rights matters. The second case of this type was *Baggs v. United Kindom* which was also found to be admissible. Both cases were settled outside of court.

The practice of the Commission and the Court was, however, not consistent. For example, the case of *S v. France* based on Article 8 of ECHR and Article 1 of the First Protocol was not admitted by the Commission on the grounds of having been manifestly ill-founded. The applicant complained about noise and other nuisance caused by a nearby power plant.

The *Powell and Rayner v. United Kingdom* case was yet another illustration of the Court's perception of environmental matters. This was also another airport case which related to noise generated by Heathrow Airport. Application was based on Article 8 and Article 1 of the First Protocol. The Court decided that the case was manifestly ill-founded on the above-mentioned grounds but found it admissible in part on the basis of Article 13 (right to effective remedy under domestic law).[59]

The Court has applied a test between community interests and those of an individual. The Court has found that the existence of large airports is necessary to a country's economic well-being and thus overrides environmental concerns. Moreover, the UK government has adopted

---

57 Application n. 7407/76, Dec. 135.76.D.R.15, p.161.

58 Application no. 9234/81, Dec. 14.7.81, D.R. 26, p.270.

59 Article 13: 'Everyone whose rights and freedoms as set forth in this Convention are violated shall have an effective remedy before a national court notwithstanding that the violation has been committed by a person acting in official capacity'.

measures in order to minimise noise and paid compensation to affected individuals.

In *Fredin v. Sweden,* however, the European Court has made a pronouncement that in 'today's society the protection of the environment is an increasingly important consideration'.[60] Thus the decision of the Swedish government to revoke for reasons of nature conservation the applicant's licence to extract gravel from his property did not violate Article 1 of the First Protocol.

The judgment in the *Lopez Ostra* case is, on the other hand, of a ground-breaking character. The applicant in this case was a resident in the city of Lorca, in Spain. Twelve metres from her house a plant was erected in 1988 for treatment of liquid and solid waste owned by a company SACURSA. Although the plant was built using municipal subsidies, it did not obtain the licence required for activities classified as causing nuisance. Fumes originating from the plant were polluting atmosphere in this town, especially affecting people living in its vicinity. In July 1988, the city council re-housed local residents free of charge, including the Lopez Ostra family and provided them with new apartments. In October 1992, the applicant and her family returned to the old flat and lived there until 1992, when they were re-housed again by the municipality which paid the rent of the new accommodation.

The applicant first lodged her claim on, *inter alia*, the following grounds: unlawful interference with her abode; impairment of her family's physical and mental health and safety. Courts of all instances in Spain, including the Constitutional Court, found the applicant's claim manifestly ill-founded and dismissed it. Having exhausted all local remedies, Ms Lopez Ostra brought the case before the European Court of Human Rights. The applicant based her claim on the grounds of Article 3 and Article 8, paragraph 1 of the ECHR. The Commission in Strasbourg considered the claim admissible on the grounds of Article 8 but not on the grounds of Article 3.[61] In the meantime, the plant was closed in 1992 on the judge's order, as hazardous to human health but re-opened again as a result of an appeal. Finally, the plant was temporarily closed in 1993.

The Commission found a causal link between emissions and the illness of the applicant's daughter. Subsequently, the Court, in connection with Article 8, decided that severe environmental pollution even without causing serious damage to health, can result in affecting an individual's well-being and impede enjoyment of their homes in such a manner as to affect their private and family life adversely.

---

60 ECHR, *Fredin v. Sweden* (1990) 13 EHRR 784, Series A, No. 192, 85.

61 ECHR, *Lopez Ostra v. Spain*, Series A, No.303-C; (1995) 20 EHRR. 277.

The Court made several other important pronouncements in this case. It decided to apply the test, based on Article 8, paragraphs 1 and 2, which would balance competing interests of an individual and those of the community as a whole. The Court has stated that the payment of the rent for the substitute apartment did not completely compensate for the nuisance suffered by the family for three years and that the state did not balance properly between individual and public interest – i.e., between general economic concern and private well-being.

It also found that although the plant was privately owned, the nuisance was attributable to the state. The plant was built on public grounds and subsidised by the municipality. Public authorities had knowledge of the harm caused by the plant.

There are several interesting legal points in relation to the environment which can be identified in the Court's judgment. For example, the quantification of environmental pollution. Pollution does not have to cause serious damage to human health but has to be severe in order to constitute cause of action. Another issue is the attributability of a claim to a state (see above).

The most important, however, is the fact that the European Court discerned environmental issues within the human rights structure and that even without explicit environmental right in the ECHR, it found in Article 8 a proper and sufficient link to connect these two. It also has to be emphasised that it was for the first time that the Court granted a 'green slant' to its decisions while weighing the interests of a public and economic nature against an individual environmental complaint.

In conclusion, it may be said that the Court in the *Lopez Ostra* case made the following important statements:

1. the serious effects of environmental degradation may affect an individual's well-being, since they may have adverse consequences on enjoyment of his private and family life;
2. public authorities have a duty to protect family and private life and the home; and
3. the conditions suffered by the family of the applicant did not amount to degrading treatment according to Article 3 of the ECHR.

2. Special Position of Children

Questions have been raised as to whether all categories of international human rights apply to children as well as adults. The answer to this question begins first and foremost at the beginning of the twentieth century, when the development of international law on the rights of the child evolved alongside the general body of international human rights law. The matter of the legal status of the child is very complicated and a thorough consideration of this problem is beyond the consideration of this book.[62] Suffice to say that the nature of this problem has been the subject of fierce debate throughout history.[63] Van Bueren divides the development of international law on the rights of the child into three stages.[64] The first stage was marked by the recognition of the international community that all persons, children included, required the protection of international law. The second stage concerns granting children specific substantive rights; this stage is still evolving. The third stage, which is also a developing area, relates to the recognition that in order to guarantee that persons are able to exercise their basic rights they must be granted the procedural right to claim these rights and freedoms.

Generally speaking, the position of the child is different from that of an adult. The child, under normal circumstances, does not have access to legal procedures or other facilities. The 1989 Convention on the Rights of the Child (CRC) was a significant landmark in that it symbolised the fundamental change of attitudes of states towards the status of children under domestic law. In consequence, the CRC can be said to be far-reaching, as is evidenced by the most contemporary constitutions of the world (such as the Constitution of the Republic of South Africa), which grant *locus standi* to children in order to address their environmental rights.[65]

Simply put, the main difference between the rights of adults and children is that they are not identical. For example, participatory rights, which are applicable and are dependent on the application of the evolving capacity of the child, so as to condition them with age and maturity. An excellent example of this is the Finnish case.[66] A further difficulty is in the precise definition of the rights of the child and also the lack of a definition as to who is a child. Article 1 of the CRC provides that 'for the purposes of

---

62 For an excellent, in-depth analysis of this development see Geraldine Van Bueren, *The International Law on the Rights of the Child* (Dordrecht: Martinus Nijhoff, 1995).

63 *Ibid.*, p. 5.

64 *Ibid.*, p. 1.

65 See Annexes I and II.

66 See Annex II, in particular the amendment to the Finnish Constitution with regards to environmental rights.

the present convention a child means every human being below the age of 18 years ...' Nonetheless, the Convention provides for state discretion; thus national laws determine when childhood should begin to count. This is a universal problem that is far-reaching and involves, for example, the areas of environmental rights and criminology. The same discretion is granted to the state in formulating the upper age limit at which childhood ends. According to the CRC, 18 years of age is the upper limit.

The right of a child to a clean environment, as all other rights of children, is conditioned by cultural and religious considerations. The right of the child to a clean environment is as special and as different as other rights of the child. According to Van Bueren, the Convention is interpreted according to new principles, the best interests of the child and the evolving capacities of the child. Can this extend to environmental law? The principles of interpretation provided for in the Convention cannot be said to be universally applicable to interpretation of the right of the child to a clean environment.[67] As is evidenced in the contributions and Annexes, the variety of legal regulations do not permit drawing any uniform conclusions as to interpretation of this right nationally or internationally.

In our view, elaboration of general principles of environmental rights of the child will develop in time, when the right itself is more specified and defined. Unlike other rights of the child, this right is still very fluid and vague, not only in relation to the child but also in general, as mentioned above. This, coupled with differences in the definition of the child and its general position in law, make it almost impossible at present to draw general conclusions. Nonetheless, the development of the right of the child to a clean environment fits certain patterns (for example see the South African Constitution), which was specified by Van Bueren in her analysis of the right of the child in a general context.

3. An Overview of the Essays

There is not any international law instrument in existence which explicitly grants a child the right to a clean environment. Nonetheless the are some international agreements which indirectly deal with this issue. The most important ones are the International Labour Organisation (ILO) Conventions which establish environmental standards for children within the work context and the general convention on the rights of a child, i.e. United Nation Convention on the Rights of the Child (CRC).

---

67 Van Bueren, op. cit. no. 62, pp. 45 et seq.

In her essay, Cullen argues that the idea of a right to a clean environment can be extended to conditions of labour. The problem at hand comprises several issues which are problematic to define, for example, the extent of child labour. The complex question of child labour is not only a relevant issue in developing countries, or countries in economic transition, but it also has been considered a problem in Western Europe. The International Labour Organisation (ILO) has conducted in-depth studies in the relation to this problem. The ILO defines child labour as both a consequence and a cause of poverty. Environmental hazards, which affect adults, will affect children even more strongly. The Convention on the Rights of the Child (CRC) contains in Articles 6 and 24 the right of the child to life and to health. Article 6 guarantees the right of the child to be free from economic exploitation. This Article does not mention environmental hazards, but does refer to an obligation to prohibit work which would interfere with health or physical development, which is implicated where environmental hazards are present. The ILO has been setting international standards on child labour since 1919. The most important document in this field is the Minimum Age Convention of 1973. Nonetheless, this Convention, even if it had been widely ratified, is insufficient to cover all children who are engaged in hazardous labour and allows member states numerous exemptions. In addition, the ILO adopted a number of conventions which relate to child labour in specific sectors, such as, the 1921 Minimum Age (Agriculture) Convention. As stated above, however, all these instruments have not proven to be entirely successful.

As far as it relates to international environmental law and international human rights law, they present limited but significant convergence, in particular, in connection with non-material values. Some relevance to child labour may be found in general environmental human rights as codified in regional conventions. The role of NGOs has to be stressed in this field. One of the problems which relates to child labour concerns justiciability to enforce the right of child workers to be protected from environmental hazards. Cullen proposes certain solutions to the problem of environmentally hazardous child labour. Along these lines, she asserts that there are two main approaches to the elimination of child labour: the 'trade' approach and the 'development' approach. Education is also seen as an important tool for the elimination of child labour, due to increased earning power in the long-term which results in the reduction of poverty. In general, she concludes that the approach to child labour protection from environmental hazards will be a multifaceted approach. To further these purposes, a new ILO convention is to be drawn up, which will relate to the most extreme forms of child labour.

It should be noted that the extent of child labour is almost impossible to assess; it can only be estimated by the ILO. It is even difficult to state with absolute certainty whether child labour has increased or decreased. The recent estimated number of child workers aged 5–14 is 250 million world-wide. Africa has the highest number of child workers in the world, with an estimated 40 per cent of children between 5 and 14 years working.[68]

Environmental hazards have harsher effects on children than adults especially in the context of labour. The ILO has specified a list of hazardous substances which affect a child worker in different fields of labour. (For example, in commercial agriculture, fertilisers, herbicides, and pesticides are often handled by children.) Children who work in food processing plants come into contact with certain substances that can be fatal for their health. In Sri Lanka, for example, mortality of children due to exposure of substances used in commercial agriculture is more extensive than from all other diseases combined. In manufacturing, such as for example the leather industry, children are exposed to carcinogens such a benzene solvent and glues which result in neurotoxicity.

Children are victims of other hazards such as noise pollution found in glass and ceramic factories. Child labour has been defined by the ILO as 'a denial of the right to education and the opportunity to reach full physical and psychological development'.

As indicated above the ILO has been establishing standards on child labour since its creation in 1919. The Minimum Age Convention (No. 138, 1973) codifies these standards. It has been, however, ratified only by 49 out of the 174 member states of the ILO. This Convention's main purpose is to reduce the age at which children may enter employment,[69] not to protect them from environmental hazards.

Cullen points out that the right of child workers to be protected from environmental hazards face the same difficulties in relation to justiciability when attempting to enforce them, as other environmental rights.

Article 1 establishes the minimum age for employment 'to a level consistent with the fullest physical and mental development of young persons'. An important provision is contained in Article 18 which sets the minimum age for hazardous work at 18, with the lower age of 16, only applicable if the health, safety and morals of a child are fully protected or she or he has received adequate training in the work. The Minimum Age

68 International Labour Organisation – Programme on the Elimination of Child Labour (IPEC), Child Labour in Commercial Agriculture in Africa, Dar es Salaam, United Republic of Tanzania, 27–30 August 1996(Geneva, 1997), paragraph 7, cited in Chapter 1.

69 Article 2 provides that the age 'shall be no less than the end of compulsory schooling and at least 15'. Developing countries may set initially the age at 14. Article 7 allows for light work for children between ages of 13 and 15 and in developing countries between the ages of 12 and 14.

Convention contains several exceptions in application which make it a weak instrument even when ratified. For example, the exclusion for developing countries is provided for in Article 5 and concerns 'family and small-scale holdings producing for local consumption and not regularly employing hired workers'. Article 4 allows member states, after consultations with employers and workers' organisations, to exclude any category of work where 'special and substantial problems arise'. The decision to exclude must be justified in states' reports to the ILO on their implementation of the Convention. According to the Convention, however, many hazardous forms of work such as mining and large-scale agriculture, must be within the scope of the Convention. It must be mentioned that the ILO has adopted conventions which relate to minimum age within particular sectors of labour, such as the Minimum Age (Agriculture) Convention, 1921. The main purpose of this Convention is 'reconciling demands of school and agricultural work for young children rather than banning it altogether'.

The ILO being mindful that many states did not ratify the 1973 Convention because it is too rigid, is at present in the process of preparing a new Convention to be ready for signing in 1999.

It is possible to be eligible for compensation once the harm has been done, through national health and safety legislation or tort/delict law, nonetheless, as in all cases of environmental damage prevention is more effective than remedies afterwards. As mentioned above Cullen identifies two approaches to the elimination of child labour. The 'trade approach' is preferred by international and non-governmental organisations (NGOs) and the development approach was elaborated by the United States and introduced in the context of the European Union. The trade approach is based on, for example, introduction of trade sanctions or consumer boycotts of products made with child labour. This approach, however, was met with opposition from developing countries which put forward the argument that boycotting products made by children does very little for child workers. Bans of this nature have often an undesirable effect such as children resorting to more hazardous forms of labour than the boycotted one.

Other initiatives proposed by the United States, such as labelling of products as manufactured without the use of child labour, are very difficult to implement on a world-wide level due to imperfect monitoring. Equally problematic is the inclusion of social clauses in trade agreements, such as the WTO/GATT Agreement, which would be against the law of these organisations.

Less controversial, but no less difficult to implement, is the 'development' approach. This would be based on assistance for developing countries and through this assistance achieving transfer of children from work to education.

There is no comprehensive international instrument which protects the child worker from environmental labour hazards. Nonetheless, existing ILO Conventions, although imperfect, provide a minimum standard.

There are, as well, numerous recommendations adopted by the ILO, which, although non-binding, provide guidance for member states, and fill the lacunae in the ILO Conventions and their implementation by member states is monitored by the ILO. The ILO has adopted several important recommendations in relation to child labour. For example in the Recommendation on the child worker in agricultural sector which supplements the 1973 Convention, it states that when it is not immediately feasible to fix a minimum age for all employment in agriculture, a minimum age should be fixed at least for employment on plantations and in other agricultural undertakings referred to in Article 5, paragraph 3 of the 1973 Convention.

Jansen's essay stresses that the key provisions of the Convention cannot be honoured and implemented without addressing the environment as a key determinant of their realisation. This applies particularly to the right to life, survival and development and to the highest possible standard of health, which are universal and part of the inalienable rights of the child. Jansen aptly points out that the Convention is an important tool to ensure environmental protection, by providing a legal and ethical framework for the effective implementation of, *inter alia*, sustainable development as envisaged by Agenda 21, with linkages between poverty, environmental degradation and impairment of children's health. It must be pointed out that there are few instruments of binding legal character, leading to the development of practices whereby the procedural bases for enforcing the right become more firmly rooted and the complaints of violations based on environmental considerations are addressed.

The contribution of Anderson and Bluck provides a detailed survey of the developments relating to children and environmental protection in India.

An examination of the legislation on children reveals that many of the statutes date back to the colonial regime of 1880. The legislation of that time did recognise the vulnerability of children to environmental harm, but at the same time it treated children as passive and helpless objects of protection. There are examples where the legislation, especially from the colonial period, does not recognise the legal capacity of children. This depravation denies children their full range of legal powers as concerns the environment.

Children have featured prominently in the NGO environmental movement in India. They have thus been shaping the environment around them. The Indian courts have been adjudicating in environmental matters, and there have been positive trends in this respect. One of areas where children can further shape the environment is to provide them with procedural capacity, and that in the event they are unable to do so, others will need to act on their behalf.

There are three important specific areas that relate to different stages of the child's life to illustrate the legal problems which may arise in formulating a child's right to a clean and healthy environment in India. These three areas are: the unborn child and environmental protection; infants and atmospheric pollution; and children and work. As regards the first area, one of the controversial questions which naturally arises is the existence of rights of the unborn child. There is clear evidence that environmental hazards can affect the unborn child and various studies show that the womb is susceptible to external environmental factors. The manner in which to formulate an environmental right is tricky, as granting legal personality to the unborn child does not seem to be the most effective solution. With regards to the second aspect, again, studies have shown that indoor air pollution is extremely detrimental to the health. Providing solutions to this dilemma is also difficult, because it is tied to religious beliefs and poverty. Finally, in the third area, children are exposed to dangerous conditions at work, and further discriminated by not being able to benefit as workers from established safety standards.

The working conditions of children employed in industry received a great deal of attention. For example, children working in the carpet industry in Kashmir are exposed to fibres and dust in the air, 60 per cent have asthma and TB. Children at work are discriminated against in terms of health and safety regulations, and in terms of self-organisation. This situation is partly due to laws in force which excludes from representation the child labour in the formal sector, such as 1926 Trade Union Act which bans children under 15 from participation in trade unions. However, about 80 per cent of children work in the informal sector, such as small businesses or at home. These children cannot benefit from health and safety standards established in the formal sector. Thus children in the informal sector are exposed to a greater extent to environmental hazards.

India has an extensive system of environmental law in the form of statutory regulation, criminal law and tort. However, the operation of the law in practice has not lived up to its standards. As Anderson and Bluck point out, the problems of using the existing environmental regime has been a key factor in the development of the constitutional route as a means of litigating environmental issues. Article 21 of the Indian Constitution has provided the opportunity for environmental conflicts to be resolved. At the same time, it is hard to see how this Article could be used in relation to some of the principal issues affecting children, such as indoor pollution, the direct cause of which is the child's family environment.

Post reviews the situation in European Community law with regard to human rights generally and focuses on the relation to possible rights of children in connection with the environment, which in his view, is very far from clear. Indeed, the only clear-cut statement that can be made is, as observed by Post, that '... in Community law, explicitly, there is no distinct right of the child to a clean environment'. However, Post does not rule out the possibility that there does exist in the European Union some indirect, general or composite rights which may 'materially amount to comparable (or more specific) guarantees as a right of the child to a clean environment, but [which] would have a more "indirect" nature'. Furthermore, according to Post, under EC law an assumption may be made that individuals (including children) – or those acting on their behalf – 'should be able to make claims corresponding to relevant substantive and procedural duties of states'; and that they should be able to do so either directly at the European Court of Justice (ECJ) in Luxembourg, or at the European Court of Human Rights in Strasbourg, or indirectly, by way of the national courts in Member States. In the latter case, Post is discussing derived rights, and in all other cases, direct rights. Still, it has to be emphasised that a direct claim under such a right, by an individual, or by a group representing its members' interests, or by a group representing the interests of others, before the ECJ, is currently virtually excluded under existing conditions in relation to interpretation of Article 173 of the Rome Treaty. When the Treaty of Amsterdam has entered into force, however, it may be assumed that greater importance may be accorded to the European Union as a guarantor of human rights. Post also finds that in the light of existing case law, the European Court of Human Rights does not seem the most logical court to develop this field. One of the more difficult aspects of a general right to a clean environment under European law is, indeed, the relationship between EU law and European human rights law. Due to the fact that the EU has neither a bill of rights nor is itself operating within the framework of the European Convention on Human Rights, it is left for the human rights court to ensure that a legal structure is maintained in which the protection of fundamental human rights is guaranteed.

As far as 'derived' human rights within European law are concerned, this term is meant to indicate that a distinction is maintained as against 'direct' rights of individuals (including children). Direct rights are explicitly guaranteed and are potentially directly enforceable at the international level, including the Community level, whereas derived rights may exist in the form of duties by Member States which by way of the direct effect can be claimed by an individual or, in the case of collective rights, by individuals or their representatives, before a national court – which, indeed, are the ordinary courts of Community law.

The definition of who is a child and whether a child is entitled to claim independently under Community law is a matter which is left to the individual member states. In fact, only in respect to some specific subjects is youth mentioned at all under European law.

As a direct beneficiary to the human right to a clean environment, the child is not referred to at all in Community legislation. Thus others, such as interest groups, claiming on behalf of children, would be the main source of the enforcement of whatever rights they may in fact have. In general, in relation to *locus standi*, EC law has two basic approaches, one is restrictive, in that only those who are directly affected by EU rules have *locus standi* and the right to invoke Community law before national law; and the other, broader approach, would allow any citizen rights under EC law, whether or not that individual is directly affected. In relation to children, however, even this broader view is not much help, since children have very limited 'subject status'. This situation, to a large extent, results in children being dependent on a citizen's action on their behalf even if they are directly affected. There are other legal obstacles under EU law which prevent children from claiming their environmental rights, such as: that a challenge to the way directives are implemented cannot be lodged, as Post puts it 'horizontally'– i.e., against private individuals; that if interest groups are involved, they encounter difficulties in convincing a court as to the substance of their claim and thus denied the granting of a remedy; and, finally, that the interest groups may be burdened with the issue of costs.

As to substantive law, there are a quite a number of provisions under EC law with direct effect which are relevant to rights of children to a clean environment. These provisions, accessible by way of national courts, may be used to challenge acts of national authorities which more indirectly lead – or may lead – to the degradation of the environment of children. In the realm of environmental provisions with direct effect, which have relevance to children's rights, secondary instruments appear to be more effective.

Post shows that under the EU Treaty there is in fact a plethora of substantive and individual rights, and that potential rights are also available. It would further seem that the most significant legal basis for EU environmental rights outside the EC Treaty itself is to be found in the Euratom Treaty. Post concludes that notwithstanding the legal obstacles that exist, the difficult situation in regard to a direct right of the child to a clean environment under EU law is mitigated to a great deal by the existence of a large body of potentially enforceable derived rights.

One of the questions which are unclear under European law is the *locus standi* of NGOs before the European Court of Justice. NGOs play a fundamental role in the development of human rights and the environmental rules. Thus there is a direct link between the procedural right of a child to a clean environment and the *locus standi* of NGOs.

One of the most important cases was launched by Greenpeace. On 2 April 1998, the European Court of Justice made an important judgment in the appeal in the Greenpeace case: *Stichting Greenpeace Council (Greenpeace International and Others v. Commission of the European Communities)*.

The Court dismissed the appeal from the order of the European Court of First Instance (CFI). As Scott stresses this case is important for various reasons, including the EU operation of developmental policy and of the environmental sustainability of the projects it finances and that it relates to the broader issue of 'access of justice' in the EU legal order.[70] The case originated from the decision of the European Commission as to release of a second 'tranche' of funding for the construction of two coal-fired power stations in the Canary Islands. Greenpeace International protested against funding of a project which, according to Greenpeace, was in contravention of the EU international commitments, i.e. in respect of elimination of carbon dioxide emission which contributes to global warming. Greenpeace claimed that such a decision was illegal in the view of a 1985 Community Directive (Council Directive 85/337), on compulsory 'environmental impact assessment' which has to be complied with prior to release of funds. Further, Greenpeace argued that the decision of the Commission to release the funds was in contravention of Community law, since the law requires that all projects which are financed from the European structural funds be consistent with environmental law and policy. Scott further elaborates that the concept of environmental compatibility is a very political one since it was introduced into the EU legislation as a result of campaign of environmental NGOs, in particular World Wide Fund for Nature (WWF).

The application was dismissed, however, on the procedural grounds, i.e. that none of the parties which brought the case before the Court including Greenpeace had the *locus standi* before it. Thus the decision of the ECJ did not enter the discussion on the merits of the case. From this

70 Joanne Scott, 'Greenpeace in Europe', 1, *Queen Mary and Westfield College Law Journal*, 1 (1988), p. 22; see also by the same author, *'Access to Environmental Justice in the European Community: Problems and Proposals'*, 4, RECIEL (1996) issue 3, pp. 206–224.

follows that the legality of the Commission's decision was not scrutinised. The lack of 'sufficient interest' constituted a bar on pleading the case before the Court. None of the parties in the case, i.e., Greenpeace (and other individual parties, such as a local fisherman, a taxi driver, doctor, windsurfer, and an ornithologist) had legal standing before the Court. This question is regulated in a very narrow manner in European law. We have to refer here to Article 173 of the EC Treaty (see above) which is based on the concept of 'individual concern'.

The individuals have to demonstrate that the contested decision affects them by reason of certain attributes which are peculiar to them or by reason of circumstances in which they are differentiated from all other persons and by virtue of these factors, distinguishes them individually just as in the case of a person being addressed. Both the CFI and ECJ found that the individuals in this case did not have sufficient legal standing because all residents of the island, present or future will be affected by the decision of the Commission in the same manner. Therefore the applicants could not claim any particular features which distinguished them from other groups in order to merit granting them *locus standi*.

The ECJ not only interpreted in a narrow manner Article 173 in relation to the individuals, but also denied legal standing to Greenpeace, an applicant association. By this the ECJ elucidated that associations do not enjoy more legal privileges than individuals and must strictly comply with the requirements of Article 173. Thus associations in order to protect common interests must prove that the individual members are 'individually concerned' so as to conform with the interpretation of Article 173.

The judgment of the ECJ is strongly criticised by Scott. She points out inconsistencies of ECJ jurisprudence. Initially it has promoted the effective application of Community law in terms of its proper enforcement against member states; and subsequently it has taken a restrictive approach as to *legal standing* of an individual who is advocating the proper application of Community law by its own institutions, such as the Commission in this case. Moreover, she argues, this decision does not allay the feelings of resentment towards the Community in relation to alienation of individuals and deepens a 'democratic deficit' of law-making within the Commission, which is not an elected body and acts on the basis of delegated power and whose proceedings are not sufficiently transparent.[71]

Concerning case studies, Argentina provides an interesting study as concerns the constitutional right to a clean environment and the NGO's participation in the implementation of this right. The Constitution of Argentina was amended in 1994 to include an explicit right to a clean environment. This reform was the result of a 1983 leading case relating to a duty of environmental impact assessment. Before the amendment of the Constitution the right to a clean environment was based on Article 33 of the Constitution which, *inter alia*, required the state to perform the necessary environmental impact assessment emanating from the state's obligation to promote the general well-being enshrined in the Preamble of the Constitution. In 1994, the amended Constitution introduced the explicit right to a clean environment which was included in the group of third generation rights (Art. 41). This Article is based on the principle of intergenerational equity. Nonetheless, the formulation of this article is rather vague and undoubtedly will give rise to many interpretations.

The legal content of this right means that any citizen has the right to a protected environment in that it can only be exploited in a way that will not degrade it, i.e., even though a citizen has no individual right with respect to natural resources, which are known by other persons or by the state, he or she has a right to claim that the activities of this state are conducted in a sustainable manner. At present, the consequences of this right are very hard to envisage. Aguilar, Doglioli and Oliva-Day claim that the right as formulated in Article 41 is not sufficient to make it operative. The procedural instrument which gives *locus standi* to a claim to a right to a clean environment is based in the writ of so-called '*amparo*'. This writ is a procedural guarantee which consists of a brief and summary action in order to protect all constitutional rights except for physical freedom which is protected by the principle of *habeas corpus*. The writ of *amparo* is applicable in cases which require summary procedure. This was also enshrined in the 1994 constitutional reform.

Fijalkowski, in her study on Polish environmental legislation provides an overview of the ecological devastation, the result of mismanagement and heavy industry of the nearly fifty years of communism. The many years of negligence and inaction have certainly left their mark, most notably with regards to the atmosphere and water. In the 1980s, for example, the residents of the most contaminated areas of the country showed signs of genetic diseases.

At present, Poland, in an effort to bring into line their legislation with that of the European Union, has set short and long-term goals. Polish environmental law dates back to 1980 and with the recent 1997 developments the environmental law will probably set a new path for the protection of the environment. Indeed, the Preamble of the 1997 Constitution pledges that citizens have a right to clean environment in addition to several constitutional provisions. The State Inspectorate for Environmental Protection plays a key role in the protection of the

71 Scott, op. cit. n. 70, pp. 23–24.

environment. The Polish Criminal Code, in force since September 1998, also considers protection of the environment.

As regards the rights of children, Poland has been pioneering in this field, having ratified the CRC in 1991. Polish legislation conforms with the most salient points of the CRC. While there is no right to a clean environment in Poland, children are ensured the right to a certain standard of living and they are also guaranteed health care.

At present Polish environmental legislation is first and foremost concerned with addressing the damage from the Communist era and to satisfy its requirements for the market democracies. Yet, recent amendments may provide legal grounds for a child to protect his or her right to a clean environment. NGOs can play an important role in stressing the particular rights of a child. Local initiatives, which involve international assistance, are significant. Finally, education can play a key role in furthering public awareness about the environment.

Elias provides a profound analysis of legislation concerning the environment and the rights of the child. He begins with an overview of Nigerian legislation. Nigeria's successive military regimes have made giving effect to international obligations at the national level of little consequence. The federal government always reserves the right to make international treaties which can apply throughout the country, with provincial governments being powerless to refuse effect.

The African Charter on Human and People's Rights has been ratified by Nigeria. The government has also drafted a Children Decree based on the CRC and the African Charter on the Rights and Welfare of the Child; these have yet to be passed into law.

There is some ground for expecting that the rules on the status of international law can provide a basis for the treaty framework of rights to a decent environment within the country. Based on his findings, Elias argues for a human rights approach to environmental protection, even if the relevant environmental rights can be assimilated to a human right provided for in a treaty to which Nigeria is a party, whereby they assume the same status as a human right.

An investigation of Nigerian national law, in particular in torts law, as concerns land, nuisance, negligence and liability is found under the rule established in the nineteenth-century English case *Rylands v. Fletcher*. The rule in this case has proved more useful from the point of view of environmental protection. The main reason for this is that the strict liability tort applies where the offender has brought onto the land in the course of a non-natural user of the land something which is likely to cause harm. The subsequent case law has indicated trends where the common law of torts has been used as a means of protecting the environment, albeit limited. Elias notes that there is usually no practical need for a separate right of a child to bring any of these actions, since children do not normally suffer separately from those they live with, who would normally bring these actions.

As regards public law, the most relevant legal principle is that of public nuisance, although efforts towards environmental protection also have been limited. The right to bring an action in public nuisance then lies with the Attorney-General. Because public nuisance is criminal in nature the conflict of interest which might arise where the polluter is a public body gives rise to interesting legal questions.

Finally, Elias provides a summary of the existing statutes in Nigerian law which relate to environmental protection. The general leading statute, the Federal Environmental Agency Decree of 1988, led to the establishment of the Federal Environmental Protection Agency. The Decree is the first attempt to set up a comprehensive environmental regime. Whilst the Agency has been active in issuing several guidelines on environmental protection, it does not have binding force. In short, the effect of this Decree, alongside related statutes, is yet to be felt. In conclusion, it can be said that the human right to a clean environment is still very much in *statu nascendi*.

Wright submits that in The Gambia there is no universal definition of child. The child is defined differently depending on statute. For example, for the purpose of criminal law, a child under seven years of age is not capable of committing a criminal act. A child, however, under fourteen but above seven years of age can be criminally liable if it can be proved that he or she is aware of the nature of the act. The Children and Young Persons Act fixes the age of a child at under fourteen years of age and of young adult at above fourteen but under eighteen years of age. The Maintenance of Children Act defines a child as someone below twenty-one years of age who sooner marries. Voting rights are guaranteed by the Constitution to persons of from eighteen years of age. Although the 1996 Constitution of The Gambia does not include a direct environmental right, it states under the chapter 'Directive Principle of State Policy' subsection 3 that '[t]he State shall pursue a policy of … protecting the environment of the nation for posterity, and … co-operation with other nations and bodies to protect the global environment'. The Constitution also grants other rights, summation of which amounts to the right to a clean environment, such as public health and safety, town and country planning, and inhuman and degrading treatment. The new Constitution includes for the first time a section on the rights of a child. These rights, however, are reflective of the obligations of The Gambia under the ILO and the CRC conventions and 1966 Human Rights Covenants.

In 1994, the Gambian Parliament promulgated the National Environment Management Act as a framework legislation to provide the control and management of the environment. The Preamble of this Act sets the goal of assurance of the fundamental right to an environment adequate for the 'health and well-being of all people living in the country; the necessity to protect and improve the health and quality of life of all Gambians; increase in environmental awareness and public participation in environmental management; prevention or control of pollution; and promotion of international co-operation in environmental protection.' The Preamble also recognises the need 'to conserve and promote the national use of natural resources for the benefit of present and future generations'.

The Act introduces the duty of an individual to maintain and enhance the quality of the environment. It also contains a very important provision namely, it confers *locus standi* on citizens, both adults and minors, to sue on their own behalf and on behalf of every other person in the country, anybody who pollutes any segment of the environment. It is not clear, however, what remedies are available to a plaintiff under this Act. This provision has not yet been tested in a court. The Gambia has introduced environmental compulsory education in schools for children.

It is hoped the Environmental Education programme will promote awareness of the environment. This programme was designed to achieve the specific objective of raising the level of knowledge and skills in environmental management and to influence the attitudes of future generations. It is worth noting that The Gambia has a policy of compulsory primary education for all children. The introduction of environmental education into the school curriculum means that a majority of children will attain early knowledge on issues relating to environmental management.

Finally, it is noted that The Gambia ratified the African Charter on 8 June 1983. Although the state is bound to observe its obligations under international law, there is no provision for the direct enforcement of the Charter in Gambian courts under Gambian law.

The role of NGOs is the subject-matter of the essays of Oliva-Day and Bistrup. Argentina can boast very active environmental NGOs. One of these NGOs is the topic of the case study, Fundación Patagonia Natural, in the province of Santa Cruz, Patagonia. This foundation organises a course which aims to introduce the children of Puerto Desuado to the history, geography and wildlife of the place they live in. The course is focused on sporting events especially designed for underprivileged and socially disadvantaged children. This course is intended to fully integrate them in the community and to assist them in acquiring the understanding of the issues that contribute to a clean environment. The foundation is based on three pillars: geography, history and the environment. It tries to educate the children in the spirit of respect and tradition. It organises the meetings with the elderly people of community. This NGO is very active in primary school education. The students have the opportunity to meet scientists, environmentalists and members of other NGOs.

Bistrup emphasises the role of NGOs in the protection of the child from environmental hazards, in particular the work of Childwatch International. This organisation monitors the situation of children in the countries which are parties to the CRC. It works very closely with UNICEF and other NGOs. It has established an extensive network of contacts worldwide, linked by the same purpose. As mentioned above, the main tasks of Childwatch International are focused on various aims deriving from the CRC. It promotes an interdisciplinary approach to child research, the effective dissemination of results of child research to the public, identification of global issues to be included in the agenda for child research and initiation of new projects.

PART I

RIGHT OF THE CHILD TO A CLEAN ENVIRONMENT AT INTERNATIONAL AND EUROPEAN LEVELS

1 The right of child workers to protection from environmental hazards[1]

HOLLY CULLEN

1. Introduction

The idea of a right to a clean environment, sometimes described as a 'healthy' or 'decent' environment, is still controversial in international law.[2] Environmental harm is often seen as too vague and 'victimless' to support the concept of a legal right. Sometimes it is conceptualised as an extrapolation of the right to life, the right to health or other existing human rights[3] but this formulation is possibly too individualist to express all aspects of the right to a clean environment.[4] Many formulations of the right to a clean environment discuss the duties of states much more than the rights of individuals, and, unlike most human rights instruments, some impose duties directly on individuals.[5] Whatever the exact substantive content of the right, Kiss identifies three procedural elements: information, participation and means of redress or remedy.[6] Although no universal binding treaty enshrining the right to a healthy environment exists, statements from the international community, beginning with the Stockholm Declaration of 1972, may show the beginnings of how such a right may be understood.[7] It is, nonetheless, too controversial for there to

1 The author would like to thank David Ong of the University of Essex for his guidance on human rights approaches to environmental issues. However, the responsibility for the final product is mine alone.

2 See the introductory essay by Susan Tanner, Executive Director of Friends of the Earth (Canada) to the section on the right to environment in Kathleen Mahoney and Paul Mahoney, (eds.), *Human Rights in the Twenty-First Century: A Global Challenge* (Dordrecht, Kluwer, 1993) at p. 517, where she calls the right to environment a new right, and places it in inverted commas. See also, Alexandre Kiss, 'Concept and Possible Implications of the Right to Environment' in the same volume, at p. 556.

3 A.A. Cançado Trindade, 'Environmental Protection and the Absence of Restrictions on Human Rights' in Mahoney and Mahoney, eds., op. cit. above, n. 2, at pp. 572–582.

4 Mary Simon, 'The Integration and Interdependence of Culture and the Environment' in Mahoney and Mahoney, eds., op. cit. above n. 2, at p. 521.

5 Alexandre Kiss, op. cit. above, n. 2.

6 *Ibid.*

7 There are, however, regional treaty provisions. Article 24 of the African Charter of Human and Peoples' Rights provides that 'All peoples have the right to a general satisfactory environment favourable to their development'. European states, along with the Commission of the European Communities, adopted in 1989, the European Charter on Environment and Health. See Maguelonne Déjeant-Pons, n. 8 below.

be much hope that a customary international law right to a clean environment may be emerging.[8]

Rights of the child are also controversial.[9] In particular, the approach of the Convention on the Rights of the Child (CRC) has been criticised because of its emphasis on the agency of children, the idea that they have the right to have their views taken into account.[10] Children's rights can be understood as having a basis in the protection of children or in the liberty of children. Some authors dispute any assertion that children might have equal rights to adults, particularly those rights based in liberty. However, the subject of this paper, the rights of child workers, demonstrates that failure to involve children in solving the problems that affect them will ultimately lead to failure of the proposed solutions.

One may question why it is worth examining the right to a clean environment in relation specifically to children. There are two primary reasons. The first is that environmental hazards will often affect children differently, and more severely, than adults. Children are still in a stage of physical development, a development that may be affected by toxins in the environment. As children are physically smaller than adults, the safe levels of exposure are likely to be much lower in any event. The second reason is the difficulty which children have in making their concerns known to decision-makers or otherwise enforcing their environmental rights. Child labour, in particular, often exists in informal, and therefore unregulated, sectors of the economy. These children will have difficulty in acquiring the necessary environmental information. Child workers are often from otherwise marginalised groups, such as ethnic or religious minorities or unfavoured castes. Furthermore, they are very rarely represented by trade unions. As a result, participation by child workers in environmental decision-making is virtually impossible where child labour is an unacknowledged problem. These factors also prevent child workers from being able to enforce their rights, including rights under health and safety legislation to protect them from environmental hazards. Therefore, in practice, they have no means of redress.

---

8 Maguelonne Déjeant-Pons, 'The Right to Environment in Regional Human Rights Systems' in Mahoney and Mahoney, (eds.), op. cit. above., n. 2, at p. 595.

9 William Lucy, 'Controversy over Children's Rights' in David Freestone, (ed.), *Children and the Law* (Hull, 1990).

10 For example, see the following: Bruce C. Hafen, 'Abandoning Children to their Autonomy: Convention on the Rights of the Child' 37 *Harvard International Law Journal* (1996) at p. 449; Laura Purdy, 'Why Children Shouldn't Have Equal Rights' *International Journal of Children's Rights 2* (1994) at p. 223; Anne McGillivray, 'Why Children Do Have Equal Rights: In Reply to Laura Purdy' *International Journal of Children's Rights 2* (1994) at p. 243.

2. The Problem of Child Labour Defined

Child labour is to be distinguished from child work. When children, particularly teenagers, work in safe conditions for relatively short periods of time which do not interfere with their education, this is generally considered benign or even useful for the child.[11] The International Labour Organisation (ILO) has defined child labour as work that is detrimental to children's physical and mental development.[12]

The extent of child labour is virtually impossible to determine. Even the ILO uses the term 'estimate' when discussing the number of child workers. These estimates have increased significantly over the past few years, largely due to better survey methods, developed by the ILO. It is difficult to say whether, overall, child labour is increasing or decreasing. One region where it is definitely increasing is Central and Eastern Europe, but it appears to be decreasing in some parts of Asia where prosperity has increased and education systems have been improved.[13] The most recent estimates by the ILO put the number of working children, aged 5–14, at 250 million world-wide.[14] Of these, approximately 120 million work full-time. 61 per cent of child workers are found in Asia, 32 per cent in Africa and 7 per cent in Latin America. Africa has the highest density of child workers, with an estimated 40 per cent of children between 5 and 14 years old working. Furthermore, there is evidence of some correlation between rates of school attendance and rates of child labour. This is particularly the case when rates of primary school completion are compared with child labour rates.[15]

Child labour is not only an issue in developing countries, or countries in the throes of dramatic economic transition. The existence of extensive participation by children in the labour market has also been considered a problem in Western Europe. The European Union adopted a Directive on young workers in 1994,[16] which follows the general principles of the relevant ILO convention, but provides more detail. In the context of the need to implement this Directive, child labour issues in the United Kingdom have been scrutinised in greater detail and more publicly than has been the case for many years. The Low Pay Unit estimates that

11 International Labour Organisation, *Child Labour: Targeting the Intolerable* (Geneva, pub., 1996).

12 International Labour Organisation – International Programme on the Elimination of Child Labour (IPEC), *Child Labour in Commercial Agriculture in Africa: Report,* Technical Workshop on Child Labour in Commercial Agriculture in Africa, Dar es Salaam, United Republic of Tanzania, 27–30 August 1996 (Geneva, 1997), paragraph 10.

13 International Labour Organisation, op. cit. above, n. 11.

14 *Ibid.*

15 International Labour Organisation, op. cit. above, n. 12.

16 Directive 94/33/EC.

approximately two million children in the United Kingdom take part in paid employment, and that, of these, 75 per cent are employed illegally.[17] Such child workers do not exist for many legal purposes, and therefore have no standing to enforce their rights, including the right to be protected from environmental hazards.[18] Chris Pond MP, formerly Director of the Low Pay Unit introduced a Private Member's Bill, the Employment of Children Bill, in Parliament, to update the United Kingdom law on child employment and to provide far more extensive enforcement of prohibitions on child labour, including the prohibition of hazardous work for children.[19] Mr. Pond agreed to withdraw the Bill when the Minister for Health, Paul Boateng MP, stated that amendments to existing legislation proposed by the Government would meet the objectives of the Employment of Children Bill.[20]

There are a number of factors which lead to the incidence of child labour in various societies. Foremost amongst the supply factors is family poverty. However, no simple causal relation can be established, since some poor areas have relatively low rates of child labour. An example is the Indian province of Kerala where full-time child labour is extremely rare,[21] (although this province has near-universal education).[22] The ILO has described child labour as both a consequence and a cause of poverty.[23] This is particularly true in agriculture, an industry where many child workers are employed. Many agricultural workers are paid on a piece-rate basis. Many female agricultural workers will bring their children along with them in such circumstances, so that the children can bring the official worker's total productivity to a level where a better wage may be earned.[24] In addition, many children work on family farms (which are often commercial outgrower or subcontracted farms rather than subsistence farms) as non-wage labour,[25] and thereby make such family farms economically viable.

17 Low Pay Unit, *Fair Play for Working Children* (London, pub., 1997). Furthermore, research cited in this report shows that, at least in some parts of the United Kingdom, over 40 per cent of children are employed during school terms, and that almost three-quarters of children have taken on paid employment at some time in their lives.

18 *Ibid.* The majority of employment undertaken by children in the United Kingdom is work usually associated with adults, usually in the service sector. While, in 1993–4, 34 major accidents at work involving children were reported, this is thought to be a poor indication of reality. Studies of working children have revealed that around one third of these child workers had experienced accidents at work. Such figures would lead to a conclusion that thousands of accidents per year are affecting child workers in the United Kingdom.

19 A summary of the bill can be found in the Low Pay Unit report, *ibid.*

20 'New law on child work hours', *The Guardian*, 14 February 1998.

21 International Labour Organisation, op. cit. above, n. 11.

22 UNICEF, *Education and Child Labour:* Background Paper (New York, 1997).

23 International Labour Organisation/UNICEF, *Strategies for Eliminating Child Labour: prevention, removal and rehabilitation – Synthesis document* (Geneva and New York, 1997).

24 International Labour Organisation, op. cit. above, n. 12.

25 *Ibid.*

On some company-owned farms, children may be required to work if they wish to live with their primary carers on the estate.[26] As a result, many children working in agriculture are not official employees, which makes enforcement of national minimum age and health and safety laws extremely difficult.

Tradition also influences the likelihood that child labour will be tolerated within a particular community, particularly where children are expected to follow the same trade as their parents. However, it is instructive to note that everywhere in the world, including the richest countries, it is children in the most marginalised groups who are likeliest to engage in child labour.[27]

The demand for child labour is often presented as being a matter of particular skills possessed by children (the so-called 'nimble fingers' argument), but ILO studies have shown that this supposed advantage is illusory.[28] In reality, it appears that the main reason is that, for employers, particularly small-scale employers with tight profit margins, children are better employees because they are more easily exploited. They are often paid less than adults, although the difference in pay may be small in relation to the final price of the goods, especially export goods. The main factor, in the view of the ILO, may be non-economic.[29] Children are more reliable employees than adults, since they are less likely to complain about poor working conditions and take orders more readily. They are less likely to steal from their employer and less likely to be absent from work. All in all, child workers are invisible workers.

3. Types of Environmental Hazards Faced by Child Workers

As stated above, the environmental rights of child workers are often particular to them. Hazards which have some effect on adults will effect children more strongly. Exposure to some hazards may cause irreversible damage to their physical development or result in permanent disabilities. Children suffer more readily from chemical hazards and radiation and have less resistance to disease. Furthermore, protective equipment designed to reduce the danger from exposure to hazardous substances is usually designed for adults. It is either less useful for children, or because of the awkwardness of size, it is not used at all by

26 *Ibid.*
27 International Labour Organisation/UNICEF, op. cit. above, n. 23.
28 International Labour Organisation, op. cit. above, n. 11.
29 *Ibid.* Also, International Labour Organisation, op. cit. above, n. 12.

children. It is necessary, therefore, to go beyond adult-oriented health and safety laws and define the right of child workers to a safe working environment in such a way as to take into account the developmental aspects of childhood.[30] It is important to remember that environmental hazards will be most acute for younger children, who are less developed and who suffer longer cumulative exposure. Asbestos exposure in young children leads to the development of lung cancer in young adulthood instead of middle age or later.[31]

Furthermore, the fact that child workers are often chosen because they are easier to exploit than adults, being less aware of their rights and of the dangers that may be in their environments, means that employers of child workers are often less likely to attempt to eliminate hazards in the working environment.

The ILO has argued that '[a]ny work that involves exposure to known human carcinogens, neurotoxins, heavy metals, and substances which sensitise skin or lungs should be banned for children.'[32] Up to 1997, the ILO set out specific industries, notably those discussed in the following paragraphs, which posed special hazards to child workers as priority areas for the elimination of child labour, although it was concerned that lists of hazardous industries and working conditions was less helpful than are more general guidelines. From 1996 onwards, it recommends a generalised ban on all work which is especially hazardous.

3.1 Commercial agriculture

> It is orthodox to imagine children working in traditional cropping or husbandry under the protective eyes of a family concerned to instruct them in farming skills necessary for adulthood, assuming that their environment is healthier than that of their urban peers. This bucolic view, which is sometimes fed by the romantic notions of urbanites who have little direct experience of rural poverty, is scarcely warranted by the current facts facing children in commercial agriculture.[33]

Contemporary farming is very heavily based on the use of chemicals, as fertilisers, herbicides and pesticides. Child workers in commercial agriculture are often employed handling these chemicals as part of their

30 International Labour Organisation, op. cit. above, n. 11.

31 *Ibid.*

32 *Ibid.*

33 Opening address by the Honourable Sebastian R. Kinyondo (MP), Minister of Labour and Youth Development, United Republic of Tanzania, reproduced in International Labour Organisation, op. cit. above, n. 12, Annex III(a). See also, International Labour Organisation, Bureau for Workers' Activities, Bitter Harvest: *Child Labour in Agriculture* (Geneva, 1997).

34 International Labour Organisation, op. cit. above, n. 12.

duties.[34] Even when child workers do not handle agrochemicals themselves, there are large concentrations of chemical residues in the air, soil and plant leaves.[35] Children working in processing plants that are often located on or near commercial farms are exposed to other toxic substances from chemicals used in food processing.[36] The effect of such substances on children can be fatal – in Sri Lanka, mortality of children from exposure to pesticides is greater than from most other childhood diseases combined.[37] Even where exposure to environmental hazards does not effect life expectancy directly, children can suffer from skin, eye, respiratory or nervous afflictions.

In addition to the direct hazards presented by the use of agrochemicals, the environment in which children work may present indirect dangers to their health and development.[38] Deforestation is one example. The distance of the forest from the family home will effect the amount of time taken up by tasks, such as gathering firewood or fodder for animals. This is time that might otherwise go to school or play. Furthermore, deforestation can lead to families keeping fewer cattle because of lack of fodder. Fewer cattle means less manure for fertiliser and eventually the need to rely on chemical fertilisers, with all the dangers to the health of children which go along with their use. Similarly, landslides can affect the ease with which children can herd cattle, and thereby affect the amount of time spent on work as opposed to other activities. Attention to these environmental situations, through afforestation or irrigation (which makes farming easier), can contribute to reducing the hazardous nature of child labour in agriculture.[39]

3.2 Manufacturing

This is the area which most people think of when child labour is discussed, although agriculture is a far more common activity. Many children working in manufacturing, particularly in Asia, work in small workshops, where maintenance is often poor, leading to exposure to dust and wastes. In the leather-working industry, children may be exposed to solvents (including benzene, a known carcinogen) and glues, which cause neurotoxicity. In construction and glassworks, children may be exposed to lead. In shoe-

---

35 *Ibid.* See also, International Labour Organisation, op. cit. above, n. 33.
36 *Ibid.*
37 *Ibid.*
38 Victoria Johnson, Joanna Hill and Edda Ivan-Smith, *Listening to Smaller Voices: Children in an Environment of Change* (Somerset, pub., 1995).
39 *Ibid.*
40 Duncan Green, *Just How Clean Are Your Shoes?* (London, pub., 1997), pp. 12–13. It is worth noting that most shoes purchased in the United Kingdom cost between £5 and £10, all of which are supplied by imports from countries with very low labour costs, including some where child labour is prevalent – see pp. 2–3 of the report.

making, the open pots of glue on the assembly lines lead to a number of health complaints, including irreversible neurological damage.[40]

In Brazil, gluing, a very unpopular task, is usually assigned to the youngest children.[41] High noise levels are common in glass and ceramics factories, which can lead to hearing impairment, as well as toxic fumes such as carbon monoxide and sulphur dioxide. In match and fireworks factories, child workers may be exposed to high concentrations of asbestos, potassium chlorate, antimony trisulphide, and various phosphorus compounds, which cause toxic reactions and dermatitis.

3.3 Mining

In gold mining, child workers will be exposed to high levels of mercury. In most mining activities, children will be exposed to a range of environmental hazards, including gases and fumes. Children work in the sulphur and coal mines of Colombia, and may wind up suffering from lung and kidney diseases from the fumes in those mines.[42]

These, and other industries, where much child labour is found, present serious environmental hazards to child workers. There are other issues of harmful child labour – practices akin to slavery (such as bonded labour), employment of very young children, trafficking in children, children in illegal activities (the drugs trade, pornography, prostitution) and other work which by its nature or the conditions in which it is carried out, is likely to jeopardise the health, safety or morals of the child. These areas are now considered the priorities for international organisations such as the ILO and UNICEF.

4. International Legal Norms Protecting Child Workers from Environmental Hazards

4.1 International norms relating specifically to child workers

Child labour has been described by the ILO as 'a denial of the right to education and the opportunity to reach full physical and psychological development'.[43] It therefore interferes with the full realisation of a number of rights of the child, including health and education. There are provisions of international law which aim at protecting child workers, either by prohibiting child labour in general, or by prohibiting the kind of work which is especially

41 *Ibid.*
42 'Into the mouth of hell for a pittance', *The Guardian*, 31 October 1997.
43 International Labour Organisation, op. cit. above, n. 11.

hazardous. At present, no specific provisions of international law address the specific issue of environmental hazards facing child workers.

The CRC contains provisions dealing with the right of the child to life and to health (Articles 6 and 24).[44] More specifically, it guarantees the right of the child to be free from economic exploitation:

Article 32:

1. States Parties recognise the right of the child to be protected from economic exploitation and from performing any work that is likely to be hazardous or to interfere with the child's education, or to be harmful to the child's health or physical, mental, spiritual, moral or social development.

2. States Parties shall take legislative, administrative, social and educational measures to ensure the implementation of the present article. To this end, and having regard to the relevant provisions of other international instruments,45 States Parties shall in particular:

a. provide for a minimum age or minimum ages for admission to employment;

b. provide for appropriate regulation of the hours and conditions of employment;

c. provide for appropriate penalties or other sanctions to ensure the effective enforcement of the present article.

This article does not mention environmental hazards, but does refer to an obligation to prohibit work which could interfere with health or physical development, which is implicated where environmental hazards are present. One other measure of the CRC is essential to ensuring that Article 32 or any other provision restricting or banning child labour will be effective: Article 7, which obliges states to ensure that children are registered immediately after birth. Without such information, minimum age legislation is unenforceable.

The CRC, which is one of the most widely ratified human rights treaties ever, reflects the contemporary view of childhood as a time of development. However, it is important to note that there is disagreement amongst researchers as to the role of work in a child's development.[46] Some have argued that all work, regardless of the conditions under which it is performed, interferes with education and play, which should be the focus of childhood. Others have countered that work, when the conditions are safe and the work does not prevent the child from being educated, is

---

[44] David Parker and Claudio Sepúlveda, 'Children's Right to Survival and Healthy Development' in James R. Himes, ed., *Implementing the Convention on the Rights of the Child: Resource Mobilisation in Low-Income Countries* (The Hague, pub., 1995) at p. 69.

[45] This clause is usually understood as referring to the relevant ILO conventions and recommendations.

[46] Johnson et al., op. cit. above, n. 38, at pp.88–89.

helpful to the development of the child's self-esteem and preparation for adult life and responsibilities. The current trend of thinking within the ILO and UNICEF, as well as many development NGOs, is that, at least for the moment, only child labour which causes harm to the child should be targeted. However, many trade union organisations, including the Workers' Group within the ILO, argue for a total ban on child labour. They do not accept that there is a possibility of making employment and education compatible with each other.

The CRC, which was opened for signature in 1989, was followed by the World Summit for Children in 1990. The document resulting from the Summit, the World Declaration and Plan of Action on the Survival, Protection and Development of Children, signed by 159 countries, called for the elimination of illegal child labour and the protection of working children.[47] The CRC and the World Declaration arguably make sufficient reference to the idea of harmful child labour to allow for environmental hazards to be covered by such provisions, but it leaves extensive discretion to States Parties, and places heavy responsibilities on implementing bodies, such as the Committee on the Rights of the Child, to ensure that such issues are addressed.

The ILO has been setting international legal standards on child labour since its establishment in 1919.[48] The Minimum Age Convention (No. 138), 1973, is the most recent version of the relevant standards. However, it has only been ratified by 49 of the 174 Member States of the ILO.[49] This, despite the fact that the ILO has included the Minimum Age Convention within its list of essential, or 'core' conventions which it expects all Member States to ratify. One attempt to deal with this problem, which the Governing Body of the ILO is currently considering,[50] is for the International Labour Conference, which represents all Member States, to adopt a solemn Declaration on fundamental rights with a follow-up mechanism. This Declaration would set out the scope of the commitments which Member States undertake when accepting the ILO constitution, whose principles have been developed in the core conventions. The implications of such a Declaration could be that Member States could be monitored on their progress in implementing the principles of the core conventions even when they have not ratified them.

---

47 International Labour Organisation, op. cit. above, n. 12. See also, several general mentions of the World Summit for Children in James R. Himes, ed., op. cit. above, n. 44.

48 For a discussion of all the relevant ILO conventions, see Lammy Betten, *International Labour Law: Selected Issues* (Deventer, 1993), chapter 8.

49 International Labour Organisation, *Legislation and Enforcement* (Geneva, 1997).

50 International Labour Organisation, *'ILO Governing Body: Proposal for a Declaration on Fundamental Rights to be Discussed'*, Thursday 6 November 1997, Press Release ILO/97/29.

The Minimum Age Convention is primarily addressed to reducing the age at which children enter the labour market, rather than protecting them from specific harms. The basic principle, set out in Article 1, is to raise progressively the minimum age for admission to employment 'to a level consistent with the fullest physical and mental development of young persons'. Article 2 provides that this age shall be no less than the end of compulsory schooling and at least 15, although developing countries may initially set the age at 14. By virtue of Article 7, light work may be permitted for children between 13 and 15, and in developing countries, 12 to 14. Under Article 3, for all countries, the minimum age for hazardous work is 18, with the lower age of 16 only applying if the health, safety and morals of the child are fully protected and he or she has received adequate training in the work.

The Minimum Age Convention, even if it had been widely ratified, is insufficient to cover all children engaging in hazardous labour, and allows Member States numerous opportunities to exempt sectors of their economies from the application of the Convention. One significant exclusion for developing countries, contained in Article 5, is 'family and small-scale holdings producing for local consumption and not regularly employing hired workers'. National legislation often goes further and excludes agriculture altogether, and often excludes all small or family businesses. Furthermore, Article 4 of the Convention allows Member States, after consultation with employers and workers' organisations, to exclude any category of work where 'special and substantial problems of application arise', although they must justify such exclusions in their reports to the ILO on implementation of the Convention. Article 5, as indicated above, allows developing countries to limit the scope of application of the Convention. In such circumstances, the Member State must make a declaration upon ratification as to which sectors *will* be subject to the Convention. However, many hazardous forms of work such as mining and large-scale agriculture, *must* be within the scope of the Convention.

The ILO also adopted, at the same time as the Minimum Age Convention, Recommendation No. 146 as a supplementary measure. ILO Recommendations are soft law measures which do not impose binding international legal obligations on Member States, although their implementation is monitored in a similar way to conventions, and they apply to all ILO Member States. Article 8 of the Recommendation is directed towards the agricultural sector, which is largely excluded from the Minimum Age Convention:

> Where it is not immediately feasible to fix a minimum age for all employment in agriculture and in related activities in rural areas, a minimum age should be fixed at least for employment on plantations and in other agricultural undertakings referred to in Article 5, paragraph 3, of the Minimum Age Convention, 1973.

Article 9 of the Recommendation exhorts states that, where they have not raised the minimum age for hazardous work to 18, that immediate steps should be taken to raise the age to that level. Also in relation to hazardous work, Article 10 provides greater guidance as to what should be considered hazardous work:

> *1.* In determining the types of employment or work to which Article 3 of the Minimum Age Convention, 1973, applies, full account should be taken of relevant international labour standards, such as those concerning dangerous substances, agents or processes (including ionising radiations), the lifting of heavy weights and underground work.
> *2.* The list of the types of employment or work in question should be re-examined periodically and revised as necessary, particularly in light of advancing scientific and technological knowledge.

This last paragraph is especially important to those who wish to protect child workers from environmental hazards, as it requires continuous review with the commitment to remove or reduce hazards as they become known.

The ILO has also, prior to the Minimum Age Convention, 1973, adopted a number of conventions relating to child labour in specific sectors, notably the Minimum Age (Agriculture) Convention, 1921.[51] This convention makes more specific provision for children working in agriculture. The aim of this convention is more towards reconciling the demands of school and agricultural work for young children rather than banning it altogether. Not surprisingly, given the nature of agriculture at that time, no provision is made for protection from hazardous forms of agricultural work. Nonetheless, this convention is in keeping with much current thinking about child labour which is non-hazardous – effort should be directed to ensuring that education does not suffer rather than demanding an outright ban. The ILO's Committee on Work on Plantations, established in 1950, has looked at questions relating to child labour in the course of its work. Its resolutions have examined issues relating to the prohibition of employment of very young children, working time for child workers and education.[52]

---

51 The older conventions remain in force for those who have ratified them, but not the later general Minimum Age Convention, 1973.

52 International Labour Organisation, op. cit. above, n. 12.

As a result of the ILO's standard-setting efforts over the past eight decades, many states do actually have national legislation banning child labour. The legislation is often, in the view of the ILO, needlessly complex. Many states have not established a single minimum age applicable to all sectors, but instead take a sector by sector approach.[53] Often there is no stipulation that work done by children should not be harmful to health or development, although there may be a list of prohibited tasks.[54] There is often incongruence between school leaving ages and minimum ages for employment.[55] Moreover, they often do not have effective labour inspection systems to enforce these laws. Particular problems arise in monitoring child labour because it is often found in small farms, in households, in small businesses and in the informal sectors of the economy.[56] Many states exclude these very sectors, which is where the majority of child labour is found. Often these sectors are excluded primarily because it is thought that it is difficult to enforce the rules in these unregulated sectors.[57] Certainly there are difficulties facing inspectors who are responsible for enforcing child labour laws. They are often understaffed and do not have the resources to reach all the locations where child labour may be found, especially outside urban areas. The International Labour Organisation and UNICEF have recommended that labour inspectorates be given the extra resources needed to enforce child labour laws more thoroughly. They also need the support of political and judicial authorities, greater training in the specific problems of child labour and the co-operation of other public authorities working with children.[58] While it is recognised that legislation and its enforcement cannot on their own deal with child labour, rooted as it is in economic, social and cultural conditions, the ILO sees legislation as an essential foundation for combating child labour, since it acts as a yardstick to what is acceptable and what is not, and as a framework for fair employment relationships.

Furthermore, many states have refused to ratify the Minimum Age Convention because it is perceived as being too rigid. The ILO has begun to draft a new convention, addressed specifically to the most extreme forms of child labour, with the intention that it should be opened for signature in 1999. This convention holds the potential to address the issue of environmental hazards facing child workers much more directly and effectively than in the existing documents.[59]

---

53 International Labour Organisation, op. cit. above, n. 49.
54 *Ibid.*
55 *Ibid.*
56 International Labour Organisation/UNICEF, op. cit. above, n. 23.
57 *Ibid.*
58 *Ibid.*
59 International Labour Office, Governing Body, Committee on Employment and Social Policy, GB.268/ESP/4, 268th session, Geneva, March 1997.

4.2 *International norms providing for the right to a healthy environment*

International environmental law and international human rights law, as noted in the Introduction to this chapter, present limited but significant convergence. This partly arises because of the similarity of aims of these two branches of international law. Both emphasise non-material values – the dignity of humanity in the case of human rights law and the preservation of nature in the case of environmental law. However, the convergence between these aims is inevitably limited, as it may be necessary in some cases to choose between the long-term protection of the environment on the one hand and human freedom or well-being on the other. Nonetheless, the aims are often synergistic. The protection of a natural environment may be essential to the protection of the rights to life or health, and the preservation of a particular natural environment may be necessary to support the way of life of a minority or indigenous group. Given that many child workers are drawn from such marginalised groups, the protection of such environments may be crucial to their well-being.

The interest in the intersection between human rights and environmental protection is a relatively recent development.[60] It can be considered useful in the context of the development of international environmental law because it 'would legitimise international supervision of the whole range of a state's domestic environmental policies, not merely of their extraterritorial effects'.[61] Not surprisingly, therefore, the international human rights instruments providing for a specific right to a healthy environment are those which have been drafted relatively recently. While the UN General Assembly noted a connection between environmental protection and human rights as early as 1968, a more active concern by the General Assembly, the Commission on Human Rights and the Sub-Commission on Prevention of Discrimination and Protection of Minorities can be seen in the few years leading up to the Rio Conference.[62] The 1980s also saw the development of environmental human rights within regional international organisations.[63] The African Charter of Human and

60 See Alan Boyle and Michael Anderson, *Human Rights Approaches to Environmental Protection* (Oxford: Clarendon Press, 1996).

61 Patricia W. Birnie and Alan E. Boyle, *International Law and the Environment* (Oxford: Clarendon Press, 1992), at p. 191.

62 Philippe Sands, *Principles of International Environmental Law I: Frameworks, standards and implementation* (Manchester: Manchester University Press 1995), at pp. 222–223.

63 Sands, *ibid.*, at p. 225, notes that the Council of Europe was unsuccessful in its attempt to have adopted a protocol to the ECHR which would have given the individual a right to protection against environmental changes which would cause 'intolerable damage or threats to his health or … intolerable impairment of his well-being'. Individuals would have been able to claim this right whether the source of the environmental change was the result of state or private action. In the event of private action, the individual would have had the right to assessment of the potential environmental harm.

Peoples' Rights 1981, Article 24, provides that 'all peoples shall have the right to a general satisfactory environment favourable to their development'. It is notable that this formulation makes the right to a healthy environment a collective rather than individual right. As a collective right of peoples, it could be difficult for child workers to establish a case of violation based on their particular circumstances. More recently, in 1988, the Organisation of American States adopted the Protocol of San Salvador to the American Convention on Human Rights. This Protocol sets out economic and social rights. Article 11 provides for an individualised right to a healthy environment:

> *1* Everyone shall have the right to live in a healthy environment and to have access to basic public services.
> *2* The state parties shall promote the protection, preservation and improvement of the environment.

Most human rights instruments, however, contain no specific reference to a right to environmental protection. In such circumstances, the right to a healthy environment may be derived from other rights. In terms of individual economic and social rights, environmental questions may arise in the context of the right to an adequate standard of living, the right to health, the right to safe and healthy working conditions, the right to enjoy the fruits of scientific progress and the right of children to protection against exploitation, some of which have already been noted.[64] The right to life and the right to health, as set out in the American Declaration of the Rights and Duties of Man, were recognised by the Inter-American Commission on Human Rights as having been violated by environmental degradation in the *Yanomami* case.[65] Collective economic rights, such as the right of peoples freely to dispose of the natural wealth and resources and the right to development,[66] may be double-edged swords. Exploitation of natural resources and economic development both can be conducted in a way which preserves the natural environment and in ways which degrade or destroy it. Furthermore, as noted above, collective rights may be inappropriate for violations which affect a sub-group, or affect them differently from the majority. Both these circumstances apply to children, and child workers in particular. Civil rights which could lead to a

64 *Ibid.*, at p. 225.

65 *Yanomami Indians v. Ecuador*, Case no. 7615 of 5 March 1985, Ann. Rep. of the Inter-American Commission on Human Rights, OAS doc. OAE/Ser.L/V/II.66, doc. 10 rev 1, 24 (1985).

66 Sands, op. cit. above, n. 62 at p. 225. On the idea of environmental rights as solidarity rights, see Alan Boyle, 'The Role of International Human Rights Law in the Protection of the Environment' in Alan Boyle and Michael Anderson, eds., *Human Rights Approaches to Environmental Protection*, op. cit. above, n. 60 pp. 57–59, and R. R. Churchill, 'Environmental Rights in Existing Human Rights Treaties', in the same volume, at pp. 104–107.

substantive right to a healthy environment include the right to protection of private life and of property. However, in practice, the institutions of the European Convention on Human Rights have been very reluctant to recognise the potential environmental implications of these rights, most notably in the case of *Powell and Rayner v. United Kingdom*.[67]

In terms of instruments of international environmental law, the starting point for all writers on the issue of a human right to a healthy environment is the Stockholm Declaration of 1972, particularly Principle I, which provides that:

> Man has the fundamental right to freedom, equality and adequate conditions of life, in an environment of a quality that permits a life of dignity and well-being, and he bears a solemn responsibility to protect and improve the environment for present and future generations.

Principle I is of particular relevance to children because of its emphasis on long-term, inter-generational responsibilities. However, this strong formulation of the right to a healthy environment has not been repeated. Many later formulations set out the duties of states without indicating whether or not individuals are actually the corresponding right-bearers.[68] Pallemaerts argues that the Rio Declaration has gone so far in the opposite direction from Stockholm on this issue that human beings are now seen as objects of development rather than subjects of rights.[69] The right to development is enshrined in Principle 3 of the Rio Declaration, but it is unclear to what extent this is a right of individuals, peoples or states.[70] The weakness of the language in the Rio Declaration represents a lost opportunity to develop concepts of human rights to environmental protection. The World Commission on Environment and Development Experts Group on Environmental Law had proposed an article stating that 'all human beings have the fundamental right to an environment adequate for their health and well-being'.[71] Similarly, a group of countries from the Economic Commission for Europe developed a draft 'Charter of Environmental Rights and Obligations', which was substantially weakened by amendments made at a full ECE meeting, and never went forward to the UNCED Preparatory Committee.[72]

67 (1990), Series A, No. 172 (European Court of Human Rights).

68 Sands, op. cit. above, n. 62 at p. 223.

69 Marc Pallemaerts, 'International Environmental Law from Stockholm to Rio: Back to the Future?' in Philippe Sands, ed., *Greening International Law* (London, 1993) at p. 9.

70 *Ibid.*

71 Marc Pallemaerts, op. cit. above, n. 69 at pp. 10–11.

72 *Ibid.*, at p. 11. Further attempts by the sponsoring countries to bring the draft forward to the Rio Conference agenda were thwarted by opposition from developing countries and some ECE Member States.

While the environmental hazards suffered by child workers are appropriate for the use of human rights language in the context of environmental protection, some commentators on international environmental law are concerned that the principles may become to anthropocentric.[73] The use of human rights language may have the effect of downgrading the importance of the natural environment itself within environmental law. As a result, the human right to a healthy environment may not address all the issues arising out of environmental degradation. Within the more specific context of child workers, it may nonetheless be possible to articulate the problems within a human rights framework, particularly in relation to a right to health. Unfortunately, the generally held view is that there is no right to a healthy environment in customary international law, so that it is necessary to extrapolate it from other existing rights in human rights treaties, with all the difficulties that such an attempt may pose.[74]

5. Solutions to the Problem of Environmentally Hazardous Child Labour

Like all questions of the right to a clean environment, there are serious issues of justiciability when attempting to enforce the right of child workers to be protected from environmental hazards.[75] It may be possible to obtain compensation once the harm has been suffered, through national health and safety legislation or tort/delict law, but even if such remedies are adequately available in the state in question, a preventative remedy would be preferable. Kiss, as noted above, includes information and participation, as well as means of redress, as part of the implementation of the right to a clean environment.[76] Given the importance of the precautionary principle in international environmental law, these two first methods should, in any event, be emphasised, rather than compensation or other redress after the damage has occurred. Information and participation elements reflect the fact that the right to a clean environment has both individual and collective elements.

At present, there are two main approaches to the elimination of child labour. These can be termed the 'trade' approach and the 'development' approach. The development approach is preferred by NGOs and by the international organisations working in this area. The trade approach has

73 See Catherine Redgwell, 'Life, the Universe and Everything: A Critique of Anthropocentric Rights', in Alan Boyle and Michael Anderson, (eds.), *Human Rights Approaches to Environmental Protection*, op. cit. above n. 60 at pp. 71–87, and Patricia W. Birnie and Alan E. Boyle, op. cit. above, n. 61 at pp. 193–194.

74 Patricia W. Birnie and Alan E. Boyle, op. cit. above, n. 61 at p. 192.

75 See A. A. Cançado Trindade, op. cit. above., n. 3, at 582-586.

76 This point is also made by A. A. Cançado Trindade, op. cit. above., n. 3.

been primarily advocated by the United States, but it has been introduced in the European context as well.

5.1 Trade sanctions and consumer boycotts

The 'trade' approach to eliminating child labour often advocates trade sanctions or consumer boycotts of products made with child labour. There have been numerous criticisms made of such measures. Some developing countries have accused developed countries of using child labour as an excuse for what are in truth measures designed to protect jobs in those countries.[77] Less emotive, but more crucial to the issue is the criticism that boycotting child labour does little for child workers. In fact, it has been argued that forcing children out of export industries without dealing with the underlying problems of poverty and inadequate provision of education simply drives children into more hazardous forms of labour.[78] Finally, it has been argued that social labelling initiatives, which guarantee that a product was made without child labour, make a promise to consumers which is virtually impossible to keep, since monitoring is extremely difficult.[79] These initiatives have primarily been attempted in the hand-knotted carpet industry, which is by no means the most hazardous form of child labour, although it has been associated with bonded labour. They exist in Germany and in the United States. More generally, Senator Tom Harkin has introduced a bill in the United States Senate to ban all products made with child labour from being imported into the United States.[80]

Many NGOs concerned with developing countries are trying to move consumer pressure away from boycotts and towards simply demanding better treatment for workers. An example is Christian Aid's Change at the Check-out Campaign, which seeks to encourage supermarkets in the United Kingdom to adopt ethical principles in their purchasing of food from developing countries and in particular to implement codes of conduct with suppliers of own-brand products, to be monitored independently. At the end of October 1997, Christian Aid issued an update on the progress towards these goals. Its report included a model code of practice, including a requirement that employment of children should be in line with the basic principles of ILO Convention 138.[81]

77 See for example, '"Dumping social" contre "protectionnisme"', *Le monde*, 1 November 1997; 'Children labour under ignorance', *The Guardian*, 4 November 1997.

78 International Labour Organisation/UNICEF, op. cit. above, n. 23.

79 Janet Hilowitz, 'Social Labelling to Combat Child Labour: Some Considerations', *International Labour Review*, 136 (1997) No. 2.

80 'Child labour, child danger', *The Guardian*, 31 October 1997.

81 Christian Aid, *Change at the Check-out?* Supermarkets and Ethical Business, http://www.oneworld.org/christain_aid/checkout.htm.

Nonetheless, there is continuing interest in the use of trade-related measures to control the recourse to child labour. The issue of child labour has been linked to arguments about the inclusion of a social clause in the World Trade Organisation agreement or other trade treaties.[82] However, as the law of the GATT stands, the use of social standards to determine trading practice is probably against the GATT.[83] The dispute resolution panels established under GATT have tended to interpret the exception clauses narrowly. While the use of prison labour allows states to restrict imports, other abusive labour practices do not give rise to such a discretion. The European Union has used its generalised system of preferences to promote labour and environmental standards, but in a promotional rather than prohibitive way. Under a proposal currently before the Council of the European Union, developing states which observe certain core labour standards, including ILO Convention No. 138, and certain environmental standards will be entitled to reductions of duty payable on items exported to the European Union.[84] The crucial element of this scheme is that the explicit consent of the state benefiting from the reductions of duty is essential – states which do not wish to have their labour standards scrutinised cannot be forced to by the threat of losing access to the European Single Market. This enables the European Union to work with developing countries to improve their labour and environmental record, rather than imposing its own view of these standards from without.[85]

5.2 Improving working conditions and mobilising social actors

Improving the working conditions of child workers is often controversial in the developed world, and is seen as encouraging the continuation of a wrong practice. However, as a matter of priorities and practicalities of enforcement, making work safer for children will often be a better route to protecting them from the environmental hazards of work in industries such as agriculture and glassworks. The ILO has called for the introduction of health and safety measures for child workers, including the provision of safety equipment specially designed for them. Other important measures recommended by the ILO include pre-employment and periodic medical

82 International Labour Organisation/UNICEF, op. cit. above, n. 23, paragraph 12.

83 Halina Ward, 'Common but Differentiated Debates: Environment, Labour and the World Trade Organisation' *International and Comparative Law Quarterly* 45 (1996), p. 592.

84 Proposal for a Council Regulation (EC) applying the special incentive arrangements concerning labour rights and environmental protection provided for in Articles 7 and 8 of Council Regulations (EC) Nos. 3281/94 and 1256/96 applying the scheme of generalised tariff preferences in respect of certain industrial and agricultural products originating in developing countries, COM (97) 534 final, OJ 1997 C 360/9, presented to the council on 30 October 1997.

85 It is worth noting that the European Union has demonstrated concern with child labour through Directive 94/33/EC.

examinations and the removal of children from the handling of chemicals.[86] Improved labour inspection is crucial to achieving any improvements, and to removing children from work which presents severe environmental hazards.

Recognising the close relationship between child labour and poverty, the Oslo Conference on Child Labour, held at the end of October 1997, emphasised the need to focus development aid on poverty reduction programmes, and advocated the 20/20 initiative.[87] This involves a commitment by developed countries to allocate 20 per cent of official development assistance to basic social programmes including education and primary health care, and by developing countries to allocate 20 per cent of their national budgets to these areas. In terms of addressing child labour problems directly, the agenda calls on states to draw up time-bound programmes of action to eliminate child labour, beginning with the most intolerable forms, which includes work which exposes children to environmental hazards. These programmes of action should also address the question of improving educational opportunities for working children. The Oslo Conference agenda for action also emphasised the mobilisation of different social actors. UNICEF has argued that 'to sustain the movement against child labour, existing efforts need to become part of a broader, consciously-directed process aimed at permanently improving the lives of the poorest and most excluded groups'.[88] Trade unions are a resource for children which have been underused. In some countries, the law prohibits young persons from being members of trade unions.[89] However, where trade unions are involved in the problem of child labour, they can be effective. Brazil's National Confederation of Workers in Agriculture (CONTAG) conducted an awareness-raising campaign which has led to greater mobilisation against the problem. The International Union of Food, Agricultural, Hotel, Restaurant, Catering, Tobacco and Allied Workers' Associations (IUF) has presented a draft code of conduct for the tea sector which includes a provision demanding that no child below school leaving age shall be employed on a tea plantation, and that workers' children should have access to care facilities and schools within a reasonable distance of the plantation.[90] It is, however, too soon to determine the effect of this draft code of conduct, which was developed in 1997. Employers organisations have also been mobilised in some cases. The Association of Tanzanian

86 International Labour Organisation, op. cit. above, n. 12, paragraphs 82 and 126.

87 Norwegian Ministry of Foreign Affairs, Oslo Conference on Child Labour, 27–30 October 1997, *Agenda for action – adopted at the conference*, http://odin.dep.no/ud/publ/97/labour/agenda.html.

88 UNICEF, *Social Mobilisation and Child Labour: Background Paper* (New York, 1997).

89 International Labour Organisation, op. cit. above, n. 12, especially paragraph 96.

90 International Labour Organisation, op. cit. above, n. 33.

Employers has identified tea and coffee plantations with high incidence of child labour and conducted workshops with the employers and managers. These have led to action plans to improve working conditions for child workers and to discourage the use of child labour.[91]

5.3 Phased removal of children from employment and into education

Education is seen as an important tool for the elimination of child labour, since it increased earning power in the long term, thus reducing poverty.[92] Education of child workers cannot, however, be secured simply be attempting to enforce compulsory education laws. It is also important to ensure that the education provided to child workers is free and is relevant to them.[93] Often families of children at school must pay fees, or for books, stationery and uniforms.[94] Sometimes, it may be more helpful, at least in the short term, to integrate educational provision and work demands. Sugar plantations in Tanzania, for example, have provided primary schools on the plantations, with the result that most of the children working there also attend school.[95] Approximately half of child workers combine work and school at present, so education policies may need, at least initially, to focus on making this possible for all child workers rather than giving a stark choice between work and school.[96] Income replacement schemes, where parents are given a subsidy when their children go to school to replace the value of the children's labour, have been attempted, but are considered an imperfect solution. These programmes, however, are seen as unsustainable in the long term, and are less likely to respond to local realities than locally-initiated programmes.[97] They can even be viewed as encouraging child labour, since parents whose children do not work are not eligible for the subsidy.

There is evidence that the problem of child labour needs to be approached with complex solutions. Bans on hazardous labour in more well-known industries, especially export industries, where trade sanctions or consumer pressure can be most acutely felt by employers and by states where child labour is prevalent, can simply lead to children moving into more invisible, unregulated and hazardous work. When a factory in Bangladesh dismissed its child workforce after a threat of a boycott by trade sanctions by the United States, most of those children

91 International Labour Organisation, *Practical Action to Eliminate Child Labour* (Geneva, 1997).
92 UNICEF, op. cit. above, n. 22.
93 *Ibid.*
94 International Labour Organisation/UNICEF, op. cit. above, n. 23.
95 International Labour Organisation, op. cit. above, n. 12, paragraph 50.
96 UNICEF, op. cit. above, n. 22.
97 *Ibid.*

moved into other forms of work, many into more hazardous work such as waste collection.[98] In contrast, the Secretary of State for International Development, Clare Short, announced at the Oslo Conference on Child Labour, that the United Kingdom, as a contribution to IPEC, would be funding a project to be run by the development NGO Save the Children. This programme will provide social assistance so that when children are withdrawn from work in export industries, in this case football stitching, they and their families will have the support that will prevent children from moving into more hazardous work.[99]

The ILO's International Programme on the Elimination of Child Labour (IPEC) is a major technical support programme that has helped a number of countries to develop multi-faceted strategies for eliminating child labour. IPEC encourages countries to prioritise children at greatest risk. This includes, along with forced labour, sexual exploitation of children and the employment of very young children, industries and working conditions which expose children to environmental hazards.[100] IPEC's strategy has been to emphasise preventing children from entering employment, particularly the extreme forms of child labour, but has also helped countries to develop removal and rehabilitation strategies.[101]

5.4 Procedural rights in international environmental law

It is perhaps easier to conceive of procedural environmental rights than substantive ones. Procedural rights, are familiar parts of the range of civil and political rights. They also avoid the problem of anthropocentricity which surrounds substantive environmental rights.[102] It is simply necessary to extend them to a new context. Many procedural rights relevant to the enforcement of environmental rights have been identified. Among these are rights to: participation and information, integration of environmental concerns into environmental policy making and remedies. Some of these rights may be difficult for children to make use of without substantial assistance and therefore may be of limited utility. In particular, the possibility of child workers to influence the development of policies which may affect the environment is limited because of their status and because of their lack of education and maturity. In terms of enforcing remedies, child workers, like all vulnerable groups, usually require representation by

---

98 Save the Children, 'A labour of necessity', http://www.oneworld.org/scf/childlab/feature.htm.

99 Speech by the Rt. Hon. Clare Short, Secretary of State for International Development to Oslo Conference on Child Labour, 27–30 October 1997, http://www.oneworld.org/dfid/news4897.html.

100 International Labour Organisation, op. cit. above, n. 11.

101 *Ibid.*

102 Patricia W. Birnie and Alan E. Boyle, op. cit. above, n. 61 at pp. 194–195.

advocates such as trade unions or members of the legal professions. Principle 10 of the Rio Declaration establishes the principle of citizen participation in environmental decision-making, which means that procedural environmental rights are more firmly entrenched in the Rio Declaration than are substantive environmental rights.[103] This is an advance over the legal situation established by the Stockholm Declaration of 1972, but Pallemaerts has argued that the right in Principle 10 is structured as a declaration of principle rather than an individual or collective right.[104] Only the second paragraph uses the language of individual rights, and there the rights of information and participation are heavily qualified.[105] The principle would imply first the right to adequate information, and the right to be consulted within the decision-making process.[106] It should also include the principle of integration, which requires that environmental concerns are integrated into policy-making in all areas.[107] Participation requires prior notification and consultation, including consultation of individuals and groups in local planning inquiries, allowing public participation in environmental assessment exercises, and even legal standing to prevent environmentally harmful policies from being implemented. In some circumstances, such as the transport of hazardous wastes, a system of prior consent may be established.[108] The 1989 Indigenous People's Convention establishes an obligation to undertake environmental impact assessments and the right of indigenous peoples to be consulted and to participate in decision making.[109]

The right to participation in policy-making processes needs to be supported by rights to remedies. Numerous existing human rights documents set out such rights, including the right of access to a court or other dispute resolution process and the right to a fair procedure. However, in cases relating to environmental issues, the European Court of Human Rights has been less than generous in enforcing the right to a remedy.[110]

International law has long recognised that states are responsible to other states for environmental harms.[111] However, the first international

---

103 Maurice Sunkin, David M. Ong and Robert Wright, *Sourcebook on Environmental Law* (London, pub., 1998), at p. 645 add that Chapter 23 of Agenda 21 elaborates the right of participation particularly with respect to inputs to environmental assessment procedures. Furthermore, the principle of participation has been included in several other international and European Union measures since the early 1980s.

104 Marc Pallemaerts, op. cit. above, n. 69 at pp. 11–12.

105 *Ibid.*

106 Maurice Sunkin, David M. Ong and Robert Wright, op. cit. above, n. 103 at pp. 34 and 641.

107 *Ibid.*, at pp. 34–35.

108 *Ibid.*, at p. 643.

109 Sands, op. cit. above, n. 62 at pp. 229–230.

110 See *Powell and Rayner v. United Kingdom*, op. cit. above, n. 67.

111 *Trail Smelter Arbitration (US v. Canada)*, Reports of International Arbitration Awards, RIAA (1938 and 1941), p. 1905, noted by Maurice Sunkin, David M. Ong and Robert Wright, op. cit. above, n. 103 at p. 646.

attempt to provide for rights to access to remedies for environmental harms was the Economic Commission for Europe draft Charter on Environmental Rights and Obligations.[112] The 1989 Indigenous People's Convention did succeed in including the right to legal remedies.[113] However, the most significant developments have been internal to states – the widespread development of class action lawsuits and public interest litigation.[114]

6. Conclusion

Environmental hazards faced by child workers are rightly seen as one of the most intolerable forms of child labour. In examining the environmental rights of child workers, we see the interdependence between the rights of people in developing and developed countries. The concerns that consumers in wealthy developed countries have over pesticide residues in the food that they and, more importantly, their children, eat are magnified for the workers in commercial agriculture in the developing world. In particular, child workers in agriculture are subject to serious environmental harms. One part of the solution is to develop and promote methods of agriculture which are less reliant on harmful chemicals. However, reducing the environmental harm suffered by child workers is only the first stage of the solution. The child worker has other rights: to economic security for his or her family; to education; and to respect for his or her views about work and education; to representation by trade unions and other bodies (one right which multinational corporations are slow to grant in their voluntary codes of conduct).[115]

Until recently, the approach to dealing with child labour issues has been fragmentary, with different countries attempting different, and often contradictory, solutions. There has been a lack of understanding of the many factors which lead to a prevalence of child labour and a failure to recognise the diversity of forms of child labour. Developed countries have often paid scant attention to the child labour problems in their own territory while being concerned with child labour in the developing world. The development of the ILO's IPEC has finally brought together the international concern with the serious problems of child labour into a single programme. Within IPEC, a wide variety of solutions are being developed and researched. The use of trade mechanisms to prohibit child labour

112 Patricia W. Birnie and Alan E. Boyle, op. cit. above, n. 61 at p. 195.
113 Sands, op. cit. above, n. 62 at p. 230.
114 *Ibid.*, at pp. 195–196.
115 Duncan Green, op. cit. above, n. 40, p. 16 and Appendix D.

seems, for the most part, to be falling out of favour, although consumer pressure campaigns to improve the labour practices of suppliers to the wealthier countries does seem to be better adapted to address the issue of hazardous child labour. A new convention on the most extreme forms of child labour will be part of this multi-faceted approach. The development of such international legal norms cannot in itself eradicate or even reduce the incidence of hazardous child labour. It does, however, complement the other aspects of IPEC. It creates widespread international publicity for the campaign to address the problem of child labour. It sets an agenda of the priority areas for the international community in addressing child labour issues.

The development of international environmental law has, even more than international trade and development law, demonstrated the effects which actions in one country have on others. There is a need for this insight to be extended to other human rights, particularly the strong concern that exists at present for the rights of child workers to be free from exploitation and environmental hazard.

2 The right of the child to a clean environment in European Union law

HARRY POST

1. Introduction

The right of the child to a clean environment in European Union law has several 'ingredients' that are quite distinct in positive law and need to be combined. However, whether or not they can successfully be brought together in a coherent manner is very much to be seen. It will, of course, very much depend on the 'recipe' and/or on the 'qualities of the cook'. The basic ingredients, as the title implies, are as follows: the right to a clean environment in both general international law and in European Union law, the right of the child to a clean environment, and, finally, the right of the child in European Union law.[1]

We are not necessarily dealing here with a 'cumulative' juridico-gastronomical process. It may be the case that a substantive environmental right (or duty) does exist in Community law and not yet in general international law (or the other way around). Such developments occur, as in environmental law.[2]

In Community law, explicitly, there is no distinct right of the child to a clean environment. Until the 1985 Single European Act even the term 'environment' was absent in the Community treaties. However, since the Single European Act has entered into force, things undoubtedly have changed rapidly. In 1995, Professor Jans observed:

> Since the entry into force of the Single European Act the environment has had a permanent place in the EC Treaty. It is reasonable to expect that a flood of Community legislation on the environment will continue to pour over us in the next few years.[3]

---

1 In the following pages, 'Community' law, or EC law, will often be used instead of European Union law.

2 After all, the EC Treaty since Maastricht was probably the first (written) international legal document in force with a provision on the precautionary principle (in its Article 130r), and, the Single European Act was equally the first instrument with a binding provision on the 'polluter pays' principle, whatever, in both cases, that precisely may mean (see the 1994 UK High Court's explanation of the EC precautionary principle: *R. v. Secretary of State for Trade and Industry ex parte Duddridge and others*, *Environmental Law Review*, 37 (1995), p. 151).

3 In the Preface to his *European Environmental Law* (The Hague, London (etc.) 1995), at p. xv. The somewhat exaggerated title of Jans's book is already quite telling. Another book on the same subject matter, although it is somewhat more narrow in scope, has a more modest title: Ludwig Krämer, *EC Treaty and Environmental Law*, (2nd edn., London 1995).

His assessment has proven to be correct. Nevertheless, in the whole construct of the European Union legal order, including the secondary legislation, there is still no human, or child, right to a 'clean' environment to be found (nor is it found in the Treaty of Amsterdam, for that matter).

The obscurity, in EC law of human, or 'basic' rights, seems primarily due to the well-known and already long-lasting ambiguous relationship between Community law and the Strasbourgian European Human Rights law. Notwithstanding, some improvement foreseen by way of the Treaty of Amsterdam, even at the end of the twentieth century, human rights can still be argued to have an embarrassingly unsettled place in EU law, at least as far as their primary addressees, European citizens, are concerned.[4]

Having said this, it should still not be excluded that a general right to a clean environment, or such a right of the child in particular, does exist, albeit in a somewhat distinct form. This right may materially amount to comparable (or more specific) guarantees as a right of the child to a clean environment, but would have a more 'indirect' nature. It would be composed of a number of duties of EU Member States in specific areas that can effectively be claimed by individuals. Along these lines, legal practice may perhaps present an unexpected and wonderfully diverse and detailed whole of environmental guarantees binding Member States and EU institutions which together, indeed, would amount to a right of the child to a clean environment. This 'composite' human right can then be claimed by them or on behalf of them. However, the legal nature of such a 'derived' human right of the child to a clean environment, as it will be called here, tends to differ from human rights as guaranteed in more conventional human rights instruments, notably in terms of enforcement or alienability, within the context of modes of claiming them. Although these efforts to derive a human or child's right to a clean environment will not be entirely unsuccessful, substantively something remains missing. What is lacking in view of our subject are rights guaranteeing environmental protection of special relevance to children, specifically geared to their needs.

In the following pages, after a first, preliminary section on matters of definition, terminology and, in particular, scope and demarcation in which the complexity of the topic is exhibited, current Community law will be examined for a 'direct' right of the child to a clean environment. Of particular importance in this section is the nature of the guarantee the EU extends to human rights to be guaranteed by the Member States due to their

4 See, among the many studies on the subject, e.g. A. Cassese, A. Clapham, J. Weiler, *Human Rights and the European Community*, 3 volumes (Baden-Baden: Nomos 1991).

obligations under the 1950 European Convention on Human Rights. Like the EU treaties, the European Convention on Human Rights does not contain any 'direct' human right to a clean environment, but recent jurisprudence nevertheless shows an important development in this respect. In two recent judgments, the Strasbourg Court has explained Article 8 of the Convention on the right to respect for private and family life in such a way that this right now appears to imply an individual legal guarantee against environmental deterioration.

In section 3, EC environmental law will be examined for relevant environmental duties toward citizens. Both substantive and procedural duties will be reviewed and considered for their potential direct effect. An important concern in section 3 is the possibility for children to claim, effectively, rights under Community law.

2. Preliminary Matters

2.1 Environment, environmental degradation and human rights

Textbooks on international law and the environment have, in an infinitely better manner than can be done here, explained what possibly could be meant by 'environment'.[5]

Environment could vary from a catalogue of phenomena in which everything should be included, to a particular definition which is usually wide-ranging, but could also be a simple 'the environment is where we all live'.[6] If we limit ourselves to definitions of environment as they occasionally tend to be included in treaty law and other (potentially) binding international legal instruments, it is remarkable that, as early as 1984, the European Community chose to define environment and to include that definition in a binding Regulation. In the EC view, environment had to be seen as 'the combination of elements whose complex inter-relationships make up the settings, the surroundings and the conditions of life of the individual and of society as they are and as they are felt'.[7] Since then, not much has been heard of the implications of this 'binding'

---

5 Cf., Patricia Birnie and Alan Boyle, *International Law and the Environment* (Oxford: Clarendon Press 1992), pp. 2–3 (see also Boyle's later observations in his chapter "The Role of International Human Rights Law in the Protection of the Environment", in: Alan Boyle and Michael Anderson (eds.), *Human Rights Approaches and Environmental Protection* (Oxford 1996), pp. 48–57; Alexandre Kiss and Dinah Shelton, *International Environmental Law* (London: Graham & Trotman 1991), pp.116–119; Philippe Sands, *Principles of International Environmental Law* (Manchester 1995), pp.17–19.

6 World Commission on Environment and Development (WCED), *Our Common Future* (Oxford 1987), p.xi.

7 EEC/1872/84 on Action by the Community relating to the Environment; in (1984) *OJ*, L 176/1.

definition for the development of EC environmental law, which perhaps is partly due to its rather blatant anthropocentricity.[8]

Somewhat less vulnerable to that critique are a number of more modern treaties in which the intrinsic value of the environment, including nature, in the sense of natural ecosystems and species, has not been disregarded. However, they usually do without a definition of 'environment', unless in a somewhat narrower sense, serving their particular purpose. The 1985 Vienna Ozone Convention is an example, steering a middle course through the 'ecocentric-anthropocentric' battleground. In its Article 1(2) the Convention defines 'adverse effects on the environment' to include 'changes in the physical environment or biota, including changes in climate, which have significant deleterious effects on human health or on the composition, resilience and productivity of natural and managed ecosystems, or on materials useful to mankind'.[9]

However, in terms of our subject-matter not much is gained by adopting one definition of 'environment' or another, except that some notion of environment (and environmental degradation) with recognised international legal relevance, may be useful in order to establish the link to (potentially) effective international human rights.[10] In section 2.3 a choice along this line will be made.

2.2 A universal right to a 'clean' environment

The (1972) Stockholm Declaration states in its first principle that '[m]an has the fundamental right to freedom, equality and adequate conditions of life in an environment of a quality that permits a life of dignity and well-being'. However, this kind of human rights perspective[11] has disappeared from the Rio Declaration. This failure should not necessarily be read as indicating that an explicit right to a decent, viable, and healthy environment is legally a superfluous or otherwise useless instrument,

---

8 See Catherine Redgwell's study on that subject, with the challenging title: 'Life, The Universe and Everything: A Critique of Anthropocentric Rights'; in Boyle and Anderson (eds.), op. cit., n.5, pp.71–87 (the nature of Redgwell's critique does not allow for much in terms of an analysis of definitions of environment and environmental rights in international legal instruments).

9 (1985) Vienna Convention for the Protection of the Ozone Layer; in (1987) *International Legal Materials* (hereafter: *ILM*), pp.1529 ff. The nature of the change is here somewhat problematic. In case of natural causes the kind of claims possible will be different from environmental degradation due to human causes. The 'famous' 1974 OECD defintion, repeated in a number of treaties, refers, e.g., to pollution as '... the introduction by man ...' (in OECD Council Recommendation C(74)224 of 14 November, 1974).

10 Philippe Sands submits that a legal definition of 'environment' is needed, because, a), it defines the scope of the legal subject (and therewith, e.g., the powers of an international organization), and, b), more specifically, it assumes significance in light of rules governing liability for damage to the environment (Sands, op. cit., n. 5, p.17). This latter aspect may at some point arise in view of environmental litigation under the *Francovich* jurisprudence, but for the time being, there are still enough other obstacles to the effectiveness of such liability claims – see, below, sub-section 4.5.2.

11 An argument could, of course, be made that Rio's 'sustainable development' perspective is also a human rights approach. However, this would then be a 'third generation' human rights perspective only.

although some distinguished authors are quite pessimistic here.[12] After a detailed analysis of the arguments presented, Boyle recognises the inherent problem to postulate a definition that is adequate in the qualitative sense. In conclusion, he observes that such problems are inherent to other concepts like, indeed, sustainable development, but that this problem

> has not rendered futile the UN's efforts to promote sustainability as the central objective of international environmental policy. Indeterminacy is thus a problem, but not necessarily an insurmountable one.[13]

The most serious of the arguments against a right to a decent, clean environment is perhaps that such a right would add only little to what exists already in environmental law. Boyle argues that, although it may be true

> that adequate environmental quality is an essential condition for the enjoyment of human rights, it is less obvious that a substantive human right to environmental quality is an essential condition for the protection of the environment.[14]

This warning about the relative significance of such a right (including that of the child) for the protection of the environment, if this term is taken in a non-anthropocentric sense,[15] seems equally important in respect to Community law.

2.3 The 'quality' of the environment

What then is to be understood by the child's right to a *clean* environment (in Community law)?[16] Here, again (and without any pretence of 'ontological' correctness) a perspective is chosen which was already embraced in a legal document, i.e., in the decision in the *López Ostra* case.

---

12 The outstanding example is, probably, Gunther Handl, in Trindade (ed.), *Human Rights, Sustainable Development and the Environment* (San José, 1992), at p. 117.

13 In Boyle and Anderson (eds.), op.cit., n.5, p.51. I am not sure that, the argument in respect to 'sustainable development' is yet a valid one. Recent history of international law knows more examples of 'concepts' that have received much support, but nevertheless did not prove all that lasting. So far, in my view, the value and endurance of the concept still has to be proved beyond the level of a still somewhat abstract ideal.

14 *Ibid.*, p.57.

15 Redgwell, op.cit. n. 8. In general it is, of course, very difficult really to apply an 'ecocentric' concept (see, also, Alan Boyle, in Boyle and Anderson, op. cit. n.5, pp.51–53), and even more so in the realm of human rights.

16 No special significance should be given to 'clean' here: 'viable', 'decent', even 'good', would also have done. Principle 2 of the Draft Principles on Human Rights and the Environment of the 'Ksentini' Report says: 'All persons have the right to a secure, healthy and ecologically sound environment' (reproduced in Boyle, in Boyle and Anderson, op. cit., n.5, p.66, see also n.21, *below*).

The simple result of freely paraphrasing on what the European Court of Human Rights argued in this decision of 9 December 1994, and partly leaving aside the particular circumstances of the case is then as follows:

> A child's right to a clean environment is a right to an environment free from pollution so severe that it affects its well being and prevents it from ordinary life adversely, without necessarily seriously endangering its health.

It is realised, of course, that this definition has the character of a bottom-line definition. Although its contents are somewhat broadened in view of the right mentioned by the ECHR in its award,[17] a number of aspects have been excluded which we might like to see included in our analysis, in particular in children's 'core' environmental right. In a study of a different nature and scope than this one, defining a right that is more specifically geared to the environmental needs of children should be undertaken. Which environment would basically fit in with their vulnerability in the process of physical and psychological development? How is this basic child environment expressed in the language of rights? The more positive European and general international law as yet does not provide much indication of what such rights will involve. We will therefore stick to the proposed bottom-line definition of the quality of the environment and, roughly, corresponding rights.

Such core environmental rights of a child are not too idealistically conceived, it seems, and have a practical orientation in accordance with Hilson's contention that 'rights without effective remedies are hardly worth having'.[18] After all, we are still talking about a beginning: an individual right to a 'clean' (decent, viable) environment which has been enforced or might proof to be enforceable, as yet, can hardly be said to exist. Other rights might either be added to the core, or find a place as more 'ordinary' duties to be guaranteed by states.

It should perhaps be emphasised that if such rights are part of EC law's 'direct effect' stratum, they, for all practical individual purposes, have a very high status in the hierarchy of individual rights, including in the legal systems of the Member States.[19]

---

17 European Court of Human Rights, Judgment of 9 December 1994, in Case no. 41/1993/436/515, *Gregoria López Ostra v. Spain*, Series A, No. 303-C, cons. 51. The court stated: 'Naturally, severe environmental pollution may affect individuals' well-being and prevent them from enjoying family life adversely, without, however, seriously endangering their health.'

18 Chris Hilson, 'Community rights in environmental law: rhetoric or reality?', in Jane Holder (ed.), *The Impact of EC Environmental Law in the United Kingdom* (Chichester, etc., 1997), p. 53 (see also, below, section 4).

19 Something similar is, in principle, the case, if, in a predominantly 'monistic' state like The Netherlands, such a right would be included in an international treaty, and then would be considered to be self-executing by the judiciary. In the Dutch system, a provision in a binding decision of an international organization can have the same status; see Article 94 of the Dutch Constitution (cf. e.g. Peter Malanczuk, *Akehurst's Modern Introduction to International Law* (7th ed. London, 1997), pp. 67–68; and n.59, below).

The 'core' right as here defined should perhaps achieve an even higher status, yet to be created, in Community law.[20]

2.4 The 'scope' of the right involved

As mentioned in the Introduction, no right to a clean environment was to be found in Community law. In that respect what Professor Boyle calls the most fundamental conclusion of the Ksentini Report, i.e., to 'a shift from environmental law to the right to a healthy and decent environment', has not yet manifested itself in Community law, at least not in an explicit way.[21] It has proved not to be so simple to transplant human rights into Community law. If the interest is effective protection of rights to a clean environment under Community law, it is to be seen how much is really gained by the inclusion of such a right.[22]

Although it is not possible to find any 'direct hits' in Community law if one is looking for the right to a clean environment (whether for children or for adults), more indirect legal protection may also be relevant or in fact, on occasion, even much more important. That is: more important in view of protection against damage to human well being due to the deterioration of the environment. As any environmental interest group would not legally sit still upon discovery that no straightforward legal provision protecting the right to a clean environment could be found, we will not do so either (although not having an activist inclination here). The result of such a bold stand, however, is that access by individuals, including those acting on behalf of children, to a wide variety of duties of Member States and of the Community, enters the scope of this examination. Notably, in EC law,[23] with a legal enforcement mechanism which is far superior in its effectiveness to that of any other international treaty, a wide variety of duties potentially accompanied by 'indirect', or better because ours is a human rights perspective, 'derived' rights to a clean environment comes in sight.

---

20 The logical step would be to think in terms of obligations *erga omnes* (see, e.g., Kiss and Shelton, op. cit., n. 5, pp.16–17) or, in particular, of (regional) *ius cogens*, as known in general international law. The outstanding quality of *ius cogens* status is that it can only be replaced by a provision with similar status.

21 Boyle (see op. cit., n. 16) refers to the study by Ksentini on 'human rights and the environment' for the UN Sub-Commission on the Prevention of Discrimination and Protection of Minorities (UN Doc. E/CN.4/Sub.2/1994/9). Ksentini's conclusion may be called quite remarkable in light of the fact that EC/EU law is not included in her survey (which after all, arguably, might be described as by far the largest body of binding international law on environmental matters!). See Annex III for full report.

22 If, e.g., a 'separate' human rights treaty for the European Union were to be concluded, its effect in terms of enforceable human rights would be quite different from an amendment of, notably, the EC Treaty, depending, generally speaking, on whether the Member State has a more 'monistic' or a more 'dualistic' legal system.

23 But equally in, e.g., the realm of the European Convention of Human Rights, such a broader approach is necessary. After all, strictly speaking, the important *López Ostra case* would fall outside the subject matter announced in the title of this study, because the case concerns above all Article 8 of the Convention which deals with the protection of the right to privacy (etc.) and as such makes no provision for anything approaching a right to a clean environment.

In view of the more specific topic here under consideration, a broad perspective on potential rights may nonetheless be useful. The rights of the child is a broad-ranging subject-matter, covering a variety of (potential) more or less specific rights, from the 'classic' civil individual rights, to rights in respect to such subjects as education, labour, health, or humanitarian rights of protection in circumstances of armed conflict.[24]

2.5 The 'kind' of rights involved

Now that the scope of rights, or potential rights, beneficial to children has been more or less defined, at least in terms of size, an additional preliminary matter must briefly be touched upon: what is the 'legal nature' of the rights we are trying to distinguish?

In the first place, of course, 'substantive' rights will be included. As appears from what was said about 'derived' rights, a broad perspective is assumed. However, in doing so, we will nevertheless eventually focus on so-called 'real' environmental rights, that is rights to a clean environment that exist even beyond, and separate from, the fulfilment of a condition that environmental deterioration is detrimental to health. This is perhaps the 'ultimate' form of a human right to a 'clean' environment so far recognised in international jurisprudence.[25] So far, to effectively claim an individual right to a 'clean' environment in jurisprudence seems almost always to require the establishment of a causal link with a health hazard of some sort to that individual. Failure to establish that causation, conforming to the often very stringent standard set in most national legal systems, is a major reason for the rejection by courts of environmental claims.[26]

Apart from substantive rights to a clean environment in Community law, procedural rights, more or less intimately linked up with these rights to a clean environment, should also be included. It seems logical to cover the more procedural rights related to duties of preventive action, such as the 'rights' to an environmental impact assessment or the right to

24 See, for the scope of the rights of the child, e.g., Geraldine Van Bueren's *The International Law on the Rights of the Child* (Dordrecht, etc. 1995).

25 As will be argued, in section 3.4, below, a major reason for the importance of the European Court of Human Rights 1994 judgment in the *López Ostra* case, is the Court's recognition that apart from the dangers to the health of the plaintiffs (especially that of Mrs López Ostra's daughter), the Spanish authorities had not adequately guaranteed the rights of Mrs Lopez Ostra under Article 8 in view of serious environmental degradation.

26 See, Chris Hilson, op. cit., n. 18, pp. 65–67, where he discusses plaintiffs' problems with causation proof in liability claims in the context of the EC's *Francovich* jurisprudence; see further subsection 4.5.2, below. In national courts, the legal impact of the 'precautionary' principle is not yet very perceptible, although the Treaty of Maastricht has inserted the principle in Article 130r.2 (but see the reference in n. 2, above).

27 Such procedural environmental 'rights' get increasing attention in the literature. See, e.g., Jan Jans, op. cit., n.3, pp. 279–292, where he labels them 'horizontal environmental legislation'; Chris Hilson, op. cit., n.18, pp.62 ff.; or Alan Boyle, in Boyle and Anderson, op. cit., n.5, pp.59–63. Many of the Principles of the 1991 Rio Declaration, as well as many articles in major instruments of environmental law are, of course, of a procedural nature, and so are a number of the principles in Part IV and V of the Ksentini Report.

environmental information deriving from environmental law itself.[27] Referring among other sources to Principle 10 of the 1992 Rio Declaration, Alan Boyle has even argued that

> [t]he narrowest but strongest argument for a human right to the environment focuses not on environmental quality and solidarity, but on procedural rights, including access to environmental justice and participation in environmental decision-making.[28]

The basic idea here is that good environmental protection requires civic participation that needs to be based on adequate information.

Somewhat more remote duties, less logically linked perhaps, but also potentially accessible to individuals or their interest groups, such as duties under the EURATOM Treaty to follow specific procedures in case of the opening of a nuclear waste plant or a major nuclear installation, the question remains if such procedures should also be included. I think that at this point it would be unwise to exclude them, in particular, because the Luxembourg Court has also allowed access to them in its case law. Moreover, the few potentially relevant examples to some extent might even be argued to boil down to 'rudimentary' environmental impact assessment duties and environmental information duties of the Member States.

> [I]t is one thing to speak the language of rights and something quite different to create effective enforcement mechanisms to protect those rights: rights without effective remedies are hardly worth having.[29]

Here a somewhat less strict point of view will be entertained than the one mentioned at the end of this citation. It is, after all, not always so easy to determine beforehand which duties and corresponding rights will in fact prove to be enforceable. However, the gist of this statement is quite recommendable.

As far as EU law is concerned, we will then assume the position that (a) individuals (children) or those acting on their behalf, should be able to claim rights corresponding with relevant substantive and procedural duties, and, (b), they should be able to do so either directly at an international tribunal, notably, here, the Court in Luxembourg or the one in Strasbourg (in the latter case: assuming for the moment an effective 'extension' of its jurisprudence to the European Union), or by the 'indirect' way of the

28 Boyle, in Boyle and Anderson, op. cit., n.5, pp.59–60.

29 Chris Hilson, op. cit., n.18, p.51. It will be apparent from the following pages that I am quite indebted to some of Chris Hilson's studies on UK jurisprudence.

national courts in the Member States. In the latter case we will be talking about 'derived' rights, in all the other cases, we will talk about 'direct' rights.

2.6 The child and environmental protection (and vice versa)

2.6.1 Who is a child?

This question easily leads the naive author into a minefield. The problem is not so much situated at the end of childhood, although there are some traps to be avoided there, as well, but in particular at the beginning. However, a primarily legal approach focusing on such banal matters as standing rights and effective remedies, makes it possible to avoid most of the minefield.[30] Article 1 of the Convention on the Rights of the Child (hereafter: the 1989 Convention), says: 'For the purposes of the present Convention a child means every human being below the age of 18 years, unless under the law applicable to the child, majority is attained earlier.'[31] After extensive discussions, the Convention leaves the States Parties the discretion to provide in their domestic law when childhood begins, and, thus, if applicable, when protection begins. Van Bueren concludes that as far as international law is concerned, it protects childhood from birth.[32] Concerning the end of childhood, the States Parties have less discretion due to the inclusion of a 'maximum' age. They are, however, free, as Article 1 of the 1989 Convention states, to determine that majority is attained earlier.[33]

The rights of the child in international law clearly differ from the rights of the adult. On the one hand, children are commonly excluded from determining their own residence and from voting. However, on the other hand, they are entitled to special protection. As the 1959 Declaration on the Rights of the Child provides:

> The child shall enjoy special protection and shall be given opportunities and facilities by law and other means to develop physically, mentally, morally, spiritually and socially in a healthy and normal manner and in conditions of freedom and dignity...[34]

---

30 Geraldine Van Bueren's book, at pp. 33–38, provides interesting reading on this matter (op. cit., n. 24).

31 The text is to be found in (1989) *ILM*, pp.1448 ff.

32 Van Bueren, op. cit., p.35. Occasionally, but indirectly, international law extends its protection beyond the date of birth: Article 6(5) of the 1966 UN Covenant on Civil and Political Rights allows the death sentence to be imposed but not to be carried out on pregnant women, whereas Article 6(4) of the 1977 Additional Protocol I to the 1949 Geneva Red Cross Conventions prohibits both imposition and execution of the death penalty on pregnant women.

33 However, some international treaties employ other ages to provide for specific forms of protection, as for instance the 1949 Geneva Convention on the protection of civilians does. Under Community law, Member States' national law is decisive. However, Community law does require '... that the national legislation does not undermine the right to effective judicial protection' (ECJ: Joint cases C-87, 88, 89/90, *Verholen v. Sociale Verzekeringsbank;* in 1991 ECR-1, p.3790). See, further, section 4.2, below.

34 As GA Res 1386 XIV, adopted on 20 November 1959, unanimously and without abstentions.

Many of the Articles of the 1989 Convention provide for detailed codification of aspects of this special protection.

2.6.2 The rights of the child and environmental protection
In view of the Declaration's text just cited, it would not have been surprising if an environmental right would also have been included in the 1989 Convention. However, the only – very limited – reference to such a right can be found in Article 24 of the Convention. This Article focuses on the establishment, access and support in the use of a wide variety of child health care programmes. Article 24(2)(c) then specifies that as a means of combating disease and malnutrition, states should take into consideration 'the dangers and risks of environmental pollution'.

2.6.3 Environmental protection and the rights of the child
Looking at our subject-matter from the opposite angle, from environmental instruments to the position of children, the results are not much better. In Principle 19 of the 1972 Declaration, education in environmental matters 'for the younger generation as well as adults', is considered essential. In the 1992 Rio Declaration special attention for 'the young' has virtually disappeared. Only Principle 3 provides a reference: 'The right to development must be fulfilled so as to equitably meet developmental and environmental needs of present and future generations.' This reference brings us, however, in the rather special realm of 'inter-generational equity'.

On the one hand, the theory of inter-generational equity can be seen as a modified version of a rather classic view, i.e., that certain cultural pursuits of humankind and natural features of the earth as well, should be preserved, i.e., are part of humankind's heritage to be passed on. The 1946 International Convention for the Regulation of Whaling refers to the interest of the nations of the world in safeguarding whale stocks 'for future generations'.[35] The idea of 'sustainable development' in the meaning of the Brundlandt Commission elaborated upon these roots: 'development that meets the needs of the present without compromising the ability of future generations to meet their own needs'.[36]

35 Text, e.g., in Patricia Birnie and Alan Boyle, *Basic Documents on International Law and the Environment* (Oxford, 1995), pp. 586 ff. et seq.

36 See also Principle 3 of the 1992 Rio Declaration, cited in the text above. Gallons of ink ever since have been spent on the 'very vague and complex concept of 'sustainable development' to make it more definite and thereby more effective ...' (Alfred Rest, 'The Aftermath of Rio: Hurdles and Obstacles in Implementing Environmental Policies and Law – Some examples of Preliminary Efforts in State Practice', in K.-H. Böckstiegel (ed.), *Perspectives of Air Law, Space Law, and International Business Law for the Next Century* (Cologne, 1996), pp. 263–264.

On the other hand, there is a particular addition that the theory of inter-generational equity brings: the heritage, both cultural and natural, should be passed on to the next generation 'in no worse condition than it was received'.[37]

In a probably somewhat weaker (and curious) variety, this 'equity' core of inter-generational equity is also to be found in Principle 4 of the Ksentini Report's Draft Principles, which states:

> All persons have the right to an environment adequate to meet equitably the needs of present generations and that does not impair the rights of future generations to meet equitably their needs.[38]

Notwithstanding the many (legal) uncertainties related to sustainable development, several of its components have already found expression in the remarkable, and controversial, judgment by the Supreme Court of the Philippines in the *Minors Oposa* case. This class suit complaining about the granting of permits for extensive logging by the government of the Philippines was filed by and on behalf of a group of minors who asserted to represent their own generation as well as 'generations yet unborn'. The Supreme Court not only admitted the class suit, but also considered the principle of inter-generational responsibility to be legally binding. The decision held also that 'although the rights to a decent environment and to health were formulated as State policies, i.e. imposing upon the State a solemn obligation to preserve the environment, such policies manifest individual rights not less important than the civil and political rights enumerated under the [Philippines'] Bill of Rights of the Constitution.'[39]

So far, 'inter-generational equity' has not left perceptible traces in Community law, beyond, if one wishes, the inclusion of 'sustainable development' among the purposes introduced by the Treaty of Maastricht.

Another, also more indirect, reference to children in light of an environmental right is when interests of 'vulnerable persons' are taken into consideration.[40] In the Principles of the Ksentini Report, this happens almost as an afterthought in Principle 25: 'In implementing the rights and duties in this Declaration, special attention shall be given to vulnerable

37 See, for example, notably, Edith Brown-Weiss, *In Fairness to Future Generations* (Dobbs Ferry, 1989).

38 To be found in Boyle, in Boyle and Anderson, op. cit., n.5, p.66.

39 The text of the judgment has been published in (1994) *ILM*, pp. 173 et seq. See for a sympathetic and critical review of the *Oposa* judgment: Alfred Rest, 'The Oposa Decision: Implementing the Principles of Intergenerational Equity and Responsibility', in *Environmental Policy and Law*, (1994) pp. 314 et seq.

40 Such particular provisions for (pregnant) women, the elderly, the sick and children are known in other areas of international law, e.g., in the humanitarian law of armed conflict (cf. the detailed Arts. 76–78 of Additional Protocol I to the 1949 Geneva Conventions, relating to the Protection of International Armed Conflict).

persons and groups'. In section 1.3, above, the importance of substantiating the specific environmental vulnerability of children has already been emphasised.

3. 'Direct' Environmental Community Rights

3.1 Enforcement by individuals of their EC environmental rights?

Since 1974, the European Community has developed a substantive environmental policy, which, apart from specific provisions in the treaties, has found expression in an impressive number of environmental legal instruments.[41] However, Community law does not mention an individual right to a clean environment, nor in the Treaties nor in this vast body of secondary legislation.[42] Moreover, on a more implicit score, as will be further explained in the next section, a 'general environmental principle of Community law' seems difficult to construct as the constitutions of the Member States hardly refer to (individual) rights to a clean ('sound', 'healthy') environment, either. Of the current Member States only the constitutions of Spain and Portugal contain such provisions.[43]

Even if an individual Community right to a clean environment could be constructed or would be developed, a direct claim under such a right by an individual, or by a group representing its members' interests (e.g. Greenpeace), or by a group representing the interests of others (e.g. Child Watch International) before the Luxembourg judiciary is currently virtually excluded.[44] Article 173 EC does allow an individual action against a Council or Commission decision, but it sets severe conditions to be fulfilled. Such actions, to be lodged with the Court of First Instance, nevertheless, are likely to become increasingly more relevant in light of the growing powers of the Community in the field of the environment (and closely related fields).[45]

---

41 In its 12th *Annual Report on Monitoring the Application of Community Law* of 1994 (95/C 254/01), the Commission examined over 120 binding instruments of secondary legislation.

42 Like a provision comparable to Article 119 EC in which each Member State is held to ensure and maintain '... the applicability of the principle that men and women should receive equal pay for equal work'. This still limited 'human right' has then been elaborated in subsequent secondary instruments into a much broader right to 'equal treatment'.

43 In the future, this picture is likely to improve somewhat as East European countries will become Members of the EU. Several of them have included environmental rights in their new constitutions See, e.g. Stephen Stec on the application by the Hungarian Constitutional Court of the new Article 18 of the Hungarian Constitution guaranteeing the right to a healthy environment (in: 'New Phase in the Legislative Struggle for Environmental Protection in Central and Eastern Europe', in *Ecodecision*, (1995) pp.23–24).

44 This categorisation of litigants suggested by Chris Hilson and Ian Cram in 'Judicial review and environmental law – is there a coherent view of standing?', in *Legal Studies*, (1996) p.2, does not, of course, avoid all overlap between categories.

45 See Jans, op. cit., n.3, p. 192, for some examples.

Some good examples, illustrating some of the problems faced in such litigation, were the *Danielsson and others* and the *Greenpeace International* cases.[46] In *Danielsson*, the claimants applied for interim measures in respect to a final position adopted 23 October 1995 by the Commission on France's nuclear tests at Mururoa and Fangataufa atolls. In their application for interim measures the claimants sought, *inter alia*, to have the operation of this final position suspended. There is no doubt that the Court of First Instance has the powers to order the suspension of a decision.[47] However, if the decision (or regulation) is addressed to another person, according to Article 146 EURATOM (or 173(4) EC Treaty, for that matter) any natural or legal person should be 'directly and individually concerned'. This condition – quite relevant in the case of the rights of children as well – cannot easily be fulfilled.[48]

It has consistently been held by the Court that a decision is of individual concern to other persons only if that decision 'affects them by reason of certain attributes which are peculiar to them or by reason of circumstances in which they are differentiated from all other persons and if by virtue of those factors it distinguishes them individually just as in the case of the person addressed'. In *Danielsson*, the Court did not consider this criterion to be fulfilled because (again *prima facie*) 'the contested decision concerns the applicants only in their objective capacity as residents of Tahiti, in the same way as any other person residing in Polynesia'.[49] The Court further added that even if the applicants would suffer personal damage linked to the alleged harmful effects of the nuclear tests on the environment or on the health of the general public,

> that circumstance alone would not be sufficient to distinguish them individually in the same way as a person to whom the contested decision is addressed, as is required by the fourth paragraph of Article 146 of the Treaty [i.e., the EURATOM Treaty], since damage of the kind they cite could affect, in the same way, any person residing in the area in question.[50]

46 Case T-219/95 R. *Danielsson et al. v. Commission* [1995] ECR II-3051, order of the President of the Court of First Instance of 22 December 1995; Case T-585/93, *P. Stichting Greenpeace Council* (*Greenpeace I International et al. v. Commission* [1998] ECR-I-nyr (2 April 1998)).

47 The French Government who, in *Danielsson* (op. cit., previous footnote) obtained leave to intervene in support of the Commission, denied that the Commission's final position was in the nature of a decision (cons. 33), but the President of the Court *prima facie* rejected the French submission (cons.64–65).

48 For example *Greenpeace International v. Commission*; also *Danielsson*, with similar problems (both cases: op. cit., n.46).

49 *Danielsson*,op. cit., n.46, cons.70.

50 *Ibid*., cons.71. The Court refers here to its judgment in *Greenpeace International and Others v. Commission*, op. cit., n.46, cons. 49–55, where the same reasoning was followed. The text of Article 173 EC is identical to that of Article 146 EUR (see *Danielsson*, cons.72, where the appeal of Danielsson and others, in respect to 'attributes or circumstances peculiar to them', is also rejected).

In the face of these rather formidable obstacles blocking the path of the individual claimant, it is not a surprise that under Article 173 the position of 'groups representing interests' is even more discouraging. In *Greenpeace International v. Commission*, for example, the Court of Justice did not consider Greenpeace to be 'directly and individually concerned' by a measure affecting the general interests of a whole category of persons, when Greenpeace members had not been allowed *locus standi* as the Court had just denied that to them.[51] Here developments in the jurisprudence will have to be awaited in order to improve the possibility of bringing claims under Article 173 EC (or 146 EUR) in respect to children's environmental rights.

3.2 The European Union and human rights obligations: an awkward matter

Among the well-known problems of Community law is its somewhat curious, if not half-hearted, relation to the legal protection of human rights, in general, and to the European Convention on the Protection of Human Rights and Fundamental Freedoms and its institutions, in particular.[52] However, Article F.2 of the Treaty of European Union says that the Union shall respect as general principles, the fundamental rights from the European Human Rights Convention and the fundamental rights 'as they result from the constitutional traditions common to the Member States'. Thus the actions of the Union, of its institutions, should be in conformity with fundamental rights. Nevertheless, in a number of pre-Maastricht decisions of the Court – largely carried by judicial creativity – 'fundamental' rights are not only applicable in respect to the actions of the Community but, within the realm of EC law, increasingly, also the Member States should act in compliance with their values.[53]

The next important questions then are: what are 'general principles of Community law' and which fundamental rights are recognised as such general principles? It could be inferred from the somewhat awkward formulation of Article F.2, that the second category of fundamental rights mentioned, those additional to the (1950!) European Convention, has to pass the test of being 'embedded' ('for a long time'?) in the constitutional traditions common to ('all?') the Member States. The jurisprudence of the Court does not bring much clarity here, despite the older decision in the *Nold* case where the Court declared that the 'general principles of law' in

51 *Greenpeace International v. Commission*, op. cit., n.46.

52 See, e.g. the impressive set of questions opening Craig and De Burca's *EC Law; Text, Cases, and Materials* (Oxford 1995), p. 283.

53 Craig and De Burca, op. cit., n. 52, p. 309.

case of conflict were supposed to take precedence over specific Community measures.[54]

It is worthwhile realising that the Member States have undertaken a diversity of international obligations to create and protect the conditions that make it possible to enjoy environmental rights. In multilateral instruments (and in bilateral ones, but they will generally be left outside the scope of this study) they have assumed duties to protect and improve the quality of the environment. Principles (or emerging principles) setting standards for the undertaking of activities which are environmentally potentially detrimental, like the (notorious) precautionary principle, norms on environmental impact assessment or the principle that environmental damage should preferably be prevented at source, whatever their current legal state precisely may be, are also among them.

Apart from international instruments, all Member States have laid down environmental obligations in their legislation and, as said, Spain and Portugal even in their constitutions. These municipal provisions occasionally thus even include the guarantee of fundamental environmental rights.[55] However, in this study of limited scope, no effort will be undertaken to examine the state of the municipal law of the Member States in the light of the condition set to the 'second' category of fundamental rights of Article F.2 of the Treaty on European Union.

Article F.2 has introduced human rights now by way of this explicit reference to the European Convention in the text of the Treaty.[56] Although the Court of Justice has already declared several times, how important an adequate relationship to the decisions made by the Strasbourg institutions is to it, the nature of the relationship remains unclear and seems to leave open all kinds of suggestions for improvement. These ideas for improvement vary widely: from the EU/EC adopting its own 'Charter of Human Rights', via a strict adherence to the protection of fundamental rights by way of a legally binding commitment thereto, to the EU/EC becoming a party to the European Convention. In respect to a human right to a 'clean' environment some of these solutions will not make an explicit

54 Case 4/73, *Nold, Kohlen -und Baustoffgrosshandlung v. Commission* [1974] ECR 491. Advocate General Warner concluded in Case 155/79, *A. M. & S. Europe Ltd v. Commission* [1982] ECR Op.1631, that 'it should be possible to distil a general principle even if the "conceptual origin" of that principle and the "scope" of its application in detail differ from Member State to Member State' (cf. also Case 17/74, *Transocean Marine Paint v. Commission*, [1974] *ECR* 1063).

55 See for an overview of the state of constitutions at the end of the 1980s: Ida Koppen and Karl-Heinz Ladeur, "Environmental rights", in Cassese, Clapham and Weiler (eds.), op. cit., n.4, pp. 22–25. More recently, environmental rights and concerns have notably found expression in the constitutions of Eastern European states (see above, n. 43, and subsection 2.1).

56 In the Preamble, the Single European Act also referred to the Convention, as well as to the European Social Charter. The latter reference (together with a new reference to the non-binding 1989 Community Charter of the Fundamental Social Rights of Workers) has been maintained in the Preamble to the Treaty of European Union, whereas reference to the European Convention has thus been 'up-graded' to Article F.2.

difference. After all the European Convention does not include such a right.[57] A right to a clean environment could, of course, be 'directly' included in the EU Treaty,[58] or be part of a separate human rights charter for the Member States. However, it should be realised that in a primarily monistic legal system as, for example, the Dutch one, the significance of human rights guarantees in a separate treaty is, in principle, quite different from the consequences of such a treaty in a primarily dualistic legal system like the English one. A decision of a Dutch judge that a provision from, e.g. the European Convention on Human Rights, the UN Covenant on Civil and Political Rights, or whatever other treaty provision has direct effect, makes this provision prevail (Art. 94, Dutch Constitution) over any contrary rule of Dutch law. Some such provisions have thus acquired tremendous importance.[59]

In a more dualistic system, the individual may have a hard time claiming an individual right guaranteed in a human rights treaty, whereas, in principle, he may be equally successful as his Dutch counterpart in claiming a 'right' under a provision with direct effect of Community law. The Court of Justice can even grant more extensive protection to individual rights than ensured by the European Convention on Human Rights.[60]

With the Treaty of Amsterdam entering into force, greater importance of the European Union as a guarantor of fundamental rights might be the result. Apart from the addition of 'sustainable development' in the seventh 'economic and social progress' recital of the Preamble and to Article B, in the light of the subject matter here under consideration notably a change in respect to Article F may eventually prove to be of relevance. Article F.2, itself has not been altered, but Article L of the European Union Treaty has been amended to include – in Article L(c) – Article F.2 as among those provisions to which the powers of the Court of Justice apply 'with regard to action of the institutions, insofar as the Court has jurisdiction under the Treaties establishing the European Communities and under this Treaty'. This amendment, although not marking a great change with the *acquis*, indicates that, at last, the European Union is on its

---

57 However, see sections 3.3 and 3.4, below, on the relevance of Article 8 of the Convention in this regard. See, also the wide-ranging papers, reports and other reflections on the future relationship between 'Luxembourg and Strasbourg', notably the semi-official Westendorp Report's para. 34 on EU or EC accession to the Convention (the Report was published on 5 December 1995 (SN520/95).

58 For the new Treaty of Amsterdam changes along the latter line have been suggested, but not accepted. For example, a new Article 8d containing an individual environmental right, including a right to (public) access to decision-making on environmental matters, and a right to adequate judicial remedies, have been mentioned; see, e.g., *Nederlands Juristenblad* 1995, p. 914 (in Dutch). See, also below in this subsection.

59 See, briefly, P. Malanczuk, *Akehurst's Introduction to international law* (8th ed. London, 1997), pp.67–68, or, in greater depth: E.Alkema, 'Foreign relations in The Netherlands Constitution of 1983', in *Netherlands International Law Review* (1984), pp. 322–328.

60 Cf. Advocate General Lenz in Case 137/84, *Ministère Public v. Mutsch*, (1985) ECR 2690.

way to its own, explicit, system of protection of fundamental rights. At least, one may presume it to be more and more unlikely that the European Union, in one way or another, will accede to the European Convention on Human Rights. However, in what way the ECJ will take the viewpoints of human rights organs into account has not been clarified by the Treaty of Amsterdam.[61]

3.3 The 1950 European Convention on Human Rights

The European Court of Human Rights does not seem the most logical court to develop environmental jurisprudence. The 1950 European Convention on Human Rights and Fundamental Freedoms does not include any individual environmental rights. Nevertheless, notably, since the Court's judgment of 21 February 1990, in the case of *Powell and Rayner v. United Kingdom*,[62] it has become clear that, at least, Article 8, which provides that

> *1.* Everyone has the right to respect for his private and family life, his home and his correspondence.
>
> *2.* ....

(and, perhaps, Article 3 as well) may involve guarantees by the (respondent) states which include the responsibility to avoid the deterioration of an individual's environment. Indirectly such responsibility is highly relevant from the perspective of the effective enjoyment of environmental rights by individuals. What can be at stake in cases regarding such rights is that individuals can no longer be presumed to be able to enjoy their fundamental human rights facing particular forms of environmental deterioration or nuisance.[63] In its *Powell and Rayner* decision the Human Rights Court came very close to deciding that in view of claimant's suffering of 'excessive noise generated by air traffic in and out of Heathrow Airport',[64] the applicant's rights under Article 8 of the European Convention could no longer be considered as adequately guaranteed. However, in view of the UK government's measures to abate noise pollution and other

---

61 See further, below, section 3.4.2.

62 *Case of Powell and Rayner*, Judgment of 21 February 1990, in: ECHR, Series A: Judgments and Decisions, Vol. 172. Already from 1976 onwards, the European Commission of Human Rights has passed judgments on complaints of an environmental nature (see the overview in Philippe Sands, 'Human Rights, Environment and the *López-Ostra* Case: Context and Consequences' in *European Human Rights Law Review*, (1996) no.6, pp. 608–611).

63 See, e.g Richard Desgagné, 'Integrating environmental values into the European Convention on Human Rights', in *American Journal of International Law* (1995), p. 265.

64 *Powell and Rayner* case, op. cit., n. 62, cons. 17.

actions, it did not decide against the United Kingdom, and in fact concluded, generally, to a wide 'margin of appreciation' in cases like this.

> [I]t is certainly not for the ... Court to substitute for the national authorities any other assessment of what might be best policy in this difficult technical and social sphere. This is an area where the Contracting Parties are to be recognised as enjoying a wide margin of appreciation.[65]

Hence, in view of this broad interpretation of Article 8.2, what was decided in the judgment of 9 December 1994 by a Chamber of the Court in the case of *López Ostra v. Spain* could come as something of a surprise . However, here the case was not concerned with the nuisance caused by one of the world's largest airports, but by the adverse effects of a local purification plant. Moreover, the Spanish authorities' behaviour seemed to be in a rather different class from that of their English counterparts.

The Chamber concluded that Spain had not acted according to its obligations under Article 8 and granted Mrs López Ostra a considerable amount of money for damages, and, in addition, for costs and expenses. By its decision, the Chamber was probably the first international tribunal ever to hold that a respondent state actually had to pay for damages (and costs and expenses) in a case where someone was suffering from a deterioration of the state of the environment.[66]

3.4 The 1994 decision in the López Ostra *case*

This case originated in an application dated 14 May 1990, under Article 25 of the Convention against Spain, by a Spanish national Mrs López Ostra. The case concerned a plant for the treatment of liquid and solid waste from several tanneries all belonging to SACURSA. This plant was built with a state subsidy on municipal land twelve metres away from Mrs López Ostra's home in the town of Lorca.

The start-up in July 1988, without the licence required from the municipal authorities, of this undertaking to improve the local environment was not entirely successful. The plant

65 *Ibid.*, cons. 44. Substantively, the Court decided on similar grounds as the European Commission of Human Rights had done in cases such as *S.v. France* (see n.75): it passed judgment on the adequacy of the measures to protect claimants' rights under the Convention taken by the governments concerned.

66 The 1938 (interlocutory) decision by the international arbitrary tribunal in the Canadian-USA *Trail Smelter* case granting a claim for damages by the United States government on behalf of the Stevens County farmers, may also be considered as the first, somewhat more indirect, case where an international tribunal 'went all the way' (in *RIAA*, Vol. III, p. 1918).

> released gas fumes, pestilential smells and contamination, which immediately caused health problems and nuisance to many Lorca people, particularly those living in the applicant's district. The town council evacuated the local residents and rehoused them free of charge in the town centre for the months of July, August and September 1988.[67]

On 8 September 1988, the town council decided to reduce the plant's activities to the treatment of wastewater contaminated with chromium. Although there remains some disagreement on the effects of this measure, expert opinions and written evidence of subsequent years show 'that certain nuisances continue and may endanger the health of those living nearby'.[68] In September 1991, the Murcia High Court ordered the plant's temporary closure. However, following an appeal by the town council and SACURSA, enforcement of this order was stayed.

After an account of the procedural stages of the applicant's (and related) proceedings in Spain, up to the Constitutional Court, including a survey of the expert reports presented and of the relevant domestic law, the European Court of Human Rights turned to the applicable provisions of the Convention.

Firstly, it reviewed, as usual, the proceedings before the European Commission of Human Rights, as well as Spain's preliminary objections (which were dismissed or considered unfounded). Next, the Court examined the 'core' alleged violation of Article 8.

Basically, the Court established whether or not the Spanish authorities took the measures necessary for protecting Mrs López Ostra's rights under Article 8. To do this, the authorities needed to strike a fair balance between Mrs López Ostra's interest of having been granted her right to respect for her home, private and family life under Article 8, paragraph 1, and the interest of the community of Lorca. Thereto the respondent state should appropriately make use of the 'margin of appreciation' expressed in Article 8, paragraph 2. In that respect the Court took into account that Lorca's municipal authorities had not only failed to take measures to protect the applicant's rights under Article 8, but had also resisted judicial decisions to that effect. As noted above, in 1991 the Spanish town's council appealed against the judicial decision of the Murcia High Court to close the plant, resulting in its remaining open until October 1993. Temporary re-housing measures that the town had taken provided insufficient redress for the nuisance and inconveniences.[69]

67 *López Ostra* case, op. cit., n.17, cons. 8.
68 *Ibid.*, cons. 9; see also cons. 18–20 of the Judgment.
69 *Ibid.*, cons. 56 and 57.

The Court decided that despite its margin of appreciation, Spain had not managed to find a fair balance between the interest of Lorca's economic well-being – that of having a waste-treatment plant – and Mrs López Ostra's rights. Accordingly, Article 8 had been violated.[70]

The damage suffered on account of the violation of Article 8, was divided into material damage – foremost as a consequence of the depreciation in value of her old flat and the obligation eventually to move – and non-pecuniary damage:

> In addition to the nuisance caused by the gas fumes, noise and smells from the plant, she felt distress and anxiety as she saw the situation persisting and her daughter's health deteriorating.[71]

In accordance with Article 50 of the Convention, the Court made an assessment on an equitable basis, and awarded Mrs López Ostra ESP 4,000,000. In addition, she received ESP 1,500,000 for costs and expenses incurred before the Convention institutions.[72]

In its judgment of 19 February 1998, in the case of *Guerra and others v. Italy*, the Court also decided that Article 8 had been violated for reasons concerning the state of the environment. In this case the violation by the Italian authorities involved their failure to act, i.e., to provide adequate information in view of a serious threat of environmental deterioration. The Court awarded each of the 40 applicants ITL 10,000,000 (plus interest) for non-pecuniary damage.[73]

3.4.1 Some observations on the Strasbourg jurisprudence

The 'environmental' jurisprudence of the Strasbourg Court leads to the following observations of some interest for the subject-matter here under examination.

(1) For a child (or for an adult) the *López Ostra* and *Guerra* awards – and something comparable has already been said about the *Powell and Rayner* case – implies a general right to a 'clean' environment. It does not seem a great exaggeration to define the quality of that environment for a child (every human being) as 'free from pollution so severe that

---

70 *Ibid.*, cons. 58.

71 *Ibid.*, cons. 65.

72 Minus 9,700 French Francs paid by the Council of Europe (see for compensation for damage and reimbursement of costs and expenses, awarded: cons. 65 and 71, respectively, in *ibid.*).

73 Judgment of 19 February 1998, in Case no. 116/1996/735/932, Case of *Guerra and others v. Italy*, not yet published, cons. 58, and, for the award for damages, cons. 67.

it affects its well-being adversely and prevents it from ordinary life, without necessarily seriously endangering its health' (see section 2.3, *supra*).

(2) From the point of view of those who have obligations to protect the environment, the duties of Contracting Parties' authorities have, of course also been made more explicit. While recognising their margin of appreciation, they have a responsibility to ensure that the actions of their authorities do not prevent an individual from enjoying an environment with the qualities just defined.

(3) In the *Guerra* decision, the Court added that 'in addition to this primarily negative undertaking, there may be positive obligations inherent in effective respect for private or family life'.[74] One of those positive duties is providing essential information to individuals in order to allow them to assess the risks they and their families might run in the face of serious environmental deterioration.

(4) The *López Ostra* and *Guerra* judgments are landmark decisions: for the first time in an 'environmental' case, the Court has decided that a Contracting Party's authorities failed to measure up to their duties under the 'margin of appreciation' (of Article 8(2)). In previous cases the Strasbourg Court and Commission always found that the Contracting Party had stayed within the realm of Article 8(2).[75] In *López Ostra* and *Guerra*, the Court has thus made the first steps in devising a standard for misbehaviour in this regard (and even awarded damages accordingly).

(5) These two awards do not seem to provide much ground for significantly narrowing down the state's margin of appreciation, at least not the one concerning noise nuisance in airport cases as was set out in the *Powell and Rayner v. United Kingdom* case (see the text at section 3.3).

(6) For the first time in international jurisprudence a right to environmental protection is acknowledged *even* if the health of individuals is not seriously endangered. In paragraph 51 of the award, the Court considered:

74 *Ibid.* cons.58.

75 In *Powell and Rayner*, but somewhat later on 17 May of the same year, the Commission declared a case inadmissible on the basis of reasonable actions by the French authorities (*S. v. France*, Application no.13728/88; in D.R. 65, at pp. 250 et seq.). Previously, cases involving airport and other noise nuisance had also been settled, or found inadmissible because no intolerable or too frequent noise levels were at stake (see, for an overview, Philippe Sands, op. cit., n.62, at p.609).

Naturally, severe environmental pollution may affect individuals' well-being and prevent them from enjoying their homes in such a way as to affect their private and family life adversely, without, however, seriously endangering their health.[76]

(7) Apart from Article 8, no other rights guaranteed in the Convention were so far effectively connected to degradation of the environment: neither Protocol 1, Article 1 (on the protection of property rights), nor Articles 2 (right to life), 3 (on inhuman or degrading treatment), 6 (right to a fair and public hearing), or 10 (freedom of expression in the *Guerra* case) of the Convention were thus considered.

3.4.2 Its significance for TEU Article F.2

What is the legal relevance of decisions such as those in the *López Ostra* and *Guerra* cases for EU law and thereby for the protection of the right of a child to a clean environment under that law? This is a difficult (and perhaps even a somewhat painful) question to ask, in view of the ambiguous relationship between EU law and (European) human rights law, referred to above in section 3.2. As the Union has neither a Bill of Rights nor itself is operating within the European Convention on Human Rights, it is left to the Luxembourg Court to ensure that a legal structure is maintained which guarantees protection of fundamental human rights. The Court has tried to do so in successive years, at least in respect to the Community institutions, leading Advocate-General Darmon to draw attention to the main reason why the European Commission of Human Rights has declared inadmissible applications directed against national decisions enacted pursuant to a Community act. This reason is 'that, through its successive judgments, the Court [of Justice] had established the principle that it reviews the Community institutions' observance of fundamental rights'.[77]

Conversely, Craig and De Burca conclude from their survey of the application by the Court of Justice of several fundamental human rights that 'the European Convention on Human Rights as interpreted by the Court of Human Rights has come to represent a standard against which the Community institutions and indeed the Court of Justice measure their "fundamental rights" performance'.[78]

76 In the *Guerra* decision (cons. 60) the Court reiterates cons. 51 of the *López Ostra* judgment. In the latter case, the Court, however, also agrees with the Commission that 'there could be a causal link between [hydrogen sulphide emissions from the plant] and the applicant's daughter's ailments' (see cons. 48 and 49; and also cons. 57).

77 In Case 49/88, *Al-Jubail Fertilizer Co. and Saudi Arabian Fertilizer Co. v. Council* [1991] *ECR* I, 3230.

78 Op. cit., n.52, p.308. Parliament, Council and Commission were in fact already committed to such performance by way of the so-called 'Tri-partite' Joint Declaration of 5 April 1977 (cf. Case 222/84, *Johnston v. Chief Constable of the Royal Ulster Constabulary;* in [1986] *ECR*, p. 1651, cons. 18).

This is probably a correct assessment of the Court's performance and viewpoint in respect to the Community's institutions, but how about the Member States? Here the situation is rather different. The Court's jurisdiction in respect to acts of Member States under the treaties is much more limited than its powers regarding acts of Community institutions. Moreover, it is still to be seen which 'fundamental rights are common to the Member States' (Article F.2) and whether the Court of Justice is accepted by them to determine this and judge their behaviour accordingly.

Whatever the position exactly is, Article 8 of the Convention has already found a favourable reception in the jurisprudence of the Court. In Case 249/86, *Commission v. Germany*, a decision about the requirement of respect for family life in the context of re-unification of families of migrant workers, covered by this Article, the Court declared:

> That requirement [i.e., respect for family life set out in Article 8 of the Convention] is one of the fundamental rights which, according to the Court's settled case-law, restated in the preamble to the Single European Act, are recognised by Community law.[79]

In this case, the Court decided that German legislation was indeed not living up to an EC obligation, because that obligation had to be interpreted, *inter alia*, in light of the requirement of respect for family life as guaranteed under Article 8 of the Convention. There is thus ground to presume that, in principle, for the interpretation of other EC obligations of Member States Article 8 should also be taken into account. A Member State might thus also be held to prevent serious environmental degradation, i.e., at least to the extent of the basic standard set in the *López Ostra* case. In an environment below that standard individuals' right to family life can no longer be guaranteed by a Member State. Hence that state may be expected either to prevent such degradation taking place, to improve the environment or to make sure the individual(s) are adequately compensated.

Recent jurisprudence of the Court where the relationship between (international) fundamental rights obligations of the Member States and general principles of Community law has been at stake, does not really seem to challenge this conclusion. In its judgment of 19 March 1998 in case T-83/96, *G. Van der Wal v. Commission*, the Court of First Instance, produced a 'reflective' paragraph on the relationship, notably, with the

[79] Case 249/86, *Commission v. Germany*, in [1989] *ECR*, 1263, cons. 10. The Court held that the Regulation concerned (No.1612/68) must also be interpreted in the light of this requirement. However, in what way the Court made use of Art. 8 in its interpretation of the Regulation is not revealed in the judgment.

European Convention on Human Rights, which seems worthwhile to quote at length:

> It is settled case-law that fundamental rights form an integral part of the general principles of law whose observance the Community judicature ensures ... For that purpose, the Court of Justice and the Court of First Instance draw inspiration from the constitutional traditions common to the Member States and from the guidelines supplied by international treaties for the protection of human rights on which the Member States have agreed or to which they have acceded. In that regard the ECHR has special significance ... Furthermore, as provided for in Article F(2) of the Treaty on European Union (etc.).[80]

However, a month earlier, on 17 February 1998, the decision of the full Court in case C-249/96, *L.J.Grant v. South-West Trains Ltd* appeared to display more of the ambiguity and complexity of the relationship Community law has with fundamental human rights, albeit apparently, primarily, with other rights than those of the European Convention.

In cons. 44 of this decision, the Court recalls that the UN International Covenant on Civil and Political Rights contains fundamental rights it takes into account 'in applying the fundamental principles of Community law'. However, the Court then draws a boundary by adding that those rights

> cannot in themselves have the effect of extending the scope of the Treaty provisions beyond the competences of the Community.[81]

It restates its more or less classical codex of interpretation: the scope of Article 119 EC 'as of any provision of Community Law, is to be determined only by having regard to its wording and purpose, its place in the scheme of the Treaty and its legal context'.[82] Here, the Court seems to draw the line between interpretation of existing Community law in light of international obligations of Member States under human rights treaties (as took place in case C-249/86, *Commission v. Germany,* referred to above) and 'transforming' such obligations into (new) obligations under Community law.

At times this boundary probably will probably prove to be a difficult one to apply, as the judgment in the *Grant* case already seems to show. The Court argued that the point of view of the Human Rights Committee established in Article 28 of the Covenant cannot constitute a basis for the

---

80 Case T-83/96, *Gerard van der Wal v. Commission*, Judgment of 19 March 1998, not yet published, at 46. This case, which was primarily concerned with information, with regard to the ECHR dealt with Article 6 only.

81 Case C-249/96, *L.J. Grant v. South-West Trains Ltd*, cons. 45, not yet published.

82 *Ibid.*, cons. 46.

Court to broaden the scope of Article 119 of the Treaty. The Court noted that the Committee is not a judicial body and that its determinations have no binding legal value (*Ibid.*, para. 46). Nevertheless, this denial of the relevance of the Human Rights Committee's opinion, albeit indeed not 'binding' as such, is remarkable. Under general international law, a 'competent organ' – as the Human Rights Committee – has powers in matters of interpretation.[83]

This reflection of the Court on the opinions of the Human Rights Committee leaves unclear what the significance (for matters of interpretation) is of decisions and opinions, whether binding or not, of the European Commission of Human Rights or of organs of other human rights treaties.[84] However, it does not diminish the relevance of fundamental rights obligations binding on all Member States, like Article 8, nor the authority of a determination by the European Court of Human Rights which, after all, is a judicial body and the decisions of which are binding on Member States.

The limited scope of this study does not permit much more than suggestions. Among them is that the duties under Article 8.1 of the European Convention on Human Rights, mentioned at the end of the previous subsection, in particular those under (2) to (4) which are inferred from the *López Ostra* and *Guerra* judgments, should also be guaranteed under Community law. If that is the case they will represent rights of the child (and other individuals) to a 'clean' environment under Community law. However, the Luxembourg Court should first provide much more clarity in respect to their guarantee in the law of the European Union.[85]

---

83 Cf. '[E]ach organ, must, in the first place at least, determine its own jurisdiction' (*Certain Expenses of the United Nations, Advisory Opinion*, (1962) *ICJ Reports*, p.168). This is, of course, not the equivalent to complete freedom to determine powers. See, the Advisory Opinion of 8 July 1996 of the ICJ on *Legality of the Use by a State of Nuclear Weapons in Armed Conflict* in response to a question asked by the World Health Organisation, where the ICJ set some important limits to the implied powers of the WHO Assembly ((1996) *ICJ Reports*, cons. 29). In light of the Luxembourg's Court own positive reference to the Preamble of the Single European Act, which at least also suggests a relationship between human rights and 'the framework of the United Nations' (e.g., in its judgment in Case 249/86, *Commission v. Germany*, cons. 10, op. cit., n.79) this putting aside of the Committee's view is also remarkable.

84 Like the organs of the International Covenant on Economic, Social and Cultural Rights, the International Convention on the Elimination of all Forms of Racial Discrimination, or the European Social Charter (although the latter Charter is referred to in the Preamble of the Single European Act), to mention a few. At the end of its Judgment in the *Grant* case (op. cit., n.81) the Court provides some rather limited kind of consolation when it refers to new Article F.1 to be brought into the EU Treaty by the Treaty of Amsterdam, which will allow Council (by unanimous decision!) to take adequate measures to fight forms of discrimination.

85 Some straightforward provisions on the observation of human rights in the Treaty of Amsterdam would have been the better approach, although the political will for more than some piecemeal progress was apparently still lacking.

4. 'Derived' Environmental Community Rights (With Special Reference to English Jurisprudence)

4.1 Environmental duties towards individuals

In EC legal discourse 'directly effective Community rights' tends to be replaced by 'Community rights'.[86] The reason thereto is that Community rights that are not directly effective could also be relevant as individual rights, i.e., where the principles of indirect effect, or liability under the *Francovich* jurisprudence[87] could be applied. From a point of view of rights to be claimed by individuals, however, neither indirect effect of rights, nor 'sympathetic interpretation' (of, notably, directives), nor the *Francovich* liability principles, although certainly of great relevance as such, belong in the category of international or European human rights to be claimed in national courts.[88] 'Derived' human rights will be used here. This term is meant to indicate that a distinction is maintained from 'direct' rights of individuals (children). Direct rights are explicitly guaranteed and are (potentially) directly enforceable at the international level, including at the Community level. 'Derived' rights may exist in the form of duties by Member States, which by way of their direct effect can be claimed as individual or collective rights by individuals or their groups before a national court, 'which are the ordinary courts of Community law'.[89] As said, both direct and derived rights share, at least the potential of being international (Community) rights and being effectively enforceable, albeit in international (Community) and national courts, respectively. A limited number of rights can be claimed by individuals in national litigation but may also be potentially enforceable at the international or Community level.[90]

86 Cf.Steiner, *Enforcing EC Law* (London, 1995), pp. 42 et seq.

87 Cases C-6 and 9/90, *Francovich v. Italy*, [1991] *ECR*. I p.5357; Joint Cases C-46/93 and C-48/93, *Brasserie du Pêcheur SA v. Fed. Rep. of Germany*, nyr, and *R v.Secretary of State for Transport, ex parte Factortame Ltd, (Factortame IV)*, nyr; could be considered to belong, respectively, as a further explanation of the *Francovich* jurisprudence, thereby specifying the conditions set for Member State liability. On the extensive literature, see, in particular: Han Somsen, '*Francovich* and its application to EC Environmental Law' in Han Somsen (ed.), *Protecting the European Environment: Enforcing EC Environmental Law* (London 1996), pp. 135 et seq.

88 Although they could, of course, be labelled Community rights, it is preferable perhaps simply to call them principles of interpretation and principles of liability, respectively.

89 *Danielsson*, op. cit., n.46, cons.77. It may not always be necessary really to 'read' the provisions of the Community instrument in place of the potentially faulty or absent domestic legislation. This might notably be the case if a claim concerns a breach of quality standards derived from an EC directive which as such has been implemented appropriately. However, it can be questioned, in my view, if such a case is a proper example of a claim for a right on the basis of direct effect (see Hilson, op. cit.,n.18, p. 52, n.4). In such a claim direct effect seems not to be at issue (neither are 'preliminary' rulings of the national courts).

90 However, this is likely to be a very limited category: see subsection 3.1, above.

The case of children, claiming for the application of provisions with direct effect is extra-difficult, because children have even more limited ways of independently claiming their rights than adults. This makes them more dependent on the *locus standi* of groups or organisations acting on their behalf. We will first turn to this matter.

4.2 Children and the enforcement of rights

How does one define a child and is a child allowed to claim independently? Not surprising, perhaps in view of the discussion in subsection 2.6, above, on the Convention on the Rights of the Child, Community law leaves this matter to the Member States. Only in respect to specific subjects, like Articles 126 and 127 EC on education, vocational training and youth, as well as in some instruments of social policy or rights of residence, is 'youth' mentioned at all in EC law.[91] However, as a direct beneficiary of a right to a clean environment the child (like its fellow human beings) is absent altogether.[92] Others, interest groups, claiming on behalf of children would be the main source for the enforcement of their rights.

Under Article 5 EC, Member States have a general duty to ensure fulfilment of the obligations arising under Community law. In its 1990 *Factortame* judgment the Court of Justice explained:

> It is for the national courts in application of the principle of cooperation laid down in Article 5 of the EEC Treaty to ensure the legal protection which persons derive from the direct effect of provisions of Community law.[93]

In doing so, the procedural conditions are not supposed to be less favourable than in respect to similar actions of a domestic nature, and, furthermore, never, in practice, may these conditions make it impossible to exercise the rights derived from these provisions.[94]

---

91 Article 126.2 on education refers to the encouragement of the development of youth exchanges as an aim for Community action; Article 127.2 singles out 'young people' as those whose access to vocational training should be facilitated and whose mobility should be encouraged. Also in secondary legislation in the areas of social policy or rights of residence, children are occasionally referred to (e.g. Article 1.f.ii of Council Regulation (EEC) 1408/71 on the application of social security schemes to employed persons and to members of their families moving within the Community, or Article 2.2 of Council Directive 90/365/EEC on the right of residence for employees, etc.).

92 Thus, perhaps not surprisingly although not wise in my view, in treatises on the rights of the child not much attention tends to be paid to European Community law, either. Geraldine Van Bueren's well-known and valuable book (op. cit., n.24), is a good example. It does cover regional organisations, but reference to the EC is virtually absent.

93 Case-213/89, *R. v. Secretary of State for Transport, ex parte Factortame Ltd*, [1990] *ECR* I-2433, cons. 19 (following a long line of judgments).

94 See, Andrew Geddes, '*Locus Standi* and EEC Environmental Measures', in *Journal of Environmental Law*, (1992), p.29.

4.2.1 Standing rights

Basically EC law has two approaches to the crucial issue of standing in national courts. On the one hand, there is the restrictive view that only those who are 'directly affected' by EC rules have standing and can invoke Community law in national courts. 'Everybody else possesses simply an interest in the application or enforcement of the law rather than a right as such.'[95] In this restricted view there is no room for action to enforce such interests – as those of children – under EC law in national courts (there may be protection, and thus enforcement possibilities, under national law, however).

A broader view, on the other hand, would allow any citizen rights under EC law, whether or not that citizen is directly affected. In terms of the rights of children, however, even the latter approach does not entirely solve the problem of standing in view of children's very limited 'subject' status. This, at least to a very great extent, leaves them dependent on 'citizen action' on their behalf, even if, within any reason, they are directly affected.

So far, the jurisprudence of the ECJ seems to have a preference for the 'restrictive' approach to standing and has not shown much inclination to give interest groups access to provisions with direct effect.[96] However, the 'doctrine of effectiveness', so coined after the Court's decision in *Verholen v. Sociale Verzekeringsbank*, may indicate an opening in this matter, perhaps of particular interest if the interest group claims for subjects who are indeed directly affected but are legally incapable to claim themselves. The Court said: '[w]hile it is, in principle, for national law to determine an individual's standing and legal interest in bringing proceedings, Community law nevertheless requires that the national legislation does not undermine the right to effective judicial protection'.[97] In his decision in the English *Thorp* case, Judge Otton seemed to decide in this spirit when he allowed Greenpeace UK standing: 'if I were to deny standing ... those they represent might not have an effective way to bring the issues before the court.'[98]

In the meantime, in several Member States the legal situation seems indeed to have become somewhat more inviting for interests groups. In his survey of preventive enforcement action in English and Welsh courts, Hilson can conclude that '[t]oday, however, the courts have adopted a much

95 Hilson, op. cit., n.18, p.53.

96 A 'classical' case here is Case 158/80, *Rewe v. Hauptzollampt Kiel*, in (1981) *ECR*, p.1805.

97 Joined Cases C-87,88,89/90, in (1991) *ECR*, I-3790. Cf. Steiner, op .cit., n.86, pp. 43–46.

98 *R. v. Secretary of State for the Environment, HMIP, MAFF, ex parte Greenpeace and Lancashire County Council*; in (1994) *Environmental Law Review*, at D-10 (Part 3).

more generous approach to standing in judicial review cases, particularly in relation to group applicants ...'[99]

4.2.2 Other obstacles to effective rights

There are more obstacles apart from standing for (legal) persons in their path to seek effective judicial remedies in national courts. For one thing, if they try to challenge the way directives are implemented, they, cannot do so 'horizontally', that is against private individuals. Moreover, in differing ways the interest groups involved may still have a hard time to convince a court from the substance of their claim and thus from the necessity to grant a remedy. Finally, from a more practical point of view, at the beginning of proceedings and often at the end as well, interest groups must face the issue of costs.[100]

Environmental cases in the United Kingdom provide some good examples. At present, the major problems interest groups encounter are persuading the court of the merits of the claim and then of the need to grant remedies. Among several reasons, which have wider importance than for the local British situation only, the following stand out. First, although the interest group has passed the hurdle of the standing, still it may not be considered to enjoy the Community rights appealed for because it has not 'directly' suffered the alleged damage. This was one of the main arguments in the rather controversial *Friends of the Earth* decision by the High Court.[101]

Furthermore, if the interest group is granted their rights, the court may, of course, still decide for a variety of reasons that these rights have not been infringed. In particular, the effective argument for the rejection by the English Court of Appeal of the claim by Friends of the Earth for substantive rights under one of the drinking water directives is remarkable here. These rights were considered as not being infringed because the implementing legislation had been approved by the European Commission and in fact by the ECJ, as well.[102]

99 Hilson, op. cit., n.18, p.59. See, more generally, Eckhart Rehbinder, '*Locus Standi*, Community Law and the Case for Harmonization', in Han Somsen (ed.), op. cit., n.87, p.153. The Commission also recognized the relevance of improving direct access to justice in respect to environmental rights and duties and is considering a new instrument to facilitate such public involvement (see its Twelfth Annual Report on monitoring the application of Community law; op. cit., n.41). However, the Treaty of Amsterdam does not show much improvement in this respect.

100 This may not be a major issue for 'rich' NGOs, but can be quite stifling for more ordinary citizens' groups. See, further, Hilson, op. cit., n.18, p.59.

101 *R v. Secretary of State for the Environment , ex parte Friends of the Earth Ltd;* in (1994) *Common Market Law Review* (CMLR), p.760 (see for the appeal where standing was no longer doubted: Hilson's note in *ibid.*, 1995, pp. 1461 et seq.); or, in respect to local authorities: *Twyford Parish Council v. Secretary of State for Transport;* (1992) *Journal of Environmental Law*, pp. 273 et seq, (see also Jans, op. cit., n.3, pp.178–179; more generally: p.182–183), and *Wychavon District Council v. Secretary of State for the Environment and Velcourt Ltd;* in (1994) *CMLR*, pp. 35 1 et seq.

102 See Chris Hilson's commentary on this complicated case, in: 'B. National Courts', (1995) *CMLR*, pp. 1461 et seq., especially at p. 1468.

In some of the more procedural British cases, mainly on quests for environmental impact assessments, even some rather pragmatic grounds, for instance economic considerations, have been invoked to reject a claim. However, whether or not such decisions will survive Luxembourg's scrutinising in the light of the principle of effectiveness mentioned above, is a good question to ask.

In respect to the Court's decisions in the *German TA Luft* cases,[103] among others Jans draws attention to Community instruments by which obligations are enacted to maintain environmental standards with a very general protective aim. Such standards almost by definition serve a 'general' interest. The Court concluded 'whenever the exceeding of the limit values could endanger human health, the persons concerned must be in a position to rely on mandatory rules in order to be able to assert their rights'.[104] This possibility would solve most of the standing and some of the other enforcement problems referred to above for interest groups and children who depend on them for effective enforcement of their environmental rights. That is, at least, in so far as enforcement of obligations with direct effect in secondary legislation that sets general environmental standards (emission standards, product standards, etc.) is concerned.[105]

4.3 Substantive environmental duties and rights

There is no lack of substantive provisions of Community law with direct effect, which are relevant for rights of children to a clean environment. These provisions accessible by way of national courts may be used to challenge acts of national authorities which, more indirectly, lead or may lead to the degradation of the environment of children. To that avail primary Community law, e.g. as found in fundamental Articles from the EC Treaty like 12, 30, 34, 36, provisions on competition such as 85, 86, 93(3) or Article 95 on taxation, the direct effect of which has already been recognised by the Luxembourg Court. However, the specific environmental duties under Articles 130r–t EC have not yet been awarded direct effect.[106]

In the realm of environmental provisions with direct effect which grant – or may grant – to children rights of more immediate relevance, secondary instruments provide a more promising range.[107]

---

103 Case C-361/88 *Commision v. Germany;* in (1991) *ECR* I-2567 and case C-59/89 *Commission v. Germany*; in (1991) *ECR* I-2607.

104 *Ibid.*, Case C-361/88, cons. 16.

105 See Jans, op. cit, n.3, pp. 185–187.

106 See the analysis by Ludwig Krämer in his 'Direct effect of EC Environmental Law', in Han Somsen (ed), op. cit, n.87, pp.113–115.

107 The articles eligible for direct effect must fulfil the familiar criteria of being unconditional and sufficiently precise (but see Jans who concludes that a much more 'lenient' approach to direct effect has prevailed in recent years, op. cit, n.3, pp. 152–153).

In 1991, the Court argued in a similar way as in the *German TA Luft* cases referred to above, about two directives on the quality of surface water for drinking:

> whenever non-compliance with the measures required by the directives in question might endanger the health of persons, those concerned should be able to rely on mandatory rules in order to enforce their rights.[108]

In *German TA Luft*, case 361/88, the Court's concern was sulphur dioxide and suspended particulates in the air.[109]

Overviewing the current state of jurisprudence, Hilson's comment on the Court's viewpoint so far, seems justified: because all the directives under consideration are explicitly intended to protect human health, as shown in their Preamble, 'those whose health may be affected enjoy personal rights under the directives which must be enforceable in national courts'.[110] He calls this nevertheless a restrictive view because whether or not a directive's Preamble explicitly lists the protection of human health 'most pollution-related directives affect human health'. As examples he mentions the groundwater directive 80/68[111] and directive 76/464/EEC on dangerous substances discharged in the aquatic environment.[112]

In his overview of a variety of environmental provisions with (or which are a candidate for) direct effect, Jans eventually reaches somewhat similar conclusions. However, apart from emission standards he also points to product standards that, in addition to purposes of market integration, like the former, often serve environmental purposes. As an example of a relevant product standard directive he mentions the 'Batteries' directive, 91/157, prohibiting the marketing of alkaline manganese batteries containing more than a specified amount of mercury.[113] He also refers to directive 82/501 on major accident hazards of industrial activities, the 'post-Seveso' directive, as an example of a directive (also) on emissions which 'would also seem, in the view of the Court [i.e., in the *Post-Seveso* case] to have created rights for individuals'.[114]

---

108 Case C-58/89, *Commission v. Germany*; in (1991) *ECR* I-5023, cons.14. The case concerned Directives 75/440 (in *OJ* 1974 L 194/34) and 79/869 (in *OJ* 1979 L 271/44), both on the quality of surface water intended for purification to drinking water.

109 Cons.16 of Case C-361/88 on Directive 80/779 (in *OJ* 1980 L 229/30).

110 In op. cit., n.18, p.56, he also based his viewpoint on Case C-59/89, *Commission v. Germany* (1991), I-*ECR*, cons. 19 and 23, at pp. 2631 and 2632, respectively) on lead in the air, and Case C-298/95, *Commission v. Germany* (nyr) on water standards for fish and shellfish.

111 In (1980) *OJ*, L 20/43, later amended. Cf. Jan Jans (op. cit., n.3, pp. 186–187) who basically agrees, but also points to the rather Dutch/French view of legal protection the Court of Justice exhibits in the relevant (Case C-131/88, *Commission v. Germany*; in (1992) *ECR* I-825).

112 In (1976) *OJ*, L 129/23, later often amended; the directive has not yet given rise to any ECJ decisions.

113 Directive 91/157; in (1991) *OJ* L 78/38, later amended.

114 Jans, op. cit., n.3, pp.185–186, referring in particular, to cons.17 of the *Post-Seveso* case (Case C 190/90, *Commission v. Netherlands*; in (1992) *ECR* I-3265). See for a more detailed account of the *Post-Seveso* Directive (in (1982) OJ L 230/1, later amended) and the case itself: Jans, *ibid.*, pp. 282–286.

In sum, under the EC Treaty, there is indeed a major source of substantive individual environmental rights and potential rights available. These rights, *inter alia*, fulfil the condition emphasised in subsection 4.1, above, that there should be a reasonable prospect of their effective enforcement.[115] However, these rights are linked to the protection of health. As was argued above, this link is also a sign of weakness: the environment is not protected for its own sake, the criterion for protection is that its deterioration might lead to health dangers which legally jeopardise rights of individuals.[116] So far, unlike its Strasbourg counterpart as we saw in subsection 3.4, above, the Luxembourg Court has not yet presented its views on the effects of a serious degradation of the environment on individual rights if such degradation does not result in health damage.[117]

The most significant legal basis in EU law for environmental rights outside the EC Treaty is to be found in the EURATOM Treaty. Notably, Chapter III on Health and Safety, Articles 30–38 of the Treaty, is of relevance. For instance, Article 30 EURATOM requires that basic standards shall be laid down for the protection of workers and the general public against the dangers from radiation.[118] According to the ECJ, the scope of the protection is to be taken in a broad sense.

> [T]he purpose of the articles referred to is to ensure the consistent and effective protection of the health of the general public against the dangers arising from ionising radiations, whatever their source and whatever the categories of persons exposed to such radiations.[119]

The question here then is, of course, whether or not the major provisions of this basic Directive under Euratom (as well as some other EURATOM provisions) must be considered to be legally relevant for the rights of a child to a clean environment and, more particularly (and intimately

115 In Henk Addink's view, generally, Dutch judges are prepared to apply Community law in environmental cases. He is under the impression that Dutch judges are more prepared to do so than their foreign colleagues (in G.H. Addink, 'Europese milieurechtspraak en (milieu) belangen: conflict of verzoening?' [European environmental jurisprudence and (environmental) interests: conflict or conciliation?]; in *Europese Milieurechtspraak* [European Environmental jurisprudence], (Zwolle, 1996), p.158).

116 See, subsection 4.5.2 on the almost unsurmountable evidential problems this limitation has so far posed, notably in respect to the requirement of establishing a *causal* link with health damage.

117 In Hilson's view 'true' environmental rights will only arise if directives, such as on nature conservation, which have nothing to do with the protection of health, are also granted direct effect (Hilson, op. cit., n. 18, p.57–58).

118 The basic instrument is Council Directive 80/836 on 'Health Protection against the Dangers of Ionizing Radiation' in (1980) *OJ* L 246/1 (with many amendments).

119 Case C-70/88, *European Parliament v. Council* (the Chernobyl-I case). Both 'primary' radiation, i.e., radiation released from nuclear plants or direct handling of fissile materials, and 'secondary' radiation, i.e. radiation from contaminated products or incidents, falls within the purposes of the articles.

connected), whether they have direct effect? All the provisions linked to the protection of persons, including children, against health hazards, in my view, should be included in the children's rights perspective just as much as the provisions of the instruments based on Article 130(r) and (s) and other provisions of the EC Treaty. Moreover, in principle, there is no reason to regard their potential for direct effect differently from the provisions of other (EC) directives; this potential should be carefully analysed on an Article by Article basis.[120]

So far, the Court of Justice has not had the opportunity to provide much guidance in respect to the EURATOM Treaty. However, it did establish that the dose limits of radiation required in the basic Directive 80/836 on the 'protection of the general public and workers against the dangers of ionising radiation applying to any activity' – at least for companies – were minimum standards and that the Member States had discretion to set a higher standard of protection.[121] Moreover, under Article 35 each Member State is required to establish the facilities necessary to carry out continuous monitoring of the levels of radioactivity in air, water and soil. The Commission shall have the right of access to these facilities. However, the Commission cannot be obliged to verify the operation and efficiency of their operation. Generally speaking, not until the 1989 Chernobyl disaster has the Commission shown itself to be active in this respect.[122] Finally, some important jurisprudence on procedural rights and duties under the EURATOM Treaty is discussed in the next subsection.

4.4 Relevant procedural duties and rights

In agreement with Hilson, a procedural right will be defined as a right to have a given procedure carried out. The most important instruments of 'horizontal environmental legislation', i.e., of 'legislation which examines a given activity from a variety of environmental viewpoints',[123] with potentially relevant direct effect rights, would include, in particular, then the Environmental Impact Assessment (EIA) Directive, the so-called

120 Henk Addink, in a careful analysis of Dutch environmental jurisprudence, expresses much confidence at this point: 'Often the duties of the Member State are also the rights of the citizens (...). This is clear from the jurisprudence in respect to EURATOM directives. The [Dutch] jurisprudence shows that, in view of the importance in spirit, structure and text of the norms prescribed therein, (direct) rights versus the State can be derived from EURATOM directives' (transl. HP); in Addink, op. cit., n.115, p. 42; cf., more generally, p.160.

121 Case C-376/90, *Commission v. Belgium*; in (1992) *ECR* I-6153. Somewhat curiously the Commission had brought an action against Belgium which had set stricter national standards than the Directive required. The Court rejected the Commission's argument, because the *travaux préparatoires* of the Directive, *inter alia*, indicated that the dose limits represented the '*dont les conséquences sur la santé des personnes, régulièrement exposées aux rayonnements ionisants, sont à la limite du tolérable ...*' (*Ibid.*).

122 Until 1992 no Article 35 EUR verifications had been carried out, e.g. in the United Kingdom.

123 Jan Jans, op. cit., n.3, p.279.

'post-*Seveso*' Directive which has been referred to already, and the Directive on the freedom of access to information on the environment.[124] In addition, attention will be brielfy given to some of the specific procedural duties under Title 2 Chapter 3, on Health and Safety, of the EURATOM Treaty.

In the 1995 decisions in *Commission v. Germany,* the ECJ made clear that several of the provisions from the EIA Directive created straightforward duties for the Member States. Articles 2, 3 and 8

> unequivocally impose on the national authorities responsible for granting consent an obligation to carry out an assessment of the effects of certain projects on the environment.[125]

In its decision of 24 October 1996 in the *Kraaijeveld* case, the EC Court has made clear that the discretion of Member States to exclude particular projects from environmental impact assessment provided for in Articles 2(1) and 4(2) of the Directive, is limited. That is, if that project is likely to have significant effects on the environment.[126] Furthermore, referring to its established attitude in this matter: if Member States are obliged to pursue a particular course of action, individuals can indeed rely on it before their national courts. Moreover, national courts are expected to independently convey whether or not the legislative or executive branches of Member States have stayed within their discretion under Articles 2(1) and 4(2).[127]

In a number of English cases applicants have also appealed to rights under the Directive on environmental impact assessment. For a variety of reasons, these claims have not been very successful. None of these cases has been referred to the ECJ under Article 177, hence it is not known whether or not the Luxembourg Court would have agreed with the judgments.[128]

An interesting case in a somewhat comparable realm was brought in 1987 under Chapter III of the EURATOM Treaty, which in several Articles provides a kind of impact assessment procedure *avant la lettre.* Article 37 EUR requires each Member State to provide the Commission with general

124 Directive 85/337 (*OJ* 1985 L 175/40, later amended), Directive 82/501 (*OJ* 1982 L230/1, later amended), and Directive 90/313 (*OJ* 1990 L 158/56), respectively. See Ludwig Krämer, *European Environmental Law* (London, 1993), pp.377–436, for some less important procedural cases of a different nature.

125 Case C-431/92 *Commission v. Germany*, cons. 40; in (1995) *ECR* I-2211.

126 Case C 72/95, *Aannemersbedrijf P. K. Kraaijeveld BV and Others v. Gedeputeerde Staten van Zuid-Holland*, cons. 50 and 53, not yet published.

127 *Ibid.*, cons. 60 and 62 (that is: if under its national law a court 'must or may raise of its own motion pleas in law based on a binding national rule which have not been put forward by the parties ...' – cons. 62).

128 It seems, indeed, quite arguable that the ECJ might not have agreed with, e.g. the judgment in *Twyford Parish Council v. Secretary of State for Transport* (in (1992) *Journal of Environmental Law*, pp. 273 et seq.), in particular since the *Kraaijeveld* judgment (see, further, Hilson, op. cit., n.18, pp.60 and 61, and, especially, 62).

data relating to any plan for the disposal of radioactive waste. On the basis of these data the Commission should then be able to determine whether or not radioactive contamination in another Member State's territory may result.[129]

In its judgment of 22 September 1988 in the *Catténom* case, the European Court had to answer the question whether the Commission should be supplied with the relevant data for its opinion under Article 37, before or after the issuing of an authorisation for discharges by the (French) authorities. The Court decided that the Commission's opinion could not be effective unless given before the Member State's decision to authorise the nuclear waste disposal.[130] It is likely from this case, which was referred to the ECJ under Article 150 EUR (similar to an Article 177 EC procedure), and brought by the German Land Saarland, together with environmental associations and private individuals, that individuals (and environmental groups) may challenge inadequacies in the Article 37 procedure. The Court said: 'knowledge of the Commission's opinion may be of use for the purpose of enabling any person concerned to assess the merits of a possible legal action against the decision granting authorization'.[131]

Article 34 EUR empowers the Commission even more: where 'particularly dangerous' experiments are involved, liable to affect the territories of other Member Sates, the 'assent' of the Commission is required. So far, only in relation to the French nuclear tests in 1995 in the South Pacific, have these powers of the Commission been (unsuccessfully) appealed to.[132] Apart from several more general provisions on surveillance and inspection in respect to possible major nuclear dangers, Directive 80/836/EUR requires the provision of information on accidental radioactive discharges.[133] Among the measures taken after the Chernobyl disaster was Directive 89/618/EUR on informing the general public about health protection measures to be applied and steps to be taken in the event of a radioactive emergency.[134]

---

129 Case 187/87, *Saarland and others v. Ministère de l'industrie and others*, the '*Catténom*' case; in (1988) *ECR*, pp. 5037 ff. Since this judgment – remarkably a long time after – the Commission has issued Recommendation 91/4 (1991 *OJ* L 6/16) indicating what information the Member States should supply under Article 37, and has given several opinions conforming with the Article (e.g. on the nuclear fuel reprocessing plant Thorp of the Sellafield complex, 1992 *OJ* L 138/36).

130 *Ibid.*, cons. 17 and 18, pp.5041–5042.

131 *Ibid.*, cons.17, p.5042.

132 In *Danielsson*, op. cit., n.46. Jans's observation that this article 'has hardly any practical significance' seems no longer fully adequate (Jans, op. cit., n.3, p.50). In the meantime the Commission, e.g. has seen fit to define 'particularly dangerous experiment' and has made clear that in its view the EURATOM Treaty also covers experiments of a military nature. More relevant national and European jurisprudence is anticipated.

133 In case of an unplanned release, Article 45(5) of the Directive, e.g. (see op. cit., n.118) requires that any anticipated accident involving exposure of the population to radiation must be notified as a matter of urgency, *inter alia*, to neighbouring states and the Commission.

134 (1989) *OJ* L 357/31.

The ECJ has not yet had a chance to clarify whether this instrument or the particular obligation under Directive 80/836/EUR, are accessible to individuals. At least in terms of remedies, there cannot be much question in this respect where Article 38 EUR is concerned: in cases of urgency, the Commission shall issue a directive requiring the Member State to take all measures necessary to prevent infringement of the basic standards and to ensure compliance with regulations. If the Commission fails to do so, Article 148 EUR allows, *inter alia*, natural (or legal) persons to complain to the Court of Justice.[135]

Whether the 'post-*Seveso*' and the 'access to information' Directives include provisions with direct effect embodying environmental rights, has so far not been clarified in the jurisprudence.[136] The 'access to information' Directive aims explicitly at ensuring freedom of access to information on the environment held by public authorities, without having to prove an interest. However, the real question is what discretion Member States have left to restrict access to such information further, even beyond the already considerable list of Article 3(2) of the Directive. In Article 4, the Directive provides for a possibility to seek judicial or administrative review of a refusal of information.[137] Also under the EIA Directive, Member States have duties to inform. According to Article 7, if significant effects on the environment in another Member State are likely, gathered information shall be forwarded to that Member State at the same time as such information is made available to the forwarding state's own nationals.

Although procedural rights will most likely be accessible for individuals, all these and other procedural rights seem rather distant from rights of a child to a clean environment. In terms of the 'traditional' language of human rights, that may be so. However, in order for the rights of the child to be 'effective', procedural rights should be included because they are a necessary precondition for effective enforcement mechanisms to protect the (potential) substantive rights under Community law outlined earlier. This overview of the state of Community law relevant for our subject will be concluded with a brief review of the third element – apart from standing and substantive (procedural) rights – of an 'effective' right of the child to a clean environment: remedies.

---

135 Under the conditions laid down earlier in Article 148 EUR; the Article is identical to Article 175 EC (see for an overview of Community law in respect to judicial protection, e.g. Henry G. Schermers, *Judicial Protection in the European Communities*, 5th edn., Deventer, etc., 1992).

136 Case C-190/90, *Commission v. The Netherlands*, in (1992) *ECR* I, pp. 3265 et seq., is not very helpful in this respect.

137 See, further Jan Jans, op. cit., n.3, pp.287–288.

4.5 Remedies

4.5.1 General remedies

If the litigant is successful in his claim in a national court, in the sense that he is allowed leave and, subsequently, that a court of law decides that his Community rights have been infringed, then still the matter of remedies can be quite problematic. In some English cases the courts seemed to have been rather pragmatic here: they pointed to the costs, as an argument to refrain from any more material remedies than, in fact, declaring that the law had been infringed (an argument which may equally be used in respect to procedural claims).[138] This leads Hilson to a deliberation on what English courts could do in terms of remedies in cases, which involve, for instance, substantive policy decisions. The interesting case here is *R v. Secretary of State for the Environment, ex parte Friends of the Earth Ltd.*[139] In this case, Friends of the Earth claimed a breach of national quality standards of drinking water where the (formal) implementation in the UK of the relevant EC Directive had been accepted by the Commission. If the standards were now, in practice, breached, has the individual (or his interest group, for that matter) still a right to claim under the EC Directive? If so, and the Court of Appeal seems to say so,[140] what does this right involve? The court can, of course, issue a one-off declaration that the Community obligation to achieve the quality standard is violated. However, what more can it do? The national court can, either, leave the action to be taken to comply as a subjective matter for the government of the Member State, or, act in a more policy-oriented way, e.g. by issuing an order that further action be taken and set conditions, like a time limit, for its accomplishment. Hilson argues that the more 'active' orders would easily lead into political controversy. He believes that the UK Court of Appeal approaches the matter in the more passive, former option.[141]

4.5.2 Francovich

If the claim relates to damage to health, the litigant trying to invoke the direct effect of a Community instrument faces a serious problem of evidence. If it is assumed that other conditions set for a claim under *Francovich* jurisprudence have been fulfilled, i.e., that ascertainable and

---

138 Hilson points to several cases in the realm of nature protection where the court took this pragmatic approach; see op. cit., n.18, p.61. As said, from the EC law perspective such decisions may be questioned in light of the principle of effectiveness (see subsection 4.2.1, above).

139 For the first instance decision in the High Court, see (1994) *CMLR*, pp.760 et seq.; for Hilson's account of, and comments on, the 1995 Court of Appeal's decision, see (1995) *CMLR*, pp. 1461–1475.

140 Although the decision is not so straightforward here. The Court of Appeal did not decide on a breach of Community law (see (1995) *CMLR*, op. cit., n.139, pp.1467–1468).

141 *Ibid.*, pp.1467 and 1471.

serious rights are conferred on the claimant, then still a formidable hurdle is to be overcome: that of proving causation. Proving the causal link between rights which are infringed and damage to health or illness, has perhaps been the great stumbling block for attempting litigation, e.g. to prevent the operation of nuclear installations or closing such operations.[142] At some point the ECJ will probably have to provide some clarity on what kind of evidence, notably of an epidemiological kind, is required in such and similar cases. So far, this matter is left to the national courts to decide.[143]

In particular the issues related to proving causation led Hilson, I believe quite rightly, to a rather pessimistic view on the possibility effectively to apply *Francovich* jurisprudence to the environmental field, that is to cases where damage to health is at the centre of claims.[144] Unfortunately, such cases are likely to include environmental claims on behalf of children on the basis of rights under Community law. An example would be the enormous number of children with asthma or other respiratory problems related to forms of air pollution. However, in other cases, more localised, involving smaller numbers of potential victims, such a 'floodgates issue' might as such be less of a barrier to a *Francovich* claim.[145] In light of such decisions as in the *López Ostra* case (see above, subsections 2.4 and 2.5) where health damage is no longer the all-decisive criterion in view of degradation of the environment, in the future effective claims for remedies may offer a somewhat better perspective. In either case additional jurisprudence would be welcome.

5. Conclusion

The relationship between European Union law and human rights is somewhat awkward in nature. This awkwardness is reflected in the way the topic of this chapter took shape. EC law as such has no references to any individual right to a clean environment. According to Article F.2 of the

142 See on nuclear cases in the UK: Jane Holder, 'The Sellafield Litigation and Questions of Causation in Environmental Law' in (1994) *Current Legal Problems*, p. 287. *Short and Others v. BNFL*, a current Irish case, may in future shed a fresh light on the Sellafield litigation, including on the matter of causation which here, in particular, is one of the long-standing issues (see Irish High Court No.119/94 no.1751p, and Irish Supreme Court no.174/95, notably Judgment of 24/7/96).

143 Here, there is no intent to engage in the *Francovich* debate. See for an excellent analysis for its applicability in principle to breaches of various environmental provisions, Somsen, op. cit., n.87, pp. 139 et seq.

144 Hilson, op. cit., n.18, pp. 66–67; see, also Christopher Miller, 'Environmental Rights: European Fact or English Fiction?'; in (1995) *Journal of Law and Society*, p. 386.

145 Notably in cases of high-dose exposure (e.g. in respect to radioactive contaminations, the possibility of successful *Francovich* claims should be viewed somewhat less pessimistically than Hilson, *ibid.*, at pp.67–68, and Miller, *ibid.*, at p.388 do, including the potential role of the ECJ in such cases.

Maastricht Treaty, the human rights of the European Convention on Human Rights, however, feed the 'general principles of Community law'. By way of its judicial creativity the Luxembourg Court over the years has stipulated that this means that not only the Community's institutions but now, increasingly, also the Member States, when acting within Community law, should comply with the values these rights represent. That is, if in addition, these rights also derive from the constitutional traditions common to them. This condition is a considerable obstacle in the case of any 'new' right like the right of the child to a clean environment. After all, even in general international law, the existence of a right to a clean environment, whatever it precisely may mean, is uncertain.

Some hope may perhaps be inferred from recent jurisprudence of the Strasbourg Court. In its *López Ostra* decision, the Court explained the 'classic' Article 8, protecting private and family life, in such a way that this individual right (including the right of a child) linked up with deterioration of the environment. The Contracting Parties have a duty under the Convention to ensure that the actions of their authorities do not prevent an individual from enjoying an environment 'free from pollution so severe that it affects its well-being adversely and prevents it from ordinary life, without necessarily seriously endangering its health'. Moreover, from the Court's decision along the same lines in the *Guerra and Others* case also a positive duty may be deduced, i.e., to provide essential information to individuals in order to allow them to assess the risks they and their families might run in the face of serious environmental deterioration.

As the rights guaranteed in Article 8 may be presumed also to belong to the constitutional traditions common to the Member States, it is not unlikely that the ECJ will consider this explanation of them to be applicable both to Community institutions and Member States. Now this may still seem a long way from a 'separate' right of a child to a clean environment under Community law which really addresses children's specific environmental needs, it nevertheless represents an opening to the creation of such a right.

Apart from this 'inroad' by way of Article 8 of the ECHR, such a direct right does not appear to exist in Community law. Its presence in the framework awaits a policy decision on the tricky subject of either adherence by the Community to the ECHR, which seems unlikely in view of the Treaty of Amsterdam, or agreement on a separate 'Bill of Rights' for the Community. However, whether this latter development would mean such a vast improvement on the current situation is still to be seen. It will mainly depend on what status such an instrument and its rights will have in the EU treaty fabric. For example, a separate treaty concluded among the Member States will not necessarily offer a tremendous potential for litigants in a

Member State with a constitutional system that is predominantly 'dualistic' with regard to the reception of international law. If the European Union (or the EC) Treaty is amended – a third possibility, now somewhat half-heartedly chosen in the Treaty of Amsterdam – the situation for litigants might eventually improve. After all, EC provisions with direct effect can offer quite impressive potential legal power to individual claimants, including to children or those representing them. Notably, such EC rights would prevail over provisions of the municipal law of the Member States. It is even imaginable that, due to their exceptional character, some of those rights might legally even become stronger, adorning them with the status of Union or Community *jus cogens*.

Although such developments are not really to be foreseen in the immediate future, that does not mean that the legal situation in the Community is without hope in terms of our topic. It may safely be submitted that there is no international treaty regime that allows enforcement of rights more effectively than the EU Treaty does. This is the result, primarily, of the phenomenon of the 'direct effect' of many of its rules of law and its specific system of preliminary rulings on behalf of the national judiciary. Since the middle of the 1970s and especially since the enactment of the Single European Act and the Treaty of Maastricht, a considerable body of environmental law (as well as instruments relevant to the protection of the environment) has been added to Community law. Several of these environmental instruments have rules with direct effect, potentially to be claimed as individual rights by litigants before their own municipal courts. Here these rights have been distinguished as 'derived' environmental Community rights. From the point of view of environmental protection and rights of the child to a clean environment, Community law (potentially) offers quite a number of such derived rights. They are of a substantive as well as of a procedural kind and, in principle, are enforceable. I do not believe it to be any exaggeration to say that this body of potentially effective rights has no equal in international law (including human rights law).

However, the picture is not in all respects as bright as the preceding sentence boldly states. A stumbling block, certainly in the field of the rights of the child is standing rights. Both municipal courts and the ECJ have often been reluctant to allow standing to individuals, but in particular to interest groups. However, recently, broader recognition of such rights seems likely, both in court and by way of the EC Commission's recognition of the problem. Another obstacle is formed by problems of evidence, in particular within the context of remedies – though not only in that context. The problem of providing proof for the causal relationship between damage to health and environmental deterioration is very difficult indeed. Perhaps, the

López Ostra decision may again be helpful here. In its award, for the first time in international litigation it seems, the Strasbourg Court acknowledged a right to environmental protection that was also separate from health damage. Although not within the scope of this examination, the increasing international legal importance of the precautionary principle (included in Article 130r.2 EC, and by way of the Treaty of Amsterdam – in a revised form – to be included in Article 100a EC), may eventually lead to somewhat less stringent scientific requirements being set the quality of evidence in legal procedures.

Notwithstanding the legal obstacles just referred to, on the whole, the rather problematic situation in regard to a direct right of the child to a clean environment in Community law must be viewed as mitigated a great extent by the existence of a promising body of potentially enforceable derived rights. As an international treaty regime, the Community must be considered very successful in terms of effective individual rights. It may not even be an exaggeration to suggest that there is no regime in international law even remotely comparable to the EC in terms of 'effective' rights of the child to a clean environment. These rights are to a great extent ready to be claimed!

Part II

Right of the child to a clean environment at national levels: selected case studies

3 Environmental rights of the child in India

MICHAEL ANDERSON AND SYLVIA BLUCK

1. Introduction

It is now well known that Indian courts are world leaders in developing and applying environmental rights.[1] The human right to environmental protection has been recognised in dozens of legal decisions since 1985, and India's robust pattern of public interest litigation in pursuit of environmental rights is probably without rival in the world.[2] The superior courts have not only developed a broad set of environmental rights based upon the constitutional right to life, they have also liberalised standing to extend to environmental non-governmental organisations (NGOs) and any person acting in the public interest.[3] Perhaps more importantly, the courts have adopted innovative constitutional remedies such as monetary compensation for environmental harm,[4] and have been in the forefront of incorporating international environmental standards into domestic law.[5] Relying upon this range of substantive and procedural innovations the courts have issued wide-ranging orders with respect to all manner of environmental matters including, lakes, forests, mines, quarries, rivers, industrial closure, vehicular pollution, coastal zone management, and environmental education.

Yet one does not need to be an observer of India's environmental litigation for long before a paradox emerges. On the one hand, the jurisprudence of the superior courts is boldly environmentalist, recognising that every individual has a justiciable right to live in a healthy environment. On the other hand, actual environmental conditions in India are often notoriously poor, ranging from life-threatening water supplies and

1 See, for example, M. Anderson, 'Individual Rights to Environmental Protection in India', in A. E. Boyle and M. R. Anderson (eds.), *Human Rights Approaches to Environmental Protection* (Oxford, 1996).

2 Useful compilations of the relevant case law include Rosencranz, Divan, and Noble, *Environmental Law and Policy in India: Cases, Materials and Statutes* (Tripathi, 1991) and Singh, Anklesaria, and Gonsalves, *The Environmental Activists' Handbook* (Gonsalves, 1993).

3 The literature on public interest litigation is now extensive. The most comprehensive account of the case law is available in Ahuja, *People, Law and Justice: A Casebook on Public Interest Litigation* (Sangam, 1997).

4 Anderson and Ahmed, 'Assessing Environmental Damage under Indian Law' *Review of European Community and International Environmental Law*, 5 (1996), p. 335.

5 Anderson, 'International Environmental Law in Indian Courts', *Review of European Community and International Environmental Law*, 7 (1998), p. 22.

severe urban air pollution to the loss of forest cover and the degradation of soil, water, and wildlife in most parts of the country. The juxtaposition of enforceable environmental rights in the courtroom with degraded and sometimes life-threatening environmental conditions in reality is an instructive irony. It points to the importance of making rights effective with well-designed enforcement strategies, as well as the limits of pursuing a rights-based approach to environmental protection without an underlying transformation in economic and social conditions.

These issues are especially important for children, who are not only more vulnerable to many types of environmental degradation, but who have particular interests in environmental protection which have gone largely unrecognised in the Indian jurisprudence to date. In the extensive legal literature on environmental rights in India, there has been little specific attention to the needs, circumstances, and political significance of children,[6] even though children are sometimes invoked in the abstract as the moral conscience of the nation. This chapter sets out to examine the promises and problems of children's environmental rights in India, with a particular emphasis on the problems of formulating and enforcing such rights. In this context, it is important to go beyond 'the right to a clean environment' since the emphasis upon cleanliness as a sole criterion of environmental quality has been widely criticised in India for its focus upon pollution-centred issues. In India, many of the most important survival issues have to do with the degradation and depletion of natural resources – particularly forest cover, fish stocks, etc. – which are relied upon for livelihood. For India's children, the issue is not simply a matter of a clean environment, although that is also important, but also an un-degraded and un-depleted environment.

2. The Significance of the Environment for Children

The environmental rights of children in India deserve separate attention for at least three reasons. First, in a country with a young demographic profile, children under 18 make up 41 per cent of the population, and thus represent a substantial social sector to be considered in overall environmental policy-making. To put this figure in a global context, India presently has some 390 million persons under the age of 18, which means that India's children

6 The environmental and anthropological writers have been more closely attuned to these questions than legal writers. For example, the magazine *Down To Earth* produced by the Centre for Science and Environment in New Delhi has a regular section devoted to children and the environment. Much of the relevant general material is now summarised in Satterthwaite, Hart, Levy, Mitlin, Ross, Smit, and Stephens, *The Environment for Children* (Earthscan, 1996). See also the useful overview with recommendations provided in Johnson, Hill, and Ivan-Smith, *Listening to Smaller Voices: Children in an Environment of Change* (Actionaid, 1995).

outnumber the population of all ages in the European Union.[7] The welfare of this large population, and its role in global environmental change, should be a matter of concern not only to Indians, but to the international community.

Second, while there has been extensive international attention given to the health, education, and social status of children in India, the relevant environmental factors in children's welfare have gone largely unrecognised. The rate of child malnutrition in India is one of the worst in the world: nearly 12 per cent of all children die under the age of 5 while 53 per cent of children under 5 are underweight by international standards, with 21 per cent severely so.[8] For many years, the conventional wisdom has attributed such poor health statistics to poverty and inadequate health care systems, but more recent studies have emphasised the role of environmental conditions in causing ill health.[9] It is not only the classic link between water pollution and diarrhoeal disease which is at issue here; the health of children can be affected by a broad range of environmental factors including air pollution, deforestation, and soil erosion (see Table 1). In many cases it is the environmental hazards associated with poverty, rather than poverty *per se* which has a direct effect upon the morbidity and mortality profile of the population under 12.[10]

Third, it is a simple consequence of age and predicted lifespan that children are more likely than their parents or grandparents to suffer from the effects of long-term environmental damage. Considered from the standpoint of 1999, the likely ecological conditions in the year 2060 hold greater personal relevance for a child of 10 than for a senior bureaucrat aged 65. Such a child is likely to witness first hand the absolute effects of accumulating deforestation, urbanisation, climate change and population increase. Even if the senior bureaucrat possesses a high degree of environmental consciousness the relevance of conditions in 2060 must be moral and conceptual rather than personal. In this sense, children have a greater stake in the sustainability, and represent a bridge to future generations. In protecting the lifelong environments of today's children, we are taking no small step toward protecting the environments of future generations. It follows that the environmental interests of children deserve a degree of legal respect which comports with their longer temporal stake in environmental outcomes.

---

7 Undated statistics derived from www.unicef.org/statis.

8 See www.unicef.org/statis/country_1Page 81.html.

9 Ramalingaswami, Jonsson, and Rohde, 'Commentary: The Asian Enigma' in UNICEF, *The Progress of Nations 1996* (reprinted at www/unicef.org/pon96/nuenigma.htm) and Satterthwaite, et al., op. cit. n. 6.

10 See for example, Burger and Esrey, 'Water and Sanitation: Health and Nutrition Benefits to Children', in Pinstrup-Andersen, Pelletier, and Alderman (eds.), *Child Growth and Nutrition in Developing Countries: Priorities for Action* (Cornell University Press, 1995), p. 153.

Table 1: Environment and child health

Environmental condition	Factors affecting children	Potential health impact
Water pollution; poor sanitation; contaminated water supplies	Biological pathogens	Diarrhoeal disease; malnutrition; death
Air pollution	Airborne pathogens, suspended particulate matter; sulphur dioxide, aldehydes	Respiratory infections; tuberculosis
Depleted or degraded natural resources, incl. deforestation, soil erosion, loss of fisheries and wildlife	Inadequate supplies of food, water, fuel	Malnutrition
Physical hazards, incl. traffic hazards, flooding, landslides, and other accidents	Children more vulnerable and inadequately protected	Injury, disability, death
Long-term environmental change, incl. depletion of non-renewable resources, accumulated waste, increase in extreme climatic conditions	Children more likely to be affected by long-term change	Long-term threat to food supplies, income, and safe living conditions

3. The Existing Legal Position of Children

There is in India, as in many parts of the world, an important question regarding the legal definition of a 'child'. Current legal definitions of the child derive mainly from the period of colonial legislation, which were in turn heavily influenced by English and Scots law of the nineteenth century. In a legal context, as many observers have noted, the term 'child' serves three main functions: 1) to denote a relationship (as with a parent in matrimonial proceedings), 2) to indicate degrees of legal capacity, and 3) as a term constituting an obligation of special protection.[11] These three legal functions are important, since they establish the conceptual framework in which children's rights must operate. The first principle, of relationship, casts the child as an adjunct of another person – normally an adult – and thereby creates rights and duties for the child which are essentially derivative of those held by the adult. This position leaves little space for autonomous legal agency. The second principle, of capacity, is a time-honoured legal principle which delimits and restricts the rights of the child in matters of contract, litigation, and so forth. It results in an inferior set of

[11] See, for example, the useful discussion in Diwan and Diwan, *Children and Legal Protection* (Deep & Deep, 1996), chap 1.

rights for the child *vis-à-vis* the adult. The third principle, of protection, complements the other principles in establishing a set of obligations – for parents, guardians, employers, and the state – to provide special protection for children. The implicit logic is that a child's limited rights are offset by special protections. As we shall see, the special protection offered acts to construe the child as a passive object of protection rather than an active agent involved in shaping her or his world.

3.1 Limited legal capacity

Any proposal to establish a child's legal right to environmental protection immediately faces the obstacle of the limited legal capacity of children in the Indian legal system. In the law of contract, for example, the colonial regime limited the much wider contractual rights previously available to minors[12] by limiting contractual capacity to those aged 18 or over.[13] Similarly, a child under the age of 7 is deemed incapable of committing a criminal offence,[14] while those over 7 are deemed to possess limited criminal responsibility.[15] Although the child may be liable in most types of tort actions,[16] and may be subject to income tax[17] through a parent, the law does not recognise an independent legal capacity for children to participate in civil litigation. A child wishing to bring a civil suit must do so through a 'next friend', and the failure to involve a next friend will entitle the defendant to have the plaint taken off the court's file.[18]

The direct consequences of legal incapacity for a child's right to environmental protection are mainly procedural. For example, a child may not enforce a contract containing provisions requiring protection of the environment. Similarly, a child cannot independently bring a tort action in respect of nuisance, trespass, or negligence for environmental damage.[19] Such procedural barriers may seem of little practical consequence, but they symbolise a more fundamental aspect of the child's legal existence – the

12 The classical schools of Hindu law provided for full contractual capacity at age 15 or 16, while Islamic law fixed contractual capacity at the age of puberty. Local customary usage varied, but married life and full participation in productive activity and public life normally began well before the age of 18.

13 Indian Contract Act 1872, s. 11, read with the Indian Majority Act 1875, s. 3. This did not apply strictly to family law questions, which continued to be governed by 'personal' laws of Hindus, Muslims, Parsis, Christians, etc. Subsequent case law has qualified the rule so that contracts clearly beneficial to the child may be enforced in certain circumstances, and contracts for service may be entered into from the age of 14 under the Apprenticeship Act 1961.

14 Indian Penal Code, 1860, s. 82.

15 Indian Penal Code, 1860, s. 84; Juvenile Justice Act 1986.

16 Singh (ed.), *Ratanlal & Dhirajlal's The Law of Torts*, 23rd edn. (Wadhwa, 1997), pp. 58 et. seq.

17 Income-Tax Act 1961, s. 64(1), as amended.

18 Code of Civil Procedure, 1908, Order XXXII, R. 1-2.

19 A minor is not prohibited, however, from filing a complaint to the police in respect of an environmental public nuisance or other alleged crime (Code of Criminal Procedure, 1973, ss. 133, 154, and 155).

relative inability for children to work the levers of the legal system so as to influence their own living environments. There is a presumption in the law that the child's interests will be protected by a parent, guardian, or other concerned adult, thus precluding the child from protecting his or her own interests.

This conceptual constant may help to explain the uncertain position of children in constitutional litigation. Since India's environmental rights are constitutional, the question is crucial: is a child legally entitled to bring an action for the enforcement of his or her constitutional rights? The answer is not entirely clear. The question turns on legal capacity to file a writ petition before either the Supreme Court or one of the several state High Courts under Articles 32 and 226 of the Constitution. It is commonly assumed that children do not possess such legal capacity.[20] Yet there do not appear to be any constitutional impediments, nor are there any reported cases of minors being denied *locus standi* on the grounds of age. There is at least one reported High Court case in which a minor's petition found a favourable hearing,[21] but there do not appear to be any definitive Supreme Court decisions on the question. Since the procedural rules of the 1908 Code of Civil Procedure have often been held in some cases to apply to constitutional proceedings, there is some support for the view that its procedural ban on minors in civil suits would apply equally to constitutional petitions, but a 1976 amendment to Section 141 of the Code made it clear that it does not apply to High Court proceedings under Article 226 of the Constitution. On the other hand, barring children from direct access to constitutional remedies might easily be impugned as a violation of Article 14 (right to equality) and Article 32 (right to move the Supreme Court to enforce fundamental rights). What is clear is that with the exception of the case mentioned above, all other constitutional cases involving the rights of minors have been brought by adults acting in either a representative or public interest capacity.[22] There is, even in the iconoclastic and imaginative framework of public interest litigation, an enduring perception that children are to be construed mainly as vulnerable objects of protection rather than active agents capable of enforcing their own rights. This view is implicit in a great deal of the protective legislation relating to children, much of which was framed under colonial rule.

20 See for example, Ahuja, op. cit. n.3, p. 228.

21 *Shrivas Rajesh Kumar v. Chairman Selection Committee* 1987 AIR 1987 Guj.

22 See, for example *Sheela Barse v. Union of India* AIR 1986 SC 1773 relating to the rights of juvenile detainees, and *Labourers Working on Salal Hydro-Project v. State of Jammu & Kashmir* 1984 AIR 177 SC on the prohibition of child labour.

3.2 The legacy of protective legislation

The idea that children should be protected from the effects of injurious, polluted, or otherwise unhealthy environmental conditions is not new. The general principle that younger people should be shielded from harm could be found in the pre-colonial Hindu and Islamic law texts, as well as regularly embodied in local 'customary' practices. Yet the temptation to romanticise the position of children before colonial rule should be resisted: during hard times children were sometimes sold into slavery, and it was not unusual for children to be exposed to environmental hazards such as contaminated drinking water and indoor air pollution from biomass sources. As Goonesekere notes, the pre-colonial legal systems of South Asia placed emphasis on the nurturing and care-giving responsibility of the family, but also endorsed a concept of almost unlimited family authority, with particular emphasis on the powers of patriarchs.[23] This latter theme picked up by early colonial rule, which guaranteed that 'the rights and authorities of fathers of families, and masters of families . . . shall be preserved'.[24] Pre-colonial understandings of child protection have left a social legacy of considerable practical importance, but the institutions and norms of the modern legal system owe much more to the legacy of colonial rule, which deferred to family practices in many ways,[25] but which gradually brought the treatment of children under state control.

Starting in the last third of the nineteenth century, the colonial government in British India began to introduce pieces of legislation designed to protect children from certain social and physical hazards. While most of these reforms involved social questions such as the age of consent, the minimum age for marriage, and so on, there was some treatment of the workplace environment in the Factory Acts and other labour statutes. The 1881 Factories Act established a minimum age of employment (7 years) for children in larger industries, and regulated the working hours of those under the age of 12. The main justifications invoked by the Act's supporters related to the long working day and the dangers of physical injury from industrial machinery, but also evident was some concern for the environmental hazards facing children – particularly the effects of cotton dust and other indoor air pollution in textile mills. Subsequent protective legislation[26] raised the minimum age of employment and further regulated industrial conditions, and thereby provided some limited degree of

23 Goonesekere, *Children, Law and Justice: A South Asian Perspective* (Sage, 1998), p. 104.

24 21 Geo III cap 70 (1781) sec 18.

25 See Anderson, 'Work Construed: Ideological Origins of Labour Law in British India to 1918', in Robb (ed.), *Dalit Movements and the Meanings of Labour in India* (Oxford University Press, 1993), at pp. 91–94.

26 The Factories Act was amended in 1891, 1911, 1921, 1934 and 1948.

protection for children in exposed to hazardous workplace environments. The colonial labour statutes have been amended and updated, but still form the basis for much of the regulatory structure relating to working children in the present day. Recent legal initiatives are not innocent of influence from this colonial legacy, and therefore the provenance and character of the legacy do warrant closer examination to better understand present-day debates.

The development of this early protection raises four general points. First, the question of the child's physical environment arose as a secondary issue in the context of industrial regulation. This was not environmental law as such, but labour law. It identified only one particular setting – the industrial workplace – as a site of potential environmental harm, and problematised the position of children within that setting. The term 'environment' was not in widespread circulation, and while there was some general concern for problems of industrial pollution, wildlife preservation, and forest management in the colonial period,[27] it would be anachronistic to attribute present-day motives to the earlier legislation. Yet the legacy of this legislation does point to a colonial concern for the particular vulnerability of children to adverse environmental conditions in the workplace.

Second, the legislation was protectionist rather than rights-oriented. Indeed, the legislation contains no explicit reference to the rights of children, and to the extent that such rights might be deemed to exist, they may be deduced only from the duties which are imposed upon factory operators. The Factory Acts adopted a protectionist approach, conceiving of children as vulnerable and relatively passive objects for state protection rather than as active agents capable of exercising legal rights. In the debates which surrounded the early factory legislation children were described in terms which emphasised their vulnerability and tender years. This was conducive to an ideology of high imperialism which was inclined to portray Indian children as impoverished and as victims of social abuses which flowed from the character of a static and backward Indian society. In this context, the colonial state could be conceived as a civilising and modernising organ which would naturally exercise a *parens patriae* power with respect to children.[28] Legislation to protect children played a role in legitimating colonial government to critics in London and Calcutta alike. As many observers have noted, the paternalistic state of the colonial period evolved directly into the developmentalist state of the independence period, bequeathing with it as well a paternalistic approach to social legislation.

27 See Arnold and Guha (eds.), *Nature, Culture, Imperialism: Essays on the Environmental History of South Asia* (Oxford University Press, 1996).

28 Singh, 'Ideological Origins of Legal Paternalism in India', *Journal of the Indian Law Institute*, 24 (1982).

The consequences for the law relating to children in India are important: there is a predilection for laws which protect children as passive and helpless victims rather than those which conceive of children as active agents engaged in the social and physical environments in which they reside.

The third point to note about the first Factory Act in India is that it was mainly promulgated not in response to perceived demand within India, but to placate the demands of the Lancashire textile industry which complained of the 'unfair' competition posed by Bombay textile mills.[29] Noting its loss of market share to the Bombay industry, the Lancashire lobby objected to Bombay's low labour costs resulting in part from the use of child labour, which had by that time been prohibited in England. The impetus for the Act emanated not from working class pressures within India, but from capitalist and allied interests in the metropole. The Act was primarily designed to appease an English rather than an Indian audience, and was thus distinctly colonial in character. Even though subsequent labour legislation was increasingly influenced by Indian working class movements, a colonial element remained pervasive until 1947.

The fourth point is that the 1881 Act and subsequent legislation on child labour also involved a fierce debate about the nature of children and childhood in India. On one hand, advocates of regulation pointed to the polluted and hazardous working conditions which children often faced, and argued that children were particularly vulnerable to such conditions and ought to be protected from hazards which adults could be expected to endure. On the other hand, opponents of the Act argued that European standards for children were not applicable in Indian social, economic, and environmental conditions. It was said that in a society where people were often married before puberty, and frequently had children of their own by the age of 16, it was perfectly ordinary to assume adult social responsibilities at an earlier age. It was also noted that in India, many children working in industrial settings did so alongside their parents: a fact which was used to argue that their health and well-being was properly supervised in a family setting – emphasising the pre-colonial idea of the family as protector rather than the Victorian notion of the state exercising a supervisory role. These arguments diluted and delayed protective legislation, but did not stop it altogether, and India came to develop laws regulating the workplace environment for children which were closely based on British models. A full explanation for these developments requires that Indian laws be

29 Anderson, 'Work Construed Ideological Origins', op. cit., n.25, at pp. 113–117; J.C. Kydd, *A History of Factory Legislation in India* (Calcutta, 1920), chap 1.

set in the context of an emerging international system for regulating production. Legislation to protect children spread to India at roughly the same time as industrial capitalism. As new technologies and modes of organising labour were disseminated around the globe, so too were prescribed social roles. This coincidence should be of more than passing interest to anyone concerned with the development and application of global human rights standards.

After 1919, the colonial influence on Indian labour law came to be mediated through its early participation in the International Labour Organisation (ILO). India had a large corpus of protective legislation in place by the time of independence in 1947, and this was augmented by a flurry of legislative activity in the first five years of Nehru's government. These factors, and the preference of subsequent governments to introduce new legislation rather than enforce existing legislation more vigorously, has resulted in over 200 pieces of labour legislation on the books today. Many of these relate indirectly to the environmental conditions of children's work, as shown in Table 2.

The same influences were felt in the process of drafting and subsequently amending the 1950 Constitution. The only passages in the Constitution relating to children deal with either employment or education, and here the approach follows the previous legislation. Article 24 of the Constitution is a Fundamental Right which prohibits the employment of any person below the age of 14 'to work in any factory or mine' or to be 'engaged in any other hazardous employment'. The only other Fundamental Right relating to children is Article 15(3) which explicitly allows the State 'to make any special provision for women and children' despite the general prohibition on discrimination contained in Article 15(1). Both of these provisions, although nestled in the chapter of Fundamental Rights, are essentially protectionist in character. Turning to the chapter on Directive Principles of State Policy, one finds in Article 39 that the state is enjoined to 'direct its policy towards securing':

(e) that the health and strength of workers, men and women, and the tender age of children are not abused and that citizens are not forced by economic necessity to enter avocations unsuited to their age or strength;
(f) that children are given opportunities and facilities to develop in a healthy manner and in conditions of freedom and dignity and that childhood and youth are protected against exploitation and against moral and material abandonment.[30]

30 Article 39(f) was inserted by the Constitution (Forty-second Amendment) Act, 1976, sec. 7.

Table 2: Rights of the child under selected protective legislation in India

Statute	Legal provision	Rights of the child	Comment
Constitution, 1950, Art 24	No child below 14 to be employed in factory, mine, or hazardous activity	None explicit. Implicit right to freedom from certain types of labour	Forms part of the Fundamental Rights Part of the Constitution and thus creates procedural rights to enforcement under Articles 13, 32, and 226
Children (Pledging of Labour) Act, 1933, ss.2–6	Parent or guardian may not pledge the labour of any person under 15	None explicit. Implicit right to freedom from quasi-slavery of pledge labour	
Factories Act, 1948, s. 67	No child who has not completed 14th year to be required or allowed to work in any factory. Does not apply to powered factories with fewer than 10 workers, or unpowered factories with fewer than 20 workers (s.2(m))	None explicit. Implicit right to freedom from certain types of labour	Successive Factory Acts have regulated child labour: 1880: min age; limited hrs. 1890: min age of 9 1911: 6 hrs/day max of child 1922: min age of 12; age 12–15 labour regulated
Factories Act, 1948, ss.68–77	Regulation of working conditions of young persons (age 15–18); certification of medical fitness; limited hours, etc.	None explicit. Implicit rights for 'young persons' to medical examination, limited hours	
Plantation Labour Act 1951, s 24	No child under 12 to work in any plantation	None explicit. Implicit freedom from labour under 12 years old	
Merchant Shipping Act 1958, s 109	No person under 15 to be employed on any ship, execpt a family-run ship if accompanied by male relative	None explicit. Implicit freedom from labour on ships unless in a family context	Does not apply to ships under 200 tons gross (i.e. does not apply to most vessels in India)
Mines Act, 1952, s. 45	No person below 18 yrs to be employed in any mine	None explicit. Implicit freedom from labour in mines	The definition of 'mine' (s.2(j)), is very broad, see *Tarkeshwar v Dar Dass Dey* (1079) 3 SCC 106
Apprentices Act, 1961, s. 3	No person below 14 may qualify as an apprentice	None explicit. Implicit freedom from many types of labour	Legislation is largely ignored in actual employment relations
Child Labour (Prohibition and Regulation) Act 1986	Employment of children (ie under 14) prohibited in 5 categories of industry and highly regulated in 11 categories	None explicit. Implicit freedom from work in certain industries; right to certain conditions of work in other industries	Possible conflict with Art 24 of the Constitution; duplicates provisions of many other Acts; has now (as of 1993) been extended to all undertakings in India

Like Article 45, which enjoins the free and compulsory education of children to the age of 14, these provisions are Directive Principles, which is to say that they are formally unenforceable in court, even though in recent years judges have come to rely heavily upon such provisions in interpreting the content of the Fundamental Rights. The point to notice, however, is that the Articles relating to work are inspired by a largely protectionist ethos.

The legacy of protective legislation for children's rights in India bears a moment's reflection. One point to note is that the legislation relating directly to the child's living environment operates mainly in the area of industrial and other large-scale employment. The other colonial legislation in the areas of environmental control – including the forest acts,[31] the smoke nuisance acts,[32] and the regulation of fisheries[33] – made no explicit provision for children or the interest of the child in environmental matters. So too the more recent environmental and pollution legislation does not acknowledge a distinct interest of children in the environment, nor do these Acts make special provision for the protection of children's environments.[34] On the other side of the same coin, the pieces of legislation introduced to protect the general welfare of children – such as the Children Act 1960 and later the Juvenile Justice Act 1986 – made no provision for the physical environment of children. Thus, we are left with the provisions relating to the working environment as a special area in which the environmental circumstances of the child were given early and continuing attention by regulators.

Examining the relevant labour legislation more specifically, to what extent does it provide children with enforceable rights? A perusal of the most important provisions summarised in Table 2 reveals that they generally take the form of proscription. These provisions do not use the language of rights as such, but contain enforceable standards which may result, indirectly, in the protection of the legal rights of children. With the exception of Article 24 of the Constitution, which may give rise to prerogative writs and other public law remedies, these provisions are enforced through fines or other punishments for non-compliance. To the

31 See Gadgil and Guha, *This Fissured Land: An Ecological History of India* (Oxford University Press, 1992), chaps 5–7; Guha, 'Forestry Debate and Draft Forest Act: Who Wins, Who Loses?' *Economic and Political Weekly* (20 August, 1994), p. 2192.

32 Anderson 'The Conquest of Smoke: Legislation and Pollution in Colonial Calcutta', in Arnold and Guha, op. cit. n. 27.

33 Reeves, 'Inland Waters and Freshwater Fisheries: Some Issues of Control, Access and Conservation in Colonial India' in Arnold and Guha, op. cit., n. 27.

34 See, for example, The Wild Life (Protection) Act, 1972, The Water (Prevention and Control of Pollution) Act, 1974, The Forest (Conservation) Act, 1980, The Air (Prevention and Control of Pollution) Act, 1981, The Environment (Protection) Act, 1986, The Public Liability Insurance Act, 1991, the National Environmental Tribunal Act, 1995, and the National Environment Appellate Authority Act, 1997.

extent that rights are created, they are implicit rights to freedom from certain employment conditions. Such legal rights are classic negative rights in that they predominantly establish a freedom from a hazardous environment rather than an entitlement to a beneficial environment.[35] But the true nature of the provisions shows through at this point, for even if one of the prohibitions is legally enforced, the normal consequence is to remove the child from the hazard, rather than removing the hazard from the environment.

The role of regulatory legislation in the protection of children is an important one, but it does not go far towards creating a rights-based approach to protection of the child's environment. For this one must turn to the Fundamental Rights part of the Constitution and the robust jurisprudence of environmental rights which has been built upon it.

4. Public Interest Litigation and the Constitutional Right to Environmental Protection

When compared with the solid but stolid traditionalism of its protective legislation, India's environmental rights jurisprudence appears bold and exciting. It is not only that the courts have recognised a constitutional right to environmental protection implicit within the right to life, but they have most crucially combined that substantive right with a broad range of imaginative procedural remedies which have gone a long way towards providing effective access to justice. The main substantive and procedural rights available under public interest litigation are outlined in Table 3. What is certainly clear is that public interest litigation has brought about a revolution in Indian environmental law, effectively supplanting the regulatory and torts-based approaches with a new rights-based legal framework.[36] Of more immediate concern here is to question whether this remarkable jurisprudence has actually provided much for the environmental rights of the child.

On a plain reading of the cases, there appears to be little in the way of the development of a specific right of the child to environmental protection. The relevant public interest litigation cases have not been brought by children, but by adults.[37] The right to environmental protection now

35 Although some industrial legislation does impose positive obligations upon employers, for instance the duty to provide shielding from machinery.

36 M.R. Anderson, 'Public Interest Perspectives on the Bhopal Case: Tort, Crime, or Violation of Human Rights?' in N. Robinson and J. Dunkley (eds.), *Public Interest Perspectives in Environmental Law* (Wiley Chancery, 1995).

37 Indeed, the majority of the landmark cases have been litigated by one activist lawyer – M.C. Mehta.

Table 3: The Constitutional right to Environmental Protection in India

Content of the Right	Legal authority	Comment
I. Substantive Rights 1. Constitutional right to life (Art 21) right to equality before the law (Art 14), and right to move the Supreme Court to enforce fundamental rights	The Constitution, 1950, contains a chapter on fundamental rights which takes precedence over ordinary statutes	Fundamental right must be read in light of the Directive Principles of State Policy
2. The right to life is not limited to the right to a mere animal existence but includes the protection of every human being	*Francis Coralie Mullin v Union Territory of Delhi* [1981] AIR 746 SC	
3. The right to life includes the right to health	*MK Sharma v Bharat Electronics* [1987] AIR 1792 SC; *Paschim Banga Khet Mazdoor Smity v State of West Bengal* [1996] AIR 2426 SC	Right to health appears to include both the right to health care and the right to healthy conditions
4. The right to life includes the right to be free from 'the slow poisoning caused by environmental pollution' includes the right to live in a healthy environment	*R.L. & E. Kendra v State of Uttar Pradesh* [1985] AIR 652 SC; *T. Damodhar Rao v Municipal Corpn. of Hyberabad* [1987] AIR 171 AP; *Koolwal v Rajasthan* [1988] AIR 2 Raj	- Subsidiary source of legal authority = Art 48A & Art 51A(g) - A general environmental right works to fill the gap in existing legislation esp relating to mines, quarries, and systemic problems
5. The right to life includes the right to 'pollution free air and water'	*Charan Lal Sahu v Union of India* [1990] AIR 1480 SC; *Subhash Kumar v Bihar* [1991] AIR 420 SC	
6. The right to life includes the right to 'ecological balance'	*R.L. & E. Kendra v State of Uttar Pradesh* [1985] AIR 652 SC; *T. Damodhar Rao v Municipal Corpn. of Hyberabad* [1987] AIR 171 AP	
7. The right to environmental protection included within the right to life should be applied with principles adopted from international environmental law: the principle of sustainable development, the principle of the polluter pays; the precautionary principle	*Vellore Citizens Welfare Forum v Union of India* [1996] AIR 2715 SC; *M.C Mehta v Union of India (Badkhaland Surajkund Lakes Case)* [1997] 3 SCC 715; *S. Jagannath v Union ofIndia* [1997] 2 SCC 87; *M.C. Mehta v Union of India (Taj Trapezium Case)* [1997] 2 SCC 411	Adopts Brundtland definition of sustainable development; Polluter-pays is very stringent: doctrine of 'absolute liability' Precautionary principle: explicitly puts onus of proof on the polluter, thus goes further than int'l law
8. Principle of intergenerational equity recognised; present generations have a duty to protect the environment for future generations	*People United for a Better Living in Calcutta v State of West Bengal* [1993] AIR 215 Cal; *Vellore Citizens Welfare Forum v Union of India* [1996] AIR 2715 SC	Not clear who may exercise this right

Table 3: The Constitutional right to Environmental Protection in India

Content of the Right	Legal authority	Comment
II. Procedural Rights 1. Right to petition either the Supreme Court or one of the State High Courts to have the environmental right enforced	Constitution, Arts 32 & 226	Direct and relatively speedy legal gateway; much faster than ordinary litigation
2. Right to have environmental statutes enforced through writs and orders	Constitution, Arts 32 & 226 Environment (Protection) Act, 1986	A gateway to have the existing law enforced
3. Wide *locus standi*; right to bring a writ petition on behalf of another person, or on behalf of public interest	*S.P Gupta v Union of India* [1982] AIR 149 SC (esp per Bhagwati)	An individual may launch a petition on behalf of a child
4. Right to petition the higher Courts by letter or postcard	*PUDR v Union of India* [1982] AIR 1473 SC	Avoids legal technicalities; court will convert letter to writ petition; may be important to give access to children
5. [Right?] to non-adversial proceedings	*Bandua Mukti Morcha v Union of India* [1984] AIR 802 SC; many other cases	Not clear whether this is a right or a matter for discretion. Import: litigants do not always have to prepare case; court-appointed committee of experts will often conduct the investigation; possibly esp important for children
6. Monetary compensation for victims of abuses of fundamental rights; unclear whether this is a right or within judicial discretion	*Rudul Sah* [1983] AIR 1086 SC; *Nilabati Behera v State of Orissa* [1993] AIR 1960 SC	Probably discretionary. Monetary compensation established as a public law right distinct from rights in tort
7. Public interest petitioners [entitled?] to an order for costs where the petition is successful	Art 32; varies on a case-by-case basis	Costs orders make public interest litigation much more possible
8. Right to enforcement of international human rights treaty provisions as part of the constitutional rights	*People's Union for Civil Liberties v Union of India* [1997] AIR 1203 SC; *People's Union for Civil Liberties v Union of India* [1997] AIR 1 SCC 301 *M.C. Mehta v State of Tamil Nadu* [1996] 6 SCC 756	ICCPR Art 9(5) [monetary compensation] and Art 17 [privacy] enforceable in Indian law; mention of Convention on Rights of the Child

recognised by the Courts is a right enjoyed by all citizens, with no special provision for children. Indeed, Article 14 of the Constitution provides that the rights should apply equally to all within the territory of India, and any special rights for children would need to be justified as derogations from this rule. In principle a differential right for children could be justified to the Supreme Court,[38] but sound arguments regarding the special environmental circumstances of children would have to be brought. Although the environmental jurisprudence has featured some abstract discussion of the needs of children and future generations as a justification for the court's actions, there have been no orders specifically tailored to address the particular vulnerabilities or interests of children.

Viewed from another angle, there is much about the current pattern of public interest litigation which is well-suited to meet the environmental interests and needs of children. The broad rules of standing do allow any concerned citizen to bring a case on behalf of a child or group of children. The rules of procedure in public interest litigation are non-technical, and allow petitioners (including potentially, children) to bring information to the court in undigested form. The widespread use of non-adversarial proceedings and court-appointed expert committees reduces the burden on the petitioner to adduce extensive complex evidence: the courts regularly rely upon environmental experts and administrators to gather and assess technical evidence. This practice has enabled petitioners (who would otherwise lack the resources and expertise to bring complex environmental evidence before the court) to prevail in litigation in environmental disputes involving highly technical information. These arrangements are particularly helpful for any potential litigation by children, who might not be able to fund and organise scientific evidence for the court. This procedural flexibility has been extended to remedies, where the courts have been willing to grant a wide range of writs, orders, directions, and injunctions. Perhaps one of the most important features is the development of monetary compensation to those whose rights have been infringed: this is likely to allow the courts to apply the polluter pays principle in an effective and flexible manner.

In addition to these procedural advantages, there are a number of substantive developments in the content of the environmental right which may be conducive to petitions from children. To begin with, the Indian jurisprudence has been highly elastic, with the courts willing to recognise new areas of environmental concern under the general heading

38 The test of reasonable classification in India is that the right to equal protection requires equal treatment in similar circumstances. Differential treatment must have a rational relation to the object sought to be achieved by statute or law being challenged.

of the protection of the right to life. Added to this, the Supreme Court has gone a long way toward incorporating the standards of international environmental law into domestic jurisprudence, so the polluter-pays principle, the principle of sustainable development, and the precautionary principle are recognised and enforceable in the superior courts through public interest litigation. This not only creates jurisprudential scope for a wider range of environmental claims (including those by children), it also raises the possibility of judicial recognition of the principles in the Convention on the Rights of the Child, to which India acceded in 1992. This is particularly important in the context of a general judicial recognition of the principle of inter-generational equity.[39] Although the principle has been recognised in only the broadest possible terms, and has not been decisive in deciding any disputes to date, it has the potential to do so. Since the interests of children and of future generations are conceptually allied, the principle may yet play a role in evolving a practical and distinctive approach to the environmental rights of children. These features of public interest litigation in India are promising, but they have not yet resulted in the creation of a cohesive view of how the rights of children to environmental protection should be secured.

5. Which Approach to the Rights of Children to Environmental Protection?

It follows from the above that there is considerable scope for the development of an environmental rights specifically tailored to children, but what form should such a right take? Children have fewer rights than adults at the moment, due to the disabilities raised above. In this context the basic dilemma is whether it is enough to simply remove the disabilities, thereby giving children rights equal to those of adults, or must one give shape to special rights particularly designed for children? Or is it possible to secure the effective protection of children's rights without making any changes to the substantive law at all?

5.1 Apply existing rights

One approach is simply to adopt the existing environmental right which applies to all individuals and deploy it in contexts specific to children. In

---

39 *People United for a Better Living in Calcutta v. State of West Bengal* 1993 AIR 215 Cal; *Vellore Citizens Welfare Forum v. Union of India* 1996 AIR 2715 SC.

other words, retain the content of the general environmental right, but to apply it and enforce it in ways more conducive to meeting the needs of children. There is a strong argument for this point of view from those who advocate a single right applicable to all, and it is the case that the existing right is defined so widely that it can be turned with good effect to a wide range of problems.

5.2 Remove legal incapacities

A second approach is to rely upon the existing conceptual structure of the right, but to remove the existing traces of the colonial and traditional legal system which disadvantage children. The various legal disabilities considered above – in particular the legal incapacity to participate in litigation – could be removed so that children might be enabled to exercise their full range of legal powers with respect to the environment. A related change is more conceptual and fundamental, and it relates to protective legislation. The current law protecting children provides few procedural gateways for children to actually participate in the management of their surroundings and lives. As discussed above, a key feature of much labour legislation was that while it did recognise the particular vulnerability of children to environmental harm, it tended to treat children as passive and helpless objects of protection rather than active agents interacting with the environment around them. In other words, the legislation construed children as objects of protection rather than rights-bearing legal subjects. There is considerable evidence that children in India can and do play a positive role in raising environmental awareness, protesting against environmental harm, and contributing to positive solutions to environmental problems. Children have been active participants in the NGO environmental movement in India, and have therefore been active agents in shaping the environment around them. For example, in one celebrated initiative, children in Delhi have held a number of public demonstrations against automobile pollution, and have even stopped heavily polluting vehicles in the middle of the road demanding that drivers clean up their emissions. Similarly, one of the most effective and well-organised lobbying groups in the aftermath of the Bhopal gas leak disaster was made up of children, including those orphaned by the death of parents exposed to the toxic gas. Given the moral and political influence which children can sometimes exercise in such circumstances, and considering the right of the child to freedom of expression and the right to be heard in judicial proceedings as provided in Article 12 of the Convention on the Rights of the Child, there is a strong argument for a legal regime which treats children as active legal agents.

5.3 Fashion a new child-specific right

A third approach would be to develop a distinct and autonomous right of the child to a clean, healthy, and ecologically sound environment. If a new right of this kind is to be developed, its precise shape is not yet clear, although it would inevitably draw heavily upon the existing jurisprudence, and might involve the removal of certain legal incapacities. The relevance of the precautionary principle and the concept of inter-generational equity may be noted for a child's right. It might be that the distinctive feature of child's environmental right would lie largely in the procedural and enforcement aspects rather than the substantive protections, which are already generous under the existing jurisprudence. Before venturing into the development of yet another right on paper, however, considerable intellectual effort would be required to show that such a right would provide effective guarantees beyond what is already available under the Constitution enforced by public interest litigation.

It is not the proper place of this chapter to venture into further speculation on the matter, however, some consideration may be given to the conceptual and practical difficulties which arise when one considers applying any environmental right – either general or specially formulated – to children.

6. Practical Issues in Formulating Environmental Rights

This section examines some practical environmental problems in India that raise difficult legal issues for the rights of children. Of course, there are many environmental issues affecting children in India that cannot be comprehensively covered here. Three specific areas that relate to different stages of a child's life have been selected in order to illustrate the legal problems that may arise in formulating a child's right to a clean and healthy environment in India.

6.1 The unborn child and environmental rights

Attributing rights to the unborn child is a controversial issue because of the potential conflict with the rights and interests of the mother. Whether it is appropriate to give unborn children rights or whether rights accruing at birth can be made more effective for damage caused to the child in the womb or even before conception, is an issue that should be considered in formulating a legal right for children. However, there is clear evidence that environmental hazards can affect the unborn child and various studies show that the child in the womb is susceptible to external environmental factors.[40] A UNEP study[41] estimates that 5–10 per cent of birth defects results from environmental factors such as exposure to chemicals. Other studies have found that exposure during pregnancy to indoor air pollution from smoky fires can lead to adverse pregnancy outcomes such as low birth weight, stillbirth or neonatal death.[42] Although in many cases, the mother may also be damaged by exposure to the environmental hazard, in some cases the foetus can be seriously affected by hazards that appear to leave the mother unharmed.

Studies of the impact of the Bhopal gas leak disaster showed much higher rates of spontaneous abortions in women who were exposed to the gas during pregnancy with one study showing a twofold increase.[43] There is also some evidence of an increase in spontaneous abortions in women conceiving after the gas leak but who had been exposed to the gas.[44] Other studies have shown that it is not only environmental hazards to which the mother is exposed in pregnancy that may affect her unborn child. Exposure of the mother to environmental hazards such as chemicals and radiation before pregnancy may affect a child conceived later in her life

How do these issues affect environmental rights for children? It is important in formulating such rights to consider how to address the health effects of environmental hazards to which they or their parents were exposed before their birth. There is in Indian law now clear authority for the view that ante-natal injuries caused by environmental damage may give rise to liability. In *Union Carbide Corporation v. Union of India*[45] the Supreme Court took guidance from UK legislation[46] in holding that those who were unborn at the time of the Bhopal gas leak and who are able to show congenital defects traceable to the toxicity of the gas are entitled to be compensated. Yet this rule accords legal rights to the child after being born for damage which occurred before birth – it does not extend legal personality to the unborn child as such. To extend legal personality directly to the unborn child does not seem to be an effective way of addressing children's needs. Rather, the interests of the unborn child should be seen in the context of the parents' needs as in most cases, damage to the child has

40 For a general overview of the impact of environmental factors on the child in the womb see Satterthwaite, et al., op. cit., n. 6, pp. 75–80.

41 UNEP and UNICEF, Children and the Environment: *The State of the Environment 1990* (UNEP and UNICEF, 1990).

42 S. Banerjee, 'The Enemy Within', *Down to Earth* (15 July 1996) which refers to studies in western India which associate a 50 per cent increase in stillbirths to exposures suffered by the region's pregnant women.

43 C. Sathyamala, 'Reproductive Health Consequences of the Bhopal Gas Leak', *Economic and Political Weekly*, 6 January 1996.

44 T. Narayan, 'The Health Impact of the Bhopal Disaster', *Economic and Political Weekly*, 18 and 25 August 1990.

45 AIR 1992 SC 248, at p. 311.

46 Congenital Disabilities (Civil Liability) Act 1976, s. 1.

resulted from damage to the parents. Although in some cases the parents, specifically the mother during pregnancy, may be apparently unharmed by exposure to an environmental hazard, it does not significantly progress the interests of children to see them in isolation from their parents. To protect a child from environmental hazards, particularly those before birth requires protection for the parents and community. It is within this context that an unborn child's special vulnerability may be most effectively considered.

6.2 Infants and the impact of indoor air pollution

Indoor air pollution is caused by smoky fires that are usually made by burning wood, crop residues and cow dung. Such fuels are used by more than three-quarters of Indian households and some estimates suggest that these smoky fires are responsible for about 60 per cent of exposure to particulates.[47] In 1991 the World Bank classified indoor air pollution in developing countries as one the four most critical global environmental problems. Exposure to indoor air pollution is major factor in acute respiratory infection (ARI) which is one of the three main causes of infant death in India.[48]

The issue of indoor air pollution is difficult because the use of biomass fuels such as cow dung is bound up with religious beliefs and cultural practices as well as poverty. It is also a difficult issue in legal terms because of the problems in distinguishing impact of indoor from outdoor air pollution; moreover, the effects of pollution are closely bound up with the effects of poverty and malnutrition. For these reasons it is hard to show the relative damage caused by indoor pollution in relation to damage caused by other factors. Although in one sense, the direct of cause of environmental air pollution is the fuel burning practices of the child's own family and community, these practices may have a less direct cause such as government policy or other factors which lead to a lack of cleaner fuel and burning methods. These are urgent health issues for children, and important environmental problems, but it is not clear that they can be addressed through a legal right. Against whom would the right be enforced? Against the child's family or community for exposing the child to the pollution, or against the state for not complying with a legal duty to ensure a clean environment for children? It is conceivable that in the context of India's ambitious prerogative writs and judicial orders, it might be possible to order

47 Banerjee, op. cit., n. 42 cites two studies by the Tata Energy Resource Institute. The first compared exposure of men women and children to indoor air pollution in a village in the Garhwal Himalaya and which found that 80–100 per cent of daily exposure to pollution was caused by indoor environments. The second study looked at infants in the slums of Delhi to establish the extent of the interaction between indoor and outdoor air pollution.

48 *Ibid.*, p. 27.

the government to provide cleaner fuel at subsidised prices, although this would raise questions regarding the separation of powers. Formulating a legal right to protect children from indoor air pollution (perhaps one of the most important hazards affecting children) will not be easy. As with environmental issues affecting the unborn child, it is clear that the child must be seen in the context of its family and community and that any environmental right must address this as well as the special vulnerabilities of children.

6.3 Children and work

The working conditions of children in manufacturing and other industries have received a great deal of attention.[49] Many examples can be given, but to take just a few: the carpets industry in Kashmir employs many children who are regularly exposed to the fibres and dust in the air. Up to 60 per cent are said to suffer from asthma and tuberculosis. Similarly, in the match factories children are exposed to dangerous chemicals, poor ventilation and accidents.[50]

Children are doubly discriminated against working in industry in India. Official government policy is to eliminate child labour and where the law is enforced, it is enforced to prevent children working at all at the particular factory. Where children are working illegally, either because they are under age or because of the type of industry in which they are working, the law does not enforce health and safety standards that apply to other workers. For this reason, children frequently do not benefit as workers from established safety standards. Despite government policy, the reality is that child labour is here for the foreseeable future and most child workers are not benefiting from the existing regime as far as it is enforced.

Not only are child workers in the formal sector discriminated against in terms of health and safety matters, they are also discriminated against in terms of self-organisation. The ability of children to organise themselves to deal with, amongst other things, the environmental hazards that they face is of critical importance in addressing the environmental hazards faced by children in India. However, because of the policy of eliminating child labour; and specifically because of the provisions of the 1926 Trade Union Act, children under 15 are not allowed to be members of trade unions. A

49 See in particular the contribution by Holly Cullen in this volume.

50 There are many studies into the working conditions of children in industry. For a general overview from an environmental perspective see Satterthwaite et al., op. cit., n. 6, at pp. 91–94; for an overview of child labour in India see Srinivasan and Gandotra (eds.), *Child Labour: Multi Dimensional Problem* (Ajanta, 1993). Specific studies include Laksar, 'Child Labour and Health: An Exploratory Study of Aligarh Lock Industry in India', *International Review of Child Health*, October 1996; and Kothari, 'There's Blood on those Matchsticks', *Economic and Political Weekly*, 2 July 1983.

recent attempt by a children's union in Delhi to be registered was refused by the registrar of trade unions and later upheld by the court.[51] This is a further example of a legal disability which restricts the rights of children to vindicate their rights to a healthy environment.

Recognising the reality of children at work and enabling children to organise may be a more effective way to improve children's environmental conditions than enforcing unrealistic prohibitions upon working relations. Ironically, it is the very laws designed to keep children out of hazardous employment which play the most important role in denying children legal capacity – and social agency – in their working environments.

The point needs to be made that roughly 80 per cent of the children who work do so in the informal sector – in small businesses, at home, or in agriculture – and so cannot benefit from health and safety standards established for the formal sector. The small and disparate workplaces also mean that children are unlikely to form effective trade unions or other organisations. Workers in the informal sector, including children, have very little formal protection from environmental hazards such as unsafe working conditions and exposure to chemicals such as pesticides. Thus formulating an effective child's right to a clean environment will be even more difficult to achieve effectively in the informal sector.

Finally relating to children at work, it is important to raise the issue of the impact of environmental degradation. Such degradation often means that it is harder to collect fuel and firewood and so it becomes more difficult for children, particularly girl children, to attend school. The damage caused to the child may not therefore be a clear physical one, but be a loss of education and other opportunities. In such circumstances, the child's interest in environmental protection arises not from immediate exposure to hazards or environmental degradation, but from the changing economic circumstances and daily working requirements which resource degradation may bring. For this reason, children in families directly dependent upon fuel and other natural resource goods have an immediate interest in the protection of those resources. This again raises difficult issues in formulating a right for children.

Although these are only three examples of the environmental issues facing children in India, they illustrate some of the challenges of formulating a child's right to a clean environment. The key points are the importance of ensuring the child's right is seen in the context of his or her family and community; and the importance of seeing the child's right in context of other issues such as poverty and gender.

51 Shankar, 'Child Workers want their Unions Recognised', Down to Earth, (15 March 1993).

7. Implementing and Enforcing Environmental Rights of Children in India

On paper, India has an extensive system of environmental law in the form of statutory regulation, criminal law and tort. However, the operation of the law in practice has not lived up to its promises on paper. In 1980 the government committee appointed to recommend reforms in environmental legislation noted that the laws were often inconsistent and poorly implemented. In particular the committee noted that criminal fines for pollution were low and infrequently applied, while remedies in the civil law were often slow and expensive.[52] Despite legislative improvements in the intervening years, the same criticisms are frequently heard today. The actual rate of prosecutions for violations of the Air Act and Water Act have increased substantially in recent years,[53] but there is also evidence that the absolute number of infringements have increased as well. While there have not been systematic surveys of the efficiency of pollution control enforcement, there is widespread dissatisfaction with the existing system on the part of citizens, businesses, and civil servants alike.

Public interest litigation cases have fared rather better due to their high public profile and the involvement of the highest courts. Yet even in such high-profile cases the anecdotal evidence suggests that enforcement is often poor or even non-existent. It appears that the Supreme Court judgements which have been most effectively enforced in other areas of fundamental rights have been those which give specific directions to state bodies to implement specific and achievable measures. Those judgements which have been very extensive in their scope, or which envisage substantial changes to systems of social and economic organisation, have proved more difficult to enforce.

Turning to the question of children's rights, it is possible to identify further inadequacies in existing legal arrangements. In the main, the problem is that issues affecting children are often not directly addressed in the law: this has led to a gap relating to indoor air pollution, environmental degradation and the impact of environmental change (such as declining fuel supplies) on schooling. Moreover, the private bodies often responsible for harm to the child's environment are not fully covered by fundamental rights. Although the courts have tried to address this by ordering the state to take

52 Report of the Committee for Recommending Legislative Measures and Administrative Machinery for Ensuring Environmental Protection, Delhi, 1981.

53 Prosecutions under the Water Act, for example, increased from 1,665 in 1987 to 4,403 in 1992. See Mehta, Mundle, and Shankar, *Controlling Pollution: Incentives and Regulations* (Sage, 1997), p. 22.

action against private companies,[54] and have in some cases actually issued direct orders to companies in order to enforce fundamental rights, the development of the law in this area is still inchoate.

8. Alternative Means of Implementation

While formal court systems have an essential role to play, they may not always be the most appropriate forum for implementing a child's right to a clean environment. They can be expensive, inaccessible and adversarial. The Indian Supreme Court judges have done a great deal to address these issues by providing easier and cheaper access and by developing more inquisitorial forms of approach. Yet delays remain a problem, and the well-described problems of finance, access to legal advice, and the geographical and cultural inaccessibility of the courts remain serious obstacles to invoking formal courts in litigation.[55]

Turning to alternative forms of enforcement, the advent of human rights commissions around the world is one of the most significant recent developments in the protection of human rights. Such commissions have a real advantage over courts in that they can initiate action and investigate patterns of rights violations, rather than focusing on single incidents and isolated individual complaints. Commissions have a great potential to identify structural problems, to generate fresh research, and to recommend courses of action to the government.

The National Human Rights Commission in India was established by the Protection of Human Rights Act 1993, and was endowed with powers to conduct investigations, intervene in legal proceedings, make inspections, and promote human rights through research and education. Empowered to inquire into any complaints regarding the violation of human rights, the Commission does not charge a fee and may initiate judicial proceedings on behalf of the person making a complaint. These powers give the Commission the potential to develop an innovative approach to a child's right to a clean and healthy environment. Although the Commission has no specific mandate in relation to environmental rights, the National Commission has taken a number of actions on fluoride and arsenic

54 See, for example, *Consumer Education & Research Centre v. Union of India* 1995 AIR 922 SC, in which the Supreme Court ordered private asbestos manufacturers to pay compensation to employees on the grounds that the right to life provided in Article 21 of the Constitution had been infringed.

55 The general literature on the inaccessibility of courts and other legal mechanisms is now large. The comprehensive survey and analysis provided by the Florence Project remains a definitive statement (see Capilletti (ed.), *Access to Justice*, 3 vols. (Sijthoff, 1978–79). More specifically, myriad problems faced by people in actually using courts in India is summarised in Perry and Anderson, 'Access to Environmental Justice in Bangalore', SOAS Law Department Working Paper No. 12 (March 1996).

contamination in public water sources, and in respect of air pollution in urban areas.[56]

Although none of its environmental actions have been specifically in relation to children, the Commission has increasingly been concerning itself with the rights of the child. In its annual report for 1995/6, the Commission reports that it 'made a concerted effort to come to grips with the major social problems affecting adversely the rights of the child'.[57] Initiatives have dealt with iodine deficiency, child marriage, female foeticide and infanticide, child prostitution, and child labour. It has an active programme on the issue of child labour in hazardous industries. The Commission has carried out research on the topic and has focused particularly on the Ferozabad District in Uttar Pradesh where up to 50,000 children are believed to be working in the glassworks and bangle industry. The Commission monitors the situation in Ferozabad through visits and meetings with government officials. Although the government has a scheme to end child labour in hazardous industries by the year 2000, the Commission is sceptical that this goal will be achieved without a more concerted and systematic approach. For this reason, in addition to working with the government and public officials, the Commission has solicited the support of each of the main political parties to make recommendations as to how each party could take action to eliminate child labour.

Most human rights commissions, such as the national and state commissions in India, are still relatively new, so it is not yet possible to make a confident assessment of their effectiveness. Yet the indications are that there is great potential to develop a realistic, coherent and integrated approach to children's rights, including those to a clean and healthy environment.

9. Conclusion

It is clear that many children in India are exposed to environmental hazards which not only pose immediate health problems, but which also affect the long-term quality of life in their communities. Although India's legal system has evolved an imaginative jurisprudence of environmental rights, it is nevertheless failing to deliver healthy and ecologically sound environmental conditions to millions of children. The existing right to environment does offer considerable scope for development, and the

---

56 Interview with R.V. Pillai, Secretary-General of the Indian National Human Rights Commission (Sylvia Bluck, October 1997).

57 National Human Rights Commission, Annual Report 1995/6, p. 26.

internal conceptual resources to achieve needed changes are available. Yet if legal rights for children are to be effective in this area, a crucial conceptual challenge is raised: how can the legal system recognise the social agency of children? An effective approach to the environmental rights of the child will necessarily treat children as rights-bearing subjects rather than passive objects of protection.

Moreover, an effective rights regime for children will need to recognise and account for the actual circumstances in which children live. Thus it is important to link a child's right to a clean environment with that of her or his family and community, as well as the child's own needs in relation to issues of poverty and gender. And finally, the procedural rights and mechanisms of enforcement should account for the specific circumstances of children by making space for non-litigious means of enforcement, such as the use of the National Human Rights Commission.

4 The right of the child to a clean environment in Poland

AGATA FIJALKOWSKI

1. Introduction

1.1 The state of the environment in Poland in 1989

Poland has one of the worst environmental records in Europe. In comparison to other Central and East European countries Poland still has a disproportionately higher level of environmental pollution. This is in large part due to the legacy of the previous political system; it was an inescapable side-effect based on the following particular features of the Communist regime:

(1) the years of long dominance of the most energy consuming and harmful industries, particularly minerals extraction and metallurgy;
(2) the construction of huge industrial plants, usually located in already heavily industrialised areas;
(3) the wasteful use of low-priced minerals, energy and water in production processes, and the resulting release of excessive quantities of waste into the environment;
(4) pricing of goods without regard for their real production costs.

Under the Communist regime, the state, as an exclusive owner of industrial facilities, was not interested in introducing strict laws to enforce the construction of pollution-control installations.[1] In consequence, Poland's natural environment deteriorated progressively, and by the end of the 1980s, Poland was one of the most polluted countries in Europe. The many years of inaction and negligence certainly have left their mark, and much work still needs to be done so that Poland meets internationally set environmental standards.

1 For an interesting discussion about the ideological dimension (i.e., Marxism–Leninism) of environmental protection, see Daniel H. Cole, *Instituting Environmental Protection: From Red to Green in Poland* (London, 1998), pp. 155–181. See also Barbara Hicks, *Environmental Politics in Poland: A Social Movement Between Regime and Opposition* (New York, 1996).

What follows is a brief summary of the state of the environment in Poland in 1989. The situation has improved, but is far from satisfactory, and the effects of the ecological devastation on the population are only now being discussed. The extent of the environmental damage forces one to discuss it in the context of human rights. Discussion about the environment are related to environmental policy and law. One of the aspects of the right to an environment involves the protection of the well being of individuals. This chapter will specifically focus on the child's right to a clean environment.

Atmospheric pollution in Poland was one of the heaviest in Europe. In 1989, Poland was the third biggest polluter after the former Soviet Union and Germany, emitting about 4 million tonnes of sulphur dioxide and 1.5 million tonnes of nitrogen dioxide from its territory.

In all the big cities, the concentrations of particulates (sulphur and nitrogen dioxides) exceeded the allowable standards. This situation was particularly critical in the Upper Silesian region, Cracow, the Legnica-Glogow region, and the Sudety Mountains (where acid rain is one of the main reasons of the extinction of the forest there). In the Sudety Mountains region, for example, there were twelve power plants which burned poor quality brown coal. Originally, none of these plants had facilities for exhaust gas desulphurisation, and emissions from this region, aptly referred to as the 'Black Triangle' accounted for 20 per cent of the European emissions of sulphur dioxide. Steps have been taken to address this problem.

Water pollution was also in a serious state. In 1989, as much as one-third of Poland's municipal sewage was dumped into surface waters without any treatment, and another 35 per cent after only the preliminary mechanical treatment. Only the remaining 32 per cent of waste was treated to a satisfactory level. Of all the Polish cities, 366, or 44 per cent, including cities with more than 200,000 inhabitants (Bialystok, Lodz, Radom) did not have any waste treatment plants. The capacities of waste treatment plants in many other large urban industrial areas such as Warsaw, Cracow, Wroclaw, Poznan, Gdansk, Bydgoszcz, and Szczecin, were far from sufficient.

As a result the quality of Polish rivers was very poor. In 1989 only 5 per cent of river length had potable (Class I) water, and along 35 per cent of it the water was below all rankings and could not be used even for industrial purposes. A particular problem was the high salinity of many rivers, the result of the bituminous coal mine effluents in the Upper Silesian region. Some of these mines had deep saline waters which had to be pumped up to the surface during mining operations (the mines constructed during the last twenty years). In 1989 the total amount of salt dumped into the Vistula and

Odra rivers everyday was 9,000 tonnes, which was enough to fill 450 20-tonne railway wagons. This resulted in huge material losses due to chlorine damage to heating systems in towns and cities located along the two biggest Polish rivers and the many industrial plants which used the river water.

Finally, of the 161 lakes that had been tested for water quality, only 4 per cent qualified for the highest purity class, while 63 per cent of the water was unsuitable for drinking, even for recreational purposes. Pollution of underground waters by community sewage, substances used in farming, i.e., pesticides and fertiliser residues, and petroleum products was also commonplace. (The last form of contamination was worst in the areas where Soviet army units were stationed.) In 1989, 65.9 per cent of the residential wells in villages and 54.2 per cent of the wells on the outskirts of urban areas had poor quality (undrinkable) water, and in five provinces over 80 per cent of such wells were so affected (Konin, Sierdaz, Kalisz, Lodz, and Leszno). The main source of their pollution was community sewage. Since 99.5 per cent of the territory in Poland is within the Baltic Sea catchment area, the sea receives most of the sewage dumped into the rivers. In 1989, of the total load of sewage dumped into the Baltic Sea by the countries of the Baltic Sea catchment area, Poland contributed 40 per cent of the phosphorus, 34.7 per cent of the nitrogen and 21.3 per cent of the organic matter.

The consequences of the long-term neglect of investing in environmental control are most apparent in Upper Silesia. Since the twelfth century, non-ferrous metal ores have been extracted in this region, which has the richest deposits of natural resources in Poland, and since the eighteenth century bituminous coal has been exploited there. It was only after World War II, however, that extraction reached levels that accelerated the process of environmental deterioration in the whole region.

In the 1980s, 62 coal mines in the Upper Silesia industrial region extracted 190–200 million tonnes of coal per year (several times more than before WWII), generating several tens of millions of tonnes of coal wastes and discharging 2.0–2.5 tonnes of salt into the rivers every year.

A substantial amount of coal extracted is burned on the spot in several large power plants and in the heating system of the Silesian conurbation, which has over 3 million residents. It is also made into coke which is then used in steelworks and chemical plants. In 1989, Katowice province extracted 98 per cent of the national output of coal and 100 per cent of zinc ores, generated 50 per cent of the national steel output, and produced 34 per cent of the coke, 41 per cent of the window glass, 50 per cent of the passenger cars and 7 per cent of the sulphuric acid. This type of production causes the emission of about 560,000 tonnes of particulates, 950,000 tonnes of sulphuric acid, 250,000 of nitrogen oxide and approximately 900 million cubic metres of sewage, of which only 24 per cent is properly treated.

Such large-scale extraction of materials and such high concentration of environmentally hazardous industry (in an area of only 6,650 square kilometres, 21 per cent of Poland's total area) has caused unprecedented ecological disaster in Poland. It is estimated that about 1 million residents of Silesia now live in areas strongly affected by toxic substances that pose a threat to human health and life. This is evident in human health indicators. The average life span there is one year shorter than in Poland as a whole, and the death rate of men in the 30–59 age group exceeds the national average by about 40 per cent. Infant mortality in this region is the highest in Poland: in 1989 it was 18.5 per cent per 1,000 live births, compared to a national average of 15.9 per cent. The children there usually have lower birth weights, and their rate of birth defects is 60 per cent higher than in other parts of Poland. Defect in the genetic code in residents of Silesia have been noted by doctors. This is the result of one-sided, long-term forced industrialisation in a region.

1.2 Environmental goals of post-communist Poland

The Council of Europe, in its 1988–1989 recommendation, expressed its concern with the state of the environment in Central and Eastern Europe, and called upon the West for assistance.[2]

In 1991, the Polish government listed the following environmental goals in their National Environmental Policy. The short-term goals to be realised (by 1995) were:

(1) improving frontier monitoring of transboundary pollution;
(2) reducing emissions from the most highly polluting industrial facilities;
(3) reducing the environmental impacts of transportation;
(4) building waste water treatment plants;
(5) remedying urban water drinking shortages; and
(6) implementing a management system for industrial and municipal solid waste and for toxic waste.

The medium-term priorities, to be realised by the year 2000, are:

(1) reducing SO_2 emissions by 2.9 million tonnes per year (eventually achieving a 30 per cent reduction over the 1980 level);
(2) reducing NO_X emissions by 10 per cent of the 1987 level;

2 'Environmental Policy in Europe (1988-1989), European Parliamentary Association, 42nd Session, Recommendation No. 1131.

(3) a 50 per cent reduction in discharges of untreated sewage;
(4) improving rural drinking water quality; and
(5) creating a waste disposal system that incorporated recycling, composting, incineration and bio-gas production.

The long-term priorities, to be realised by the year 2020, are:

(1) integrating environmentally sound techniques into all aspects of the production process and supporting clean technologies over end of pipe treatments; and
(2) repairing environmental damage and instituting systems to prevent its recurrence.

Following the OECD Environmental Performance Review, the suggested areas of concern were air pollution, water resources, waste management, and conservation.

2. Environmental Legislation in Poland

Polish environmental legislation can be traced back to the pre-war period, such as the resource ordinances of the 1920s governing forestry and hunting. Polish legislation on water was groundbreaking for its time – and it remained in force well into the 1960s.[3] Indeed, the environmental legislation of the pre-war period served as a basis – at least as an important point of reference – for present-day environmental legislation.

The notion of 'environmental protection' first appeared in the 1970s: state and citizens' environmental rights and responsibilities were first defined in 1976 in two constitutional amendments: Article 12(2), 'The Polish People's Republic ensures the protection and rational shaping of the environment'; and Article 71, 'Citizens ... have the right to utilise the values of the natural environment and the obligation to protect it'.[4] The provisions are vague and appear to have been a means to 'introduce' environmental protection as one of the aspirations of the socialist state. These provisions were, in fact, a precursor to the 1980 Environmental Protection and Development Act. The comprehensive statute was the basis for protecting individual elements of the environment, as well as regulating its economic use:[5] sections of the statute cover air, noise, vibration, waste,

---

3 Waclaw Brzezinski, *Legal Protection of the Environment in Poland* (Wroclaw, 1974).
4 *Dziennik Ustaw* (Daily Laws) (1976), No. 7, item 36.
5 *Dziennik Ustaw* (1980), No. 3, item 6.

radiation and conservation. This particular piece of legislation marked the beginnings of a more complex vision of the environment on the part of the state. The 1980 law, for example, established environmental protection duties, and obligated all economic enterprises and persons engaged in economic activities to protect the environment.[6]

It should also be noted according to the 1969 Penal Code, polluters who intentionally created a threat to human life, health, and property could be imprisoned for up to ten years.[7] The Environmental Protection and Development Act complemented the Criminal Code provisions in adding new offences ranging from causing pollution to water contamination. Of course, progressive legislation means nothing when it is not enforced; this was the case in Poland, and considering the dire environmental situation of 1989, one can conclude that penal sanctions were rarely enforced by the courts against suspected polluters.[8]

The 1980 statute has been amended in 1997 to strengthen the state's commitment to its citizens in, *inter alia*: protecting the environment (Article 1(1)); providing for legal remedies in the event the environment is not used in the public interest (*idem*); and safe and clean production, whereby the organisation, technical, and technological methods of production do not endanger human health (Article 3(4e)).

Post-Communist environmental legislation is based on the notion of sustainable development. The 1991 Statute on Nature Conservation, which is the framework for management and protection of the natural environment, the 1991 Statute on the State Inspectorate for Environmental Protection, and the 1991 National Environmental Policy are the three key components of Polish environmental law.

The 1997 Polish Constitution also refers to environmental protection. Article 5 states that the 'Republic of Poland . . . shall ensure the protection of the environment pursuant to the principles of sustained development'.[9] Under the 'Economic, Social, and Cultural Freedoms and Rights' chapter, Article 74 reiterates that '(1) public authorities shall pursue policies ensuring the ecological security of current and future generations; (2) [p]rotection of the environment shall be the duty of public authorities; (3) [e]veryone shall have the right to be informed of the quality of the environment and its protection; and (4) [p]ublic authorities shall support the activities of citizens to protect and improve the quality of the environment'.

---

6 See *ibid* and Cole, pp. 43–61.

7 *Dziennik Ustaw* (1969), No. 13, item 94.

8 For information on and an excellent analysis of the administration of justice in Poland under the Communist regime, see Maria Los, *Communist Ideology, Law and Crime* (London, 1988).

9 *Dziennik Ustaw* (1997), No. 78, item 483.

Thus, sustainable development has become a basic principle of government policy, and has been so since 1991. Economic policy measures are guided by the polluter-pays principle. The state's commitment to the rule of law (Article 2) means a broader sphere of judicial review over regulations and administrative decisions; this will pave the way in guaranteeing the constitutional right to an environment. An independent judiciary (Article 10) should, with time, find the appropriate balance between competing interests.

It should be mentioned that the new Polish Penal Code of 1998 has a chapter (XXII), Articles 181–188, on 'Crimes against the Environment'.[10] The provisions punish offenders who damage the environment (Article 181); contaminate water resulting in a human health risk (Article 182); or handles dangerous substances (Article 183); they can risk imprisonment of up to five years, depending on the *mens rea*. It should be noted that in none of the aforementioned pieces of legislation is the child mentioned as having a special right to a clean environment.

As mentioned above, the State Inspectorate for Environmental Protection (hereinafter SIEP) is responsible for enforcing environmental laws and regulations. In contrast to municipalities which are charged with issuing facility permits, SIEP monitors and enforces compliance. SIEP also has the authority to shut down some or all operations at facilities it considers threatening to the health and the environment. In 1989, SIEP compiled a list of 27 regions which were severely polluted, and 80 facilities which were considered a serious threat to the environment.[11] Already in 1993 it shut down partially, or in total, 22 facilities emitting the most pollution and, in 1997, 72 were shut down, or partially shut down, because sections of the facilities hadn't complied with environmental standards. In total, SIEP manages nearly 35,000 small, medium, and large facilities throughout Poland.

SIEP operates at national and local levels: the provincial inspectorate reports to the chief inspectorate, which is directly answerable to the environmental minister. In addition to their power to prohibit activities which violate environmental standards, SIEP also collect data on the state of the environment.

An equally important function is fulfilled by the Sanitary Inspectorate, which monitors the effects of environmental conditions on human health and inspects domestic and imported food. This agency is a part of the Ministry of Health and Social Welfare.

10 *Dziennik Ustaw* (1997), No. 88, item 553.
11 Telephone interview with Andrzej Miloszewski, Director of SIEP, 11 October 1997.

Several research institutes which report to the Ministry of the Environment are the Institute of Environmental Protection, the Institute of Ecology in Industrial Areas, and the Institute of Meteorology and Water Management. Scientific advisory boards to the government are the National Centre for Environmental Education, the State Council on Environmental Protection, and the Environmental Council Advising the President.

There are over 100 environmental groups in Poland, most of them with a local emphasis. These NGOs have a consultative role on policymaking, and draft environmental laws are reviewed by environmental groups before their submission to parliament. Furthermore, NGOs can bring legal claims before administrative tribunals. The competency of the High Administrative Court was expanded to hear complaints on administrative and adjudicatory decisions in 1995.

The role of provinces (*wojewodztwa*) and municipalities (*gminas*) is especially important in Poland. Each province has its own Department of Environmental Protection, which operate their own environmental funds, and are granted the power of setting stricter standards for emission and effluent limits. Half of Poland's pollution load is concentrated in six of its 49 provinces, so the local role is of great significance.[12]

Green Lungs of Poland is one example of a German–Polish collaboration that has transformed itself into an international programme which seeks to ensure the protection of the unspoiled region in Central and Eastern Europe. It is an experimental regional conservation strategy among five provinces, involving local administrations and international assistance. The initiative includes policies on industrial development, conservation, forestry, organic farming and eco-tourism. The Green Lungs initiative may become a model for regional cooperation in other parts of Poland.

3. The Rights of the Child in Poland

As noted above, Poland does not have specific legislation guaranteeing the right of the child to a clean environment. Children do, however, have the right to normal health standards and are protected by the state from the harms laid out in the law. Poland ratified the Convention on the Rights of the Child on 7 June 1991. Article 27(1) of the Convention states that 'State Parties recognize the right of every child to a certain standard of living

12 It should be noted that at the time of writing Polish local self-government was undergoing a radical change, in effort to meet EU standards.

adequate to its physical mental, spiritual, moral and social development'. The family is mainly responsible for the realisation of this, but the state is obligated to intervene where the family is unable to provide this support.

Articles 68 and 72 of the 1997 Polish Constitution are of particular importance in considering the rights of the child in Poland. Article 68(1) states that each citizen has the right to healthcare. Article 68(3) further states that public authorities are responsible for providing the appropriate healthcare for children. Recalling the Convention on the Rights of the Child, in Article 72 the state guarantees the protection of children. In the course of seeking remedies, the Office of the Ombudsman for the Rights of the Child was constitutionally created to assist children in ensuring that their rights are protected. The Office of the Ombudsman for the Rights of the Child is a relatively new institution and has had an increasingly prominent role in the promulgation of the rights of the child. It is unfortunate, however, that no Ombudsman has been chosen. (There has been an Ombudsman for Citizens' Rights since 1987.) An organ which has been fulfilling the role of Ombudsman is the Committee for the Rights of the Child. The Committee has been active in Poland since 1981. Its main concerns, however, do not address ecological or environmental issues, but rathet matters relating to the prevention of abuse, ensuring that the child receives appropriate healthcare and education. It will take some years before awareness of environmental issues is a significant concern of society, which in turn possibly develops into a concrete goal of the future Ombudsman or Committee in the protection of children's rights.

Polish family law, which dates back to 1964, on the rights of the state and family in the realisation of the rights of the child, may provide some answers, although not concrete ones. Article 100 of the Code on Family Law, whose text is compatible with that of the Convention, foresees state intervention where the child's rights are not protected. This particular Article provides an important remedy to the child – the family court – to ensure that the child is provided the proper care, and that the child's family is given the proper means to give the child all means for development as outlined in Article 27 of the Convention.[13]

Another source of law which makes the state responsible for the child is Article 572 of the Code for Civil Procedure. This law places the court in the role of guardian, and is significant in the realisation of the rights which are foreseen in the Convention on the Rights of the Child. Article 61 of the Code for Civil Procedure extends this responsibility to all citizens. A decree

13 For an excellent analysis of the Convention on the Rights of the Child and its impact on Polish legislation see Adam Lopatka (ed.), *Kowencja o prawach dziecka a prawo polskie* (The Convention on the Rights of the Child and Polish Law) (Warsaw, 1991).

of the Ministry of Justice from 1965 requires that all organs of childcare provide all of the necessary means for the realisation of the child's development to the family and the child. The focus, however, remains on the moral upbringing of the child, and to ensure that the child is given the proper care and brought up in the best possible circumstances.

In general it can be said that Polish law is in conformity with the Convention, and it is enough to bring to the attention of all the relevant organs the violation of child's rights to see to it that this is rectified. The responsibility of the state in the protection of the rights of the child has a highly significant role, although the state itself is not responsible for bringing the child up. The state must organise, assist, watch over, protect, and coordinate the activities of the child. It is not surprising, therefore, that the Convention is geared towards the state, so that it sees to it that the rights embodied in the Convention are realised. Article 7(1) of the Law on Procedure in Matters related to the Child requires that the state be informed of all situations where the rights of the child are violated. According to Article 30(4), the state then is obligated to inform the court of violations of the said rights of the child; assist the child in resocialisation; intervention in cases where the parents have failed to fulfil their role in providing for their development of the child. This Article also permits the other related organisations, such as the Polish Red Cross, or the Committee for the Rights of the Child, to intervene and to fulfil the necessary role related to a particular gap in the child's development.

Finally, the responsibility for the child's local environment is the parents' and the school's. This is further extended to social organs. The child has the right to safe surroundings which ensure its normal development. This remains the main responsibility of the state, and is in accordance with Article 19 of the Convention. This responsibility is further developed in the family code and in the Code of Civil Procedure. It should be noted, however, that Polish law has not interpreted this as far as the ensuring that this includes a clean environment.

4. Conclusions

To date, Polish law does not specifically mention the right of the child to a clean environment, nor does Polish environmental law. Such rights simply did not exist during the Communist era. It was not in the interest of the state, which promoted industrialisation at all costs, the results of which we see today. In present day, we can identify a growing environmental interest, which is supported by SIEP, yet the main environmental concerns are focused on global integration.

Polish environmental law is first and foremost concerned with addressing the damage from the Communist era and to fulfil its desire to integrate with other free market democracies. Its present priority is to restructure harmful and wasteful processes, essential to its economic survival. Environmental improvement is one of the key requirements to integration with the world community, namely the European Union, for which environmental protection is an important criteria.

NGOs can play an important role in emphasising this particular right of the child. Local initiatives which involve international assistance, such as UNICEF are significant. For example, finding a solution to high rates of infant mortality is one of the goals for the year 2000. In Poland, the environment must be a key consideration if, for example, the rights of the child in the ecologically damaged Upper Silesian region is considered. It is possible that the recent tragedy of the mass flooding of the Western region of Poland may also impact decisions. Since the flooding several towns and villages have had to contend with serious environmental problems with severe consequences to the health of families residing in the area, which is forcing the state to fulfil its responsibility as guaranteeing the protection of the environment. It must be said, however, that environmental awareness is still not part of the community awareness in Poland. It is still too early in the transition. Nonetheless, there are measures being taken in schools, where the implementation of special courses on the environment are gradually being introduced. Likewise, courses are being organised for raising the level of awareness and qualifications among those employed in relevant positions.

In summary, three areas will play a significant role in the future implementation of the right of the child to a clean environment:

(1) ***Normative law:*** as a general body of law which focuses on the protection of the environment. Also the role of NGOs is significant. The Committee for the Rights of the Child reviews all relevant draft legislation before it goes to parliament. SIEP also introduces its recommendations;

(2) ***Politics:*** where the government takes the initiative to see that the relevant Ministries, e.g., Ministry of Environment, in particular in promoting the role of SIEP in this area, and requiring that the Ministry and its agencies report to parliament regularly on the realisation of the specified goals. It would be beneficial for agencies to cooperate with each other;

(3) ***Education***: where specific programmes, dedicated to addressing these issues are gradually introduced at schools (at elementary and secondary levels) and in the workplace.

5 The right of the child to a clean environment in Nigeria

OLUFEMI ELIAS[1]

1. Introduction

The existence of a legal right to a clean environment is the subject of familiar controversy. This is the case even in relation to adults, and the initial suspicion must thus be that it will be at least (if not more so) as difficult to demonstrate the existence of this right as it pertains to children. In discussing this matter in the context of Nigerian law, this chapter will focus on two things. First, the status of international law on the matter within the Nigerian legal system will be analysed. In doing this, the intention is not to attempt to answer the question whether an international legal right to a clean environment exists *in substance*; that issue, as has been mentioned, has been dealt with exhaustively in the literature.[2] The debates surrounding the suitability of a human rights approach as a method of deriving the right to a clean environment and, more specifically, the extent to which other human rights can be interpreted as providing for a right to a clean environment, will not be analysed here.[3] The aim here is to place Nigeria within the debate on the existence of such a right, particularly as it pertains to children. An examination of the status of the relevant international law within Nigeria is thus an essential prelude to a discussion of whether that international law provides a basis for the claiming of the right to a clean environment within the Nigerian legal

1 I am grateful to Olga Thomas, Philly Desai and Tunde Ogowewo for their comments on an earlier draft of this essay.

2 See Anderson and Boyle 1997, *Human Rights Approaches to International Environmental Law*, (Oxford; Clarendon Press 19970, and P. Okonma, 'The Right to a Clean Environment in the Nigerian Delta', 41 *Journal of African Law*, (1997), at pp. 51 et seq. (specific reference to Nigeria).

3 Certainly as far as international custom is concerned, the more common view is that no *independent* right to a clean environment exists, but that such a right may be derived from other, better established rights, such as the right to life, health and property. Writing in 1992, Birnie and Boyle argue that 'reference to human rights instruments affords no clear conclusions concerning the individual or collective character of the right to a decent environment, or the extent to which it can be derived from other rights' (*International Law and the Environment*, p. 193; see generally pp. 190–197). There is also the additional problem of defining the content of the right as a matter of general custom. Birnie and Boyle state that it can be concluded that the right exists only where 'public bodies afford individuals little or no protection against the most seriously harmful pollution or environmental nuisance' (at pp. 192–193). The case law of the European Court of Human Rights would appear to support this conclusion, especially given its jurisprudence on the parties' 'margin of appreciation'; see, e.g. *Powell and Rayner v. United Kingdom*, judgment of 21 February 1990, Series A no. 172, esp. para. 37. See further, Sands, *Principles of International Environmental Law* (Manchester, 1995), pp. 219–230.

system.[4] Second, the relevant rules under Nigerian national law will be examined to see the extent to which they provide for the right of the child to a clean environment.

2. The Status of International Law in the Nigerian Legal System

2.1 Treaties

Nigeria is a party to a number of treaties from the provisions of which the rights of the child to a clean environment can be found more or less (but mostly less) directly. For example, Nigeria acceded to the International Covenants on Economic, Social and Cultural Rights and on Civil and Political Rights of 1966.[5] Also, Nigeria is a party to the African Charter on Human and Peoples' Rights.[6] More specifically, it is also a party to the United Nations Convention on the Rights of the Child,[7] while the African Charter on the Rights and Welfare of the Child is not yet in force.[8] The issue here is to examine the effect of the international law obligations contained in these treaties in Nigerian national law.

The position adopted in Nigeria regarding treaties has always been the 'transformation' doctrine. This is reflected in section 12(1) of the most recent Constitution (1979) which provides that

> No treaty between the Federation and any other country shall have the force of law except to the extent to which any such treaty has been enacted into law by the National Assembly.

This is based on the separation of powers doctrine under which treaty-making power lies with the executive. This is a reflection of Nigeria's

---

4 It is well-established that it is not permissible for a state to plead the peculiarities of its national laws as an excuse for not performing its international obligations. See: Article 27 of the Vienna Convention on the Law of Treaties, *International Legal Materials*, 8 (1969), p. 679; *Alabama Claims Arbitration*, Moore, *International Arbitration*, 1 (1872), p. 495 at p. 656; *Exchange of Greek and Turkish Populations* case, *PCIJ Reports*, 1925, Series B, No. 10, p. 20; *Maritime Delimitation and Territorial Questions* case, *ICJ Reports* (1995), p. 6.

5 In 1993. Nigeria is not, however, party to the Optional Protocol to the International Covenant on Civil and Political Rights (999 UNTS. 302). This is quite significant, considering that Article 1 of that Protocol recognises the 'competence of the [Human Rights] Committee to receive and consider communications from individuals subject to its jurisdiction who claim to be victims of a violation by that State Party of any of the rights set forth in the Covenant'.

6 *International Legal Materials*, 21 (1982), p. 59.

7 *International Legal Materials*, 28 (1989), p. 1448.

8 *African Journal of International and Comparative Law*, 3 (1991), pp. 173–190. Nigeria is also a party to the 1989 Basle Convention on the Control of Transboundary Movement of Hazardous Wastes and Their Disposal (since 1991), the 1992 United Nations Framework Convention on Climate Change (since 1994), and the Vienna Convention for the Protection of the Ozone Layer of 1985 (since 1988).

British colonial legal heritage.[9] However, this constitutional position is not always reflected in practice, owing to the fact that, for twenty-seven out of thirty-eight years of independence, Nigeria has been ruled by various military governments under whose practice these constitutional rules have had little consequence. The normal position in this context is that both the executive (including treaty-making) and legislative functions are performed by the head of the federal military government. The paradoxical result of this position, however, is that it could actually facilitate the operation of treaties within Nigerian national law. This is because treaty-making power (which is an executive function) and the power to make treaties effective in national law (a legislative function) become vested in the same organ of government. The duality inherited from British practice, whereby the state could be bound at the international level while the courts of that state remain powerless to give effect to those international obligations at the national level, could thus be easily bypassed, in the way that the constitutions of some countries require parliamentary approval before the treaty is concluded at the international level. Furthermore, there is another way in which the position in Nigerian practice could facilitate the applicability of international treaties in domestic law. In some federal states, jurisdiction over certain issues, such as human rights, depends on the constitutional allocation of power between the federal and the provincial (or state) governments. In Nigeria, however, the federal government, military or civilian, always reserves the right to make international treaties which can apply throughout the country, with provincial governments being powerless to refuse that effect.[10] However, in spite of these apparently favourable observations, the reality is that ratification, when it happens, is not always followed by implementing legislation. In this respect, the African Charter on Human and Peoples' Rights is a notable and pertinent exception. It was ratified and transformed in its entirety by an Act of the National Assembly under civilian rule in 1981. In contrast, the government drafted a Children's Decree based on the United Nations Convention on the Rights of the Child[11] and the African Charter on the Rights and Welfare of the Child,[12] but it is yet to be passed into law.

Furthermore, even when there is such legislation, the implementing provisions are weak or even positively abrogated. For example, the successive military governments have always issued Decrees attempting to

9 See C. N. Okeke, 'International Law in the Nigerian Legal System', *California Western International Law Journal*, 27 (1997), p. 311 at p. 337, for further discussion. See also F. Nlerum, 'The Application and Some Implications of the Hamburg Rules for Nigeria', *African Journal of International and Comparative Law*, 9 (1997), p. 386.

10 *Ibid.*, p. 343, esp. n. 143.

11 See n. 6 above; this was ratified in March 1991.

12 See n. 7 above.

oust the jurisdiction of the courts in relation to many issues, especially human rights. The African Commission on Human and Peoples' Rights considered the effect of one such provision of a Decree, namely section 13(1) of the Political Parties (Dissolution) Decree No. 114 (1993), which provides that

> notwithstanding anything contained in the Constitution of the Federal Republic of Nigeria 1979 ... the African Charter on Human and Peoples' Rights (Ratification and Enforcement) Act or any other enactment, no proceeding shall lie or be instituted in any court for or on account of any act, matter or thing done or purported to be done in respect of this decree.[13]

The Commission found that such provisions did not affect Nigeria's obligations under the African Charter.[14] This may not be surprising, but ultimately, the only powers of enforcement vested in the Commission are political and promotional, rather than legal or judicial. It is thus to the attitude of the Nigerian courts that we must turn in order to determine the real status of these treaties. Nigerian courts appear to take treaties seriously, particularly human rights treaties.[15] Recent confirmation of this can be seen in the Federal Court of Appeal case of *Fawehinmi v. Abacha.*[16] The case concerned the effect of the African Charter in the face of Decrees issued by the military government, which purported to oust the jurisdiction of the courts. Their Lordships stated that:

> the provisions of the Charter are in a class of their own and do not fall within the classification of the hierarchy of laws in Nigeria ... It seems to me that the learned trial judge acted erroneously when he held that the African Charter

13 See also the Nigerian Constitution (Modification and Suspension) Decree no. 7 of 1993 for a provision to the same effect.

14 *Account of the Internal Legislation of Nigeria and the Disposition of the African Charter on Human and Peoples' Rights*, Doc. II/ES/ACHPR/4, at p. 3.

15 An example is provided by the unreported case of *Garuba v. Attorney-General for Lagos State* (ID559/90). There a judge of the Lagos State High Court, after stating that the African Charter on Human and Peoples' Rights had been transformed into local law, went on to hold that even if it may have been the subject of a purported modification or suspension by local law, 'the international aspect cannot unilaterally be abrogated. We dare not breach any of the terms without incurring the frowning of our international friends'. Even more telling is the unreported case of 5 May 1996, also of the Lagos High Court, referred to by R. Murray, 'Decisions by the African Commission on Individual Communications under the African Charter on Human and Peoples' Rights', *International and Comparative Law Quarterly*, 46 (1997), p. 412, at p. 416, n. 30. She states: 'The Constitutional Rights Project of Nigeria published two decisions by the Commission concerning Nigeria in its magazine *Constitutional Rights Journal*, July/September 1995. One of these was used by a Nigerian judge, Justice Morounkeji Omotayo Onalaja, to take a case which it would not have been possible to do under national legislation'. The case, which is unreported, is *Constitutional Rights Project v. The President* (see S. Amadi, in the Nigerian newspaper *The Vanguard* of 16 December 1997, at p. 8). The judge also referred to the case of *Oshevire v. British Caledonian Airways Ltd* [1990] *Nigerian Weekly Law Reports* (*NWLR*), Part 163, p. 507, at pp. 519–520.

16 [1996] *NWLR*, Part 475, at p. 710. See also *Ogugu v. The State* [1994] 9 *NWLR*, Part 366, p. 1 at p. 27 (*per* Bello C.J.N.).

> contained in Cap. 10 of the Laws of the Federation of Nigeria is inferior to Decrees of the Federal Military Government ... While the Decrees ... may override [sic] other municipal laws, they cannot oust the jurisdiction of the court ... in relation to matters pertaining to human rights under the African Charter. They are protected by international law and the Federal Military Government is not legally permitted to legislate out of its obligations.[17]

The Court of Appeal went on to state that the Charter 'is in full force and *because of its genesis* it has an aura of inviolability unlike most municipal laws and may as long as it is in the statute book be clothed with vestment of inviolability (by reason) where a decree specifically repeals it'.[18]

It is true that this 'vestment of inviolability' arises primarily because the Charter has been incorporated by domestic legislation.[19] But there seems to be recognition of a further source for the inviolability of the Charter and perhaps human rights treaties generally. Three other possible reasons for this exalted status are suggested. The first is the international law origins of the treaty. Justice Musdapher stated that 'the fundamental human rights stem from the attributes of human beings which justify their international protection'; that the provisions of the Charter 'are in a class of their own and do not fall within the classification of the hierarchy of laws in Nigeria' and that the Act of 1983 incorporating the Charter into Nigerian law was 'legislation of international flavour', so that the 'ouster clauses ... cannot affect its operation in Nigeria'.[20]

This aspect of the judgment augurs well for the derivation of rights from international instruments. The second reason for the aforementioned exalted status that can be gleaned from the judgments is the actual mode of incorporation of the Charter. Justice Pats-Acholonu stated that the ratification of the treaty at the international level alone did not connote its enforceability 'within the *corpus iuris civilis* of Nigeria. Our national government however went further and incorporated the spirit of that treaty into our law thereby giving due notice that *it is to be recognised and applied and enforced by the three arms of government,* giving message to all the signatories to the convention that it has adopted the treaty in toto'.[21] He also stated that by 'not merely adopting the African Charter but enacting it into our organic law, the

17 *Ibid. Per* Musdapher JCA, at pp. 746–747.

18 *Ibid. Per* Pats-Acholonu JCA, at pp. 758–759 (emphasis added).

19 *Ibid.* At p. 756, Justice Pats-Acholonu stated that 'Where there is no enactment to give effect to the spirit of a treaty notwithstanding its adoption and recognition, and due regard by a sovereign government, it cannot be justiciable in a municipal court', and at p. 758: '... the government could have avoided being irretrievably immersed into the nuances of this charter by not incorporating it into the law of the land. In that case the attitude of the court would have been different'.

20 *Ibid.* at pp. 746–747.

21 *Ibid.* at p. 756 (emphasis added). Bello C.J.N. also stressed the same point in *Ogugu* (see n. 16 above), which lends some support to this argument.

tenor and intendment of the preamble and section seem to vest that Act with greater vigour and strength than mere decree for it has been elevated to a higher pedestal'.[22] This may suggest that the particular way in which the treaty was incorporated it to be scrutinised in order to determine its status *vis-à-vis* other sources of law in Nigeria. This second consideration would therefore suggest, negatively, that not all incorporated treaties can thereby enjoy the same status as the Charter simply because they are incorporated. The third possible reason for this higher status suggests natural-law type reasoning. As seen above, it was stated that the provisions of the Charter 'were clothed with vestment of inviolability (by reason)'.[23] The parenthesised phrase is ambiguous; it is unclear what 'reason' is being referred to here, but it could be a reference to the content of the law in question (i.e., human rights). Also, Justice Musdapher, as mentioned earlier, referred to the fact that 'fundamental human rights stem from the attributes of human beings which justify their international protection',[24] and this may be seen to reflect naturalist thinking. These three considerations are all suggested with increasing levels of diffidence from the first to the third, but they all suggest a special position occupied by treaties within the national legal system. It may be argued that all treaties to which Nigeria is a party, *provided they have been incorporated*, occupy a special position on the basis of any of these considerations, especially the first (i.e., the international law basis).

But even where there has been no act of incorporation, it would seem that the treaties will still have some effect, although it is difficult to say exactly to what extent this will be the case. It was stated that even where there is no incorporation of the relevant treaty into municipal law, 'the courts seemed to be very vigilant in ensuring that treaty obligations are not treated with levity'.[25] He had referred earlier to English case-law on the use of treaties as an aid to construction of domestic law.[26] Treaties would thus appear to enjoy some status in national law even when they have not been incorporated into national law.[27]

---

22 *Ibid.* at p. 758.

23 See n. 18 above.

24 See n. 20 above.

25 [1996] NWLR, Part 475, at pp. 758–759.

26 *Ibid.* at p. 756 ff.

27 There is evidence in the practice of the English courts relating to the provisions of the unincorporated European Convention on Human Rights which is pertinent in this regard. In a number of cases (which have not always gone unchallenged), the courts have given effect to the provisions of the treaty 'through the back door'. See, e.g. *Cassell v. Broome* [1972] AC, 1027, at p. 1133 (*per* Lord Kilbrandon); *Ahmad v. Inner London Education Authority* [1978] QB, 36 at p. 48 (*per* Scarman LJ); *Attorney-General v. BBC* [1981] AC, 303, at p. 354 (per Lord Scarman), and p. 352 (per Lord Fraser); *Attorney-General v. Guardian Newspapers (No. 2)*, [1990] 1 AC, 109, at p. 283, *per* Lord Goff; *Derbyshire C.C. v. Times Newspapers* [1992] QB 770 (*per* Balcombe LJ). Decisions of the United Kingdom courts are frequently referred to as the basis of judgments in the Nigerian courts, again a consequence of Nigeria's colonial legal heritage. The extent to which Nigerian courts will follow this lead in the future should be of interest.

There is thus some ground for expecting that the rules in Nigeria on the status of international law can provide a basis for the treaty framework of rights to a decent environment within the country. The idea that the foregoing considerations may be of use only in the context of fundamental human rights must be noted. Nevertheless, regardless of its problems, this is simply an argument for the human rights approach to environmental protection;[28] if these relevant environmental rights can be assimilated to a human right provided for in a treaty to which Nigeria is a party, then they must occupy the same status as that human right. This augurs well for the judicial applicability of propositions like that contained in Article 24 of the Charter ('All people shall have the right to a general satisfactory environment favourable to their development'), even if the content of that right may pose problems; Article 16(1) ('Every individual shall have the right to enjoy the best attainable state of physical and mental health'), Article 16(2) ('state ... shall take the necessary measures to protect the health of their people ...'), Article 4 (the right to life), and Article 25 (the duty to promote and ensure, through teaching, education and publication, the respect of rights and freedoms). The enactment of the Children's Decree mentioned earlier would go a very long way towards completing the picture.

2.2 Custom

Regarding international custom, it is difficult to find cases in which it has been applied directly. The only authorities on the matter are the pronouncements of jurists, which are again generally based on British and Commonwealth practice which influenced Nigerian constitutional law, to the effect that rules of customary international law form a part of national law, in contrast to the position regarding treaties. The closest the Nigerian courts have come to dealing with international custom explicitly is in cases concerned with sovereign immunity.[29] But even then, as has been pointed out in other contexts,[30] those cases are often, as is the case with the Nigerian courts, dealt with in terms of determining a national rule on the jurisdiction of the courts in question, rather than applying a rule of customary international law as such. The controversial nature of the rights in question here under international custom would add to the difficulty. What is clear, however, is that given the frequent recourse to English common law,

28 See n. 3, above.

29 See, e.g., Y. Osinbajo, 'Sovereign Immunity in International Commercial Arbitration: The Nigerian Experience and Emerging State Practice', *African Journal of International and Comparative Law*, 4 (1992), p. 1.

30 See, e.g. J. Dunbar, 'The Myth of Customary International Law', *Australian Yearbook of International Law* 8 (1978–80), p. 1.

international custom would seem to be automatically incorporated into Nigerian law. The significance of cases like *Minors Oposa v. Secretary of the Department of the Environment and Natural Resources*[31] could be quite far-reaching in this context.

There has been no case in which the right of the child to a clean environment based on international law has been in issue before the Nigerian courts (as is the case with adults). But this section has attempted to see whether, if such a right exists at the international level, the possibility exists for the judicial enforceability of such rights. The conclusion is that it is quite possible.

3. Nigerian National Law

3.1 Private law rights

The torts of trespass to land, nuisance and negligence, and also liability under the rule in *Rylands v. Fletcher*, are very much a part of Nigerian law, and they are of obvious relevance to environmental protection. However, the limitations of these as a means of guaranteeing a right to a clean environment have been much commented upon.

As regards trespass, the tort is committed when a person, without lawful justification, directly places or projects any material object upon land which is in the possession of another. It has been written that this should be a more fruitful avenue for environmental claims than experience would suggest, since trespass to land is actionable *per se* and the plaintiff does not need to prove intention or negligence on the part of the defendant to found an action;[32] and there is no need to prove damage. However, liability in trespass requires that the placing or projecting of the offending material on the plaintiff's land must be direct.[33] The consequence of this, it has been written, is that for example, 'while the deliberate dumping of industrial waste on farmland is direct and will found an action in trespass, the dispersal of waste being transported in open trucks on to private property will at best found an action in nuisance'.[34] As regards private nuisance, the simple requirement is significant interference with the use of land. This tort is of even more limited utility, because it can only be

31 *International Legal Materials*, 33 (1994), p. 173.

32 See Okonma, 'The Right to a Clean Environment in the Nigerian Delta', *Journal of African Law*, 41 (1997), p. 42, at p. 48.

33 G. Kodilinye, *Nigerian Law of Torts* (1982), pp. 177 and 180.

34 B. Ogunsanwo, 'Liability and Compensation for Environmental Damage', in Ajomo and Adebowale, (eds.), *Environmental Law and Sustainable Development in Nigeria* (1994), p. 48, at p. 58.

successful where the interference in question is with the rights of the plaintiff only, or with the rights of the plaintiff in a unique manner. In cases of environmental pollution, the damage will normally be caused to other property users in the area, and this will be fatal to a claim in private nuisance. This reflects the limits of these torts in the context of environmental protection; the environment as such is not the object of protection. Rather, the concern is with the rights of the users of property. For most children, this would, in practice, mean that these torts would not come within the right to a clean environment.

The rule in *Rylands v. Fletcher* has proved a little more useful from the point of view of environmental protection. The main reason for this is that it founds a strict liability tort where the plaintiff has brought onto the land in the course of a non-natural user of the land something which is likely to do mischief if it escapes. In *Umudje v. Shell BP*[35] the plaintiff complained that the defendants had blocked and diverted a natural stream, thus interfering with their fishing rights, and also that the accumulated oil waste on land under the defendants control had escaped onto his land and had caused damage. The plaintiffs were held liable for the second complaint. In *Ikpede v. Shell*[36] it was held that for the purposes of establishing liability under this rule, the laying of pipes carrying crude oil through swamp forests is a non-natural user of land. The balancing process involved in establishing liability under this rule, however, may result in a judge holding in favour of the polluter, if it is found that their activity was not unreasonable.[37] Also, negligence, which 'is regarded as the single most important cause of oil pollution in the Niger Delta' (the oil-producing part of Nigeria), is not without its problems from an environmental point of view. The main difficulty is the requirement of proof of negligent conduct. The cases here appear to stipulate a high burden of proof. For example, in *Chinda v. Shell*[38] the plaintiffs brought an action for the heat, noise and vibration resulting from the alleged negligence of the defendants, but the court held that they had not proved negligence in the management and control of the flare set, and accordingly, the claim was unsuccessful. Similarly, in *Seismograph Services v. R. K. Ogbeni*[39] the plaintiff brought an action for damage to his buildings caused by the operations of the defendant while the latter was prospecting for oil. The claim was unsuccessful because the plaintiff could not prove that the defendants had been negligent.

35 (1975) 4 SC, p. 85.
36 (1973) MWSJ, p. 61.
37 See *Cambridgeshire Water v. Eastern Counties Leather,* [1994] 1 All ER, p. 53, at p. 59 (*per* Lord Goff).
38 (1974) 2 RSLR., p. 1.
39 (1976) 4 SC, p. 85.

Again, these cases illustrate the limitations of the common law of torts as a means of protecting the environment.

In any event, there is normally no practical need for a separate right of the child to bring any of these actions (which would be done through the child's next friend), since children do not normally suffer separately from those they live with, who would normally bring these actions. Of course, were the right to be suffered directly by the child alone somehow, then the right, subject to all the difficulties discussed above, does exist.

3.2 Public law rights

In common law, the most immediately relevant legal principle is that of public nuisance. Claims in private nuisance, as mentioned earlier, and particularly in the oil sector (a source of much pollution in the south of Nigeria), have generally not been successful because of the requirement that the plaintiff must prove that she has suffered damage over and above that suffered by the general public. In *Amos v. Shell*[40] the plaintiffs, in representative capacity, claimed that the defendant company had made a large earth dam across a creek, resulting in flooding upstream and dryness downstream, with all possible negative consequences for commercial and agricultural activities. It was held that since the creek was a public waterway, the action sounded in public nuisance. The result was that the plaintiffs claim failed, because they were unable to show the requisite special damage over and above other sufferers. The right to bring an action in public nuisance then lies with the Attorney-General; public nuisance is criminal in nature.[41] The conflict of interest which might arise where the polluter is a public body will be discussed below.

It would appear, however, that under Nigerian law, this position may have been modified as a result of case-law of higher courts on the interpretation of section 6(6) of the Nigerian Constitution of 1979. That provision states in part that judicial powers shall extend to 'all matters between persons, or between government and authority and any person in Nigeria, and to all actions and proceedings relating thereto, for the determination of any question as to the civil rights and obligations of that person'. It would appear that the concern of this provision is with the scope of the general judicial function, certainly because any constitution must provide a constitutional base for the exercise and limits of the judicial function in general, and perhaps because of the fact that the country had

40 (1974) ECSLR, p. 486.

41 See, e.g., section 234 of the Criminal Code Act, Cap. 42 (1958), and section 7(m) of the Public Health Act, Cap. 165 (1958).

been used to military rule and ouster clauses in the thirteen years immediately preceding the enactment of that constitution. In any event, the specifics of the judicial function are dealt with fully in section 236(1). Nevertheless, the courts, apparently based on the judgment of the Supreme Court in the case of *Adesanya v. President of Nigeria*[42] have interpreted section 6(6) as laying down a rule of *locus standi.* The Supreme Court in *Adediran v. Interland Transport Ltd*[43] stated that:

> Where the determination of the civil rights and obligations of a person is in issue, any law which imposes conditions is inconsistent with the free and unrestrained exercise of that right, is void to the extent of such inconsistency. Thus the restriction imposed at common law on the right of action in public nuisance is inconsistent with the provisions of section 6(6)(b) of the Constitution, and to that extent is void.

While this jurisprudence on the part of higher Nigerian courts has been the subject of cogent criticism,[44] it should have the effect of freeing the restrictions placed on the right of action described earlier in cases of public nuisance. There should be some interesting cases in the near future, given the high profile attending the situation in the oil-producing areas of the country in the last few years.

Again, these rights would exist in the case of children as well as adults, though it is likely to be invoked less frequently by children.

3.3 Statute

The leading general statute is the Federal Environmental Protection Agency Decree of 1988, which creates the Federal Environmental Protection Agency. The creation of this Agency was actually delayed due to pressure from the Nigerian National Petroleum Corporation, the government agency responsible for the management of the oil industry in Nigeria.[45] Still, the FEPA Decree is the first attempt at a comprehensive environmental regime in Nigeria.[46] The Agency's main duties are the protection, development and

42 [1981] *All Nigeria Law Reports*, p. 1.
43 [1991] 9 NWLR, p. 155, at p. 180, *per* Karibi-Whyte JSC.
44 See T. Ogowewo, 'The Problem with Standing to Sue in Nigeria', *Journal of African Law*, 39 (1995), p. 1. See also the judgment of Ayoola J in *F.A.T.B. v. Ezegbu*, [1994] 4 NWLR, p. 149, at p. 236.
45 The NNPC has itself been described as a major polluter, being an active participant in upstream and downstream activities. It is also a major shareholder in the oil companies operating in Nigeria. The result has been that certain regulations in place, for example Regulation 25 of the Petroleum (Drilling and Production) Regulations issued under section 8 of the 1969 Petroleum Act, could not be enforced. This is an example of the conflict of interest referred to earlier. See Okonma, op. cit., n. 31, at pp. 46–47.
46 A. Ibidapo-Obe notes the general paucity of environmental regulation especially in the field of oil production; see his 'Criminal Liability for Damage Caused by Oil Pollution', in J. Omotola (ed.), *Environmental Laws in Nigeria* (1990).

management of the Nigerian environment, and it is charged with advising the government on environmental policies and priorities. But while the Decree prohibits and criminalises discharge in such harmful quantities of any hazardous substances, section 20 thereof states that the provisions of the Decree will not apply where the activity is authorised by any law in force. This is a significant weakness, because there are many laws in force which permit pollution in certain cases. For example, section 4 of the Oil in Navigable Waters Act 1968 permits the discharge of oil where necessary for, *inter alia*, the prevention of damage to a vessel or cargo or accidents, and also the discharge of effluents where there are no practical options. Also, section 5(6)(a) of the Merchant Shipping Act of 1962 permits the discharge of oil for the purpose of preventing an obstruction.[47] There are powers to institute criminal proceedings under the Decree, which have not been used much thus far. The Agency has however been active in issuing several guidelines on environmental protection on Nigeria.[48] These however do not have binding force. Nevertheless, although it has not been done, there would seem to be nothing standing in the way of an action for breach of statutory duty against the Agency if it were considered not to be fulfilling its obligations.[49]

Environmental Protection Agencies also exist at the state level with similar powers, and there may appear to be more activity taking place here than at the federal level. In December 1997, a major textile manufacturing company, Hong Kong Synthetic Fibre Limited, was closed down by the Chief Executive of the Ogun State Environmental Protection Agency (OGEPA). The company had allegedly been discharging its effluents with the result that, according to inhabitants of the affected areas, 'their health, especially that of their children, has been impaired ... Aquatic life has been destroyed, while no crop in the area flourishes because of the contaminated land'. There was also evidence of 'heavy groundwater pollution' and pollution of water wells. The Chief Executive had made 'fruitless efforts

47 These and other observations have been made by Okonma, op. cit., n. 32, at pp. 47–48. He concludes that the 'inescapable conclusion can therefore be that although the FEPA Decree gave fillip to the environmental awareness engendered by the dumping of toxic wastes at Koko in 1988, not much has been achieved in terms of policing the oil industry if the Agency is merely to play a "supportive" role to the NNPC [as provided by section 23 of the FEPA Decree]'.

48 See, e.g., the *National Guidelines and Standards for Industrial Effluents, Gaseous Emissions and Hazardous Waste Management in Nigeria* (1991), Government Notice of 1991; the *National Environmental Protection (Pollution Abatement in Industries and Facilities Generating Wastes), the National Environmental Protection (Effluent Limitations) Regulations.*

49 See, e.g., *Société Générale de Surveillance SA v. Rastico Nig. Ltd*, [1992] 6 NWLR, p. 93, which held that a plaintiff need not show that the primary intention of the statute is to protect a particular class of persons of which she is a member. This contrasts with the position under English law, where the plaintiff needs to show that the obligation imposed by the statute was imposed for the protection of a such a class of persons. See T. Ogowewo, 'Transposition of Securities Legislation to an Emerging Market: The Case of the US Federal Securities Law and Nigeria', *Journal of International Banking Law*, 6 [1996], p. 239, at p. 243.

to get the management of the company to get their effluents filtered before passing them out as waste products'.

The other notable statute is the Harmful Wastes (Special Criminal Provisions) Act of 1988, which relates to the dumping of harmful wastes, following the Koko incident when a chief of a rural coastal community accepted vast amounts of toxic waste from an Italian company in exchange for money. Several inhabitants of this community, including children, suffered, and some died, as the chemicals had leaked into local streams.[50] The Act imposes criminal liability on corporate bodies[51] and civil liability on any person who deposits, dumps or imports harmful waste causing damage as a result. There is, however, an exception where the damage was due wholly to the fault of the person who suffered it or where the damage was suffered by a person who voluntarily accepted the risk.[52] This may be a loophole; the recipients in the Koko incident do not appear to have been aware of the risk, so that their voluntary acts should not be allowed to exempt the supplier of the wastes from liability. The implementation of the Act lies primarily, at the moment, with the FEPA and with the Minister of Works and Housing. In any event, there have not been any prosecutions on the basis of this Act, not even in relation to the Koko incident itself. As Eguh points out, the Act 'appears to be a public relations exercise to save face'.[53]

There is also the Environmental Impact Assessment Decree of 1992, which makes it an offence to embark upon any activity or project that may have significant environmental effects, without having first undertaken, and submitted to the FEPA, an environmental impact assessment. Significantly, the term 'environmental effects' is defined as any change that a project may cause to the environment, regardless of whether such changes occur within or outside Nigeria, as well as any changes in health or socio-economic conditions. This is potentially, therefore, more relevant to children, and it seems quite specific. Section 4 of the Act contains a list of rather stringent requirements as to the issues that the impact assessment must address. These include a description of the proposed activities, a description of the environment likely to be affected, an assessment of the likely or potential environmental impacts of the proposed activity and the alternatives, including the direct or indirect, cumulative, short-term and long-term effects, an identification and description of measures available to mitigate or address the environmental impacts of the proposed activity an assessment of those measures, and an indication of whether the

50 See E.C. Eguh, 'Regulation of Transboundary Movement of Hazardous Wastes: Lessons from Koko', 9 *African Journal of International and Comparative Law*, (1997), p. 130.

51 See section 7.

52 See section 12.

53 Op. cit. *supra* n. 49, at pp. 146–147.

environment of any other state or local government area, or areas outside Nigeria, is likely to be affected by the proposed activity or its alternatives. The effect of this Act again, is yet to be fully felt.[54]

In sum, the position under Nigerian national law is not as encouraging as it could be. In particular, there has not been any specific reference to the protection of children from environmental hazards, which is not surprising given that the position in general has not focused in a meaningful way on environmental protection.

4. Conclusion

From this overview of the position in Nigeria, it appears that there is still a considerable way to go before it can be said that there is effective protection of the right of the child to a clean environment in Nigeria. It is true, as has been noted, that the limitations on the existence such right as may be derived from international law appear to exist only as far as there are difficulties in the identification of a human right to a clean environment in international law; recent judicial pronouncements are encouraging as regards the status of international law in Nigeria. This would also seem to be, as mentioned earlier, an argument in favour of the human rights approach to environmental protection, because of the importance the judges appear to attach to human rights treaties.[55] But as far as the domestic situation is concerned, little attention is directed towards the right of children to a clean environment; after all, the regulation of pollution in general is itself quite weak. However, with the activities of non-governmental organisations such as the Constitutional Rights Project, Ecowatch and the Child Welfare League and events such as the Koko incident, one can expect that increasing attention will be diverted to these issues. The current concern, as far as children are concerned, is with more established civil and political/social and economic rights, such as child labour and slavery, and environmental protection has not come to the forefront of concerns as yet.

54 Mention should also be made of section 245 of the Criminal Code which imposes criminal liability on any person who 'corrupts or fouls the water of any spring, stream, well, tank, reservoir, or place, so as to render it less fit for the purpose for which it is ordinarily used'. Section 234 makes it an offence to violate the atmosphere in any place so as to make it noxious. There is also the National Primary Healthcare Decree of 1992, which imposes obligations to educate and inform the public about sanitation and related matters, but there are no specific enforcement mechanisms attached to this.

55 See Okonma, op. cit. *supra* n. 2, and Amadi, op. cit., n. 15, for a discussion of the status of human rights treaties in Nigeria, including economic and social rights.

6 Does the Gambian child have a right to a clean environment?

VERONIC WRIGHT

An answer to this question will firstly require an examination of the Constitutional provisions on the protection of the basic rights of the person. This is the starting point of this chapter. It will look at the 1996 Constitution of the Second Republic of The Gambia to see how much has been attempted to protect the right of children to a clean environment. The chapter will also attempt to answer the question by looking at other national laws that directly address environmental issues, specifically, the National Environment Management Act 1994 and the work of the National Environmental Agency in this area. It will then consider some International Conventions which deal with the issue of children's rights to a clean environment, to which The Gambia is signatory and try to assess how far their implementation or non-implementation affect the protection of children from a harmful environment.

1. What is the Meaning of Environment?

Although definitions of the term 'environment' are varied, it is generally understood to encompass the elements of earth, air and water. In fact most international conventions have simply not produced a definition of the term perhaps because of the inherent problems that may be posed by a definition. In The Gambia however, the term has been defined in the National Environment Management Act to mean the physical factors of the surroundings of the human being including land, water, atmosphere and climate. It includes sound, odour, taste, the biological factors of fauna and flora and the social factor of aesthetics and both the natural and built environment.

In the view of the present author, having a clean environment means having the physical surroundings without any form of pollution or the ability to enjoy the social factor of aesthetics without interference. This of course is impossible, because of the fact, among other things, that the very nature of human development gives rise to pollution. Moreover, our rights to enjoy aesthetic values will have to be enjoyed in conjunction with other rights and needs and the rights of others. Thus the right to a clean environment must be viewed and understood to be with limitations just like any other rights that are enjoyed by human beings.

There is no universal definition of 'a child' under Gambian law. A child is defined differently in various statutes that deal with children. For purposes of the criminal law, a child under 7 years of age is not capable of committing a crime, but a child between 7 and 14 years of age can be criminally liable if it can be shown that he or she can appreciate the wrongful nature of his or her act. The Children and Young Persons Act fixes the age of a child at under 14 years and a young adult at above 14 but under 18 years. The Maintenance of Children Act defines a child to be someone 'below 21 years old who sooner marries'. For purposes of eligibility for voting at elections, the Constitution enfranchises a person of 18 years. In effect there is no standard age for the definition of a child. For convenience, the universally accepted age of 18 years for adulthood will be assumed here.

2. Constitutional Provisions

In September 1996, The Gambia through a referendum, adopted a new Constitution that replaced the 1970 Republican Constitution and ushered in the Second Republic. Chapter 4 of the Constitution consists of the Bill of Rights therein entitled 'Protection of Fundamental Rights and Freedom'. This chapter, which spans 21 sections, does not contain any provisions regarding the rights to a clean environment or any environmental protection whatsoever.

An initial reaction would be one of discouragement and surprise that at the dawn of the twenty-first century, when environmental concerns are in the forefront of the world's agenda and that considering the work so far done and planned in the field of environmental protection in The Gambia, we still did not see it fit to guarantee ourselves the right to a clean environment. But after further readings of chapter 4, and having in mind a broader meaning of environmental protection, this initial reaction may change. This is because although there is no direct mention of environmental protection, there are other rights relating to public health and safety, town and country planning, inhuman and degrading treatment, for example, which have an environmental element in them. These rights shall be discussed later. Under section 215, which comes under the chapter entitled 'Directive Principles of State Policy' subsection (3) states, 'the state shall pursue a policy of ... (d) protecting the environment of the nation for posterity, and (e) co-operation with other nations and bodies to protect the global environment'. The Constitution falls short of imposing an obligation on the state to protect the environment; instead it simply directs that the state shall pursue a policy of protecting the environment. Even such direction is not mandatory in that section 211 specifically excludes the justiciability of this provision.

Section 211 states:

> These principles of state policy in this Chapter shall form part of the public policy of The Gambia for the establishment of a just, free and democratic state. These principles shall not confer legal rights or be enforceable in any court but
>
> (a) Subject to the limits of the economic capacity and development of The Gambia, the Executive, the Legislature and all other organs of the state in taking policy decisions, making laws and in the administration of The Gambia, shall according to their respective functions be guided by and observe them with a view to achieving by legislation or otherwise the full realisation of these principles; and
> (b) the courts are entitled to have regard to these principles in interpreting any laws based on them.

This is in direct contrast to the situation in the Philippines where section 16 of the Constitution provides for a 'right to a balanced and healthful ecology'.

This right was recognised and enforced in the famous *Minors Oposa* case by the Philippines Supreme Court. Although the main focus of the case was whether or not the plaintiffs had *locus standi* to institute the action, the case also has the effect of bringing to light the fact that environmental protection could be achieved through the enforcement of human rights. It further brings into play the interrelationship between environmental law and human rights.

However, section 211 in a way echoes the fears expressed by Judge Feliciano in his separate concurring judgment in the above case, that although the 'right to a balanced and healthful ecology' is 'fundamental' to the Constitution, it is not 'specific' and is too 'open-ended'.

3. The Rights of Children: Section 29

For the first time in Gambian constitutional history, there is a specific provision for the protection of the rights of the child.

Section 29 states:

> (1) Children shall have the right from birth to a name, the right to acquire a nationality and, subject to legislation enacted in the best interest of children to know and be cared for by their parents. (2) Children under the age of sixteen years are entitled to be protected from economic exploitation and shall not be employed in or required to perform work that is likely to be hazardous or to interfere with their health or physical, mental, spiritual, moral or social development. (3) A juvenile offender who is kept in lawful custody shall be kept separately from adult offenders.

This is reflective of a willingness to observe treaty obligations under the International Labour Organisation (ILO) and the Rights of the Child Convention. As in most countries of the developing world, it is not uncommon to find children at work in The Gambia. Children are found working for pay as domestic workers, paid apprentices, selling wares for their parents or generally helping in the farm or other workplaces with their parents. Some of the conditions in which children work are sometimes very hard and leave little room for educational and leisurely pursuits. Girls are sometimes denied education completely or removed from school to be married off at a very early age (e.g. 14 or even 12 years). At home with their husband, they are expected to cook, pound coos or rice, do farm work, fetch water and firewood from long distances, and also bear children. All these are obviously 'hazardous' and 'interfere with their education' and are 'harmful to their health and physical and mental development'. This provision is therefore a welcomed development in the fight to better the lot of the child in The Gambia.

However, although this right is clearly justiciable, its enforcement becomes a real problem for the following reasons. First, there is a very high incidence of illiteracy in the country and most people who are affected are not even aware of the provision to be able to rely on it. Second, the fact of children working to help raise money for the family or helping in the family farms has been generally accepted as part of our tradition and culture. But it does become a problem where it interferes with the child's education and development. As such, non-governmental organisations (NGOs) and even government have to tread cautiously in enforcing this right less they be seen as trying to break up family values or even disintegrating the home.

Thirdly, this right would not be enforceable so long as there are no alternatives for the parents to raise the money or labour that the children would otherwise have brought in. In the absence of an adequate social structure to address the poverty that drives parents to make their children earn a living, this right will remain in the statute books and unenforceable.

4. The Right to Life: Section 18

This section states as follows:

> No person shall be deprived of his or her life intentionally except in the execution of a sentence of death imposed by a court of competent jurisdiction in respect of a criminal offence for which the penalty is death under the laws of The Gambia as they have effect in accordance with subsection (1) and of which he or she has been lawfully convicted.

It is quite common in the peri-urban and rural areas of The Gambia to find uncovered landfills for domestic rubbish situated very close to human settlements. Children could be found playing in these fills or scavenging for odd bits and pieces to make toys or even leftover food. Sometimes fires are started by someone throwing a cigarette in the fill or neighbours trying to reduce the rubbish and to get rid of the smell. These fires do sometimes cause explosions of pressurised containers, which may injure the children playing nearby. Needless to say that other diseases could be contacted by the children while they are playing in the fills or from the items they pick out of the fills. The authorities responsible for depositing the rubbish into the fills and for maintaining the fills are the local authority councils, who seem to do little or nothing to contain the problem of child scavenging. Although there has been no actual complaint in which a child's illness has been categorically linked to the landfills, it is in the opinion of the author that such incidents may very well be quite common. The reason for the absence of any complaint may be due to ignorance on the part of the community and lack of adequate investigations into the cause of a child's health condition by health authorities.

In case a child dies as a result of an explosion in a landfill while he/she is playing in it or he/she dies from disease (e.g. cholera) contracted while playing in the landfill, could the local authority be held responsible under Section 18 for depriving that child of his/her life? An obvious answer to this question would be in the affirmative. This is because the authorities have duty to the communities they serve to properly dispose of the rubbish they are paid to collect and dispose of and also to properly manage their disposal sites. This latter duty includes proper siting of landfills away from human settlements.

Although such a matter has not yet been before the Gambian courts, it is hoped in the light of the jurisprudence that is developing worldwide in this area, that if one day such a case should be brought against a local authority the courts will impose liability. By analogy to the *Lopez Ostra* decision, it is considered that the state could even be joined as a party in the suit. In that case the state's liability was based on the fact that it 'allowed the plant to be built on its site and the state subsidised the plant's construction'. In the Gambian set-up the Department of State for Health is charged with the duty of inspecting landfills and generally ensuring the preservation of public health and the National Environment Agency for monitoring environmental quality standards. The scenario described above not only raises the issue of liability for the local authorities, but also the Department of State for Health and the National Environment Agency for failure to perform their duties.

There is also the problem of open sewers in the capital city of Banjul right in the midst of homes. A fitting example of this problem is a very big gutter situated in an area where most schools are concentrated. In the Tobacco Road area of Banjul there are about five primary and secondary Sschools and a skills centre. This gutter is an obvious breeding place for the malaria – virus-carrying-type mosquito. The mortality rate from malaria in The Gambia is one of the highest in the world. No doubt, many children could contract the disease and die or are at risk of death as a result of the poor sewerage system in the city. It is submitted that the failure of the state to eliminate the sewerage problems and thereby reduce an obvious health hazard constitutes a breach of the fundamental right to life stated in the Constitution. Although this is an obvious environmental problem it is directly linked to the right to life in that it is a killer. Examples of breaches of the right to life in this context are just too numerous to be recounted here.

5. Freedom from Deprivation of Property and the Right to Privacy of the Home

The Constitution also guarantees freedom from deprivation of property (s. 22) and right to privacy of the home (s.23) subject generally to public interest considerations.

According to the provisions of section 22, nobody is to be compulsorily deprived of his or her property or any rights therein except under certain conditions which include reasons of defence, public safety, public health, town and country planning or for the public benefit generally.

The right guaranteeing a person the privacy of his or her home, correspondence, etc., under section 23 is subjected to curtailment in the 'interest of national security, public safety, economic well-being of the country, for the protection of health or morals, for the prevention of crime or for the protection of the rights of others'.

Although these are clearly civil rights, from the point of view expressed by the European Court of Human Rights in the *Lopez Ostra* case they do have an environmental perspective. Indeed a deprivation of one's home and a disruption if one's family life arising from an environmental nuisance is clearly a breach of these rights. The decision in *Lopez Ostra* is not of binding authority on Gambian courts. However, being a decision of such an eminent judicial body, it may be of persuasive authority even if only to serve as an indication of the international trend in the enforcement of fundamental human rights particularly in relation to environmental rights protection.

Like the sections discussed above, sections 22 and 23 have not yet been challenged in the light of protection of environmental rights. As such there are no judicial decisions on the point but it is submitted that if or when the Gambian courts do take account of such matters, they cannot ignore the international trend and decisions like *Lopez Ostra*.

Unlike the unjusticiable environmental provisions of section 215, the provisions contained in chapter 4 are clearly justiciable. They are intended to be 'respected and upheld by all organs of the executive and its agencies, the Legislature and, where applicable to them, by all natural and legal persons in The Gambia, it shall be enforceable by the courts'. So that the question of the justiciability of these rights is in no doubt. Indeed numerous cases have been instituted and successfully fought against organs of the state for breaches of various provisions of chapter 4, albeit not as breaches of environmental rights but as pure and simple civil and political rights breaches. It is submitted therefore that should a case be brought under this chapter in relation to an environmental matter, it will be addressed.

However, like all countries with a common law tradition, prosecution of environmental cases raises the problem of *locus standi*. The principle of *locus standi* in English law means that a complainant or litigant must be able to show that he/she has suffered damage or injury that could be traced to the act or omission complained about.

In the topic under discussion (i.e., the right of a child to a clean environment) the parent of a dead child may be able to sue the state or local authority for causing the death of her/his child through malaria contracted from mosquitoes from the open sewer maintained by the local authority. Short of showing that the malaria was caused by mosquitoes actually bred in the sewer, such a parent would not have problems proving *locus standi,* because he/she has clearly suffered a loss – the death of his/her child. However, in the example of class actions of parents living in the area to complain that the right of their children to life was being threatened by the mosquito-breeding sewer, they would be hard-put to show *locus standi* since they had not suffered any damage or loss. In effect the principle of *locus standi* is saying that 'wait until you have suffered loss or injury, then come and ask for damages'. This, it is submitted does not augur well for environmental protection because in most cases the damage caused may be irreparable.

The problem of proving *locus standi* becomes more acute in the protection of the rights of future generations. Except for the non-justiciable provision of section 215 where the state is to pursue a policy of environmental protection for posterity, the Constitution does not seem to recognise any rights relating to future generations. So that if, for example, children of the present generation want to bring an action to ensure the protection of the forest, or the River Gambia as part of their cultural heritage, not only will they have difficulty in proving *locus standi* on their own behalf, but more so for children yet unborn. They may have to look at other laws and international instruments, but they definitely will not find much help from the Constitution.

6. The National Environment Management Act 1994

In May 1994, Parliament enacted the National Environment Management Act as framework legislation to provide for the control and management of the environment. The preamble to the Act set out very noble goals, namely: the assurance of the 'fundamental right to an environment adequate for ... health and well-being' of all people living in the country, the necessity to protect and improve the health and quality of life of all Gambians, increase in environmental awareness and public participation in environmental management, prevention or control of pollution and promotion of international co-operation in environmental protection. The preamble most importantly recognises the need 'to conserve and promote the national use of natural resources for the benefit of present and future generations'.

One would have thought that having realised in the National Environment Management Act that a healthy environment is a fundamental right of all persons living in The Gambia, in 1994, it would therefore be logical to protect that right in a Constitution adopted two years later in 1996. Although it is a generally accepted constitutional law principle that laws get their validity from the Constitution and not vice versa, as a matter of consistency, and to exhibit that environmental protection is not only a matter of rhetoric alone this right should have been protected in the Constitution. The records of the debates of the Constitutional Review Commission set up to draft the new Constitution, have not yet been put in the public domain, so that one does not know why environmental and related rights have not been protected by the Constitution. It is hoped that with time, this may come to light. Another reason that may also be advanced is that the National Environment Management Act was passed by a different parliament under the former regime of ex-President Sir Dawda Jawara and the new

Constitution was negotiated and adopted under the present regime of Rt Hon Colonel Yahya Jammeh. The two regimes have different approaches and divergent views on many issues.

The Act consists of 67 sections to put into effect the goals set out in the preamble. For the purposes of this chapter, it will be interesting to look at section 3 (duty to maintain a decent environment); section 4(1) (capacity to bring public interest action); section 7(c) (duty to interpret environmental issues in economic and social planning) and the various duties of the National Environment Agency established to implement the provisions of the National Environment Management Act.

Section 3 provides as follows:

> *(1)* Every person shall have a duty to maintain and enhance the quality of the environment including the duty to inform the Agency of activities that affect or are likely to affect the environment adversely.
> *(2)* The Agency shall on its own volition or upon receipt of information referred to under subsection (1) instruct the person whose activities affect or are likely to affect the environment adversely,
> *(3)* to discontinue such activities, or
> *(4)* subject such activities to environmental monitoring or auditing as may be necessary.
> *(5)* The Agency may instruct any public officer to take measures to prevent or discontinue any act deleterious to the environment.

Clearly, every individual in The Gambia has a duty towards the environment – or duty to preserve/maintain it – and also to report to the National Environment Agency activities that harm or are likely to harm it. It is then for the Agency to take the steps necessary to ensure that such activities as damage the environment are stopped. In addition, the Agency may petition the Attorney-General to institute a public interest action against a person who breaches the duty imposed by section 3, this is in addition to the power to institute criminal proceedings against any polluters under sections 38 and 39.

Perhaps the most important provisions for the public (including children) for ensuring a safe and healthy environment is subsection (2) of section 4. It states that every person shall have the capacity to bring a public interest action to protect the environment provided that the fiat of the Attorney-General authorising such action is first obtained.

This provision confers *locus standi* on the citizens (minors and adults alike) to sue on their own behalf and on behalf of every other person in the country, anybody who pollutes any segment of the environment. Although this section does not confer rights as such, it does however confer very wide powers, albeit powers that can only be exercised with the fiat of the Attorney-General. These powers could even be described as vague and 'open-ended'. It is not clear from the Act what remedies may be available to a plaintiff or plaintiffs under this section. Again the efficiency of these sections has not yet been tested in the courts, perhaps because the Act is still in its infancy.

The National Environment Agency is established by the Act as a body 'responsible for the management of the environment' to 'co-ordinate all activities of the Government in the field of the environment' (s.9(2)). It is a body corporate with legal capacity to sue and be sued. (s.9(3)). The Agency's duties include, *inter alia,* promoting public awareness through information dissemination. It is also expected to publish periodic reports on the state of the environment (s.10(h)). The first state of the environment report is due to be published in early 1998.

The National Environment Management Act 1994 was preceded by the adoption in 1993 of the Gambia National Environmental Action Plan (GEAP) which was developed through a nation-wide participatory process. It lays out an environmental policy for the country. Thus, in the implementation of its duties, the agency is guided by both the Act and the GEAP.

One of the programmes of the GEAP, which is also echoed by the Act in section 10(h), is the Environmental Education Programme. The programme being co-ordinated by the Agency, involves environmental education in the formal (i.e., schools and other educational institutions) non-formal (i.e., through extension services, community development programmes, NGO programmes etc.) and informal sectors (i.e., environmental education acquired 'in-passing' through other media, e.g. newspapers). For the purposes of this chapter, the environmental education at the formal sector is of more relevance. It is designed to achieve the specific objective of raising the level of knowledge and skills in environmental management and to influence the attitudes of those at whom it is targeted.

The Gambia has a policy of compulsory primary education for all children. This means that the vast majority of Gambian children do acquire a primary education. Introducing education about the environment into the school curriculum means that the majority of children in The Gambia are exposed at an early age to issues relating to environmental management.

Environmental education is considered to be an important component in the effort to ensure and achieve a safe and clean environment the world over, especially in the context of sustainable development. This was realised at UNCED when delegates agreed that 'education is critical for promoting sustainable development and increasing the capacity for people to address environmental and developmental issues'. Starting environmental education at an early age ensures that children develop a culture of 'environmental responsibility'. This responsibility may even be described as a duty of care which they owe to the rest of society, but which also the rest of society owes to them.

In effect, environmental education properly structured may have the dual effect of teaching the children about their duty towards the environment, but also enlightening them about their expectations from the present managers of the environment. This in turn places a duty on the people who 'manage' the environment, who are also responsible for teaching the children about the environment, to so manage the environment as to leave it in no worse condition as they had inherited it from previous generations of 'managers', if not better.

It is a trite principle of English common law, that, where there is a legal right conferred on an individual by statute, but the statute does not provide a remedy for the breach of the right, then the appropriate remedy is an order of mandamus. This is especially so where the provision has the effect of imposing an obligation which arises out of the official status of the respondent and is therefore of a public character.

Applying this general principle to the various sections of Act that have just been examined, one would see the following scenarios arise:

1. The Agency can petition the Attorney-General to bring public interest action or institute criminal prosecutions against a polluter;
2. Any member of the public may report to the Agency any incidents of pollution for the Agency to take appropriate action to stop the pollution or seek the fiat of Attorney-General to bring a private prosecution.

The following questions could be raised:

(a) Can the Agency compel the Attorney-General to bring a public interest action against a polluter? or

(b) Could a member of the public compel the Agency to prosecute a polluter or

(c) Could a member of the public compel the Attorney-General to give his/her fiat for a private prosecution?

Even though an order of mandamus could be used to compel public officers to perform a duty, the authorities tend to show that in the case of the Attorney-General in the performance of his duty as keeper of the public interest he cannot be compelled by court order. In *Gouriet*, the Attorney-General had refused his fiat to the plaintiff to bring relator proceedings for an injunction.[1] The plaintiff then issued a writ in his own name. The trial judge refused to make the order on the ground that he had no power to grant it. On appeal to the Court of Appeal, the innovative Lord Denning MR, overturned the decision, on the ground that 'in the last resort, if the Attorney-General refuses leave in a proper case or improperly or unreasonably delays in giving his leave, or his machinery works too slowly, then a member of the public, who has a sufficient interest can himself apply to the court itself. He can apply for a declaration and in a proper case for an injunction, joining the Attorney-General, if need be, as a defendant'.

According to this decision, an individual who seeks the fiat of the Attorney-General in order to prosecute a polluter but is refused the Attorney-General's fiat, can bring an action in his own name provided he can prove sufficient interest. But the House of Lords rejected this ruling and held that the discretionary power of the Attorney-General to grant or refuse his fiat cannot be enquired into or reviewed by the court. It is interesting to note that even Lord Denning at some point conceded that a court could not enquire into the giving of consent by the Attorney-General although he maintained that if the Attorney-General refuses to grant this fiat, that decision may be subject to review by the courts. Lord Wilberforce was of the view that 'public rights can only be asserted by the Attorney-General as representing the public. ... It is the exclusive right of the Attorney-General to represent the public interest even where individuals might be interested in a larger view of the matter'. He went on to state that 'the decision to be made as to the public interest are not such as the courts are fitted or equipped to make'.

This principle had also been stated earlier in *London County Council v. the Attorney General* by Lord Halsbury LC, that 'it is for the Attorney-General and not the courts to determine whether he ought to initiate litigation … or not'.

It is the present writer's view that the position as stated in *Gouriet* is good law in The Gambia for the simple reason that the Privy Council is still the final court of arbitration in The Gambia and decisions of the House of Lords are of binding/persuasive authority. Moreover, the fact that the statute that confers the power on the public to bring our action also categorically requires that the fiat of the Attorney-General must first be obtained, demonstrates that Parliament intended to safeguard the powers of the Attorney-General as guardian of the public interest.

1 *Gouriet v. Union of Post Office Workers* [1978] AC 435; [1977] 3 WLR 300; [1977] 3 AU ER 70.

The present position of the law is not problem free. The Attorney-General may refrain from bringing an action against a polluter for purely political reasons, e.g. the action may result in the closure of a polluting factory which will mean putting a lot of people out of work.

These very reasons could motivate him/her to refuse to grant his/her fiat to an aggrieved member of the public or group of persons, to bring an action against the owner of the factory to stop or reduce the pollution. A political interest of the government of the day may have been served by the Attorney-General's refusal, but a problem of a different nature would have been allowed to continue which could affect generations yet unborn.

Another aspect of the problem is that rarely does the Attorney-General bring a public interest action against a public body or authority. In fact there is no known case in recent history in The Gambia in which the Attorney-General has brought an action against a public body for not carrying out any aspect of its public duty. For example, the management of waste collection and disposal which each local authority in the country is under obligation to carry out has always been in a shambles and this is evident to all who live in or visit The Gambia, but, up to now, never has the Attorney-General brought an action, in the interest of the public whose health is at risk, to compel the responsible authorities to do their duty. Political and economic considerations might be the reason for the inaction, but it would be interesting to see whether the Attorney-General would grant his fiat to an aggrieved person who wants to sue a polluter. It would also be more interesting if the suit is intended to protect the rights of children born or perhaps yet unborn!

7. International Obligations

7.1 The African Charter on Human and Peoples' Rights

The Gambia like most common law countries (e.g. Nigeria and Sierra Leone) has a dualist system of enforcement of international agreements. This means that an international agreement having been signed and ratified must be incorporated into national law by legislative process before it can be enforced by the national courts.

The African Charter was ratified on 8 June 1983. It has not however been wholly incorporated into Gambian law. The effect is that direct enforcement of the provisions of the Charter cannot be sought in the Gambian courts. The state is however bound to observe its obligations under international law. Complaints may be made to the African Commission, which has powers to investigate complaints against state parties. But the Commission can only bring the allegation to the attention of a state against whom it had been made, ask for its response, find whether or not there has been a breach of the Charter provisions, and make recommendations to the state to remedy the situation. The Commission lacks judicial powers and cannot therefore legally enforce its recommendations against a state party. It is hoped that the situation will be remedied with the establishment of the African Court of Human Rights.

At the national level, fragments of the Charter provisions can be found in relevant laws, for example, cultural rights protected in section 32 of the Constitution. These are directly enforceable by the national courts, which may take into consideration the provisions of the Charter in interpreting the rights.

The Charter has generally been recognised as the first international agreement to make the link between environmental protection and human rights. Article 24 states that 'All people shall have the right to a general satisfactory environment favourable to their development'. The extent of this right is unclear and 'open-ended' in that the Article does not go further and throw light on the nature of this right. It is clear however, that the obligation of state parties are limited to taking 'legislative or other measures to give effect to them'. In The Gambia, it could be said that the provisions of the National Environment Management Act and the Constitution discussed above are aimed at achieving the purposes of Article 24.

The Charter is indeed silent in relation to the protection of the child against an unclean or unhealthy environment. But it is arguable that this right could be subsumed under the umbrella of the 'right to a general environment satisfactory to their development'. Be that as it may, the right to a clean environment cannot be specifically enforced under the Charter unless it has been granted by national legislation.

7.2 Convention on the Rights of the Child

Like the African Charter, the Convention on the Rights of the Child even though signed and ratified, has not been directly incorporated into Gambian law, so it cannot be directly enforceable. Again, fragments of the Convention provisions can be found in national laws. For example, there is a constitutional provision for the protection of the rights of the child. As mentioned earlier, this appears for the first time in the Gambia's constitutional history. This was perhaps done in realisation of the obligations arising out of the Convention. There is also a national co-ordination committee that is responsible for the preparation of the country's report on the implementation of the Convention. In the latest draft report the country is reported to have a National Programme of Action for the Survival, Protection and Development of The Gambian Child which has been in operation since 1992 and is expected to last until 2003. It consists of a Maternal and Child Health Programme, a Nutrition Surveillance Programme and an Expanded Programme on Immunisation. These programmes are implemented in observance of the state obligations under Articles 6 and 24 relating to the survival and development of the child, and the right to health and healthcare

8. Conclusion

What has emerged from the analysis undertaken in this chapter is that there is no specific right of the child to a clean environment. Neither the Constitution nor the National Environment Management Act provides for this right. But the right is realisable through the enforcement and application of other related rights that are protected by the Constitution. Other procedures also exist under the National Environmental Management Act, which may be utilised to realise the right to a clean environment. However, due to the high incidence of illiteracy in the country, people are not fully aware of these rights and procedures. They do not therefore make use of them and the responsible authorities are hardly ever challenged. Consequently, the courts are not called upon to interpret the existing laws on environmental protection so as to throw light upon how far they may be relied upon to protect environmental rights. It is, however, hoped that with the passage of time and the growth of the Environmental Education Programme, people will become more aware of their rights and obligations as regards the environment and the picture will change.

7 Constitutional reform in Argentina and environmental education in Patagonia[1]

Soledad Aguilar; Maria G. Doglioli; Marcos Oliva-Day

1. Introduction

Argentina's Constitution was originally sanctioned in 1853 and based on the United States Constitution. It did not contain any specific reference to a right to a clean environment. However, before the 1994 constitutional reform introduced this right in the legal system, the Argentinian courts recognised its existence in a 1983 leading case.[2] The plaintiffs filed a complaint seeking the prohibition of fishing a special kind of dolphin (*toninas overas / Cephalorhynchus Commersonii*) in Argentina's sea until a proper environmental impact assessment was done. The judge considered that every man has an individual right to a clean environment, and that even if it had not been expressly provided for, it existed in the terms of Article 33. This Article establishes that 'the declarations, rights and guarantees that are enumerated in the Constitution, shall not be construed to deprive of other rights and guarantees that have not been enumerated, but that emanate from the principle of sovereignty of the people and the republican form of government'. He also stated that the duty of the state to perform the necessary environmental impact assessment emanated from its obligation to promote the general well being in the terms of the Preamble of the Constitution. In 1994, the Constitution was reformed and the right to a clean environment was included in Chapter II, entitled, 'New rights and constitutional guarantees'. The constitutional reform marked the recognition of 'third generation rights' in Argentina's legal system. In the following study we will analyse the implications of the recognition of this right and the obligations it gives rise to for the state and the citizens. We will then discuss the means available to exercise this right, and the possibilities provided by the Constitution for the conservation

1 Sections 1–5 of this article have been written by Soledad Aguilar and Maria G. Doglioli. Sections 6-8 have been written by Marcos Oliva-Day.

2 'Kattan, Alberto E. y otro c. Gobierno nacional (Poder Ejecutivo)', (La Ley, t-1983 – D, 576).

of the environment for the children. To conclude, a case study concerning an environmental education programme that has been implemented in Puerto Deseado, a small town in the region of Patagonia, will be described.

The Argentinian constitutional system establishes the following hierarchy among different norms:

1. The Constitution, followed by treaties with constitutional status (including the Convention of the Rights of the Child).[3]
2. The remainder of treaties ratified by the state.
3. All legislation approved by the National Congress.
4. All other decrees and resolutions of the Executive Power.

This pyramid of norms comprises the federal legal system that has to be respected by all other domestic legislation.

2. The Constitutional Right to a Clean Environment

After the 1994 reforms, the Argentinian Constitution defined the right to a clean environment in the first paragraph of Article 41, as the right of all inhabitants to a 'healthy and balanced environment, which allows for human development and productive activities to satisfy the needs of the present generation, without compromising the possibility of future generations to satisfy theirs'. The interpretation of the first part of this phrase will probably give rise to legal disputes, because the terms 'healthy and balanced' are vague and contain an emotive burden that makes them totally dependent upon the values of the interpreter. To pretend that someone can determine when the environment is 'balanced' evidences a conception of the environment as something static when, in reality, it is completely dynamic and subject to permanent change.

However, the second part of this phrase is more useful because it uses the concept of sustainable development to define the right to a clean environment. This is the 'development which meets the needs of present generations without compromising the ability of future generations to meet their own needs'.[4] In other words, the right to a clean environment would be equivalent to the right to sustainable development. Even though these terms are still imprecise, the concept of sustainable development is accepted world-wide and it is easier to transform it into operative terms.

---

3 Article 75(2) of the Argentinian Constitution.

4 World Commission on Environment and Development, *Our Common Future* (Brundtland Report), London (1987).

The legal innovation in this article is the fact that any citizen has the right for the environment to be exploited in a rational way. Thus, even though a citizen has no individual right with respect to natural resources owned by other persons or by the state, he or she has a right to claim that the productive activities of third persons are not conducted in an unsustainable way.

The consequences of this right are vast and difficult to envision. Its definition suggests that it can be exercised against any person who engages in an economic activity of any type. To be able to claim a right there must be a person with the legal duty to respect it, either by performing the activity that is being claimed, or by omitting to perform an activity in violation of such right. The right to a sustainable development requires a positive action from third parties because it limits the ways in which economic activities can be performed. In order for the right to sustainable development to be effective, a correlative obligation from all citizens to perform any economic activity in a sustainable way must exist. However, there has not yet been any authoritative precedent regarding the standing to be sued.

The first paragraph of Article 41 ends by stating that 'all inhabitants have ... the duty to preserve [the environment]'. Consequently, the correlative duty to the right to sustainable development is not a duty to perform any economic activity in a sustainable way, but a duty to preserve the environment. The questions that arise are: What does the 'duty to preserve it' mean? Do the duties to perform all economic activities in a sustainable way and to preserve the environment coincide?

The second paragraph of Article 41 refers to the obligation of the state to 'provide towards ... the rational use of natural resources, the preservation of the natural and cultural capital, and of the biological diversity ...'. Here the difference between sustainable use (equivalent to sustainable development), and preservation of the environment is clear: both are duties of the state. The meaning of the words 'will provide', however, weakens the duty because it does not compel the state to perform any activity. In other words, the state could do nothing and still act according to the law.

This analysis of Article 41 shows how the recognition of a right is not enough to make it operative. Even if the Argentinian Constitution recognises the right to a clean environment, neither its contents nor the standing to be sued are unmistakably stated. This situation is further complicated by the fact that the legal standing to sue has yet to be regulated. Therefore, the effective enforcement of this right is still dependent upon courts' sensitivity towards environmental matters, who make efforts to make environmental rights effective.

3. Procedural Means Available to Claim the Right to a Clean Environment

The most important available procedural instrument to claim the right to a clean environment in Argentina is the writ of 'amparo'. This writ is a procedural guarantee which contemplates a brief and summary action destined to protect all constitutional rights, excepting physical freedom which is protected by the writ of *habeas corpus*. The writ of amparo applies in those cases where an ordinary trial would be too long to provide an effective protection to these rights.

This guarantee was enshrined in the 1994 constitutional reform. However, two leading cases mark the praetorian creation of this institution in the Argentinian legal system. The first case was decided in 1957.[5] The owner of a publishing company that had been shut down by the police authorities of the Province of Buenos Aires submitted a complaint in the form of an *habeas corpus*, alleging that this measure violated his right to freedom of expression and work. The Court of First Instance and the Appellate Court ruled against the plaintiff, taking into account that the writ of *habeas corpus* is aimed to protect the physical freedom of citizens. The plaintiff appealed to the Supreme Court. He alleged that he had not filed a writ of *habeas corpus*, but a petition in order to get the protection of the courts. The Supreme Court allowed the action on the basis that constitutional rights and guarantees are self-executing and protect the individuals by the mere fact of being in the Constitution, irrespectively of any regulatory legislation. These rights are compelling for the individuals and the state, and have to be protected by the courts even in those cases where no procedural means to achieve the objective exist. Therefore, the absence of an equivalent of the writ of *habeas corpus* directed to the protection of constitutional rights other than physical freedom, should not leave the citizen defenceless in those cases in which an ordinary trial would be too long to be effective.

The second case was heard in 1958, but this time the institution was applied against actions performed by citizens.[6] The workers of a company started a strike that was declared illegal by the administrative authorities. The employers compelled the workers to restart working but fired two of them, who were representatives of the union. A month later, the administrative resolution was annulled, and both the employers and workers were compelled to resume their activities. The employers refused to admit the workers that had been fired, and these and other fellow workers then

---

5 'Siri, Angel s/interpone recurso de habeas corpus' (La Ley, t- 89, 531).

6 'Kot, Samuel SRL s/ recurso de habeas corpus' (La Ley, t- 92, 627).

occupied the factory paralysing its activities. The owner of the factory filed a possessory action trying to regain possession of the plant. The Court of First Instance dismissed the case because it considered that this was not a case of dispossession aimed to exercise property rights over the factory. The plaintiff appealed and in the same day that the Appellate Court was due to try the case, he filed a writ of amparo, alleging that he had been deprived of his property rights and freedom to work. The Appellate Court dismissed the action as it considered that the writ of *habeas corpus* was aimed to the protection of physical freedom and not at the protection of other constitutional rights.

Finally, the case was heard by the Supreme Court that allowed the claim. It considered that the plaintiff had not filed a writ of *habeas corpus* but a writ of amparo, as it had been defined in the previous precedent (*Siri*). The Court stated that even if the cases were different because in that previous case the restriction on the constitutional rights had been caused by an act of the governmental authorities, whereas in the present case the unlawful conduct had been performed by private parties, that difference was not essential. It considered that the writ of amparo as a means seeking protection of constitutional rights would apply if the illegality of the actions was evident, and the ordinary procedure would cause a grave and irreparable harm to the plaintiff, regardless of the character of the person performing the conduct.

In 1966, a law regulating the writ of amparo was sanctioned which considered this procedural institution to protect constitutional rights violated by governmental authorities, while the National Procedural Code established it to counteract violations performed by civil parties. Finally, this procedural institution received constitutional status having been incorporated under Article 43 of the reformed Constitution in 1994. Its scope will be analysed in the following sections.

4. The Writ of Amparo in the 1994 Constitutional Reform

4.1 Situations in which the writ of amparo should proceed

This procedural institution has been regulated to give protection to individual and collective rights:

1. When a public agent or a private party, by act or omission, has manifestly illegally affected a citizen's rights, in order to stop that conduct.

2. Provided there is no other similarly efficient procedural means to achieve the same goal. This is crucial because, if the citizen can be granted judicial protection by another means, as efficiently as through the writ of amparo, it will not proceed.

4.2 Legal standing to sue

Article 43 gives legal standing to sue the:

1. 'affected' person,
2. 'Defensor del pueblo',
3. associations which have legal personality.

Before considering the different interpretations that the term 'affected' has received, we will analyse different concepts that have been applied by the courts when dealing with environmental issues. These are the concepts of 'individual right', 'legitimate interest' and 'simple interest'. The person who is directly harmed by a certain conduct holds an 'individual right' to sue. When a person suffers a harm in an indirect way, his or her legal standing to sue will be based on a 'legitimate interest'. In those cases where a citizen files a writ of amparo in the interest of the environment without having suffered any specific harm, he or she holds a 'simple interest' to sue. The doctrine[7] tends to support a broad interpretation of the term 'affected'. They consider that a co-ordinated interpretation of the terms 'affected' and the incorporation of 'third generation rights' would give legal standing to sue to those individuals who have not been directly or indirectly damaged by an act or omission of the state or another civil party, but who have a 'reasonable interest' in protecting collective interests.

This position has been used in different judgments. The leading case in these matters is *Schroeder, Juan v. Estado Naciona.*[8] In 1994, Juan Schroeder, a citizen of a small town in the province of Buenos Aires, sued the National Government's Secretary of Natural Resources in order to annul a public bid for the installation of a waste-treatment plant. He alleged that

---

7 O.A. Gozaini, 'La noción de "afectado" a los fines de acreditar la legitimación procesal en el amparo', La Ley 6.8.96; M.A. Gelli, 'La silueta del amparo después de la reforma constitucional', La Ley Suplemento Especial del 15.11.95; D. Sabsay, 'El amparo como garantía para la defensa de los derechos fundamentales', *Revista Jurídica del Centro de Estudiantes*, no. 6, (1996); M.G. Carattini, 'El amparo en la reforma constitucional de 1994' (La Ley, t-1995 – A, 874); J.R. Walsh, 'El medio ambiente en la nueva Constitución Argentina' (La Ley), SDA, Año 1, no. 1 (6.12.94); G. Bidart Campos, 'Tratado Elemental de Derecho Constitucional Argentino', t- VI; G. Bidart Campos, 'La reforma constitucional de 1994', Ediar, Bs. As. 1995; G. Bidart Campos, 'La legitimación procesal activa en el párrafo segundo del art. 43 de la Constitución', El Derecho, 6.2.96; A.M. Morello, 'El amparo después de la reforma constitucional', Revista de Derecho Privado y Comunitario, no. 7 (1994).

8 'Schroeder, Juan c. Estado Nacional – Secretaria de Recursos Naturales' (La Ley t- 1994-E, 449).

the government had not taken into account the environmental impact of the project. The Appellate Court, who allowed the action, considered that Schroeder had legal standing to sue in this case on the basis of two facts: his status of inhabitant of the province of Buenos Aires, and Article 41 of the Constitution that established the right to a clean environment and the duty of every citizen to protect it. The Court considered that 'when dealing with the protection of the rights related to the environment, the "affected" has legal standing to sue. This condition has been fulfilled by the direct and personal interest that the plaintiff has in this case'. The Court took specially into account the fact that the plaintiff was not redressing any damages but only trying to force the government to fulfil the usual procedures of an environmental impact assessment.

Another two cases should be noted. The first claim was filed by a citizen of a Buenos Aires neighbourhood against the local government of this city.[9] The complaint addressed the situation of some homeless that had illegally settled in a park. She tried to have them given shelter in another place alleging sanitary and environmental reasons for her plea. The Court considered that the fact of being a neighbour of that area entitled her to claim the protection of the environment under Article 43 of the Constitution.

In the second case,[10] the mayor of the municipal area of Vicente Lopez filed a complaint against the national government, in which he sought to stop the cutting of trees and reduction of green areas that were being performed by a licensee in charge of the construction of a motorway. The plaintiff based his legal standing to sue in Article 41 of the National Constitution and every citizen's duty to protect the environment.

Some authors[11] consider that the term 'affected' only includes the victim, the directly injured. Their position is supported in different cases[12] in which some courts have considered that the reform hasn't introduced a new type of claim aimed at the protection of 'third generation rights'. The Congress is considering different projects of legislation regulating the writ of amparo. These projects adopt the restrictive view and give legal standing to sue to the victim and they establish that those who do not have that status should seek protection of this right via the ombudsman or the associations that have legal personality.

---

9 'Seiler, María Leticia c. MCBA s/ amparo' (El Derecho, t-165, 215).

10 'Municipalidad de Vicente López c. Estado Nacional (M.E.O. y S.P.- Secretaria de Obras Publicas y Comunicaciones – Organo de Control de las Concesiones de la Red de Accesos a la Ciudad de Buenos Aires) s/ amparo' (El Derecho, t- 161, 354).

11 Rodolfo Carlos Barra, 'La acción de amparo en la constitución reformada: la legitimación para accionar' (La Ley, t- 1994 – E, 1087).

12 'Consumidores Libres Coop. Ltda c. Estado Nacional' (La Ley SJDA, 06.12.95).

Having considered the most important precedents in this subject, it should be noted that only a broad interpretation of the term 'affected' would give effective meaning to the incorporation of the right to a clean environment. The courts are willing to support a broad interpretation of the legal standing to sue in the writ of amparo but in Argentina's legal system precedents are not binding. Future sentences could adopt a different point of view.

The 1994 reform established the new public position of Defensor del pueblo. This post is similar to the one known in Europe as 'Ombudsman'. Article 86 of the revised Constitution establishes that his or her duty is the protection of human rights and every other right or guarantee recognised either by the Constitution or any other law, against violations performed by the governmental authorities. According to the National Law no. 24.284, modified by the National Law no. 24.379, the *defensor del pueblo* can act *ex-officio*, or following a complaint of a citizen, and has legal standing to sue in cases in which he represents the interests of the citizens as members of the society, and not individually.

Finally, the associations that have been granted legal personality and aim at the protection of the environment can also claim rights within the context of the writ of amparo. These organisations could be NGOs incorporated under the Argentinian legal system. It is generally interpreted that they would have legal standing to pursue the respect for collective rights, such as the right to a clean environment. They litigate in their own name, and it remains to be seen if the courts require – such as they do in other countries – some degree of representativity, in other words, that some of its members qualify as 'affected parties'. In this respect, it is important to note a case that has been recently heard by a Federal Court of First Instance in the Province of Buenos Aires. In this case,[13] an NGO filed a writ of amparo seeking the annulment of an authorisation to capture twelve dolphins and four whales, on the basis that the Ministry of Production of the Province of Buenos Aires (which had granted the authorisation) had no jurisdiction to issue such an authorisation. The Court considered that the plaintiff's argument was not valid, but nevertheless allowed the action. It stated that the authorities had not required an environmental impact assessment and that this was enough reason to annul the authorisation. The Court did not analyse the NGO's legal standing to sue, as it considered that it stemmed from Article 43 of the Constitution. This precedent is coherent with the ones previously analysed but, as we are dealing with new legal institutions, it is yet to be seen if other courts will follow this legal interpretation.

13 'Fundación Fauna Marina c. Ministerio de la Producción de la Provincia de Buenos Aires' (El Derecho, 10.10.97).

4.3 Different types of rights protected

The Constitution has established this guarantee not only for the protection of constitutional rights, but also for those rights recognised by treaties to which the Argentinian state is party, and those rights recognised by the national and provincial legislation.

The possibility of applying this procedural institution to rights recognised by a decree, ministerial resolution or local regulation has been argued amongst Argentinian constitutional scholars.[14] A broad approach has been considered to suit better the present regulation of the amparo. A restriction in the type of rights to be protected would be against the spirit of the institution.

4.4 Is the constitutional norm self-executing?

Even if Argentina's Legislative Power has not passed a law regulating the writ of amparo, this should not be an obstacle for individuals and authorities willing to make use of this procedural institution. The majority of the writers consider that constitutional rights and guarantees are self-executing and that they do not need regulation in order to be exercised. The contrary would allow that the delay of the national authorities in the regulation of certain rights and guarantees resulted in the dilution of these rights and the consequent harm to the citizen and society as a whole.

5. Conclusion

The rights of the child to a clean environment in Argentina must be studied within the framework of rights to a clean environment in general. Argentinian law does not make a difference between constitutional rights for children or adults. The right to a clean environment has been recognised by the Constitution, the supreme law of the country, together with the rights of children (Convention on the Rights of the Child), therefore, the legal framework for the effective recognition of these rights has been set. The effective implementation of these legal norms is now a role that the society must assume, to turn the formal legal texts into positive results.

14 Alberto Antonio Spota, 'Análisis de la acción de amparo en los términos del art. 43 de la Constitución Nacional' (El Derecho, t- 163, 767).

6. Case study: Environmental Education in Patagonia

'The main objective of Environmental Education is to defend the community against ignorance and passivity'.[15]

6.1 An international perspective on environmental education

The origin of international environmental law can be traced back to the efforts of the first major international organisations to address environmental issues. In October 1948, a conference was held with the assistance of the United Nations Educational, Scientific and Cultural Organisation, which created the International Union for the Protection of Nature (IUPN) to promote the preservation of wildlife and the natural environment and to enhance *public knowledge, education,* scientific research and legislation.

The United Nations Conference on the Human Environment (Stockholm, 1972) proclaimed that '[t]hrough our ignorance or indifference we can do massive and irreversible harm to the earthly environment on which our life and well-being depend. Conversely, through fuller knowledge and wiser action, we can achieve for ourselves and our posterity a better life ... man must use knowledge to build, in collaboration with nature, a better environment'.[16]

Principle 19 states: 'Education in environmental matters, for the younger generation as well as adults, giving due consideration to the underprivileged, is essential in order to broaden the basis for an enlightened opinion and responsible conduct by individuals, enterprises and communities in protecting and improving the environment in its full human dimension.'[17] Environmental education aims at developing an understanding of the complex dialectic that exists between social and financial development and the conservation and improvement of the environment. It has become clear in recent times that the necessity of developing a coherent policy on environmental education is urgent.

In the same way, Principle 10 of the 1992 Rio Declaration recognises the importance of public education and provides that 'states shall facilitate and encourage public awareness and participation by making information widely available'.[18] Principle 22 provides that '[I]ndigenous people and

15 Dino Bellorio Clabot, *Tratado de Derecho Ambiental* (Buenos Aires: Ed. Ad-Hoc., 1997), pp.292, 630.
16 Declaration of the United Nations Conference on the Human Environment (Stockholm, 16 June 1972), reprinted in *International Environmental Law: Documents* (The Hague: T.M.C. Asser Instituut, 1997), pp. 5–8.
17 *Ibid.* See also P. Sands et al., *Documents in International Environmental Law* (Manchester: Manchester University Press, 1995), pp. 10-13.
18 The Rio Declaration on Environment and Development (Rio de Janiero, 13 June 1992), reprinted in *International Environmental Law: Documents* (The Hague: T.M.C. Asser Instituut, 1997), pp. 12–14.

their communities, and other local communities, have a vital role in environmental management and development ... States should recognize and duly support their identity ...'.[19] Chapter 36 of Agenda 21 establishes three programme areas: reorienting education towards sustainable development; increasing public awareness; and promoting training, while the 1987 Montreal Protocol calls on parties to co-operate in promoting public awareness of the environmental effects of the emissions of controlled substances and other substances that deplete the ozone layer. The 1989 Convention on the Rights of the Child specifies that education should include 'development of respect for the natural environment'. Over the past fifty years global environmental law has pushed us towards taking an active role in educating children about their environment. Environmental Education believes that the best way of realising the goals stated in international treaties' and educating the general public, as well as instilling values, is through examples and practice.

These developments have inspired a fundamental change in that direction in the Argentine legal system.[20] The right to a clean environment has been partially recognised by some important judicial awards since 1983: the difficult path comprises four areas:[21]

1. *Civil, penal, labour and administrative law*: municipal rules and provincial laws related to neighbourhood problems (noise, smell), security and hygienic work conditions, and industry settlements.
2. *National laws* related to the environment as concerns the 1972 law on the preservation of air resources (Ley 20.284) and the law on the conservation of wild fauna (Ley 22.421) which, in introducing the citizen's duty of wildlife protection, prepared the ground for the jurisprudence in the leading case of *Kattan y otro v. National State*, in March 1983.
3. *Provincial constitution reforms*, since 1986.
4. *National constitution reform* in 1986.

It is worth taking into account the encouraging role carried out by a growing community consciousness over the importance of the preservation of the nature. This development was essential in the effort of NGOs, including the help of the media.

Article 41 of the revised Argentinian Constitution was ground-breaking in that it followed the legal structure generally given in other constitutions.[22]

19 *Ibid.*
20 Daniel Sabsay et al., *La Constitucion de los Argentinos* (Buenos Aires: Errepar, 1994), p. 141.
21 Bellario Clabot, op. cit. n. 15.
22 S. Ball and S. Bell, *Environmental Law* (London, 1995), p. 9.

In its first paragraph, following the mission of the 1972 Stockholm Conference, the Constitution directly acknowledges the inhabitants' right to an environment – one that is healthy, balanced and suitable for human development. It establishes that activities must meet present needs without risking those of future generations. It marks, also, the citizen's obligation to preserve the environment, and the duty to repair environmental damage.

More importantly Article 41 orders the authorities to protect this right, to rationally use natural resources, to preserve natural and cultural inheritance and biological diversity and to give environmental information and education. It is significant that Article 75 acknowledges the ethnic and cultural pre-existence of indigenous people, guarantees to respect their identities and their right to a bilingual and intercultural education.

The Santa Cruz Province (Argentine Patagonia, discussed below) reformed its Constitution in 1995. Article 73 of this document establishes that all the people have the right to enjoy an adequate environment for their personal development. The provincial state and the individuals are obliged to protect and preserve the environment.

7. Difficulties in Protecting What is Little Known

7.1 A need for the project

The famous fresco of 'The Child and the Dolphin', painted four thousand years ago at the palace of Knossos in Crete, shows the ancient friendship that has existed between these two mammal species.

Taking an anthropocentric approach to this issue, even beyond the dolphins' natural right to life and freedom, we have the right to enjoy our environment, which includes the happiness we always feel when we watch a dolphin swimming. Furthermore, these animals also constitute an economic resource through their usefulness in medical treatments and as tourist attractions.

The southern Atlantic Ocean is home to the Commerson Dolphin, a beautiful dolphin that has been studied very little. In Argentina this dolphin is known as the *tonina overa*, due to its short nose and because all of its 1.35 metre body is black and white. Like other marine mammals, its gregarious instinct keeps it in a basic family structure. If one of the important family members is lost or removed, then the rest of the family may decline or even die.

In January 1978, the Argentine government, without having carried out any previous studies, authorised the capture of four dolphins in the

Ria Deseado, so that they could be exhibited at an aquarium in Japan. The capture was carried out without any scientific advice or official control, executed with the boats and nets used by the local fishermen. Two dolphins died of asphyxia during the process, and four captured dolphins were placed in a children's canvas pool (3m x 2m) to await their transfer to Japan. Three died during the trip, and the surviving one – as a result of non-compliance with applicable legislation – was rescued by the US authorities on its way to Japan and placed in an aquarium to be examined. It had a paralysed side fin and was swimming only with its pectoral fins. It took him three months to die.

With very few exceptions, the people of Puerto Deseado, possessing little or no information, passively watched the dolphins' capture. Today, almost twenty years later, showing how little the population has recovered from that loss, only approximately twenty dolphins live in the Ria Deseado. The present author has the comfort of having collaborated with the report made by Dr Rae Natalie Posser de Goodall, that was used as strong evidence in the leading case *Kattan,*[23] which prevented the capture of fourteen Commerson Dolphins in 1983.

7.2 Patagonia

Patagonia is a huge territory of more than 900,000 km^2 shared by Chile and Argentina, alongside the western and eastern ridges of the Andes mountains, respectively. Its northern border is the Rio Colorado river and its southern limit is Tierra del Fuego, where the American continent falls into the ocean. In Argentina, Patagonia consists of the following provinces (almost one-third of Argentina's land mass): South of La Pampa, Rio Negro, Neuquen, Chubut, Santa Cruz, and Tierra del Fuego.

7.3 Puerto Deseado

This little town located in southern Patagonia, in the Province of Santa Cruz, on the Atlantic coast, has 9,000 inhabitants. Its name comes from Sir Thomas Cavendish's main ship (the British corsair), *Desire*. He sailed into this natural port in 1584. Puerto Deseado was founded in 1884 by Don Antonio Oneto, an Italian seafarer captain who was working for the Argentinian government.

During the last ten years the local economy has switched from the exploitation of sheep to fishing activities, doubling the population.

23 'Kattan, Alberto E. y otro v. Gobierno nacional (Poder Ejecutivo)', (La Ley, t-1983 – D, 576).

8. Getting to Know our Home[24]

> *'Young people must be given banners.'* JOSE INGENIEROS (Argentinian philosopher)

8.1 Objective

The course, 'Getting to Know our Home' intends to introduce the children of Puerto Deseado to the history, geography and wildlife of the place they are living in, by giving them nautical sports experiences. There is a particular focus on making the course accessible – through sports – to underprivileged and socially disadvantaged children, because only in this way can the need for a clean environment be fully integrated into the community's identity. The commitment to defend the environment becomes deeper if we add to a general knowledge of it some notions of its geography (a space dimension) and history (a time dimension) in order to get an interrelated and integrated knowledge.

Every house has its own history and is able to give interesting answers when asked: Who built it? How was it built? Who were the first owners? The rooms in every house have their particular place – as the geography of the house – and it is difficult for the inhabitant of the house to get lost in there. Every house also has something to embellish it: photographs and pictures hanging on the walls, different flowers, souvenirs; each little thing has its own meaning. So, at the beginning of the course, the children are asked to search for these things in their own houses, and are encouraged to ask their parents, grandparents and the elderly people of the neighbourhood.

In the same way our region has its particular history, from its geological conformation to the first inhabitants, the European explorers and the founders of the town. The islands, channels, bays and creeks are the 'rooms' of the house: its geography. The birds, the sea lions, and the dolphins, are some of the things that embellish it.

We tell the students that it would be embarrassing if a foreigner came to our own house and we were not able to explain to him where the kitchen or the living room is, nor the meaning of the photographs. The same would happen if a foreigner came to our town and he explained to us about the location and names of the islands and where the penguins are nesting.

---

24 The course, 'Getting to Know our Home', has been supported by the Fundacion Patagonia Natural (FPN), Fundacion Vida Silvestre Argentina (FVSA) and CADACE (Caleta Olivia), as well as municipal, provincial and national organisations. The course has received an annual scholarship Alparamis, consisting of a one-week visit to a nature reserve in El Bagual, in the province of Formosa. Two adolescent assistants and a teacher participate in this experience, guided by a biologist. They also deliver letters from the children of Puerto Deseado to the children of Formosa and vice versa, and give lectures about the course in different schools of that province.

A foundation consisting of three supports – geography, history and environment - is stronger than one with a sole support, and the 'feeling of belonging' developed through the courses has proved to be the best defence against attacks on nature.

One important aspect of environmental education is to teach the students to be brave in standing up for their rights.[25] Children and young people take part in cleaning beaches, recovering birds covered with oil, and assisting scientists in their fieldwork. With their kayaks, they directly control fuel spillage and waste being thrown into the local river and can submit the pertinent reports. In that way they discover the need for environmental law and the need for its enforcement.

Learning about their own place has proved to be an excellent 'enthusiasm alarm clock'. The children start to be proud of their 'big house', *the knowledge of which is none other than the etymological meaning of the word 'ecology', from Classical Greek,* oikos (*house*) and logos (*study*). Soon, many of them begin to co-operate with the teaching as instructor assistants. They become aware that their effort is being valued by other children and by the local community. Regularly this feeling makes the younger ones re-evaluate themselves improving their self-esteem, replacing – in some cases – their own lack of family help and social skills.[26]

At the same time it is intended to fill children's free time with enriching sport activities, which they enjoy during their time in getting to know their home. There is acceptance of a controlled risk practising nautical sports in cold water, strong sea currents and sometimes violent winds while developing children's self assurance, and fostering their desire for adventure. Many authors think that risk and adventure are natural and positive human inclinations that have made humanity advance.[27]

Since 1983 the practical part of the course has been given gratis to about a hundred and twenty boys and girls per year, and the theoretical part was given to ten-year-old pupils in primary schools. Delegations of other schools of the province have also participated in the practical lessons. It has helped many of them to improve their confidence and self-esteem, to respect themselves, people and nature, to appreciate their history and their culture, to acquire valuable physical skills and to become good citizens interested in community problems and in participating actively in its solutions. This voluntary work for the benefit of the community awakens

25 Peter Mencke-Glucker, Former Head of Germany's Environmental Agency. 'Dialogos con lideres de politica ambiental', Fundacion Ambiente y Recursos Naturales (FARN), Buenos Aires.

26 'Society – Crime Prevention – A fighting chance', *The Guardian*, 16 August 1997.

27 F. Furedi, *Culture of Fear* (London: Cassell, 1997) and D. Morris, *The Naked Ape, Trilogy* (London: Jonathan Cape, 1994).

and strengthens their wish to be citizens who participate actively, and encourages the development of young leaders in the field of environmental conservation. The school's *leitmotiv* is 'respect and love'.

8.2 Development

This course, given by the local nautical club, takes advantage of Puerto Deseado's favourable geographic situation, as well as its fascinating history and rich wildlife.

8.2.1 What is in a name?

Our course starts with the explanation of the name 'Patagonia'. The name was given by Magellan's 1520 expedition after the indigenous people that they called 'Patagones'. The most common theory about the name's origin suggests that the Spanish crew saw big footprints in the sand and thought that they belonged to a people with big feet. The word 'pata' in the Spanish language means animal's foot, and its 'increased' form could be 'patagon'. It is probable that the sand marks had been big because the natives used to wear fur shoes filled with a kind of grass.

However another answer mentions that the word 'patagon' does not exist in the Spanish, Portuguese, and Italian languages, the mother tongue languages of Magellan's crew. The European average height was about 1.60 metres in the sixteenth century, while the Tehuelche's was about 1.85 metres, which means that there were many natives of two metres height. In those times, without radio and television, chivalry novels were very popular, even among illiterate people who used to gather in public places to listen to the stories told in a loud voice by rambling 'lecturers'. There was a well-known novel in Magellan's time: its hero was a giant appropriately named 'Patagon'.

In the same way, since we live on the shore of a ria, we must know what ria means. The word 'ria' defines a dried river bed occupied by the sea. The Ria Deseado is unique in South America. The sea comes 45 km into the land, occupying the place left by the old Ria Deseado, approximately twenty-five thousand years ago. The rocks of the cliffs date back to the Jurassic period, 168 million years ago. Taking into consideration the richness of its wildlife, it was declared a Provincial Natural Reserve in 1967.

The kayak classes are open to children aged 5 and up. The only exception was Emanuel, the youngest pupil, 3 years old. His father used to tie his kayak with a rope to his own boat. In this practical part the children are taught how to put on a lifejacket, how to get in a kayak, and how to grasp the paddle. Once on the water, the Ria Deseado is transformed into a big classroom and it is used as a *sui generis* educational natural reserve. Children with more experience help the younger ones. Boys and girls have a very important role in the teaching and surveillance of the children: in this way a bond is formed.

8.2.2 Respect and tradition

From the very beginning of the course it is intended to teach respect and gratitude towards elderly people. One example is the case of Dr Mateo Tafra, an old fisherman who used to teach the children to swim. He, as well as other elderly citizens, have been interviewed by the pupils and asked about the origin of local names (such as the *Muelle de Ramón*) and about the life of the pioneers. 'The ability to give and accept praise is fundamental to relationships'.[28]

The importance of knowing and respecting older people leads us to speak about the real owners of the land, the indigenous, tall and strong people. In Southern Patagonia, the Tehuelche or Aonikenk tribe lived in Santa Cruz, and their 'cousins' the Ona or Selknam lived on Tierra del Fuego Island. On Tierra del Fuego, the Yámanas tribes used to paddle in canoes made of bark trees. They spent most of their lives hunting and travelling in canoes, maintaining a fire inside it. The canoe was considered the woman's property.

Ushuaia, the capital of the province of Tierra del Fuego, is the place where a British missionary called Thomas Bridges settled in 1870. Ushuaia was the first European settlement on Tierra del Fuego, and Bridges' son, Lucas, was the first white man born on the island. Unfortunately, greed, transmitted illnesses, and the deep sadness for the loss of their culture wiped out the indigenous people. Nowadays, only a very few remain. One of them, a Yamana descendant, is Ursula Calderon, who lives on Navarino Island and has the sad privilege of having her photograph in the Patagonian Exhibition at the Museum of Mankind, even though she is still alive.

Some indigenous words are taught in order to transmit to the pupils a great respect for those almost extinct cultures. Hence the pupils who have native ancestors can become proud of that instead of trying to hide it.

8.2.3 History and song

Another aspect of the course is the possibility of meeting famous seamen such as Marcel Bardiaux, a Frenchman, who visited the port sailing on his own. It was his third time sailing around the world at 78 years old. Almost all the greatest sailors of the sixteenth, seventeenth and eighteenth centuries

---

28 Marianne Talbot. 'Brasenose College – Oxford', *The Guardian*, 18 August 1997.

entered into the natural port of Ria Deseado. For example, the Dutch expedition of Lemaire and Schouten, which is credited with the discovery of Cape Horn, arrived in 1616. Some engraving works present particulars of the geography: events of their stay as well as their interaction with the wildlife.

The richness of Puerto Deseado's history also appears with the remains of H.M.S. *Swift*, a British warship which sank near the coast in 1770. Members of the Club Nautico discovered the wreckage in 1982. The pieces recovered from the ship were donated to the community and in this way the museum of the town was established. Owing to these traditions, learning and singing sea-shanties are encouraged in the course. According to Susan Digby, regular singing raises self-esteem, improves behaviour and learning standards, facilitates communication and makes students calmer and more focused.[29] Sailing and marine games, like tug of war, are practised, as well as races in different towns in Patagonia. These activities allow children to visit different places and to share experiences with other children.

Gradually the children get the opportunity to live closely with nature and 'touch' its geography, as in the case of a natural monument on the front coast of the town, called Piedra Toba, formerly known as Tower Rock. Charles Darwin named it Britannia Rock in 1833 and to the Tehuelches it was known as Okl Shon (Eagleman).

8.2.4 The wildlife of the ria

Slowly the young paddlers become acquainted with wildlife, which encourages their curiosity and makes them wish to learn more. The students can approach the white cliffs where cormorants nest and have a close look at the grey one – also called the Red-Legged Cormorant – an uncommon species in Patagonia, which came from the Pacific Ocean area 15,000 years ago, during the last glacial period. The children can play with sea lions, as well as Austral and Commerson dolphins in their kayaks. (A French scientist of Bouganville's expedition (1764) classified the latter marine mammals.) The children uncover the rich fauna that surrounds them and develop a feeling of respect: the possibility of meeting Patagonian penguins during the first little expeditions allows us to show how the local wildlife, history and geography can be looked at in an integrated way.

Penguins apparently received their name after the Welsh word, 'Pen gwyn', which resembled a similar seabird of the Northern hemisphere, spotted by Drake's or Cavendish's crew.[30] Magellan, in March 1520, was the first to see them, probably in Puerto Deseado, as this species concludes its emigration to the north here in April.

---

29 *The Guardian*, 20 August 1998. (Concerning Susan Digby, who founded the Voices Foundation).

30 Merriam Webster *Collegiate Dictionary*, 10th edn.

Learning about penguins provides an example of how we can also learn about history and geography. They received their name from the Magellan expedition and the main colony on the *ria* is on Chaffers Island (named after the officer of the Fitz Roy expedition, helmsman of the *Beagle*'s boat which transported Charles Darwin to the interior of the *ria*). This island is located on the entrance to the *ria*. These penguins also nest in many islands inside the Ria Deseado; sometimes the pupils visit those places while collaborating with biologists in their field work. In addition, the variety of avifauna shows us three kinds of tern nesting in the area, and nature teaches us about their survival system as the camouflaged colour of the chicks lets them blend into the ground.

Similar to the study of penguins, viewing fur seals leads us through tragic history, namely unjust episodes of indiscriminate killings. Hundreds of thousands of fur seals used to breed on the Patagonian coast. This marine mammal species' skin has two layers of hair, one longer than the other. In 1750 the Chinese discovered a method to get rid of the longer one, getting a clean and soft-haired skin. Once the British and later the Americans 'borrowed' the method, a terrible slaughter of fur seals began. Cabo Blanco (White Cape), near Puerto Deseado, with only 500 animals, is the only continental fur seal colony that remains in Argentina. (There are others, but only on islands.) The species was almost exterminated in Tierra del Fuego. Archaeologists consider this one of the reasons that contributed to the Yámanas tribe extinction – the fur seals, with their high calorie meat, were the main ingredient of their diet.[31]

8.2.5 The course and expeditions

The above-mentioned ideas are presented once a week in one-hour-long lessons at primary school. The lessons are taken by adolescents who have previously studied the subjects. They are helped in this work by the support and training of visiting scientists, environmentalists and members of NGOs. The classes run from August to December.

This activity creates in these adolescents a strong commitment and a responsibility towards the preservation of nature. Meanwhile, in giving part of their free time to the community, their sense of solidarity is strengthened. The pupils (aged about ten years old) see the adolescents as closer in age than an ordinary teacher, and this awakens in them the desire to teach in the not very distant future, perhaps in the same classroom.

Co-operation with scientists is likewise part of the learning. Thus members of the club helped a cetologist working on an Austral Dolphin

---

31 A. Schiavini and E. Piana, *Revista Ciencia Hoy* (Buenos Aires – Argentina).

accidentally captured by a fishing ship's net. Events like this result in constructive dialogue about economic activities and wildlife interaction.

Concerning kayaks, it must be stressed that the safety measures are very strict. The children learn how to do the Eskimo roll. When a kayak capsizes there is a body movement – invented by the Inuits – that allows them to turn the boat up. The more that the experience of kayak navigation grows, the further their expeditions go. Camping in the interior of the *ria* are first steps. The difficult art of living together under uncomfortable conditions and the spirit of collaboration are practised. The interior part of the *ria* offers a good chance to advance in long distance trip learning. (Darwin, using a little boat, explored this area. Conrad Martens, Fitz Roy's expedition artist, drew this landscape.)

Penguin Island, seventeen marine miles off Puerto Deseado, represents an additional step. Here Drake, Cavendish and other seamen took a large amount of penguins to feed their crews. More than twenty thousand Magellan Penguins nest on its surface. But they are not alone – a little Rock Hopper Penguin colony of about five hundred seabirds is also nesting in a small gap in the rocks. Apparently this group – discovered in 1985 in a sea kayak trip – has only recently been set up and would have come from the main colony of Malvinas/Falklands Islands where the number of birds of this species has plummeted to only one-third during the last fifty years; probably due to overfishing. Sometimes it is possible to find a 'cousin' among them, known as the Maccaroni Penguin.

Isla Chata (Flat Island) is located in front of Penguin Island. The biggest colony of Imperial Cormorants in Argentina lives there. Its excrement – called 'guano'– is used as soil fertiliser and had a great price at the end of last century. The War of the Pacific pitted Chile against Bolivia and Peru, mainly due to guano property problems.

Penguins and cormorants share a common natural enemy: the voracious grey gull. Numbers of grey gulls, as well as of other seagull common species, have notably grown in the last years because they easily find their food in the fisheries' waste.[32] Taking into account that the gulls prey on eggs as well as penguin and cormorant chicks, this may upset the ecological balance and may damage the regional biodiversity. *National Geographic Magazine* has reported that seagulls, in eating parasites from right whales' backs, are injuring these marine mammals. But the most dangerous foe of wildlife continues to be the human species.

32 P. Gandini and E. Frere, personal report (on file with author).

8.2.6 Pollution

Waste, besides being visually offensive, can also kill sea lions and dolphins. The former, when playing, may accidentally put their head into the aluminium ring used to seal fish packages, which ends up asphyxiating them, while the latter may eat plastic bags. Oil spills usually coming from ships erode the natural resources of seabirds. The seabirds become cold because their feathers soak, so they are forced to leave the water; they cannot eat, and become weaker until they die. Sometimes oil-stained penguins are poisoned to death in their attempt to rid the oil with their beaks.

From kindergarten age, the children are told about this problem and shown how to clean an oiled penguin. The relationship between the vegetal covering and penguins' life is also explained. This theme introduces us into the desertification problem.

Direct contact with nature and the special knowledge of the place where they live encourages the children to defend wildlife. They work cleaning the shore, denounce and protest against untreated sewage, rubbish from ships, and oil spills from beached or sunken ships.

8.2.7 The feedback

The sports content of the course is also taken into account. One of the members of the Club was three times an Argentine White Water champion and had the chance of participating in two World Championships, in Europe and the United States of America.

The last part of the course comprises long distance expeditions, following not only a sporting interest, but also a cultural one. During the expeditions, observations and reports about nature, history and geography are written and given to universities, museums, libraries and NGOs. Wildlife, places and experiences are photographed, sometimes filmed and always shown to the children; in that way the long distance adventures are the feedback of the course.

The coastline of Santa Cruz Province (1,200 km, approximately) was travelled in a two-summer season. During this occasion Piedra Buena's house on the Santa Cruz river is visited. He was the first Argentine to live in that province, defending the Tehuelches, risking his sailing boat and his life, making many extremely difficult rescues in high seas, and facing strong winds in a very hostile environment. After reaching Punta Dungeness in the south of the province, the oriental mouth of Magellan Strait was paddled from Santa Cruz to Tierra del Fuego. Expeditions have been made also in the Andes. In Lake General Carreras, Chile, kayak classes were given to the children in Chile Chico town.

The Staten Island expedition, called Chuanisin from the aboriginal name, gave the author and the other members of the group the possibility of visiting the remains of the lighthouse in the uttermost part of the world, which inspired one of Jules Verne's novels. Kayaking is the method used to explore the Ria Deseado. A group of adolescents, who had previously acquired basic knowledge of local archaeology in order to make a report about the area, walk along the river.

The course honours its children's projects and is proud of the respect towards nature that the children have acquired. The course strives to meet the ideal of the German poet, Conradin Kreutzer: 'Man is like a flower, the more he digs his roots into the ground, the more he reaches up to the sky.'

Part III

Right of the child to a clean environment: the role of international organisations and non-governmental organisations (NGOs)

8 The susceptible child – does the child have a right to a healthy and a safe environment?

MARIE LOUISE BISTRUP

1. Childwatch International

In 1993, Childwatch International emerged from a process of informal consultation between child researchers from different parts of the world. With a variety of disciplinary backgrounds and thematic interests, they represented a broad spectrum of academic and research institutions. The researchers shared a desire for regular contact and collaboration. They wanted a good overview of research activities within the respective disciplines, to exchange information and to initiate new projects in areas of common concern. One common concern was the possible implications of the United Nations Convention on the Rights of the Child on their research. The Convention on the Rights of the Child provides a common platform for discussing how research could benefit children and support the implementation of the Convention.

The establishment of Childwatch International coincided with an increasing demand for knowledge and information on the situation of children and children's rights raised by those involved in the practical implementation of the Convention on the Rights of the Child. Governments, intergovernmental organisations and non-governmental organisations were looking for contributions from the research community. Childwatch International aims at playing a role in facilitating this dialogue between researchers, policy-makers and practitioners. Childwatch International works with UNICEF and various non-governmental institutions. The Committee on the Rights of the Child has also approached Childwatch to request more research related to monitoring children's rights.

Childwatch International defines itself as a response of the international research community to the challenges posed by Convention on the Rights of the Child and other efforts to improve the situation of children. In addition to alerting researchers to issues related to the implementation of the Convention on the Rights of the Child, the network is encouraging researchers to address policy-makers and decision-makers at the global and national levels with the outcome of their research.

2. The Network

The research network now has a core of about 30 institutions world-wide that work together to establish Childwatch International as a tool for their international co-operation. In September 1996, the directors of these institutions met in Charleston, South Carolina, USA, to review their further collaboration and to discuss new projects, particularly with a view to support capacity enhancing within child research. The network has a small secretariat based at the University of Oslo in Norway that serves as the co-ordinator for dialogue, co-operation and various activities.

2.1 Objectives

Childwatch defines its objectives as follows:

- to promote an interdisciplinary approach to child research and a broader understanding of children;
- to promote effective dissemination of the results from child research to the general public;
- to encourage and support a dialogue between researchers and decision-makers on the development of strategies for the implementation of the Convention on the Rights of the Child and other international agreements concerning child welfare;
- to identify new issues to be included in the global agenda for child research and initiate projects to address them; and
- to support capacity-building and capacity-strengthening within child research, especially in countries in the process of developing child research.

2.2 Activities

Since its inception, Childwatch International has explored a variety of ways to promote the network and to gain experience. Activities initiated by Childwatch International include: research projects, such as indicators for children's rights in an effort to identify existing data that can be used in monitoring implementation of the Convention and in testing its applicability in selected countries; identifying new research areas or defining new approaches to old ones, in the areas of children and environment, child labour and child work, and street children; facilitating and assisting activities to develop and strengthen research capacity in areas relevant to children's development and well-being; and taking advantage of the Internet and other electronic communication tools, to develop effective information exchange and interaction between researchers and research institutions, and to create databases on ongoing child research.

Childwatch activities are carried out and co-ordinated in co-operation between the key institutions and their partners and the secretariat. The development of States Parties to undertake to promote and encourage international co-operation with a view to achieving progressively the full realisation of the right recognised in the present article. In this regard, particular account shall be taken to the needs of developing countries. Article 24 as follows is thus interpreted: States Parties, and all sectors of society and international co-operation shall promote the rights recognised above. Without protection from environmental harms Article 24, section 1 cannot be fully implemented. This is interpreted to mean that the child has the right to protection from hazards and risks from environmental pollution and has the right to hygiene and environmental sanitation. These statements make it plausible to look at the relationship between child's health and environmental pollution and protection from the perspective of the rights of the child.

The Convention Part II, Article 42 acknowledges the rights of the child and its caregivers to know about the rights in the Convention on the Rights of the Child. The Article provides, 'States Parties undertake to make the principles and provisions of the Convention widely known, by appropriate and active means, to adults and children alike'.

2.3 Forms of environmental pollution

Environmental pollution comes in many forms:

- visible and invisible;
- local, regional, national and global;
- chemical and organic;
- tangible and intangible;
- tangible, such as particles, pollution or waste;
- intangible, such as non-odoriferous chemical pollution or chemicals hidden in goods and products; and
- other forms and combinations.

The child does not feel, see, smell or perceive all forms of environmental pollution; the child has relatively few ideas about and means of preventing exposure from environmental contaminants. The child is thus a victim of environmental pollution in the sense that she or he depends on adult activities to prevent exposure to environmental contaminants and to ameliorate harm.

Where does the environmental pollution come from? Environmental pollution originates:

- as a result of actions by individual people, such as pollution in the street;
- as a result of industry: for example, emission of poisonous gases as waste material from production;
- as a result of public activities; and
- from other forms and combinations.

The child cannot control the mechanisms that produce environmental pollution and generally has little or no knowledge about them. The child depends on adults to provide protection from harms from the environment.

In the context of environmental justice children are vulnerable and potential victims.[1] Children have the capacity to become actors and there are examples of young people and children having become environmental activists. As the environmental justice movement is growing probably more young people will be involved in fighting health threatening and hazardous environments. The Growing Up in Cities projects, supported by UNESCO and Childwatch, is an action research project with research teams in eight countries and with a focus on children's participation in urban planning. This project gives attention to urban policy development through young people's own presentation and evaluation of their community environment and development of strategies and proposals for improvement.

2.4 Who is responsible for environmental protection?

Environmental pollution is recognised as an area of common societal concern in almost all countries. Reactions to environmental pollution comprise two main approaches. First, a public approach carried out by ministries, agencies, international institutions and other bodies in the framework of environmental protection and planning. Second, a private approach is carried out by concerned citizens: for example, by using new cleaner technology in industry and by environmental interest groups such as Greenpeace, in the framework of protests, appeals to the public, horror

---

1 See Sharon Stephens, 'Reflections on Environmental Justice: Children as Victims and Actors', *Social Justice*, 23 (1997).

stories, etc. In addition to these two modes come all kinds of variations and the fact, that increasingly, young people and children are becoming environmental activists.

In the best of circumstances, reactions to environmental pollution appear in a dialogue and co-operation between everyone engaged in this matter. National ministries and intergovernmental organisations establish standards for environmental protection. The European Union, for example, sets limit values for the emission of various chemicals. A limit value can be changed over the years, sometimes because research has produced evidence of the harmful effects of that chemical and policy-makers take note of this research. Policy decisions on so-called acceptable values for environmental pollution, including chemical emission, are based on findings and research on the effects of the substance on the body of adults. The characteristics of a statistical average adult body – most often of a man – do not represent the characteristics of the child body and its sensitive development.

2.5 The susceptible child

Children are more sensitive to environmental pollution than adults. Children's development and behaviour differ from the adults. Children eat and drink more per unit of body weight and breathe more air per unit of body weight. Children grow rapidly – especially in some periods of their development.

According to the US Environmental Protection Agency, more than 75,000 new chemicals have been released within the last fifty years. This comprises an enormous pressure on the environment and subsequently on human health. Testing and assessing the environmental effects on children of 75,000 chemicals and possible co-variations, synergistic and additive effects of all 75,000 chemicals seems like an insurmountable task. A more feasible strategy is to reduce emission.

Most environmental legislation is based on findings on how environmental contaminants react in adults. When international or national organisations establish limit values for environmental emissions of a product, the child's special susceptibility is seldom taken into account.

The following are some of the health challenges

- Asthma deaths among children and young people have increased tremendously in the last decade. Asthma is now the leading cause of hospital admission for children.
- Children exposed to tobacco smoke at home have 16 million more days of restricted activity, 10 million more days of bed confinement, and miss 7 million more school days each year than do other children.

- Lead poisoning affects as many as several million children age 5 years and under.
- Millions of children under the age of 12 live within 7 km of a toxic waste dump or live on a waste dump.
- Polluted waters can affect children when they have contact with rivers or lakes and when they eat certain freshwater fish.
- Children may face developmental effects from problems such as the potential effects on the endocrine system from pesticides and other chemicals.
- Children are more at risk from toxins because their systems are still developing and because they consume more food and fluids than adults do relative to their body size.
- Children have unique behaviour, which causes more exposure to pollutants and related health risks.

2.6 Lead is still a threat

Lead in gasoline is one example in which children's susceptibility has been taken into consideration. In Europe, Canada and the United States, lead has been removed from gasoline because of evidence of harmful effects on child health. But lead comes in many other forms. Lead is found in paint, in crayons, modelling clay and painted toys. Children do not have to eat paint to absorb it. If children fuddle with the paint and the painted material, they can get lead particles on the fingers and perhaps suck their fingers.

Lead is believed to affect a child's ability to concentrate and learn. At a lead concentration of 10 mg per 100 ml of blood, development is disturbed. In tests in the United States, the IQ of children is reduced by approximately 5 percentage points if the concentration of lead increases from 10 to 20 mg per 100 ml of blood 3.

2.7 Initiatives on the relation between the susceptible child and environmental health

Within the last two years important initiatives have put the susceptible child on the agenda. In the United States, the 1st National Research Conference on Children's Environmental Health was held on 21–23 February 1997, organised by the Children's Environmental Health Network. The conference focused on research, practice, prevention and policy. The purpose of the network is to protect the environmental health of children. On 5–6 May 1997, the Declaration on Children's Environmental Health was adopted. The declaration affirms the priority of children's environmental health in bilateral and multilateral agendas. Leaders agree to co-operate on environmental research, risk assessment and standard setting, and point to the need to promote research to understand the particular exposures and sensitivities of infants and children to environmental hazards and to exchange research results and information on regulatory decisions.

A major study based on regional studies was presented at the National Symposium entitled What on Earth?: Environmental Contaminants and the Implications for Child Health, 25–27 May 1997 in Ottawa, Canada.

On 3 September 1997, the US Environmental Protection Agency and the Human Health Services moved to establish the first federal research centres to protect children's health. An Office of Children's Health Protection was established building on the National Agenda to Protect Children's Health from Environmental Threats, September 1996. 'We must meet the challenge of protecting our children from toxins in our environment', said Carol Browner, Administrator of the US Environmental Protection Agency at the opening of the Office. 'An awareness of children's unique susceptibility and exposure to toxic threats must guide every action we take to protect public health and the environment.'

2.8 Proposal for a European research and information network on environment and child health

The initiatives in North America serve as an inspiration for developing that kind of awareness of children's susceptibility in Europe. The ideas and proposal for a European network has been debated between researchers and child rights advocates.

Research into policies on and promotion of the relationship between children's health and environmental health are needed to promote environmentally healthy and child-friendly neighbourhoods. The role of an network on environment and child health could be to co-ordinate and consolidate existing research and to initiate new research, to influence policy.

A wide array of children's health problems can be brought on by environmental risks. The formation of a European Network on Environment and Child Health can be an approach to providing children with stronger health protection. Creating European sister networks that can co-operate with networks already established in the United States and in Canada and with other regional networks can initiate a world-wide platform to deal with health issues of children associated with shared and transboundary environmental influences.

2.9 *Mission*

In order to get started and function effectively, the network would be led by a co-ordination committee. Possible activities in the network:

- to identify and bring the users into the process;
- to identify supporters of the co-ordination group;
- to build a platform of multi-disciplinary knowledge, identify experts and existing research;
- to participate in and organise expert meetings;
- to identify major research themes and gaps in the research;
- to identify children's special vulnerability;
- to identify the most dangerous environmental contaminants;
- to examine the role of lead;
- to summarise the results of studies on the effects of environmental contamination on children;
- to identify the major hazardous effects of environmental contamination on children;
- to develop a greater awareness among health professionals about children's health and the environment;
- to elevate public awareness of environmental hazards to children;
- to prepare information sheets;
- to identify opportunities to minimise childhood exposure to environmental contaminants;
- to initiate policy review and future directions in research in the field of children's environmental health;
- to promote activities that enhance all of the above goals.

3. Current Activities of Childwatch International

Childwatch International was represented at the National Symposium on Environmental Contaminants and the Implications for Child Health, 25–27 May 1997 in Ottawa, Canada, and was further inspiration to develop future activities.[2]

Childwatch co-operates with the Dutch Association of Environmental Medicine and the International Society of Doctors for the Environment. With the Dutch Association of Environmental Medicine Childwatch is preparing the establishment of a European research and

2 What on Earth? A National Symposium on Environmental Contaminants and the Implications for Child Health, 25–27 May 1997, Ottawa, Canada, Canadian Institute for Child Health, 1997.

information network on environment and child health, along the lines mentioned above.

4. Conclusion

Children need the respect and autonomy that are granted by the Convention on the Rights of the Child. Children need protection from environmental hazards. Policies that reflect this vulnerability are needed. Research on children's special susceptibility to environmental exposure is needed. A European research and information network can become a vehicle for this movement.

It is important to appreciate the different kind of environmental problems that affect children in the world. The problems of children in newly industrialised countries are different from those in industrialised countries or of those in developing countries. A variety of problems related to the environment and child health are best dealt with at the regional level, and other environmental problems are global and are best dealt with by international co-operation. An expanded goal is to establish a world-wide network and to assist regions in establishing related networks.

9 Children and the right to grow up in an environment supporting their health and well-being: A sound environment, provided for and encapsulated in the Convention on the Rights of the Child

MAAIKE JANSEN M.SC.[1]

1. Introduction

'We will work for common measures for the protection of the environment, at all levels, so that children can enjoy a safer and healthier future... There can be no task nobler than giving every child a better future.' (World Declaration on the Survival, Protection and Development of Children, World Summit for Children 1990.)

Deteriorating environmental conditions have their most profound impact on infants and children. All children are exposed, from the prenatal phase, to a barrage of environmental threats to their health and survival. It costs millions of children their lives, and impedes the growth and progress of countless others. The state of the environment is a key determinant of foetal growth, whether a child survives the first year of life, and their further physical and mental development. Growing children are particularly vulnerable, as their physical characteristics, childhood activities and natural curiosity, put them at greater risk from environmental hazards.[2] Furthermore, environmental pollution and resource degradation are among the underlying causes of poverty, malnutrition, population growth and

1 The views expressed are the author's, and do not necessarily reflect the views of UNEP or UNICEF. The author wishes to thank Sabine Hoefnagel and Aiko Bode for their valuable comments.

2 Disabled children are even more vulnerable, for environmental threats are both disabling and can make disabilities more serious.

deterioration in livelihoods, of which the ramifications are most severely manifested on children, especially those living in ecologically vulnerable areas. In this context, it may be contended that an environment which is supportive of child health and well-being is one that is free from major health hazards and is conducive to healthy living, free from disease and pollution, and one that is ecologically in balance.[3]

Every child has the right to grow in an environment which is supportive of their health and well-being. This right is not stipulated in any specific provision of the Convention on the Rights of the Child, the most widely ratified human rights treaty, in fact such an explicit right is conspicuously absent. How is it then possible to contend that such a right is provided for and encapsulated in the Convention? In the first instance, it is important to recognise that many of the legal obligations and moral aspirations encapsulated in the Convention, not least the right to life itself and the right to the highest attainable standard of health, are, in their word and spirit, dependent on the provision of a sound and safe physical environment, as well as on the fulfilment of the wider goals of sustainable development. Furthermore, as noted in the *UN Manual on Human Rights Reporting Under Six Major International Human Rights Instruments*,[4] the Convention on the Rights of the Child 'pays particular attention to environmental problems and their impact on health. In fact, mention is made of the dangers and risks of environmental pollution for children's health, as well as the importance of information on environmental sanitation as a means of protecting the environment and preventing its degradation.'

In this context, it is necessary to explore the intimate link between the state of the environment in which a child is nurtured, and his or her survival and health; and in turn, to illustrate how these cause-and-effect linkages are allied to specific provisions in the Convention. Subsequently, it is necessary to describe how a growing societal understanding of how environmental degradation affects child health, coupled with a substantial body of scientific evidence in this field, is slowly but surely galvanising the protective measures, which are essential in order for States Parties to be faithful to the commitments made in the Convention. Although, in legal terms it remains a subjective proposition, the evolution of this trend in the area of children's environmental health, means that the right of a child to

3 For more on the concept of a 'supportive environment for health', see *WHO Health and Environment in Sustainable Development: Five Years after the Earth Summit*, WHO, 1997, p. 13.

4 As noted in the section on the Convention on the Rights of the Child, by Marta Santos Pais (Part Two, p. 458), in the *UN Manual on Human Rights Reporting Under Six Major International Human Rights Instruments*, United Nations, Geneva, 1997 (Office of the High Commissioner for Human Rights, UN Institute for Training and Research and the UN Staff College Project).

a supportive, clean environment is slowly entrenching itself, and hence could be considered to represent a derivative, *de facto* child right.

2. Children and Their Environment and Allied Provisions in the Convention on the Rights of the Child

A child has the right to grow in an environment supportive of their health and well-being. This may be distilled by considering, in the context of a child's unique vulnerability to environment threats, the essential meaning and spirit of the various articles of Convention on the Rights of the Child, in particular;

(i) the right to life, survival and development,
(ii) the right to the highest attainable standard of health and the right to an adequate standard of living, as well as,
(iii) a right which also confers duties, namely, that the education of the child shall be directed to development of respect for the natural environment.

2.1 'Every child has the inherent right to life' (Article 6.1, Convention on the Rights of the Child)

The degradation of the environment can pose a fundamental and constant challenge to the child's right to life. The fulfilment of this most basic substantive right, from which all others derive, is dependent on a sound and clean environment. Adverse environmental conditions cause a deterioration in living conditions, which in turn can constitute a threat to life, although not necessarily directly accompanied by death. In most cases, environment-related risks threaten child survival as a contributing and exacerbating causal factor, in the mainly cumulative 'process' of child death (most under-5 deaths are caused by an interplay of a series determinants).

Diarrhoea, largely brought about by a lack of clean water and/or a dirty, unsanitary living environment, causes 19 per cent of 5s deaths.[5] Acute respiratory infections, in many instances caused or intensified by indoor and outdoor air pollution, causes another 19 per cent of global under-5 deaths[6]. Malaria, spread by spiralling mosquito populations that are thriving due to land-use and climate changes, causes another 5 per cent of under-5 deaths.[7] Malnutrition, which intensifies when land is not able to yield

5 *Global Burden of Disease*, World Health Organisation, World Bank and Harvard University, 1996, as adapted and cited in *The Progress of Nations* 1997 UNICEF, p.28.
6 *Ibid.*
7 *Ibid.*

enough food or when vital calories are consumed by doing household chores that are made more difficult due to natural resource degradation, although alone accounting for only 3 per cent of under-5 deaths, plays a contributing role in more than half of all child deaths in developing countries.[8] Climate change which is likely to disturb ecological systems, can cause, *inter alia,* freak weather storms, floods and drought, as well as worsening several existing problems, triggering a host of mainly adverse effects on human health,[9] which can directly threaten a child's life. Moreover, chemical pollutants pumped into the air, water, food and soil can fatally poison children and cause miscarriages.

States Parties to the Convention on the Rights of the Child, are committed to act with a view to ensuring and respecting the right to life, through the adoption of all appropriate measures. These measures should be affirmative and thus designed to protect life, including taking steps to reduce infant mortality (*'States Parties ... shall take appropriate measures to diminish infant and child mortality',* Article 24.2 (a)), combating disease and rehabilitating health, providing adequate nutritious foods and clean drinking water.[10] By further allying this clause to ensuring *'to the maximum extent possible the survival and development of the child'* (Article 6.2), the essential value of States Parties actions is stressed. As such the state and the international community as a whole is bound to strive to enhance child health, including by looking at the often interdependent causal factors. Moving to reduce and ultimately eliminate risks, including the perils posed by an unclean and degraded environment.

2.2 Every child has the right 'to the highest attainable standard of health'
(Article 24.1, Convention on the Rights of the Child)

and

Every child has the right 'to a standard of living adequate for the child's physical, mental and spiritual, moral and social development'
(Article 27.1, Convention on the Rights of the Child)

A sound environment is a vital cornerstone of human, and especially child, health and physical and mental development. Estimates suggest that poor

8 *Ibid.*
9 The main conclusion of the UNEP, World Health Organisation (WHO), World Meteorological Organisation (WMO) study Climate Change and Human Health, 1996.
10 Op cit. n. 4 (Part Two, p. 424).

environmental quality is directly responsible for 25 per cent of all preventable ill-health and indirectly contributes to an additional significant portion of the global burden of disease. Furthermore, as much as two-thirds of preventable illness caused by adverse environmental conditions occurs among children,[11] particularly those living in extreme poverty and fragile ecological areas.

Placed in the environmental context, the right to the highest attainable standard of health, can essentially be interpreted to mean the provision of an environment supportive of child health. An analogous provision deals with the child's development, stipulating that every child has the right to a standard of living adequate for the child's physical and mental development. The Convention on the Rights of the Child outlines that States Parties should pursue the full implementation of the right to the highest attainable standard of health, citing, within the framework of primary health care, the provision of '*clean drinking water, taking into consideration the dangers and risks of environmental pollution*' (Article 24.2 (c)). Thus strategies for fulfilling the right to health, should incorporate the minimisation of environmental risks, as an integral element, at each stage of a child's mental and physical development, including possible threats while in the mother's womb. In this regard, prenatal threats to child health and well-being are also acknowledged in the Convention on the Rights of the Child, stating that '*the child, by reason of his physical and mental immaturity, need special safeguards ... before as well as after birth*' (Preamble).

In this context, it can be contended that child health depends at least as much on the control of root environmental causes of poor health, as on clinical responses to disease. Thus measures to improve the environment may be considered the most fundamental step in preventing child illness and absolutely vital to the attainment of the highest standard of child health. As is stated in Agenda 21:

> Many important communicable diseases remain for which environmental control measures are indispensable, especially in the field of water and sanitation such as cholera, diarrhoea disease, leishmaniasis, malaria and schistosomiasis. In all such instances, the environmental measures, either as an integral part of primary health care or undertaken outside the health sector, form an indispensable component of the overall disease control strategies, together with health and hygiene education and in some instances, are the only component.[12]

---

11 Op cit. n. 3, p.199.

12 Agenda 21, outcome of the UN Conference on Environment and Development (UNCED), Rio de Janeiro, June 1992, Chapter 6 Protecting and Promoting Human Health, para.10.

Preventative environmental health interventions help to combat illness by reducing exposure to adverse environmental conditions and promoting behavioural change. Such interventions fortify purely health-based programmes, and help to reduce burdens on often strained health care systems, as well as lowering treatment costs for diseases which are environmental in origin. Bearing this mind, it is essential to take a holistic approach to health, whereby both prevention and care are placed within the context of environmental policy, supported by effective management systems and plans of action and incorporating targets that reflect local needs and capacities.[13] In this regard, and as pointed out in a report to the United Nations by a Special Rapporteur on human rights and the environment,[14] the right to health can also be constructively viewed from an environmental perspective in the light of the principles of sustainable development embraced by the international community, namely the indivisibility of environmental protection and the development process. As is stated in the Rio Declaration (UNCED, 1992), 'human beings are the centre of concerns for sustainable development and are entitled to a healthy and productive life in harmony with Nature'. Thus, it is recognised that health is an essential prerequisite for sustainable development, as without health it would not be possible to engage in development, combat poverty, and protect and take care of children and the environment.

Child health and development are most seriously challenged by, *inter alia*, the following environment-related problems:

(a) the lack of clean water and environmental sanitation,
(b) environmental pollution, including indoor and outdoor air pollution, and chemicals in food, water and soil,
(c) vector-borne diseases, and
(d) malnutrition.

2.2.1 (a) The lack of clean water and environmental sanitation

The Convention on the Rights of the Child specifically recognises '*the provision of clean drinking water* and *hygiene and environmental sanitation*' (Article 24.2 (c), (e)) as essential for the implementation of the right to the highest attainable standard of health. The lack of access to safe

13 This point is made in the Habitat Agenda, outcome of the UN Conference on Human Settlements (Habitat II, Istanbul, Turkey, June 1996), Section C.5 Environmentally Sustainable, Healthy and Liveable Human Settlements, para. 128.

14 Final report on Human Rights and the Environment for the UN Commission on Human Rights Sub-Commission on the Prevention of Discrimination and Protection of Minorities Review of Further Developments in the Fields with which the Sub-Commission has been Concerned, by Mrs Fatma Zohra Ksentini, Special Rapporteur. E/CN.4/Sub.2/1994/9 (UN ECOSOC), (p.47, para. 184).

water, its pollution and over-exploitation are amongst the most serious environment problems affecting society, with even more serious repercussions for future generations. Rapid population growth, urbanisation, industrialisation and the drive for food security are placing increasing pressure on water quantity and quality. As UNEP's Global Environment Outlook report states 'Every day, 25,000 people die as a result of poor water quality, and water-borne diseases still represent the single largest cause of human sickness and death world-wide ... In addition, an estimated one quarter of the world will suffer from chronic water shortages in the beginning of the next century'. This will be the major impediment to development in many regions.

More than a fifth of people do not have access to safe drinking water and over half of humanity lacks adequate sanitation, with devastating repercussions for child health. Sanitation, hygiene and water supply are essential elements of the basic rights for life and health, and fundamental for development (as was recognised by the UNICEF/WHO Joint Committee on Health Policy). WHO estimates that 90 per cent of diarrhoeal problems result from an 'unhealthy' environment.[15] This strikingly underscores the fact that such debilitating and fatal ailments are largely preventable if a child can grow up in an environment that is supportive of health, with access to clean water, free from biological pathogens, and a clean immediate environment, with adequate environmental sanitation. In this sense, environmental sanitation goes beyond a narrow focus on latrines and personal hygiene to encompass waste management and environmental health issues, behavioural changes, development and mobilisation of community action for environmental management and disease prevention. Unsanitary conditions help spread and exacerbate, *inter alia*, diarrhoea, infectious diseases, AIDS and helminth infections.[16] Urbanisation and the growth of poor urban slums have exacerbated these risks.

2.2.2 (b) Environmental pollution

The Convention on the Rights of the Child explicitly recognises *'the dangers and risks of environmental pollution ...'* (Article 24.2 (c)) in relation to the right to the highest attainable standard of health. Children have rapidly developing nervous, reproductive, immune and respiratory systems, thus they are more sensitive to poisons pumped into water, soil

15 Op cit. n. 3, (pp. 172–175).

16 Helminths, a general term for parasitic worms, afflicts over 2 billion people with debilitating pain. UNICEF estimates that 200 million children aged 5–14 years old are ill due to intestinal worms crawling in their bellies and under their skin.

and air[17]. Their body compositions and behavioural characteristics put them at greater risk from exposure to chemicals and other pollutants, which can disrupt their development and cause irreversible damage. The environment to which a pregnant woman is exposed has marked effects on foetal development. Chemicals shared with babies in the womb and during breastfeeding can interfere with natural chemical messengers that tell infants how to develop. These have been termed 'endocrine disruptors'. Infants are particularly at risk due to the organisational role the endocrine system plays during early stages of life. Research is only beginning to understand how endocrine disruptors can affect the ability to fend off disease, learn, integrate socially and reproduce. However, ultimately they can reduce the potential of each exposed child.

Air pollution predisposes children (who by inhaling more air per unit of body weight than adults, can take in up to twice the pollutants) to viral and bacteria infections of the lungs and respiratory tract. According to WHO, an estimated 60 per cent of severe respiratory infections are associated with 'unhealthy' environments.[18] Indoor air pollution is the most significant air pollution hazard in developing countries and a particularly grave problem in rural areas. It is responsible for about 93 per cent of the three million premature, air pollution attributable, deaths. Indoor air pollution is primarily due to smoke from household (bio-mass and coal) fires trapped in poorly ventilated homes, resulting in exposure levels that are higher than in the most polluted cities. Acute respiratory infections from indoor air pollution are aggravated by poor environmental management, child malnourishment, and a lack of appropriate health care. Women and children, who spend the most time indoors, are the primary victims, including infants who are exposed while resting on their mothers' backs as they tend fires. As acute respiratory infections can not be prevented by immunisation, efforts to reduce them depend on an integrated approach which minimises childhood exposure to air pollutants. It is estimated that if environmental improvements were made to eliminate exposures to severe indoor air pollution in developing countries, 60 per cent of current global acute respiratory infections could be avoided in a genuinely sustainable manner.[19]

Outdoor urban air pollution also has marked effects on the development of the embryo, foetus and child. Epidemiological studies have

17 Chemicals polluting water are linked to industrialisation, run-off from populated areas and intensive agricultural activity (pesticides, and nitrate in fertilisers – which converts into nitrite inducing methemoglobinemia, a reduction in the blood's oxygen carrying capacity). Metals of greatest concern to health are lead and arsenic (an especially acute problem in Bangladesh and East India). Exposure to other metals such as cadmium and mercury is more sporadic. Pesticides and other chemicals (lead and mercury) also contaminate food and soil, bio-accumulating in the food chain, i.e. in fish, which is a main protein source in many (coastal) communities.

18 Op cit. n. 3, (pp.172-175).

19 *Ibid*.

demonstrated a close association between outdoor air pollution and incidences of respiratory infections and pulmonary disease. As a result childhood acute respiratory infection deaths are high even in nations with low infant mortality rates. Pollutants include: sulphur dioxide, nitrogen oxide, carbon monoxide, ozone, lead and suspended particles. The major causes of outdoor air pollution are: rapid urbanisation with increased combustion of fossil fuels, industrial processes, growing car use and congestion (which puts children who live on and around the streets especially at risk), and the use of domestic fuel (i.e., coal and wood).

Lead poisoning is one of the best researched and the single most preventable ailment associated with outdoor air pollution. Growing epidemiological evidence suggests that lead in a child's body, even in small amounts, can cause disturbances in early physical and mental growth, and later in intellectual functioning and academic achievements, hindering the child's ability to reach full potential. Childhood lead poisoning, at low levels can cause: a reduction in IQ and attention span; reading and learning disabilities; hyperactivity and behavioural problems; impaired growth and visual and motor functioning, and hearing loss. At high levels, lead poisoning in children can cause: anaemia, brain, liver, kidney, nerve and stomach diseases, coma, convulsions and death. The effects of lead poisoning on children are long-term and potentially irreversible, and intensified with repeated exposure and accumulation of lead in the body. Experts estimate that children living in cities may suffer as much as a four point IQ loss compared to those living in the suburbs due to lead exposure[20] (cars that rely on leaded gasoline account for up to 95 per cent of airborne lead pollution in developing countries).

Children are also uniquely susceptible to pesticides which, due to their physiological immaturity, behavioural characteristics, and greater exposure, can adversely affect child mental and physical development. Socio-economic, nutritional and health status factors also influence the vulnerability of infants and children to pesticides. Studies have revealed that children are more than twice, even ten times, as sensitive as adults to certain pesticides.[21] Nevertheless, regulations often ignore their special vulnerabilities. Children can be exposed to pesticides from the pre-natal phase. In pregnant women pesticides, that can be readily absorbed through the skin, pass through the placenta and can endanger the foetus. Parental

20 Studies have estimated that in Bangkok, between 30,000 and 70,000 children risked a loss of 4 or more IQ points (The Urban Environment: World Resources 1996-1997 UNEP, UN Development Programme, World Bank, World Resources Institute 1996, p.22). In Cairo, it is estimated that more than 800 infants die annually due to their mother's exposure to lead (World Bank, June 1996).

21 The US National Research Council Pesticides in the Diets of Infants and Children National Research Council Committee on Pesticides in the Diets of Infants and Children, National Academy Press Washington DC, 1993. The report concluded that the relative differences in toxicity between children and adults were about 10-fold (p.3).

exposure to pesticides has been linked to birth defects in their children. Children can be exposed to and accumulate pesticide residues from diverse sources, such as contaminated food, water, soil, and air. Of great concern is that most pesticide residues ingested by mothers find their way into breast-milk. Thus, a significant number of infants may be exposed to higher than tolerable levels of pesticides for a short time.[22]

2.2.3 (c) Vector-borne diseases

Vector-borne diseases, such as malaria, yellow and dengue fever, are also intimately related to environmental causal factors. Human activities, such as water and agricultural development and urbanisation, imperil the natural ecological balance, increasing the incidences, severity and distribution of vector-borne diseases. It is estimated that 90 per cent of the current global malaria burden could be sustainably avoided if environment-related interventions were made.[23] It is estimated that two billion people are at risk from malaria, transmitted by mosquitoes breeding in still standing water, with 100 million affected at any time. With environmental change these immense figures are rising. The brunt of this scourge is borne by children and pregnant women. A child dies from the disease approximately every 30 seconds. Malaria threatens life, and debilitates, causing malnutrition and anaemia, in turn stunting mental and physical growth.

2.2.4 (d) Malnutrition and the environment

In the context of the right to the highest attainable standard of health, the Convention on the Rights of the Child specifically recognises the need to, '*combat disease and malnutrition ... through the provision of adequate nutritious foods ... supported in the use of basic knowledge of child health and nutrition ...* '(Article 24.2 (c), (e)). Child nutrition and the protection of the environment in which a child is nurtured, are closely linked. On the one hand, the environment must be clean to break the conspiracy between malnutrition and infection which pulls children down in a spiral of poor growth and early death. On the other hand, the environment must be able to support adequate and sustained food production for household food security. Foetal development hinges on a mother's nutritional status. Under-nutrition during pregnancy and in early childhood can adversely affect physical and behavioural development. Malnourished children can be listless, not demanding enough stimulation needed for development, which can lead to poor school performance and disadvantages in later adult life.

---

22 However, it must be stressed that the expected negative impacts due to pesticide residues in breast milk are lower than overall benefits derived from breast-feeding practices.

23 Op cit. n.3 (pp. 172–175).

More than three quarters of malnutrition related deaths are linked not to severe malnutrition but to mild and moderate forms. As UNICEF states, these are 'silent emergencies'.

The environment in which a child is raised must be clean to break the synergetic interaction between malnutrition and infection. Disease spreads more easily in an unclean environment, threatening child health and growth. Malnutrition increases chances of infection and infection undermines nutritional status, with devastating consequences for children, for as a result minor illnesses can become life threatening. As UNICEF has pointed out, new research suggests that child growth can be harmed in unhygienic surroundings even before acute infections occur. This is captured in the 'dirty chicken' analogy which holds that a dirty chicken grows poorly.[24] It suggests that the impaired growth of poultry or livestock reared in unsanitary conditions is comparable to what occurs to children in developing countries, namely, early childhood nutritional deficits coupled with an unsanitary environment leading to impaired growth and a failure to maximise genetic potential. For even if a child is not obviously sick, a dirty environment poses a constant threat to the immune system. Nutrients from food which should help a child to grow, instead will be used by the body to support its immune system, thus impairing growth. This forms the basis of the conceptual linking of sanitation to health and growth and in turn to nutrition.

Natural resource degradation and pollution (dwindling forests, encroaching desertification, crippling drought, flooding, salination, and soil eutrophication caused by improper pesticide and fertiliser use) can all threaten food supplies, as they make farming and sustained land use more difficult. When environmental degradation compromises food security, children are most vulnerable. Unsustainable agricultural practices strip soil of nutrients, threatening harvests and spawning malnutrition. Thus it can be contended that increasing child nutritional deprivation is a direct side effect of environmental degradation, including the nutritional deprivation of soils.

Another dramatic manifestation of poverty and environmental degradation on nutritional status and health, is the energy and time spent by women and girls collecting water, fuel and fodder. They often have to walk long distances, a situation aggravated by lack of access to clean water, and deforestation (with the added danger that food will not be well cooked or water not well boiled to kill bacteria, or that food requiring longer cooking is rejected causing nutritional imbalances). A UNICEF sponsored study in Nepal, underscored the critical health implications that

---

24 See UNICEF State of the World Children 1997, Panel 5 'Growth and Sanitation: what can we learn from chickens?' (p.26).

calorie loss due to water collection assumes in light of low socio-economic, nutritional and health status. It was calculated that the extra energy spent consumes up to a third of daily energy intake of already malnourished women and girls, aggravating their poor health and malnutrition. This weak physical state is compounded by energy lost due to anaemia, diarrhoeal disease and worm infections. These factors leave less energy for women to perform essential tasks including: income generation, agricultural activity, child care, breast-feeding, hygiene, food preparation, visits to health centres, education and rest from daily chores. As a consequence, children are affected in terms of their health, development and school attendance.

It is impossible to draw up an exhaustive list of how environmental degradation endangers the right of the child to the highest attainable standard of health, the enjoyment of which is already very much influenced by underdevelopment and poverty. The preceding section is intended to give an illustrative overview. However, it is indisputable that adverse ecological factors can threaten the health, development and well-being of each and every child protected under the Convention on the Rights of the Child, especially those from poor populations, and those that have been displaced due to adverse environmental conditions (environmental refugees).

2.3 *Rights confer duties:*

'States Parties agree that the education of the child shall be directed to... the development of respect for the natural environment.' (Article 29.1(e) Convention on the Rights of the Child)

As eloquently noted in the *UN Manual on Human Rights Reporting Under Six Major International Human Rights Instruments*,[25] in the Convention on the Rights of the Child,[26]

> 'in a very innovative way, a reference is also made to the development of respect for the natural environment. Thus, the Convention clearly shows the close link existing between a healthy environment and the enjoyment of fundamental rights, while indicating the relevance of promoting the preservation and protection of the environment from a very early stage in life. Having stressed, in Article 24, the risks and dangers arising to the child's health from environmental pollution, ... it now emphasises the importance of including the protection of the environment as an essential element within the school curricula'.

It can be asserted that with the right of the child to grow in an environment supportive of his or her health and well-being, there are also

25 *Ibid.*, op. cit. n. 4 (Part Two, p. 458).
26 *Ibid.*, op. cit. n. 4 (Part Two p. 467).

corresponding duties and responsibilities which children have to assume as they mature, namely to preserve the environment for the current and future generations. Inherent in the concept of sustainable development is inter-generational equity, or the duty of present generations to ensure that in using natural resources, they do not compromise the ability of future generations to meet their needs. This concept brings children to the forefront of the environment agenda, with equity between generations involving duties and rights. The Convention on the Rights of the Child explicitly recognises the importance of environmental education and fostering a child's respect for the natural environment. Environmental education through informal and formal channels can enhance the life skills of women and children. It can provide children with appropriate environmental knowledge. It is an investment in children, laying the foundations for sustainability by engendering respect for the world, for human rights and fundamental freedoms, and by preparing them to assume their role and responsibilities. However, it must be stressed that a child's ability to assume stewardship of the earth is a function of them acquiring the rights that would enable them to do so.

3. Beyond the Convention on the Rights of the Child

The weight of increased understanding and scientific evidence in the field of children's environmental health in developing a de facto right of the child to an environment supportive of their health and well-being.

Tracing the influence of environmental effects on human health is still a relatively new science. However, the interdependence between environment and health, and more specifically the need to safeguard children from environmental health threats has been acknowledged at the highest international political level. The *Programme for the Further Implementation of Agenda 21*[27] explicitly recognises that, 'protecting children from environmental health threats and infectious disease is particularly urgent since children are more susceptible than adults to those threats'. This echoes what has been accepted in numerous fora and agreements including: *Agenda 21*,[28] the *Habitat Agenda*,[29] *the Programme*

27 Adopted at the 19th Special Session of the UN General Assembly, New York, June 1997.

28 'The health of children is affected more severely than other population groups by malnutrition and adverse environmental factors' (Chapter 6.19).

29 'The needs of children and youth, particularly with regard to the living environment, have to be taken fully into account.... Parents and other persons legally responsible for children have responsibilities, rights and duties, consistent with the Convention on the Rights of the Child, to address these needs' (Para. 13).

of Action of the World Summit for Social Development,[30] and the 1997 *Declaration of the Environment Leaders of the Eight on Children's Environmental Health,* which was the outcome of a meeting of the G7 countries plus Russia, in Miami, Florida, May 1997. Children's environmental health was the central topic for discussion at that meeting, which also resulted in an annexed paper on *Implementation Actions on Protecting Children's Health and Environment Which the Environment Leaders of the Eight Have Agreed to Promote Within Their Governments and Countries.* The two documents are intended to provide a framework for domestic, bilateral and international efforts to improve the protection of children's health from environmental threats and specify concrete actions that the Eight will undertake to begin the process of incorporating characteristics of infants and children into environmental science, risk assessments and protection regimes. The subsequent *Communiqué of the Denver Summit of the Eight* (June, 1997), taking into account the results of the Miami meeting, declared:

> Protecting the health of our children is a shared fundamental value. Children throughout the world face significant threats to their health from an array of environmental hazards, and we recognise particular vulnerabilities of children to environmental threats. Our governments will explicitly incorporate children into environmental risk assessments and standard setting and together will work to strengthen information exchange, provide for microbiologically safe drinking water, and reduce children's exposure to lead, environmental tobacco smoke and other air pollutants (para. 25).

These declarations made by the international community, can be considered to represent an acknowledged set of fundamental values, which have evolved over the last quarter of a century. In 1972, the Stockholm Declaration made at the UN Conference on the Human Environment, categorically understood that man's environment, both the natural and unnatural, is essential to his well-being and to the enjoyment of basic human rights – even the right to life itself. By definition this applies equally to children. As the UN Special Rapporteur noted in her report on human rights and the environment,[31] the Stockholm Declaration already signified a recognition of the right to a healthy and decent environment, which is inextricably linked both individually and collectively to universally recognised fundamental human rights standards and principles, and which may be demanded as such by their beneficiaries.

30 '... Recognising that improving people's health is inseparably linked to a sound environment' (Para. 35 (g)), UN World Summit for Social Development, Copenhagen, 1995.

31 Op. cit. n. 14 (pp.10–11, para.31).

These links between child health and environment, have also increasingly and repeatedly found reflection in domestic instruments,[32] a measure of the degree to which national policies are consistent with rights defined in the Convention.[33] Although seldom explicitly outlining the right of the child to a clean environment, domestic legislation which supports the fulfilment obligations under the Convention, can in certain incidences be found to refer to a general expression of a right to adequate conditions of life or a healthy environment.[34] Governments in their role as promoter, co-ordinator and facilitator of child rights, are contributing to the ideal of a clean and safe environment, by instigating such legal measures, which can lead to the adoption of certain safeguards. This represents a shift, however subtle, from environmental law to a right to a satisfactory environment.[35]

One concrete example of such domestic measures can be taken from the United States, a country which – along with Somalia – is unique in the fact that it has yet to ratify the Convention on the Rights of the Child.[36] The US Environmental Protection Agency recently established an Office for Children's Health Protection, set up under a Presidential Executive Order in April 1997. It was conceived in recognition of the fact that children are directly and uniquely affected by the environment. One of the aims of the office is to ensure that, on the basis of sound scientific evidence, legal limits and guidelines on exposures to environmental contaminants take into account the unique vulnerability of children, including through multiple exposures.

Such international and domestic efforts, underpinned by a growing body of scientific evidence, are mirrored and spurred by the advocacy efforts made by a myriad of non-governmental organisations and community groups, which are multiplying at an enormous rate. One has only to search for children's environmental health on the Internet, or in the library, to discover the range of organisations dealing with different facets of the field.[37]

Efforts relating to the field of children's environmental health can also be traced throughout the work of the United Nations. UNICEF's mission to contribute to child survival, protection and development, is dependent on

32 For more detailed account of relevant domestic measures, please refer to other chapters in this book.

33 It is important to recognise the differing ways that States Parties regard their obligations under Conventions.

34 For example, the South African Constitution (adopted 27 April 1994) directly states that, 'every person shall have the right to an environment which is not detrimental to his or her health or well-being' (section 29). As cited in, *Ibid.*, op. cit. n. 14 (p.81, Annex III, no.2).

35 The Costa Rican Supreme Court in 1993 affirmed the right to a healthy environment, to live in an environment free from contamination. As cited in *ibid.*, op. cit., n. 14 (p.92, Annex III, C.2).

36 However, it can be contended that nonetheless, the US is bound under international law to respect any agreement signed by US negotiators. Article 18 of the Vienna Convention on the Law of Treaties of 1969 says a State that has signed 'is obligated to refrain from acts which would defeat the object and purpose of a treaty' until 'it shall have made its intention clear not to become a party' (i.e., ratified or not).

37 For example, the US NGO the Children's Environmental Health Network.

a safe physical environment. UNICEF is guided by the Convention on the Rights of the Child, it has been adopted as the central premise of its mission, with a formal recognition that the pursuit of children's rights is a fundamental purpose of the organisation, and that its work is guided by the principles and standards established therein for the overall protection of the child. Its mission statement explicitly states that UNICEF is 'mandated to advocate for the protection of children's rights, to help meet their basic needs and to expand their opportunities to reach their full potential'.[38] As such, UNICEF strives to ensure the provision of an enabling environment for the promotion, appropriation and defence of children's rights, and has accordingly shifted to an integrated and child rights-based programming approach.

This approach implicitly recognises that in the Convention there is a broad scope of substantive articles, but that it is imperative that their essential indivisibility (that they are all equally important and touch every aspect of a child's life) and their interdependence (that they are mutually supportive and complement each other) are respected. Child rights also imply universality, meaning that they apply to everybody equally, imposing the imperative that all children, not just the majority, are reached. With this in mind, it is necessary to have a comprehensive and holistic vision of child rights, going beyond developing sound sectoral policies, to a coherent framework that builds on complementarily and synergy between interventions on behalf of children. Within this approach, environmental issues can be said to permeate and be integral to practically every aspect of UNICEF's sectoral work on health, water and sanitation, nutrition, education, as well as on women, urban and child protection.

Much of UNICEF's work to enable women and children to enjoy, on an equitable basis, their rights, contributes in some way to the realisation of a child's right to an environment supportive of their health and well-being, even through seemingly unrelated efforts (such as reducing illiteracy and girls' education). The acquisition of life skills is a necessary condition for the exercise of child rights. Life skills include, essential basic knowledge on health, nutrition, and environment-related information that affects child well-being. Families have a right to know such basic information, as dangers to the new-born from the environment (and whether they are life-threatening) depend in large measure on how well the family and community can manage them.

More concretely, as a response to UNCED, UNICEF's Executive Board adopted a decision (1993/14) on incorporating the Primary Environmental

38 The mission statement goes on to state that UNICEF 'works with all its partners towards the attainment of the sustainable human development goals adopted by the world community ...' (UNICEF, 1996).

Care (PEC) perspective as an integral part of UNICEF assisted programmes and projects. PEC, is an integrated community-based development approach, comprised of three inter-related elements, namely, meeting basic needs, the empowerment of local communities and ensuring the protection and optimal use of natural resources. The PEC concept was widely discussed during preparations for UNCED, and was envisaged as a strategy to create an environment supportive of health, recognising the need for the participation of every member of the community. UNICEF Executive Board subsequently adopted an analogous decision (1995/22) on water and environmental sanitation (WES) strategies. The WES strategies advance an integrated approach, which stresses the need to enhance linkages with health, environment, education, nutrition and other development programmes, exploiting synergies among all sectors that support child survival, protection and development. A central pillar of the WES strategies is community management of the water environment, within the context of Agenda 21 and PEC, reflecting the growing concern about environmental degradation and a recognition of water's role in the local environment and thus in health and livelihoods.

UNICEF could still profit from an enhanced mainstreaming of environment-related considerations into its programmes and projects, taking incremental measures within existing programmes to manage the local environment as it pertains to the health and development of children and women. There is a need to ameliorate the overall understanding of how environmental factors are integral to and impact UNICEF's work in striving to fulfil the rights of the child. In a basic analysis of the causes of why child rights are not being met, the broader aspects of the problems that women and children face should be covered, and thus by definition should include the environmental situation. Children cannot be seen in isolation from their families, communities and the larger environment in which they live. In many circumstances, the roots of gross poverty and the consequential deprivation in nutrition, health education and other essential human needs suffered by children, are quintessentially linked to environmental degradation. Such an enhancement of environmental considerations is in fact wholly in line with UNICEF's adoption of an 'integrated management of childhood illness' approach, which addresses in a holistic manner, all the maladies to which children are prey.

Recently, UNICEF has enhanced its partnerships in the field on children and the environment, notably through the signing of a Memorandum of Understanding between UNICEF and UNEP in March 1997. The agreement was made in recognition of the need to address the close relationship and interaction between environmental factors and the survival, protection and development of children, and to combine the relative strengths of both organisations in this regard. The ultimate objective is to support programme implementation through the best scientific and environmental information that bears on children and child health, especially at the field level in developing countries. It is essentially a synergistic partnership that extends UNEP's sound environmental policy guidance role to the country level through UNICEF's field network.

The partnership has focused its efforts largely on children's environmental health issues. It has recently published a UNEP-UNICEF booklet on *Childhood Lead Poisoning: Information for Advocacy and Action*, which is intended to be the first in a joint informational series on environmental pollutants and their effects on child health. The second in the series is due to address Childhood Pesticide Poisoning. Such informational and advocacy booklets are aimed at placing basic information on how children are affected by environmental pollutants, in the hands of policy-makers, communities and all those caring for children. Giving in layman's terms an overview of current scientific knowledge, as well as showing various measures that can be taken to combat the effects of such pollutants on child health, at the local, national and regional/international levels. Such information is very important to bring official and public attention to previously neglected areas. Child rights strengthen the role of such advocacy efforts, as they engender a heightened a sense of obligation and commitment and allow the engagement of a wide stake holdership. In this sense, the full power of the Convention on the Rights of the Child can and should be exploited through such advocacy efforts.

This is by no means an exhaustive list of initiatives in the field of children's environmental health, but is intended to illustrate the understanding that has developed and thus the momentum that is being generated to develop, what may be considered as a *de facto* right of the child to grow up in an environment that supports the fulfilment of their basic rights to life and health, as stipulated in the Convention on the Rights of the Child.

4. Conclusion

The Convention on the Rights of the Child is a groundbreaking piece of human rights legislation, it represents an internationally agreed set of legal and ethical standards. States Parties to the Convention have a legal and moral obligation to advance the cause of child rights, for as stated in Article 2, States Parties have committed themselves to *'respect and ensure the rights set forth in the Convention'*. This means that they should refrain from any acts that would prevent the fulfilment of child rights, while simultaneously working to ensure adequate conditions for the enjoyment of those rights. States Parties are further obligated to *'undertake all appropriate legislative, administrative, and other measures for the implementation of the rights'* (Article 4).

Various provisions of the Convention on the Rights of the Child can not be honoured or implemented without addressing the environment as an integral determinant of their realisation. This applies in particular to the substantive provisions on the right to life, survival and development and to the highest attainable standard of health, which are universal and inalienable child rights and carry a sense of entitlement. A child needs to grow in an environment supportive of their health and well-being, with minimal exposure to the dangers and risks of environmental pollution, for environmental degradation can lead to severe violations of these fundamental child rights. This may be distilled by considering the essential meaning and spirit of the right to life and the right to health. These articles cannot be disassociated from environmental considerations, and thus form a strong ethical basis for a child's right to an environment supportive of health and well-being. Consequently, to be faithful to the child rights which States Parties have proclaimed, agreed upon and ratified, they have a duty to work towards their realisation, and an obligation to engage in affirmative activities designed to promote sustainable development and a safe environment, as a prerequisite for the achievement of other child rights. The Convention on the Rights of the Child provides a powerful tool to ensure environmental protection, providing a legal and ethical framework towards sustainable development as envisaged in Agenda 21, with the linkages between poverty, environmental degradation, impairment of children's health, and community participation at its core.

The right to grow up in an environment supporting child health and well-being may be considered a substantive right, as it is a matter of major importance to all, and in essence a derivative of the right to life. It should be held to exist for its own sake and constitute part of the normal legal order of society. There is a need for a clearer understanding and consensus on the content of such a right, to give it practical expression, through a conscientious development of strategies to implement substantive aspects, in conjunction with related procedural aspects that can provide effective remedies and avenues for legal redress.

In working towards an understanding by the international community on components of such a right to a healthy environment, it will be essential to build on normative developments, not least in the outcomes of the series of conferences, which started with the World Summit for Children and UNCED and included Habitat and the Summit on Social Development. In addition, it is important to recognise that a large number of national, regional and international instruments have strengthened the legal basis of the right to a clean environment and stressed the intrinsic link between environment, development and the promotion of environmental rights. This has entailed corresponding duties for the state and institutions and/or obligations for individuals and communities, manifested in a trend towards environmental awareness at all levels of society, and supported by a growing body of scientific studies of the repercussions and risks of environmental degradation on child health.

Although, currently few instruments have a binding legal character, direct links between the environment and health have been established. This in turn can lead to the development of practices whereby the procedural bases for enforcing the right become more firmly embedded and the validity for complaints of violations based on ecological considerations can be recognised, and a body of case law and legal pronouncements built up. Other avenues to increase the normative weight of such a right to a healthy environment, could be by further increasing research and policy development in terms of the special vulnerability of children as they face ecological hazards, and how to protect them in this regard (including by human rights organisations). Attention should be focused especially on the most vulnerable children, including those living on or around the streets. The right to a safe environment should also be rationally incorporated into the activities of organisations that work to ensure the protection of child rights. The cumulative effect of these efforts, can slowly but surely, help to create a set of norms consolidating the right to a supportive environment. In this sense, it is an evolving right.

Children are extremely vulnerable to the consequences of environmental degradation and are entitled to effective protection. For, as stated in the Plan of Action for the Implementing the World Declaration on the Survival, Protection and Development of Children in the 1990s, 'children have the greatest stake in the preservation of the environment and its judicious management for sustainable development as their survival and development depends on it'. In *de facto* terms it can be contended that every child has the right to grow in an environment supportive of their health, as a derivative of the right to life and the right to health, provided for and encapsulated in the Convention on the Rights of the Child.

Concluding remarks

The concluding remarks are divided in two parts. The first part addresses the issues related to the 'United Nations Convention on the Rights of the Child' (CRC), i.e., whether the right of a child to a clean environment exists expressly or impliedly in this Convention, it being the international instrument of greatest importance and enjoying wide participation.[1]

In the second part we investigate whether the right of a child to a clean environment does exist, direct or indirect, in other national and international instruments, and, if so, what is its extent. Our conclusions will be based on the results from the field research and on conclusions drawn by the contributors of this book.

Part One

The United Nations Convention on the Rights of the Child and the Right to Environmental Protection

In general, the Convention guarantees many fundamental rights to the child.[2] In so far as the environment is concerned, the Convention mentions it explicitly in its text twice in Article 29, paragraph e and in Article 24, paragraph 2.[3] The Convention also refers to the environment implicitly in Articles 6 and 27.[4]

1 Convention on the Rights of the Child, G.A. Res. 44/25, UN GAOR, 44th Sess., UN Doc. A/RES/44/25, reprinted in 28 ILM 1448, 1465–66 (1989). For a general overview of the Convention, its historical development and related documents, see Geraldine Van Bueren, *The International Law on the Rights of the Child* (Dordrecht: Martinus Nijhoff, 1995), in particular Chapter One. See also Susan Brice, 'Convention on the Rights of the Child: Using a Human Rights Instrument to Protect Against Environmental Threats', 7 *Georgetown International Environmental Law Review* (1995), pp. 377–630.

2 For example, the right to life; the right to highest attainable standard of health; the right to adequate standard of living; the right to education; the right to name and nationality; the right to be protected against discrimination; the right to be protected against abuse, neglect, or other injury; the right to express one's views in matters affecting him or her; the right to be protected against economic exploitation or hazardous work; the right to leisure; the right to be protected against torture; the right to freedom of thought, conscience, association, religion, and expression (to some degree); and the right to have the 'best interest standard' be primary consideration in proceedings affecting the child.

3 For example, Article 24 paragraph 2 states that: '...States Parties shall pursue full implementation of this right and, in particular shall take appropriate measures: ... to combat disease and malnutrition ... taking into consideration the dangers and risks of environmental pollution ...'; Article 29 paragraph (e) states that: 'States Parties agree that the education of the child shall be directed to ... [t]he development of respect for the natural environment.'

4 Article 6 refers to the 'inherent right to life' and Article 27 refers to the 'adequate standard of living'. Both require that fulfilment of these basic rights depends on an environment free of pollution.

According to Brice, the meaning of the explicit and implicit environmental references in the CRC is unclear and open to different interpretations.[5] Moreover, the *travaux preparatoires* do not appear to indicate the intention of the drafters of the Convention to grant a separate human right to clean environment to a child. Nonetheless, the increase in importance of environmental matters resulted in attempts at a new understanding by proponents of environmental human rights, who assert that this Convention should be viewed as granting the right to a clean environment to a child. Brice also argues that textual interpretation of the CRC, coupled with its negotiating history, allows at the very least interpretation that it obliges State Parties to consider environmental factors when promulgating legislation resulting from the Convention's provisions. Its provisions, as far as environmental protection of a child is concerned, may be assessed in four different ways: (1) The CRC imposes an obligation on states to protect the environment or at least to provide safe, clean drinking water; (2) The CRC obligates states to recognise that children need a healthy environment; (3) The CRC only refers to environmental issues; and (4) The CRC ignores the environmental issues. Brice is of the view, however, that neither textual interpretation nor the *travaux preparatoires* merit the argument in favour of the existence of the right to a clean environment in the Convention.[6]

We, however, adhere to the view expressed by Madame Ksentini, outlined in her Report (see Annex III) where her list of fundamental rights which are accorded to children by the CRC, such as right to life, right to health, right to an adequate standard of living, and the right to education entail environmental concerns. Thus, she concluded that the proper implementation of the aforementioned rights implies the existence of an environmental right in this Convention. This interpretation has found its affirmation in the Committee on the Right of the Child Special Rapporteur's note which states that State Parties to the Convention should also provide relevant information on measures adopted, for example, to combat the risk of environmental pollution.[7] Furthermore, the CRC's monitoring policy has resulted in the promulgation of national laws for protecting children from environmental harm.

There are several procedural rights contained in the CRC. For example, Article 13 states that the child has a right 'to seek, receive and impart information and ideas of all kinds regardless of frontiers', which contribute

5 See Brice, *supra* n. 1, p. 591.
6 *Ibid.*, p. 596.
7 Section 97, UN Doc. E/CN.4/Sub2/1992/7 (1992).

to the fulfilment of the right to a clean environment. This right to individual and unrestricted access to information was confirmed by the 1992 Rio Declaration, in Articles 18 and 19, for example.

The conclusion may be drawn that is a far-fetched assumption, in the light of textual interpretation and the *travaux preparatoires* to the CRC, that the Convention contains the explicit and direct right to a clean environment for a child. Taking into consideration, however, all the implicit references to environmental matters contained therein, the developments in intervening years, such as the 1992 Rio Conference on Environment and Development and the growing number of environmental concerns, we argue that the provisions of the Convention will have to be interpreted in an environmental manner. Our claim has been corroborated by state practice, as indicated in the submitted states' reports and as interpreted by Madame Ksentini in her report, whose views were confirmed by the above-mentioned Special Rapporteur's note.

Part Two

The Existence of the Right of a Child to a Clean Environment on International and National Levels

At the international level, only two regional human rights instruments expressly recognise environmental rights, the 1981 African Charter and the 1988 San Salvador Protocol to the 1969 Charter of Human Rights (see Introductory remarks). The 1989 Convention Concerning Indigenous and Tribal Peoples in Independent Countries merits mentioning, as it refers broadly to environmental matters. Nonetheless, there are no direct provisions which would grant a child the right to a clean environment. The question which arises is twofold: first, whether in the absence of a general right to a clean environment children may still benefit from the current environmental legislation. Second, whether under the workings of general rights, the right to a clean environment granted to a child can be found.

As regards the first question, on the basis of existing case law, field research and other sources, we argue that the right of a child to a clean environment may be inferred from existing rights, as codified in two 1996 Human Rights Covenants on Political and Social Rights, in particular from the right to life, the right to health, the right to education. For example, the Inter-American Children's Institute, which is a specialised organisation of the Organisation of American States (OAS), has organised several meetings on the 'child and the environment'. OAS mobilises existing rights under existing international instruments, including in particular the CRC, with an environmental view. Moreover, this organisation intensifies its effort in this area, on the basis of Article 11 of the San Salvador Protocol which grants the general environmental right. American states are convinced that environmental education plays a crucial role in the development of the environmental protection of a child. As early as 1984, the Sixteenth Pan-American Child Congress was held in Washington, DC entitled: 'Ecological situations that influence the physical, psychological, and social well-being of children and families, with emphasis on the influence of education and the media'.

Furthermore, the European Court of Human Rights has interpreted the 1950 European Convention on Human Rights in an environmental manner in the *Lopez Ostra* case, where the environmental rights of a child were involved (see above).

We would also like to stress the crucial and fundamental participation of NGOs in assisting the implementation of the existing human rights in a way as to interpret them in an environmentally advantageous manner in relation to a child. This can be exemplified by the work of the Mannerheim League for Child Welfare in Helsinki, Finland. This NGO was set up for the environmental co-operation between children, adults and authorities. It is very active in monitoring the implementation of the CRC in conjunction with a CRC observation committee. Despite the fact that Finland is environmentally active, the outcome of the observation finds that the implementation of the CRC in Finnish legislation in relation to environmental matters is not very encouraging. The League is actively involved in efforts to follow Agenda 21 in so far as environmental education is concerned. As observed by Jansen, the environmental right of a child has to be interpreted and implemented within the framework of the concept of sustainable development, as envisaged by the above-mentioned document. Thus, this right has to be linked to combating poverty and raising of the standard of living. The key document in this respect is Madame Ksentini's Report, who does not consider environmental rights in isolation. In general, it may be said that the situation of a child should be considered in its entirety. For example, combating exploitation of child labour, through the action of the ILO (see Cullen) constitutes part and parcel of the same problem.

Although at the international level there are many unsatisfactory factors as to the full implementation of the right of a child to a clean environment, there is a noticeable trend to interpret existing international legislation in relation to children's rights with an environmental slant. It would be premature to say that there is an explicit right to a clean environment which is internationally recognised. It must be stressed, however, that environmental matters play an increasingly more significant role, in large part through the implementation of other rights, through education, and mostly due to the efforts exercised by international and national NGOs.

At the national level, the constitutions of more than fifty states contain a right to a clean environment. Again, questions may be asked as to the applicability of these constitutions to a general right of a child, justiciability of this right and the position of a child in the absence of such a right.

Indian legislation is illustrative. India has a wide system of environmental law in the form of statutory regulation, criminal law and tort. And, although Article 21 of the Indian Constitution has provided the opportunity for environmental conflicts to be solved, it has the potential to be interpreted in a wider manner in relation to some of the key issues affecting children, specifically in relation to the right of a child to a clean environment. Thus it is through indirect laws that a child's right to a clean environment is realised.

The constitutional right to a clean environment is usually very general. The problem which arises in relation to this general right is whether it offers *locus standi* when it involves environmental litigation. In the *Minors Oposa* case, the constitutional right formed the legal basis for the action. Dissenting Judge Feliciano expressed his doubts as to justiciability of this right, claiming that this provision was of a political character rather than granting legal rights. Further developments have proved that Judge Feliciano was right; due to procedural law in the Philippines, the case is still pending in the courts of first instance. The Philippines are an example of yet another country where education plays a crucial role in promoting development of environmental rights to the child. Although there are several governmental agencies involved with the welfare of the child, it is the more than seventy NGOs which are the most effective in the promotion of the rights of the child, including the right to a clean environment. The Philippines is thus an example of a very progressive country in respect to child and the environment, though nonetheless it still has insufficient domestic legislation which would enable full implementation of a constitutional right. The pronounced role of NGOs in relation to a human right to a clean environment in general is a common denominator in all the states, even in those states where the right to a clean environment does not yet play a prominent role, such as Nigeria (see Elias).

The most progressive is the Republic of South Africa, where the 1997 Constitution provides explicitly for the right to a clean environment for a child. This right is not an empty right. Section 38 of the Bill of Rights grants *locus standi* in the case of infringement of constitutional rights, thus also in the case of infringement of Articles 24 and 28 of the Constitution (see Annex II). This is an exceptional regulation in the countries surveyed.

The South African case is comparable to that of Argentina. Argentina provides for substantive and procedural rights in environmental matters.

Finland is also representative of the current legal situation. Amendments to the Finnish Constitution (967/95), which entered into force in 1995, have introduced important changes in relation to the right of a child to a clean environment. Section 5, paragraph 3 states that children shall be permitted to influence matters affecting them according to their degree of maturity. This is a general rule which has to be read jointly with the new section 14a, which states that with respect to the environment public authorities shall strive to ensure for everyone the right to a healthy environment, as well as the opportunity to influence decision-making concerning everyone's living environment. Prior to 1995, the Constitution of Finland did not include any explicit provisions which would grant the right to a clean environment. There has been, however, a number of specific Acts with respect to use and protection of the environment. For example, the Parliament has promulgated on 10 June 1994 (468/94), the Environment Impact Assessment Act. The Act requires that needs of various population groups, including children, must be taken into consideration, in issuing building permits and zoning. The environmental impact of building and zoning must be assessed from children's point of view and they are permitted to take part in the decision-making process. Finland also provides for extensive educational programmes on environmental matters. At the junior level (forms 1–6) environmental studies constitute a compulsory subject. The Ministry of the Environment has developed means to take into account the needs of children in community planning. It produced a handbook for the use of citizens, decision-makers and planners on the planning of a living environment friendly to children. The situation is nevertheless unclear whether the substantive right is justiciable and gives *locus standi* in cases which relate to the right to a clean environment.

The situation in the European Union conforms with this broadly outlined legal framework. Although absent as a direct right, the right to the clean environment for a child can be claimed through a body of potentially enforceable derived rights.

We arrive at the conclusion that a child has a substantive right to a clean environment. This right is either directly guaranteed by constitutions and forms a part of a general right to a clean environment, or it is derived from other rights, or is contained in other legislative instruments. This substantive right however does not automatically grant *locus standi* in cases where it is breached. This right as contained in constitutions is considered to be too general and more like a political statement than a legal right. Thus the situation in the Republic of South

Africa, as stated above, is quite unique since the substantive right corresponds with procedural ones. In most cases, rights which pertain to the clean environment for a child, and that appear to be justiciable, have to be contained in legislative instruments other than the Constitution. For example, in India the courts have consistently held that the right to life under Article 21 of the Constitution is only enforceable against the state. The courts, however, have applied this Article to private bodies by doing so indirectly; by requiring the state to take action against the private body in question. Anderson and Bluck conclude that where the state has a duty to act in cases of environmental pollution or degradation caused by private companies, it appears that the Article can be enforced against such private actors. Nonetheless it is difficult to see how Article 21 could be used in relation to some of principal issues affecting children, such as indoor air pollution, the cause of which is the child's own family, or where communities are forced to degrade their own environment in order to survive (i.e., deforestation).

In our view, the most important factor is 'access to justice'. Since NGOs play the fundamental role in securing and promoting environmental rights, we are of the view that they should have access to justice in environmental matters. 'The question is no longer so much *whether* non-governmental actors should play a role, but the extent and modalities of and procedural rules for such participation'.[8] There is a trend in many Member States of the European Union to grant access to justice to the NGOs. The extent of this access is, however, very varied. Germany and Great Britain appear to be the least developed as concerns *locus standi* for environmental NGOs. Other countries, such as Ireland, Spain and Greece, have very relaxed rules relating to *locus standi* in general, which permit almost any citizen to bring an action against at least some environmentally harmful decisions of authorities. In France, The Netherlands, Belgium and Italy, access to justice for NGOs does not only involve the right to challenge administrative decisions that affect the environment, but also enables an environmental organisation to take part in criminal proceedings as a '*partie civile*', and/or to bring directly an action against a private person or company urging the defendant to cease ongoing pollution or to claim damages for past activities. It must be said, however, that in Ireland, the law, while allowing any citizen or organisation to sue a private investor, does rule out any action against most projects of the public sector. As Ormond aptly states, the formal access to courts in environmental matters does not

8 Cameron and Mackenzie, 'Access to Environmental Justice and Procedural Rights in International Institutions', in Boyle and Anderson (eds.), *Human Rights Approaches to Environmental Protection* (Oxford: Clarendon Press, 1996), p. 152.

mean that the remedies are necessarily effective.[9] For example, French procedural law, which strictly adheres to the separation of powers, enables the plaintiff in principle only to demand the nullification of an administrative act, and excludes mandatory injunctions against administrative authorities. Finally, the high costs of counsel and experts have a detrimental effect on environmental litigation in some countries.

We must also stress participatory rights in environmental decision-making, which were explicitly recognised in Agenda 21 and Principle 10 of the Rio Declaration. These rights form part and parcel of access to environmental justice.

The importance of these rights was corroborated by signing of the United Nations Economic Commission for Europe (ECE) Convention on Access to Information, Public Participation in Decision-Making and Access to Justice in Environmental Matters (the Aarhus Convention) in June 1998. Mary Robinson, the UN High Commissioner for Human Rights said, *inter alia*, as follows:

> [t]o secure the [fundamental rights] we need to have access to environmental information and so I welcome the proposed convention – making such access binding – and I look forward to the implementation of the details of the convention ... This will put demands national and local authorities but it will also lead to better environmental management and to sustainable development. Another important meeting point of human rights is the access to justice ... In [regard to] NGOs as having a public interest 'watch dog' role which is vital in our all societies and in need of our strong support.[10]

This Convention for the first time links environmental and human rights, by expressly stating that there is a right to clean environment.[11] The Resolution of the Signatories to THE Aarhus Convention emphasises the key role of parliaments, regional and local authorities and NGOs in addition to that of governments to be played in implementing this Convention. The Resolution focused as well on the importance of environmental education.

---

9 Thomas Ormond, ' "Access to Justice" for Environmental NGOs in the European Union', in Sven Deimann and Bernard Dyssli (eds.) *Environmental Rights: Law, Litigation and Access to Justice* (London: Cameron May, 1995), pp. 71–86.

10 Cited in Katy Brady, 'Aarhus Convention Signed', *Environmental Policy and Law* (EPL), 28/3–4 (1998), p. 171.

11 Article (objective): 'In order to contribute to the protection of the right of every person of present and future generations to live in an environment adequate to his or her health and well-being, each Party shall guarantee the right of access to information, public participation in decision-making, and access to justice in environmental matters in accordance with the provisions of this Convention.'

Annex I

Summary of responses and questionnaires

Summary of responses

Selected ministries and international organisations were surveyed on the right of the child to a clean environment. Some of the responses are summarised below.

The following Ministries of Justice and Foreign Affairs of states were included: in Europe (Finland, Poland, Spain, the United Kingdom); in Africa (Kenya, Rwanda, South Africa); in Asia (India, the Philippines, Singapore, Thailand); in South America (Argentina, Brazil, Peru); in North America (the Province of Ottawa, Canada; State of California, United States; Mexico).

International organisations included: the universal organisations of the United Nations (Commission of Sustainable Development; Sub-Commission on the Prevention of Discrimination of Minorities; United Nations Environment and Development; UNESCO) and the World Bank; and regional organisations (Council of Europe; Organisation of American States; Organisation of African Unity; United Nations Commission for Europe).

Generally speaking the responses may be summarised in the following manner:

1. States

1.1 Europe (Finland and Poland)

Finland ratified the UN Convention on the Rights of the Child in 1991 and it entered into force on 20 July 1991. The rights of the child are found in various legislative instruments. The Finnish Constitution states that children should be treated equally as individuals and shall be permitted to influence matters affecting them according to their degree of maturity (Section 5, para. 3). In Section 14a, respect for the environment that public authorities strive to ensure for everyone is outlined in detail. The responsibilities over children have been divided between ministries and depends on their competencies in various areas. For example, the Ministry of Education oversees planning educational structures (e.g., possible environmental educational programmes). The Department of Environmental Health, on the other hand, is the responsibility of local authorities and the Ministry of the

Environment participates in a number of experiments where the child's point of view has been admitted into the planning process and which aims to provide an environment which is good for children and young people.

Finland has a strong tradition of presenting nature and the environment in the most accessible manner to children. The Mannerheim League for Child Welfare has conducted environmental work which demonstrates that the 'consciousness of environmental authorities' is not fully aware of the problems concerning the child's environment.

Poland provided information on general considerations concerning the rights of the child.[1] In the Polish legal system, there is no single act which would contain all the rights and liberties of a child in a manner which was consistent with the Convention on the Rights of the Child. The following rights are most frequently mentioned in the statutes and regulations: the right to care and protection; the right to personal dignity and inviolability; the right to an adequate standard of living; the right to the freedom of thought, speech, and outlook on life and religion; the right to participate in the social life of the institution; the right to privacy; the right to appeal against decisions regarding the child in care and the right to know one's rights. The rights of the child are propagated by government agencies and NGOs, such as the Committee for the Protection of the Rights of the Child which disseminates knowledge on the Convention.

1.2 Africa (South Africa)

The existence of the right of the child to a clean environment in the Republic of South Africa was outlined by the Department of Foreign Affairs, which sent detailed information. According to this department, Sections 24 and 28 of the Bill of Rights contained in the 1997 Constitution grants everyone the right to a clean environment ('that is not harmful to the health or well-being') and the environment is protected 'for the benefit for future generations' (in paragraph 24). Paragraph 28 enumerates specific rights of children. These rights included, *inter alia*, protection from 'malnutrition, neglect, abuse, or degradation' and that 'a child's best interest is of paramount importance in the matter concerning the child'. There are several NGOs in the Republic of South Africa which operate in the area of the child and the environment, such as, *inter alia*, the Wildlife Society,

1 T. Bulenda and A. Kremplewski, 'Rights of the Child and their Protection in Polish Resocialisation Institutions', in E. Verhellen (ed.), *Monitoring Children's Rights* (Dordrecht, 1996), pp. 727–744 and *idem.*, 'Propagating Knowledge of the Rights of the Child in Residential Care Institutions in Poland', in W. de Boer (ed.), *Children's Rights and Residential Care in International Perspective* (Dordrecht, 1996), pp. 155–161.

Ecoling, Molo Songololo, Seaworld, Umgeno Water, Shell Education Services, and environmental education is currently under revision. The Republic of South Africa has ratified the Convention.

1.3 Asia (The Philippines)

The Department of Legal Affairs of the Ministry of Foreign Affairs of the Philippines elaborated on children's rights and environmental protection. There is a general right to a clean environment, as provided in Section 15 of the Constitution. This right was confirmed in the landmark *Minors Oposa* case decided by the Philippines Supreme Court on 30 June 1993. The case was decided on the right to a balanced and healthy ecology, and on the concept of intergenerational equity (see above, Introductory remarks). The Philippines has ratified the Convention. All three branches of the government are active in implementing the Convention. The Child Rights Centre of the Commission of Human Rights was established to monitor the violation of human rights. Equally important is the existence of some seventy NGOs involved in an environmental programme. There is a developed system of secondary education related to the rightsof the child in connection with the environment. As regards higher education, there are several courses at universities and medical schools related to environmental sciences.

1.4 South America (Peru)

In Peru, the protection of the rights of the child, in particular the right to a sound environment, is found in Article 3 of the Law on Children and Adolescents which states that 'all children and adolescents have the right to live in a healthy and ecologically balanced environment'. The ratification of the Convention in 1990 obligated Peru to adapt relevant codes to the Convention's provisions, including Peruvian national legislation. This, in turn, has resulted in the creation of several NGOs, such as El Instituto Nacional de Bienestar Familia (INABIF), which, as a decentralised public body, focuses on the welfare of the child, adolescents, women, and the elderly.

1.5 North America (Mexico, the United States (State of California))

According to the Mexican Legal Department of the Ministry of Foreign Affairs, the Mexican Constitution has provisions for the right to a clean environment and in protecting the environment the state must ensure 'the right to preserve the minimum standards necessary for physical and mental health' (see Articles 30, 40, and 123). Provisions for a clean environment can also be found in the Civil and Labour Codes. There are special provisions relating to child labour and social security which secures ample rights. Mexico has also ratified the Convention. There has been a pioneering legislative movement to assure the right to a clean environment. There are numerous NGOs, such as CEMEDIN, Centro Mexicana para los Derechos de la Infancia, and the Fondo para Ninos de Mexico. The Ombudsman, in further ensuring the right to a clean environment, has introduced environmental education.

The Secretary for Environmental Protection for the State of California provided a detailed reply. There is no specific procedural right to a clean environment. California does have extensive environmental codes, addressing the safety of air, soil, and water for adults and children. The California Environmental Protection Agency oversees several environmental departments. In setting scientific standards for danger levels of various pollutants, the special risks associated with children are considered. Special cleaning attention is attached to contaminated sites where children commonly congregate. There are several important private non-profit agencies involved with environmental issues in California, such as the California Public Interest Research Group (CALPRIC). At the elementary school level, there is a programme called 'A Child's Place in the Environment'.

2. International Organisations

2.1 Universal

2.1.1 United Nations

The replies from some of these agencies, such as the High Commissioner for Human Rights, Centre for Human Rights, as well as the Commission on Human Rights and UNESCO, were based on the Ksentini Report (see Annex III).

2.1.2 UNICEF

Many issues that UNICEF has traditionally dealt with, such as health, water, education, and nutrition, will be addressed in the rights perspective. The child's right to a clean environment is one of the issues that is fast becoming important to UNICEF. The organisation has supported many activities that are related to the child's environment, including drinking water provisions, environmental sanitation, and hygiene education. A growing emphasis is being placed in the development of educational programmes concerning the environment. At present, over 90 per cent of UNICEF-supported country programmes have a water and sanitation sub-programme, of which hygiene is an important part. One of the divisions of UNICEF, the Water, Environment and Sanitation Cluster, is planning to organise an internal workshop on the rights of the child to a clean environment, of which UNICEF does not yet have any procedures to monitor this right, but is very much interested in developing.

2.1.3 World Bank

The World Bank, Office of the Vice Presidency for Environmentally Sustainable Development creates policies which do not specifically deal with the right of the child to a clean environment, but does work with children's rights in relation to the Convention. The first operational policy statement on environmental aspects of the Bank's work was issued in May 1984. The Bank has become the first multilateral development agency to screen projects for their environmental consequences and to adopt guidelines for the future lending operations. The Bank introduced in 1989 an operational directive relating to environmental assessment, namely all investment projects must be screened for potential environmental effects. Recent directives concerned the following: indigenous people (1991), water resources management (1993), and forestry (1993). The directive relating to involuntary resettlement recognises that this resettlement may cause several long-term hardship, impoverishment, and environmental damage, unless appropriate measures are planned and executed.

3. Regional

3.1 Organisation for African Unity (OAU)

The adoption of the African Charter on the Rights and Welfare of the Child in 1990 was a step towards bringing awareness to Member States of the need to create an enabling environment in favour of the African child. The establishment of the African Network for the Prevention against Child Abuse, as a continental body with observer status with the OAU, is also another step in implementing the decisions and rights of the African child.

3.2 Organisation of American States (OAS)

The Inter-American Children's Institute, a specialised organ of the OAS, is the body which deals with the right to a clean environment. The

'Additional Protocol to the American Convention on Human Rights in the area of economic, social and cultural rights', Article 11 of the Protocol of San Salvador, includes the right to a healthy environment. The Institute, through its Legal and Social Affairs Committee, co-operates with regional governments in the implementation of the Convention, carrying out actions related to the rights of the child to a normal and healthy environment. Although no special educational programme has been established, some isolated actions have taken place. The Convention constitutes a link between the action of the national legislator and that of an international legislator in various child-related issues.

3.3 Council of Europe

The Council of Europe does not deal with the issue of the right to a clean environment. Concerning the general problem of the right to a clean environment and case-law of the European Court of Human Rights (see above, Introductory remarks), the general documents sent included the *Lopez Ostra* case and the European Charter on the Right of the Child.

Questionnaires:

TO SELECTED GOVERNMENTS (Ministries of Justice & Foreign Affairs):
Europe: Finland; Poland; Spain; United Kingdom (also UNED-UK)
Africa: Kenya; Rwanda; South Africa
Asia: Singapore; Thailand; India; Philippines
South America: Brazil; Peru; Argentina
North America: Ottawa, Canada; California, United States Mexico

Proposed Questionnaire:

1. Is there a constitutional general right to a clean environment, and in particular does there exist the right of the child to a clean environment?

2.a. Is there any procedural right (as opposed to substantive right) to enforce the substantive right?

2.b. Were there any cases brought before the court? (i.e. Philippines, *Minors Oposa* claim)

3. Are there specific regulations pertaining to the rights of the child in the constitutional executive legislation?

4. Is the State a party to the 1989 Convention on the Rights of the Child?

5.a. What are the legislative acts implementing the Convention?

5.b. What are the organs of the State which implement the Convention?

6. Are there at present any NGOs in your country operating in the area of the child and the environment?

7.a. Is there any general education about the child and the environment offered in secondary education, in university education, or in medical schools?

7.b. If so, what type of course is available at each level?

TO REGIONAL ORGANIZATIONS

I. Europe

1.1. Council of Europe

1. How does the Council of Europe address the problem of the right of the child to a clean environment?

2. Did the Council of Europe establish any monitoring system relating to the right of the child to a clean environment in the Member States?

3. Did the Council of Europe create any educational programmes related to the right of the child to a clean environment?

4. What is the current, if any, programme of the Council of Europe related to the right of the child to a clean environment?

1.2. UN Economic Commission for Europe

1. Does the Committee on Environmental Policy address the issue of the right of the child to a clean environment?

2. Has the Committee on Environmental Policy established a programme on the right of the child to a clean environment?

II. Organization of American States

1. Is there any special organ which deals with the right to a clean environment, and in particular the right of the child to a clean environment?

2. Does the Organization monitor the policy of the Member States towards the development of the right of the child to a clean environment?

3. Has the Organization established a special educational programme relating to the right of the child to a clean environment?

III. Organization of African Unity

1. Is there any special organ which deals with the right to a clean environment, and in particular the right of the child to a clean environment?

2. Does the Organization monitor the policy of the Member States towards the development of the right of the child to a clean environment?

3. Has the Organization established a special educational programme relating to the right of the child to a clean environment?

TO THE UNITED NATIONS ORGANIZATION

I. Sub-Commission on the Prevention of Discrimination and Protection on Minorities

1. How does the Sub-Commission address the problem of the right to a clean environment for the child?

2. a. What are the findings of Madame Ksentini's report relating to children and the environment?

2. b. What were the commentaries of governments to which the draft reports were submitted?

3. How does the Sub-Commission, if at all, supervise the activities of Member States in relation to the child and the environment?

Preliminary Questionnaire

UN Economic Commission for Europe – Legal Department

1. Does the Committee on Environmental Policy address the issue of the right of the child to a clean environment?

2. Has the Committee on Environmental Policy established a programme on the right of the child to a clean environment?

Preliminary Questionnaire

Council of Europe – Legal Department

1. Within what framework does the Council of Europe work in relation to the question of the right of the child to a clean environment?

2. How does the Council of Europe address the problem of the right of the child to a clean environment?

3. Did the Council of Europe establish any monitoring system relating to the right of the child to a clean environment in the Member States?

4. Did the Council of Europe create any educational programmes related to the right of the child to a clean environment?

5. What is the current, if any, programme of the Council of Europe related to the right of the child to a clean environment?

Preliminary Questionnaire

Organization of American States – Legal Department

1. Is there are special organ which deals with the right to a clean environment, and in particular the right of the child to a clean environment?

2. Does the Organization monitor the policy of the Member States towards the development of the right of the child to a clean environment?

3. Has the Organization established a special educational programme relating to the right of the child to a clean environment?

TO THE UNITED NATIONS ORGANIZATION

I. United Nations Environment & Development

1. How does UNED support the right of the child to a clean environment.

2. Does the Anti-Poverty and Regeneration Programme of UNED have bearing on the emerging right of the child to a clean environment?

3. How does UNED's Education Programme shape the emerging right of the child to a clean environment?

TO THE UNITED NATIONS ORGANIZATION

I. Commission on Sustainable Development

1. How does the Commission address the problem of the right to a clean environment for the child and sustainable development?

2. What is the role of the NGOs in relation to the right to a clean environment and the child in the framework of sustainable development?

3. How does the Commission, if at all, supervise the activities of Member States in relation to the child and the environment, and within sustainable development?

WORLD BANK

I. To the Vice Presidency for Environmentally Sustainable Development

1.a. What is the World Bank's policy in relation to the human right to a clean environment?

1.b. How does this shape the World Bank's lending policy and financing of projects?

2. Does the World Bank, within its framework of environmental policy, take into account the special rights of the child?

Annex II

Responses

European representation Ministry of Foreign Affairs The Kingdom of Finland[1]

General information

The total area of Finland is 338,145 sq km. Approximately 70 per cent of the land surface is forest, 15 per cent cultivated land, settlement or roads and 15 per cent wasteland, such as swamps, arctic fells and sand. The population of Finland in January 1996 was 5,098,754. The average population density is 16.7 inhabitants/sq km of land, which varies from 130 in the industrialised south to between 2 and 3 in the sparsely populated regions in the north.

Question 1

a. Is there any procedural right (which corresponds to the substantive right to a clean environment with special emphasis for the child), and if so, how is it enforced?
b. And if so, how does it work in practice?
c. Were there any cases brought before the court?

Response

The provisions concerning the fundamental rights included into the Constitution Act of Finland have been amended. These amendments (969/95) entered into force 1 August 1995. In the amended Section 5, paragraph 3, it is stated that children shall be treated equally as individuals and shall be permitted to influence matters affecting them according to their degree of maturity.

In the new Section 14a it is stated with respect to environment that public authorities shall strive to ensure for everyone the right to a healthy environment as well as the opportunity to influence decision-making concerning his living environment. This was new since the Constitution Act of Finland did not include any provisions concerning the right to

1 Please note that the responses which appear in Annex II are printed in their original form.

environment although there are specific acts with respect to use and protection of environment.

The physical environment is in many ways important for children's lives. In 1993 the Government submitted a Bill to Parliament on environmental impact assessment (HE 3 19/93) and the new Act was passed 10 June 1994 (46 8/94). The Act requires that the needs of various population groups – including those of children – be considered in zoning and in issuing building permits. The environmental impact of building and zoning must be assessed from the child's point of view, and children must be heard both directly and indirectly.

Question 2

Is the state party to the 1989 Convention on the Rights of the Child?

Response

Finland has ratified the said Convention in 1991 and the Convention entered into force 20 July 1991. Finland did not make any reservations to the said Convention upon ratification.

Question 3

a. What are the legislative acts implementing the Convention?

Response

In Finland, the relationship between domestic and international law is generally understood as having been resolved according to the dualistic model.

Section 33, paragraph 1, of the Constitution Act of Finland states that the relations of Finland with foreign powers shall be determined by the President. Treaties concluded with foreign States shall, however, be approved by Parliament if they contain provisions within the legislative sphere or if the consent of Parliament is otherwise required by the Constitution.

The most frequent method of implementing international treaties in Finland is incorporation either through an Act of Parliament in *blanco* or through a similar Government Decree. In the first case, a Government Decree accompanies the Act of Parliament, as well. The Convention on the Rights of the Child was implemented by an Act of Parliament in *blanco* and accompanied by a Government Decree.

b. What are the organs of the State which implement the Convention?

Response

In Finland the implementation depends on the substance of the matters included to the Convention. The responsibilities concerning children have been divided between all the ministries, according to their responsibilities in the various fields. Therefore, there cannot be distinguished any specific instance.

For instance, the Ministry for Foreign Affairs was responsible for the national implementation of the Convention. It is also responsible for the periodic reports submitted by the Government of Finland to the Committee on the Rights of the Child.

The Ministry of Justice is in general responsible for the legislative measures. The Ministry of Interior is responsible for the general administrative matters. The Ministry of Finance is responsible for the general aims of the financial politics. These decisions have naturally a great impact on children as well.

The Ministry of Education is responsible for the planning of educational structures. For instance one of the compulsory subjects at the junior level (forms 1–6) is environmental studies. The Ministry for Social Affairs and Health is responsible for arranging day care for children under seven years old.

Environmental health is the responsibility of the local authorities, and involves environmental hygiene, control of foodstuffs and poisons, occupational health and veterinary medicine. Environmental health covers drinking water, clean air and noise control.

The Ministry of the Environment has developed means to consciously take into account the needs of children in community planning. The Ministry has participated in a number of experiments where children's points of view have been admitted into the planning process and which aim at creating an environment which is good for children and young people.

The Ministry of the Environment has produced a handbook for the use of citizens, decision-makers and planners on the planning of living environments friendly to children (*Lapsiystäivälliseen elinympäristöön*). It describes the components of an environment which is good for children and the characteristics of children as active users and planners of their environment.

In the control of land use, the best interest of children first received attention as early as the 1970s; a provision was added in the Building Decree to the effect that sufficient space for playgrounds and for free-time activities must be reserved in each city block zoned for housing. The purpose of the provision was to safeguard the best interest of children as opposed to the need for parking space for cars.

Traffic has a marked effect on the children's living environment, leading to efforts to safeguard the best interest of children in decisions regarding both traffic safety and traffic planning.

Question 4

Are there at present any NGOs in your country operating in the area of the child and the environment?

Response

There are several organisations working with children and for their welfare, e.g., the Mannerheim League for Child Welfare which has, *inter alia*, developed methods for hearing children in environmental decision-making and published a handbook on the subject (*Lapset ympäristön tutkijoina*).

Question 5

a. Is there any general education about the child and the environment offered in secondary education, in university, or in medical schools?
b. If so, what type of course is available at each level?

Response

Environment is a wide notion therefore it is difficult to give an exact answer, for instance, in the teacher's education the environment is one part of the general studies which naturally includes a wide range of various subjects. However, it is possible to take courses with respect to environmental questions as optional courses. Also the kindergarten teachers have studies on natural sciences as part of their education. Also many of the organisations for protection of nature have youth sections and special projects for children.

Annexes
– Environmental co-operation between children, adults and authorities.

Annex to Finland

Mannerheimin Lastensuojeluliitto

KAIJA KESS

The Mannerheim League for Child Welfare Environmental co-operation between children, adults and authorities

The challenge

The environment has great importance in a child's development. In Finland a child stays outdoors from 4 to 6 hours approximately daily, usually regardless of weather. *A child thoroughly knows his environment*, from trees to ditches. Very few adults have so much information about their environment. However, it's the adult who makes the decisions about environment.

It's a Finnish heritage to *offer pure nature and environment for children*. The tradition in bringing up children emphasizes outdoor activities for the healthy growth of children. In many day care centres the ecological way of thinking is a part of daily life. The school system gives great importance to physical education and studies of natural science.

There are today, however, *many threats to endanger this tradition*. In a global view, the danger to the environment posed by the uncontrolled exploitation of the earth's natural resources is universally recognized. Locally children's environment is radically narrowed by urban structures. This means that children's social contacts are limited and their possibilities to learn and develop themselves through spontaneous experiences are hindered. Children are also losing contact with their local culture and natural environment. This is also one of the alarming trends in Finland.

During the environmental work of the Mannerheim League for Child Welfare (the League) it has also appeared that the *consciousness of environmental authorities is defective* concerning problems of children's environment. This especially concerns the authorities responsible for planning communities, traffic connections and designing playgrounds. These authorities don't know about the needs and expectations of children concerning their environment. There is a severe lack of method both to gather information from children and to use the gathered information in decision-making.

The legislation

Future generations have the same right as we have to clean air, clean water and green forests. 'Towards sustainability' embodies the central theme of the 1992 Earth Summit, the *United Nations Conference on the Environment and Development* (UNCED) as set out in the Agenda 21 document. The idea is that we cannot freely use or abuse the earth's environment. The environment has a value and a price which must be recognized. The Brundtland Report 'Our common future' 1987 included the definition of the sustainable development: 'A development which meets the needs of the present without compromising the ability of future generations to meet their own needs.'

Chapter 25 in Agenda 21 concerns children and youth. It sets aims for directing the education towards sustainability, increasing environmental consciousness among children in a way that their possibilities for participating in environmental decision-making will be better, and guaranteeing a safe and healthy future for children.

Finland has adopted the Agenda 21 document. Finland has also many *national strategies* concerning the environmental education in schools and nurseries.

The United Nation Convention on the Rights of the Child was ratified by Finland in 1992. By signing this convention Finland has committed itself to promoting the well-being and interests of children and youth. Article 3 includes an obligation for the authorities in all their acts to give priority to the rights of children and youth. Article 12 obliges the authorities to pay attention to the views of children according their age and state of development. Article 12 also emphasizes that the authorities have to offer a special opportunity for children and youth to be heard.

Like all the countries ratifying the United Nation Convention on the Rights of the Child, Finland had an observation committee. The outcome of the committee was depressing: the authorities did not pay attention to the rights of children and youth in the way the Convention requires. The situation is not so much due to the state of Finnish national legislation, but instead is a reflection of it's way of thinking and working.

It's the matter of turning words into action. There are many international conventions and national legislation and strategies but fundamentally it's the question about the way the rights of children are respected in everyday actions.

The response of The Mannerheim League for Child Welfare: Co-operation between children, adults and authorities

The League celebrated its 75th anniversary in October 1995. The League has 65,000 members, 600 local societies, 13 district associations and the headquarters in Helsinki. The headquarters carries out the national projects and is responsible for lobbying both in Finland and abroad. The district associations and the local societies do the same work in their provinces and communities. The district associations and the local societies have also their own ways of working arising from the local needs. Traditionally the activities of the League have been within reach of everybody, regardless of the membership of the League.

During the years the League has done much to better the children's environment. The main point has been in questions about health and education. In 1997–1999 environmental work is one of the main points in the League's work. The environmental work of today aims to response to the demands of the present world. The work has three main goals:

1. **The consideration** of children's rights in all environmental design and planning.
2. **The participation** of children and youth in environmental decision making and management.
3. **The creation** of a common terminology and methods of co-operation for environmental authorities and children.

Successful approaches have been developed to achieve these goals. The choice between the procedures followed locally depends on many things, e.g. the nature of the situation or the existing pattern of co-operation. The main approaches are the following:

1. The agents for children's environmental issues

The League educates voluntary agents for children's environmental issues. In May 1996 there were 350 voluntary agents all over the country. In addition there are 200 voluntary workers in local societies of the League in charge of environmental actions. Represented among the agents are housewives, as well as police officers and architects. Their task is to affect locally planning and decision-making for a better environment for children. They organize events, take initiatives, promote discussion and draw attention to environmental issues. The League aims to have at least one voluntary agent in every community of Finland.

The agents have dealt with a wide range of questions. For example:

- The agent in Hartola community has participated in road planning in order to get the children's and families' opinions considered.
- The agent in Lieksa community has studied the planning documents dealing with this community and set up a meeting between the environmental authorities, the League's local society and children in order to discuss the important matters.
- The agent in Oulu city has opposed the restrictions for children's play in the courtyard of a block of flats.
- The agent in Kuusankoski city has drawn public attention to the hazards of the train traffic transporting dangerous materials through the community, e.g., oil, nuclear waste and chemicals.
- The agent in Ylöjärvi community has demanded inspections to find out if there is mould in school buildings.

2. The co-operation between voluntary agents and environmental authorities

The voluntary agents co-operate with children, youth, parents and teachers. Their main task is to get them and the environmental authorities to meet, discuss and co-operate. The subject of meeting is usually a concrete problem in the neighbourhood, e.g. a dirty playground or the lack of a pedestrian crossing. The League supports the co-operation by organising meetings and offering expertise when it's needed.

An example of this kind of co-operation are the inspections of playgrounds and schoolyards. Every year hundreds of inspections are made by voluntary agents all over in Finland. The results of these inspections are given as a report to the community authorities responsible for maintaining playgrounds and schoolyards. The League offers a simple form for these volunteers to help their work and reporting.

3. Maintaining the network of volunteers

The League maintains the interest and the knowledge of voluntary agents in many ways. The League's periodical *Lapsemme* regularly includes articles about environmental issues. The voluntary agents receive three letters per year dealing with topics of current interest. The League also offers consultation on legal questions. The mass media is giving more and more attention to children's environmental issues and to the work of voluntary agents. As a result, this network of volunteers is expanding.

4. Conferences, seminars, meetings

The League organizes conferences and activities which deal with environmental issues for children. The topics vary in accordance with the current interests and co-operators. The conferences have dealt with topics such as mouldy buildings, traffic, school yards and radioactive emissions. Voluntary agents especially are invited to these events, as well as environmental, social welfare and health authorities.

In these occasions the League introduces methods to guarantee the participation of children in decisions concerning their environment. There are many methods used, e.g. colouring or using the symbols in a map according to preference, studying the surroundings by taking a walk with children, building a miniature to describe the visions of children, and making a plan according to the same information the real planners are receiving.

5. The Forum of Experts

Twice a year the League calls experts in environmental issues to gather as a forum. Participants in the work of Forum include architects, pedagogists, doctors, psychologists, engineers, lawyers, and biologists. They are a great help in outlining the present problems and future visions in children's environmental issues.

6. The participation in environmental legislation

The League participates in legislative process by giving statements, joining committees and being heard as an expert by the Parliament. On these occasions the League emphasises that the Articles 3 and 12 of the United

Nations Convention on the Rights of the Child have to be observed in all environmental legislation, decision-making and management.

The use of these experiences in the other countries

Countries and their environment vary between each other. Also the child friendliness in societies differs. There are some indications which help to create the own approaches in other countries. The following points are based on the experiences in the environmental work of the League:

Start with individuals, both adults and children. Their needs, fears and visions are crucial to the progress of the work.

Carry out activities that are easily accomplished. The success will lay a good basis for more ambitious efforts.

Bring different groups together to discuss, form an action team or meet the authorities. Networks are useful, nowadays even obligatory if you want to advance.

Use the interest of the media to support the efforts.

Use the influence of non-governmental organizations to broaden the participation of children in decision-making and planning. The support from a respected organization helps them to get their opinions heard.

Strengthen the co-ordination between every groups, organizations and authorities to have more resources, ideas and supporters.

Remember that your 'client' is always the child.

Conclusions

In all environmental planning, decision-making and management it's crucial to pay particular attention to the needs of children and youth so that the environment would contribute to their development into physically, socially and psychologically healthy, creative, responsible and active members of their societies. This particular attention requires special knowledge about the needs of children and youth. It also requires new methods to guarantee the actual participation of children and youth in the process of environmental decisions.

Publications

1. Taivaan merit ('Signs of the sky') 1992; about environmental education in early childhood.

2. Sinä ja sininen planeetta ('You and the blue planet') 1993; about the ecological way of life in home, schools and kindergartens.

3. Ensiaskel vaikuttamiseen – Ympäristöopas ('First steps in active participation – Environmental guide') 1995; about knowledge and advice for a local agent in children's environmental issues.

4. Lapset ja tieympäristön suunnittelu ('Children in planning the road environment') 1997; about theory and exercises based on an actual project in Masku community.

5. Metsäretki ('Hike in the woods') 1997; four fairy-tales for the family hikes in the woods in every season.

For further information, please contact:
The Mannerheim League for Child Welfare
Kaija Kess
Legal Adviser in Environmental Issues
Box 141
FIN-00531 HELSINKI
Tel. +358 9 3481 1500
Fax +358 3 6549 259

North American representation Ministry of Foreign Affairs Mexico City, Mexico

Con relación a la existencia de derechos procesales que correspondan a un derecho sustantivo, acerca de un ambiente propicio con especial énfasis para los niños, y cómo se trabaja en la practica en México, los derechos del menor se encuentran establecidos al mas alto nivel Constitucional al señalar que los padres tiene la obligacién de preservar el derecho de los menores a la satisfación de sus necesidades y a su salud física y mental; estas disposiciones se encuentran en el párrafo quinto del artículo 40. Constitucional, que se complements con lo señalado en el articulo 30 y 123 apartado 'A', fracciones 11,111; V;XXIII;XXIX; apartado 'B' fraccion X, de la Constitución Federal de la República, y en los artículos 22,35, 54, 77, 84, 89, 93, 292 y 640 del Código Civil; así como en el artículo 50 fracción 1, 22,23, 29 y 178 de la Ley Federal del Trabajo.

Asimismo el artículo 40 Constitucional señala que el Estado tiene la obligación de proteger al menor desamparado; protección que queda a cargo de las instituciones públicas según lo establece el artículo 30. Constitucional en su párrafo 18; y en la Ley General de Población y su Reglamento que establece bases para la creación y funcionamiento del Plan Nacional de Desarrollo Integral de la lnfancia y la Familia (DIF), organisms publico descentralizado al que corresponde la ejecución de políticas gubernamentales de asistencia social.

Cabe mencionar que el derecho laboral mexicano lleva implícita no solo la reglamentación del trabajo, sino que también establece una amplia protección a los niños a través de la previsión y la seguridad social.

Igualmente, las disposiciones mismas de la Convención sobre los derechos del niño, al ser ratificada, se integran a la legislación nacional conforme al artículo 130 Constitucional.

En general, en gran parte de la legislación nacional relativa a la política social se refleja el espíritu de la Convención, por lo que no fue necesario llevar a cabo grandes reformas o enmiendas.

Una importante acción legislative fue la realizada en 1993, con el objeto de reformar los artículos 3 y 31, fracción I de la Constitución Politica de los Estados Unidos Mexicanos, publicada en el Diario Oficial de la Federación el 5 de marzo de 1993.

Al promover la reforma antes mencionada, se reafirmó el derecho a la igualdad de oportunidades de acceso al sistema educative nacional, sin mas limitaciones que satisfacer los requisites expresados en las disposiciones aplicables, los objetivos primordiales de esta reforma son:

- acceso a la educación que aparece ahora como un mandato a la autoridad para que ejecute o permita que se efectúe una acción determinada.
- obligación del estado de abstenerse de expedir cualquier resolución que impida el acceso a la educación.
- la educación primaria y secundaria son obligatorias.

En general, del Programa Nacional de Acción se desglosan programas nacionales específicos que son:

Seis Programas en el Área de Salud

Programa de planificación familiar
Programa materno infantil
Proramas relacionados con la condición nutricia del niño
Programas de prevención y control de enfermedades diarreicas
Programa de vacunación
Dos programas preventives (retraso mental y floruracion de la sal)

Dos Programas de Educación

Educación básica
Educacién para adultos

Dos Programas de Saneamiento Básico

Programa de agua potable
Programa de saneamiento básico

Once Programas para menores en circunstancias dificiles

Acciones preventives en favor de los menores
Menores en la calle
Menores trabajadores
Menores maltratados
Menores farmacodependientes
Menores institucionalizados
Menores minusvalidos

Hijos de trabajadores migrantes
Menores indigenas en situación de extrema pobreza
Menores refugiados
Menores repatriados

Como puede observarse los programas están conceptuados por los grupos de problemas y no por razón de género.

El Estado mexicano es parte de la Convención sobre los Derechos del Niño, que fue adoptada el 2 de noviembre de 1989, con vigencia de 2 de septiembre de 1990, ratificada por México el 21 de septiembre del mismo año y publicada en el Diario Oficial de la Federación el 25 de enero de 1991.

Los actos legislativos o leyes que implementan la Convención se citaron al principio del presente documentoy en relación con los órganos del Estado que también lo hacen podemos citar:

- DIF (Sistema Nacional de Desarrollo Integral de la Infancia y la Familia) que establece programas para el desarrollo integral de niños y jóvenes.
- MECED Programa de menores en circunstancias difíciles.
- MSS (Instituto Mexicano del Seguro Social).
- ISSSTE (Istitute de Seguridad y Servicios Sociales para los trabajadores del Estado).

Aunando a los anteriores, el Programa Nacional de Acción se convierte en instruments formal, a traves del cual son Ilevadas a la práctica disposiciones contenidas en la Convención por medio de programas sectoriales, que para su aplicación cuentan con recursos federales y en algunos casos se han legado a diseñar programas municipales.

En México también se cuenta con organizaciones no gubernamentales que operan en ese ámbito, de entre las cuales podemos citar las siguientes:

CEMEDIN Centro Mexicano para los Derechos de la Infancia A.C.
COMEXANI Colectivo Mexicano de Apoyo a la Niñez.
Federación Iberoamericana contra el Maltrato Infantil.
Fideicomiso para la Salud de los Niños Indígenas de México.
Aldeas Infantiles S.O.S. México.
Ayuda a Juventud Desadaptada.
Casa de la Juventud 'José Joaquin Fernández Lizardi'.
Colectivo de Acción por la Juventud.
Fondo para Niños de México.
Por último y en relación a la educación sobre los derechos de los niños ofrecida en educación básica, media y superior, podemos afirmar que

dentro de la educacién bisica y media el Plan Nacional de Desarrollo concerniente señala que en los libros de texto, gratuito se incluyen capitulos concernientes a la Declaración de los Derechos del Niño, La Comisión Nacional de Derechos Humanos y la defensa de los mismos a través del 'ombudsman' mexicano.

North American representation California Environmental Protection Agency Sacramento, CA, USA

Question 1

a. Is there any procedural right (which corresponds to the substantive right to a clean environment with special emphasis for the child), and if so, how is it enforced?
b. If so, how does it work in practice?
c. Were there any cases brought before the court (i.e., Philippines, *Minors Oposa* claim)?

Response

California does not have a procedural right to a clean environment which specifically focuses on children. California does have extensive environmental codes addressing the safety of air, soil, and water for adults and children. (For example, water quality is protected pursuant to the California Water Code, while air and soil safety are protected by the California Health and Safety Code.) Under the authority of these codes, the California Environmental Protection Agency (Cal/EPA) oversees several environmental departments. These departments are involved in preventing the spread of new contaminants into air, soil, and water, and in cleaning contamination that occurred in the past. They also monitor the production of toxic materials and ensure they are transported, treated, recycled, and disposed in a safe manner.

In setting scientific standards for danger levels of various pollutants, the departments take into account the special risks associated with children. For example, they take into account that small children may ingest soil, and that older children are likely to have dermal contact with soil through their play. Furthermore, persons cleaning contaminated sites are routinely required to eliminate threats to sites where children congregate, such as schools, day care centers, and parks.

Each year, the California courts handle many environmental law cases. I am not aware that any appellate level court has specifically stated that children, in particular, have a right to a clean environment.

Question 2

Are there at present any NGOs in your country operating in the area of the child and the environment?

Response

There are several private, non-profit organizations active in environmental protection in California. An organization which, though not exclusively dedicated to children's issues, appears to be very concerned about children's environmental safety is the California Public Interest Research Group (CALPIRG). CALPIRG, which may be contacted at 11965 Venice Blvd. #408, Los Angeles, California, 90066, describes itself as a non-profit, non-partisan consumer and environmental watchdog organization with 60,000 members in California.

This organization is actively supporting the 'Children's Environmental Health Protection Act', which will be reintroduced in the United States Congress during 1997. This bill is authored by Representative Frank Pallone and Representative Ed Markey. If you would like more information about this bill, you should contact Mr Pallone or Mr Markey at the United States Capitol in Washington, D.C.

An organization which targets its efforts more specifically at children's issues is Mothers of East LA, which may be contacted at 924 South Mott Street, Los Angeles, California, 90023.

Question 3

Is there any general education about the child and the environment offered in secondary education, in university education, or in medical schools? If so, what type of course is available at each level?

Response

You would need to contact individual colleges and universities for information about courses they offer on children and the environment. At the elementary level, there is a program called 'A Child's Place in the

Environment', prepared by Dr Olga Clymire. Dr. Clymire may be contacted at the Lake County Office of Education, 1152 South Main Street, Lakeport, California, 95453.

The questionnaire was completed by:
Mr Robert P. Hoffman, Chief Counsel and
Mr Dennis H. Mahoney, Senior Staff Counsel.

South American representation Ministerio de Rélaciones Exteriores Lima, Peru

Tengo el agrado de dirigirme a ustedes en relación al asunto de la referencia, a fin de hacerles llegar las respuestas a las interrogantes planteadas a la Dirección de Asuntos Legales de esta Cancillería; las mismas que son:

Pregunta No 1

1.a Actualmente, la protección de los derechos del niño, especialmente el derecho a un medio ambiente sano está consagrada en el artículo 30 del Código de los Niños y Adolescentes, que señala: 'Todo niño y adolescents tiene derecho a vivir en un ambiente sano y ecológicamente equilibrado'.

Al respecto, el Código de los Niños y Adolescentes determine un procedimiento especial, el cual tiene como objetivo fundamental mantener o restituir el respeto de los derechos del niño y del adolescents.

1.b En ese sentido, se dispuso la creación de los **Juzgados del Niño y del Adolescente**. Igualmente, se sometió el ejercicio de la potestad jurisdictional del Estado en asuntos del niño y del adolescents a las **Salas de Familia**.

De la misma manera, se implements un sistema de Fiscales del Niño y el Adolescente, que implicaba un mayor concocimiento de las áreas del derecho destinadas a la protección de los menores.

Todo este sistema, se encuentra reforzado por **Organos Auxiliares** que apoyan la labor de los **Jueces y Fiscales de los Niños y Adolescentes** y colaboran a una eficaz administración de justicia. Dichos órganos son: el **Equipo Multidisciplinario** (conjunto de médicos, pedagogos, psicólogos y asistenciales que tienen como funciones emitir los informes que le solicited el Juez y el Fiscal, emitir dictámenes técnicos respecto al seguimiento de las medidas, entre otras), la **Policía Especializada** (encargada de auxiliar y colaborar con los organismos destinados por el Estado en la educación, prevención y protección del niño o adolescente), la Policía de Apoyo a la Justicia (encargada de efectuar notificaciones por mandato de la autoridad judicial y fiscal competente y de colaborar con las medidas tutelares que dicte el juez en favor de los menores) y, el **Servicio Médico Legal del Niño y Adolescente** (que es un servicio especial y gratuito, del Instituto de Medicina Legal, para niños y adolescentes).

En lo que corresponde al procedimiento que protege el Derecho del Niño a un Medio Ambiente Sano, la ley contempla un procedimiento especial, que está señalado en los artículos 30, 1840 y 2040 del Código de los Niños y Adolescentes, en tanto que se establece que es de su competencia el conocimiento de los procesos acerca de la protección de los intereses difusos e individuales que atañen a los niños y adolescentes. En ese sentido, y según el articulo 820 del Código Procesal Civil del Perú, 'interés difuso es aquel cuya titularidad corresponds a un conjunto indeterminado de personas, respecto de bienes de inestimable valor patrimonial, tales como la **defensa del medio ambiente** ...'

l.c Al respecto, no tenemos conocimiento de proceso alguno seguido sobre el tema en cuestión.

Pregunta No 2

El Estado Peruano es parte de la Convención sobre los Derechos del Niño. Dicha Convención fue aprobada mediante Resolución Legislativa No 25278 el 3 de agosto de 1990. El instrumento de ratificación de dicha Convención fue depositado el 4 de septiembre de 1990. En consecuencia, la Convención entró en vigor para el Perú el 4 de octubre de 1990.

Pregunta No 3

3.a La ratificación de la Convención sobre los Derechos del Niño, obligó al Estado Peruano a redactar un nuevo código para la infancia y la adolescencia, el mismo que adpatara la legislación nacional a los nuevos concepts de la doctrina international sobre la materia.

El **Código de los Niños y Adolescentes** fue el resultado del trabajo de una comisión integrada por profesionales de diversos sectores tales como funcionarios públicos, catedráticos, magistrados, abogados en ejercicio, asistentes sociales y representantes de organizaciones no gubernamentales; conformación que permitió lograr una visión integral del problema de la niñez en el Perú.

El 24 de diciembre de 1992, mediante Decreto Ley 26102, el Gobierno del Perú promulgó el Código de los Niños y Adolescentes elaborado por la mencionada comisión, el mismo que entró en vigencia en junio de 1993. Entre las principales virtudes del nuevo Código destaca la de promover la participación de la sociedad civil conjuntamente con el estado para lograr el bienestar de la niñiez peruana.

El Título Preliminar del Código de los Niños y Adolescentes formula importantes declaraciones y deslindes y además demarca cronológicamente el ámbito de los niños y el de los adolescentes, locual es considerado acertado ya que permite, a través de la normatividad, efectuar una diferenciación con el fin de obtener una mejor interpretación.

De igual manera, puede apreciarse que no hay posibilidad de distingo por razón de raza, color, sexo, idioma, religión, opinión política, nacionalidad, origen social, posición económica, etnia, impediments fisico o mental o cualquier otra condición, aun de sus padres resposables.

El Código de los Niños y del Adolescente recoge además los diferentes derechos que les correspondent entre ellos el derecho a vida, al nombre y a la identidad, a la nacionalidad, a vivir en familiar a la salud, al trabajo, así como las libertades que les son propias, como la libertad de expresión, de pensamiento y de creencia, de opinión, de asociación y de tránsito, las mismas que se encuentran amparadas en el libro primero del Código de los Niños y Adolescentes.

Como consecuencia de la vigencia del Código de los Niños y Adolescentes, todos los esfuerzos estuvieron dirigidos a lograr su adecuada difusión, particularmente con la capacitación de los jueces, personal de juzgados y fiscalías de los niños y adolescentes.

3.b Los órganos del Estado encargados de implementar la Convención son:

- El ente rector del Sistema Nacional de Atención Integral al Niño y al Adolescente está encargado de dirigir y formular las políticas, planes y programas sectoriales e institucionales de atención al niño y al adolescente. Dichas funciones han sido transferidas al Ministerio de Promoción de la Mujer y del Desarrollo Humano mediante la primera disposición complementaria del Decreto Legislativo No 866 de la Ley de Organización y Funciones del Ministerio de Promoción de la Mujer y del Desarrollo Humano.

- El Instituto Nacional de Bienestar Familiar (INABIF), organismo público descentralizado que tiene como función la atención de niños, adolescentes, mujeres y ancianos en situación de riesgo y abandono, a través de la conducción de establecimientos y la administración de servicios de atención a dichos grupos. El INABIF ha sido incorporado a la estructura del Ministerio de Promoción de la Mujer y del Desarrollo Humano como organisms público descentralizado.

Actualmente, el INABIF viene implementando desde comienzos de 1994, el Programa Nacional del Niño y del Adolescente trabajador y de la calle, con la asesoria técnica del TJNICEF y el apoyo financiers del Banco Interamericano de Desarrollo (BID).

Este programa ha sido diseñado como alternative orientada a la protección y la promoción de los niños y adolescentes que trabajan en la calle, así como aquellos que viven en ella.

El Programa de Educadores de la Calle ha establecido casas de formación, semi-abiertas, administradas a tiempo completo por educadores de la calle; albergan a nifios, adolescentes y a madres solteras con sus respectivos hijos.

Actualmente, dicho programa ha incluido dos nuevos puntos para su ejecución. Uno de ellos seria el establecimiento de una comunidad terapéutica con el objetivo de atender en un lugar especifico y con atención especializada a los niños y adolescentes consumidore de drogas en la calle. otro punto, que se encuentra en ejecución, es el funcionamiento de un colegio mixto de nivelación con curricula especial para los niños de la calle, de duración aproximadamente de 1 a 3 años (este punto tiene como objetivo primordial buscar la resocialización de los niños y adolescentes para que en el futuro puedan integrarse a un colegio formal).

Finalmente, este programa tiene como meta expandirse en otras ciudades del país, incorporando a 12,000 menores como beneficiaros.

Las defensorías del niño y del adolescents constituyen un mecanismo que permite que integrantes de la sociedad civil organizada o de instituciones del Estado se constituyan en defensores de los derechos de la niñez. Las defensorías tienen la atribución de presenter las denuncias de casos de maltrato ante las autoridades competentes. Además, las defensorías podrán actuar en el campo social atendiendo las necesidades de la niña maltratada como son la atención psicológica o médica en caso de ser necesario.

La atención de casos se basa en la conciliación de las partes involucradas para llegar a acuerdos y superar los problemas. Dichos acuerdos son registrados en un acta que requiere un adecuado seguimiento para determiner si el caso debe derivarse a las instancias correspondientes cuando los referidos acuerdos no son cumplidos.

Las defensorías han sido incorporadas a la estructura orgánica de las municipalidades (Defensorlas Municipales del Niño y el Adolescente) A la fecha, se ha realizado el registro de 243 defensorias y se conoce la existencia de otras 77 defensorías en funcionamiento, haciendo un total de 320 a nivel nacional.

Cabe precisar, que el programa de defensorías cuenta con el apoyo del Fondo de las Naciones Unidas para la infancia (UNICEF).

Pregunta No 4

Efectivamente, la organización no gubernamental 'Red Ambiental Peruana', la cual participa en los siguientes programas para niños de 6 a 15 años:

a) Premio Global 500 para jóvenes.
b) Concurso Internacional de pintura infantil.
c) 'Salvemos nuestro planeta: protejamos, para el siglo XXI, la belleza de nuestros océanos, cielos y bosques de hoy'.

Pregunta No 5

5.a Como curso, no se dicta en los colegios; pero sí se ha participado en programas y eventos internacionales COMO: 'El Programa Global' (iniciativa de Estados Unidos), y en el del 'Premio Global 500'.

En las universidades, el tema referents al Medio Ambiente es tratado de acuerdo al área de especialización y no en relación a niño-medio ambiente.

5.b Educación Ambiental

1 'Programa Regional de Desarrollo Educativo de la OEA' (Secundaria y Superior).

2. 'Programa Global' (Programa Educativo Internacional para estudiantes de Colegios Nacionales de Primaria y Secundaria con el fin de fomentar la concientización y conocimiento del Medio Ambiente Global).

Asian representation Ministry of Foreign Affairs Manila, The Philippines

Question 1

1 a Is there any procedural right (which corresponds to the substantive right to a clean environment with special emphasis for the child), and if so, how it is enforced?

b. And if so, how does it work in practice?

c. Were there any cases brought before the court?

Response

1. a-c The foregoing questions can be answered through a landmark case decided by the Philippine Supreme Court on 30 July 1993 in *Oposa v. Factoran, Jr.* (224 SCRA 792).

In this case, the complaint focused on one specific fundamental right – the right to a balanced and healthful ecology which, for the first time in constitutional history, is solemnly incorporated in the fundamental law of the Philippines.

Specifically, it touches on the issue of whether the petitioners, the minors as represented by their parents, have a cause of action to 'prevent the misappropriation or impairment' of the Philippines rainforests and 'arrest the unabated haemorrhage of the country's vital life-support systems and continued rape of the Mother Earth.'

The complaint was instituted as a taxpayers' class suit and alleges that the plaintiffs (petitioners-minors) 'are all citizens of the Philippines, taxpayers, and are entitled to the full benefit, use and enjoyment of the natural resource treasure that is the country's virgin tropical rainforest'. The high court added that the case has a special and novel element – petitioners minors assert that they represent their generation as well as generations yet unborn. The court went further by saying that 'their personality to sue in behalf of the succeeding generations can only be based on the concept of intergenerational responsibility insofar as the right to a balanced and healthful ecology is concerned. Such a right, XXXX, considers the "rhythm and harmony of nature".'

Question 2

Is the State a party to the 1989 Convention on the Rights of the Child?

Response

Yes, the Philippines signed the said Convention. The Philippines later on ratified it through Senate Resolution No. 109 passed on 26 July 1990. By virtue of such ratification, the Philippines became the 31st State Party.

Question 3

3 a. What are the legislative acts implementing the Convention?

3 b. What are the organs of the State which implement the Convention?

Response

Since the ratification of the Convention in 1990, there are a number of legislative enactments. Among which are as follows:

RA 6972	–	Barangay-Level Total Development and Protection of Children Act or the Day Care Law (I 990)
RA 7610	–	Special Protection of Children Against Child Abuse, Exploitation and Discrimination Act (I 992)
RA 7600	–	Rooming-In and Breastfeeding-In and Breastfeeding Act (1992)
RA	–	Magna Carta for Disabled Persons (1992)
RA	–	Drug Prevention in the Curriculum Act (1992)
RA 7658	–	Prohibiting Employment below 15 years of age (1993)
RA 7797	–	Lengthening the School Calendar to Not More than 220 Days

RA 779 – Amending the Education Act of 1982 Regarding Stock Education Corporations

RA 7846 – Requiring Immunization Against Hepatitis-B

RA 7880 – Providing for the Fair and Equitable Allocation of Department of Education Culture and Sports Budget to Capital Outlay

RA 7875 – National Health Insurance Program

RA 8043 – The Intercountry Adoption Act (1995)

RA 8044 – Youth in Nation Building Act (1995)

RA 8172 – Salt Iodization Act (1995)

But noteworthy is the fact that the Philippines has a law preceding the Convention by sixteen (16) years which provides and recognizes the rights of the child. This is Presidential Decree No. 603 or otherwise known as the Child and Youth Welfare Code (CWC).

Response

The three branches of the government – the Executive, the Legislative and the Judiciary – are effectively involved in the implementation of the Convention.

There are number of proposed legislative measures pending in the Congress that tackle the provisions of the Convention. The Philippines Legislator's Committee on Population and Development has formulated a legislative agenda for children using the Convention as an overall framework.

At the judiciary level, there are efforts to sensitize the bench on the rights of the child. There are several decisions of the court that reiterate the basic principles of the Convention specially the best interests of the child.

At the executive department, the Council for the Welfare of Children (CWC) is in the forefront in monitoring and reporting the implementation of the Convention on the Rights of the Child. The Council is composed of the following agencies:

Department of Social Welfare and Development;
Department of Education, Culture and Sports;
Department of Health;

Department of Labor and Employment;
Department of Justice;
Department of the Interior and Local Government;
Department of Agriculture;
National Economic and Development Authority;
National Nutrition Center;
Council for the Welfare of Children; and
Three private individuals concerned with the welfare of children and youth with no dual role as a government employee and with at least one (1) being an active member of a legitimate youth organization.

The Council proper reviews existing policies and proposes legislation consistent with the principles enshrined in the Convention. Each of the above agencies, on the other hand, implement programs and services for children toward national compliance with the Convention.

The Child Rights Center of the Commission on Human Rights was established to monitor the violation of children's rights particularly the Protection Rights.

In 1992, the President Corazon Aquino issued Proclamation No. 855 adopting the Philippines Plan of Action for Children: 2000 and Beyond (PPAC). This is the blueprint of all efforts for children. PPAC was formulated in response to the World Summit Declaration on Survival, Protection and Development of Children and to the Convention on the Rights of the Child.

In the said proclamation, the President ordered the Council for the Welfare of Children to co-ordinate the implementation of the plan through its national and sub-national mechanisms including the local government units and non-government organizations.

In 1992, President Fidel Ramos reiterated the implementation of the PPACV through Memorandum Order 39 and 40.

Effectively, the entire government machinery has been mobilized to ensure the country's compliance with the obligations required as a State Party to the Convention.

The non-government organizations have also formed a coalition to assist in the implementation of the Convention and in monitoring the country's implementation of the same.

Question 4

Are there at present any NGOs in your country operating in the area of the child and the environment?

Response

According to the Department of Environment and Natural Resources (DENR), there are more than seventy (70) non-governmental organizations involved in environmental programs. According to an NGO Coalition representative, there are also child-focused agencies that have environmental protection concerns but none of them focuses on the area of the child and environment.

Question 5

5.a Is there any general education about the child and the environment offered in secondary education, in university education, or in medical schools?
5.b If so, what type of course is available at each level?

Response

Yes. Based on the said matrix, the right of the child and environment are two (2) concepts embodied in the existing Desired Learning Competencies (DLC). These concepts are discussed either singly or interrelatedly. In line with these concepts are related ideas which become the foci of the discussion. Some of these related ideas include the following:

1. Man has the responsibility to develop an appreciation and respect for the rights of others over the use of natural resources.
2. Man has a moral responsibility for his environmental decisions.
3. Environmental management has effects on individuals and social institutions.
4. Individual citizens should be stimulated to become well informed about the resource issues, problems, management procedure and ecological principles.

Side by side with the acquisition of knowledge on environmental education, the inculcation of values is also addressed. Equity, justice, self-discipline, social responsibility, cleanliness, tidiness, orderliness and concern for others are some of the values integrated into environmental education at all year levels.

According to the Commission on Higher Education and the University of the Philippines, the following are some of the courses offered in the universities/medical schools in the Philippines:
BS Major in Environmental Science;
Family Life and Development Program;
BS/BA Psychology;
Psychiatry;
Pediatrics; and
BS Education.

African representation Department of Foreign Affairs Pretoria, South Africa

Question 1

1 a. Is there any procedural right (which corresponds to the substantive right to a clean environment with special emphasis for the child), and if so, how is it enforced?

Response

Sections 24 and 28 of the Bill of Rights contained in the new South African Constitution, which will enter into force during 1997, and deals respectively with the environment and with children provide as follows:

'*24 Environment* – Everyone has the right:

(a) to an environment that is not harmful to their health or well-being; and
(b) to have the environment protected, for the benefit of present and future generations, through reasonable legislative and other measures that –
  (i) prevent pollution and ecological degradation;
  (ii) promote conservation; and
  (iii) secure ecologically sustainable development and use of natural resources while promoting justifiable economic and social development.'

'*28 Children* – (1) Every child has the right:

(a) to a name and a nationality from birth;
(b) to family care, parental care, or appropriate alternative care when removed from the family environment;
(c) to basic nutrition, shelter, basic health care services, and social services;
(d) to be protected from maltreatment, neglect, abuse, or degradation;
(e) to be protected from exploitative labour practices;
(f) not to be required or permitted to perform work or provide services that

   (i) are inappropriate for a person of that child's age; or
   (ii) place at risk the child's well-being, education, physical or mental health, or spiritual, moral, or social development;

(g) not to be detained except as a measure of last resort, in which case, in addition to the rights a child enjoys under sections 12 and 35, the child may be detained only for the shortest appropriate period of time, and has the right to be-
   (i) kept separately from detained persons over the age of 18 years; and
   (ii) treated in a manner, and kept in conditions, that take account of the child's age;

(h) to have a legal practitioner assigned to the child by the state, and at state expense, in civil proceedings affecting the child, if substantial injustice would otherwise result; and
   (i) not to be used directly in armed conflict, and to be protected in times of armed conflict.

(2) A child's best interest is of paramount importance in every matter concerning the child.

(3) In this section, 'child' means a person under the age of 18 years.

As far as enforcement of the Bill of Rights is concerned, section 38 provides:

'Anyone listed in this section has the right to approach a competent court, alleging that a right in the Bill of Rights has been infringed or threatened, and the court may grant appropriate relief, including a declaration of rights. The persons who may approach a court are-

(a) anyone acting in their own interest;
(b) anyone acting on behalf of another person who cannot act in their own name;
(c) anyone acting as a member of, or in the interest of, a group or a class of persons;
(d) anyone acting in the public interest; and
(e) an association acting in the interest of its members.

Question 2

Is the State a party to the 1989 Convention on the Rights of the Child?

Response

The Republic of South Africa ratified the Convention on the Rights of the Child on 16 June 1995.

Question 3

3.a What are the legislative acts implementing the Convention?

3.b What are the organs of the State which implement the Convention?

Response

The South African Constitution. Other implementing legislation is in the process of being drafted.

Response

Parliament
National Youth Commission
Various Government departments
Human Rights Commission

Question 4

Are there at present any NGOs in your country operating in the area of the child and the environment?

Response
There are several NGOs operating in the area of the child and the environment. The Wildlife Society, Ecolink, Molo Songololo, Seaworld, Ekko Clubs, Delta Environment, Seaworld, Umgeni Water, Enviro Teach, Shell Education Services, Two Ocean Aquarium, are only some of the NGOs. Organizations, such as the Girl Guide Association, Boy Scouts, Voortrekkers and other youth groups, are also involved.

Question 5

Is there any general education about the child and the environment offered in secondary education, in university education, or in medical schools?

Response

The curricula are currently under review and there are developments in this regard which will include the environment in all spheres – some documents that can be attached to the reply (omitted from this text).

The Director General
M.E. Olivier
(Route HREG8)

Annex III

Commission on Human Rights

Sub-Commission on Prevention of Discrimination and Protection of Minorities Forty-sixth Session

Human rights and the environment

Review for further developments in fields with which the Sub-Commission has been concerned.

FINAL REPORT PREPARED BY MRS FATMA ZOHRA KSENTINI,
SPECIAL RAPPORTEUR[1]

Introduction

1. The environment, development, democracy, human rights: these are the key issues which characterize the close of this century and pose a continuing challenge to the establishment of an order in which, in conformity with the Universal Declaration of Human Rights, the rights set out therein can be fully realized. Revolt against oppression, the quest for justice, the search for progress and the pursuit of development are fundamental concerns of mankind. They were apparent in the acts of the Founder and King of Babylon, Hammurabi, who, 16 centuries before Jesus Christ, sought to bring in the reign of justice to protect the weak from being wronged. They also emerge from the thoughts of the Confucian Meng-tzu who, 300 years before Jesus Christ, asserted: 'The individual is infinitely important; what matters least is the person of the sovereign.' They also mark Antigone's act of revolt when she invoked her right to disobedience in order to transgress the orders of the King, and Spartacus' courage when he led the slaves to break their chains.

2. When, on 10 December 1948, the international community solemnly proclaimed the Universal Declaration of Human Rights, it acknowledged the dynamics of the triptych of oppression–revolt–repression, and underscored in two essential preambular paragraphs that 'disregard and contempt for human rights have resulted in barbarous acts which have outraged the conscience of mankind, and the advent of a world in which human beings shall enjoy freedom of speech and belief and freedom from fear and want has been proclaimed as the highest aspiration of the common people' and that 'it is essential,

1 Please note that the information covered in Annex III contains extracts of the original document.

if man is not to be compelled to have recourse, as a last resort, to rebellion against tyranny and oppression, that human rights should be protected by the rule of law'.

3. The Universal Declaration also underscores the full importance of the legal expression of human rights and of establishing a legal framework that provides effective remedies. The protection of human rights by the rule of law indeed remains one of the means of democratic expression of claims, within a structured framework that guarantees legal action while fostering dialogue

4. For the particular purposes of this study of human rights and the environment, it is equally important to establish the legal framework for pursuing what have become the essential demands of this century, in order to take up the legitimate concerns of our generation, to preserve the interests of future generations and mutually to agree upon the components of a right to a healthy and flourishing environment.

5. The Special Rapporteur remains convinced that providing the various agents and beneficiaries of this evolving right with the legal framework and means of expression, communication, participation and action will reinforce the channels for dialogue, discussion and co-operation nationally, regionally and internationally, thereby making it possible to define the mutually agreed component of this right as well as its harmonious application, in conformity with the universally recognized fundamental principles of human rights. Human rights would thereby gain a new dimension. In addition, they should make it possible to go beyond reductionist concepts of 'mankind first' or 'ecology first' and achieve a coalescence of the common objectives of development and environmental protection. This would signify a return to the principal

[...]

(a) A universal awareness of the scale, seriousness and complexity of environmental problems;

(b) The need for appropriate national, regional and international measures to address such problems;

(c) The close link between the environment and human rights. Some human rights violations are allegedly the causes of or factors in environmental degradation; moreover, deterioration of the environment affects the enjoyment of human rights (life, health, work, information, participation, self-determination, the right to development, to peace and security, and so on);

(d) Specific regional and other development projects were advanced as illustrations of environmental degradation and infringement of human rights;

(e) The Sub-Commission and the Commission on Human Rights should focus greater attention on the environmental problems that affect human rights.

B. Terms of reference of the Special Rapporteur

12. In response to the requests of the Sub-Commission and the commission, Mrs. Ksentini submitted a note to the Sub-Commission at its forty-second session containing a number of proposals for a study of the environment and its relation to human rights (A/CN.4/Sub.2/1990/12). After examining the note, the Sub-Commission adopted resolution 1990/7 on 30 August 1990 requesting the Special Rapporteur to submit a preliminary report to it at its forty-third session. That request was approved by the Commission on Human Rights, in resolution 1991/44 dated 5 March 1991, and by the Economic and Social Council, in decision 1991/244 dated 31 May 1991. The Sub-Commission, after considering the preliminary report (E/CN.4/Sub.2/1991/8), adopted resolution 1991/24 dated 29 August 1991, whereby it requested the Special Rapporteur to submit a progress report. The Commission on Human Rights in decision 1992/110 dated 28 February 1992, and the Economic and Social Council, in decision 1992/252 dated 29 July 1992, endorsed this request.

13. The Sub-Commission examined the progress report (EICN.4/Sub.2/1992/7 and Add.1) containing an analysis of national and international provisions and the decisions and comments of human rights bodies relating to human rights and the environment as well as information on the results of the United Nations Conference on Environment and Development held in Rio de Janeiro from 3 to 14 June 1992, in which the Special Rapporteur participated as an observer.

14. In resolution 1992/31 dated 27 August 1992, the Sub-Commission took note with appreciation of the progress report and requested the Special Rapporteur to continue her study and to submit to the Sub-Commission at its forty-fifth session a second progress report containing additional information and an analysis of decisions and views of international human rights organs and other relevant organs, as well as information on and an analysis of national laws and practice. The Commission on Human Rights endorsed this request in decision 1993/144 dated 10 March 1993.

[...]

Chapter III concerns other aspects of the relationship between human rights and the environment. Chapters IV and V analyse the impact of the environment on vulnerable groups and on the enjoyment of fundamental rights. In chapter VI, the Special Rapporteur sets out her conclusions and recommendations. The annexes contain a draft declaration of principles on human rights and the environment, an overview of consultations with non-governmental organizations and a summary of national legislation and practices compiled by the Special Rapporteur, essentially on the basis of replica by governments.

25. Regulation of global transboundary pollution has made it possible to define a range of relevant principles which, according to Michel Prieur, 'may be considered as binding upon States'. 5/ in this respect he cites the following principles:

'Before engaging in any activity that may have perceptible effects on the environment of another State, the State under whose jurisdiction or control the activity is to take place must assess its consequences;

It must inform the other State and transmit to it relevant details of the project, provided they constitute information and data whose transmission is not prohibited by national legislation or by relevant international treaties;

In the case of activities liable to damage the environment of another State, it must consult the State concerned if the latter so requests;

States must urgently inform the other States likely to be affected, cooperate by providing mutual assistance in order to take the necessary preventive measures and, where necessary, eliminate, mitigate or repair the environmentally harmful consequences;

If the activities that take place within the jurisdiction or under the control of a State damage, or are liable to damage, the environment of another State, the latter's residents who are affected or liable to be affected by them must be able to have access to the administrative and judicial procedures of the State in which the environmental damage originates, on the same conditions as residents of that State. If persons living abroad have already suffered damage, the same remedies must be available to them as to residents. During these procedures, non-residents must receive the same treatment as residents;

A State must not discriminate in its legislation or in the application of that legislation on the basis of the location of the environmentally harmful effects, by applying less stringent rules to activities whose adverse environmental effects are felt beyond its frontiers.'

26. As early as 1968, in resolution 2398 (XXII) dated 3 December 1968, the General Assembly underscored the consequent effects of impairment of the quality of the human environment on the condition of man and on his enjoyment of basic human rights. In the same year, the Proclamation of Tehran drew attention to the fact that, while recent scientific discoveries and technological advances had opened vast prospects for economic, social and cultural progress, such developments might nevertheless endanger the rights and freedoms of individuals and would require continuing attention (AICONF.32141, Proclamation, para. 18). The Stockholm Declaration of 1972 went on to recognize the relationship between the environment, man and his basic rights, even the right to life itself.

27. The Declaration of the 1972 United Nations Conference on the Human Environment 6/ contains, in addition to its 26 principles, an Action Plan for the Human Environment, which made possible the establishment of the United Nations Environment Programme, decided upon by the right to a healthy and decent environment, which is inextricably linked, both individually and collectively, to universally recognized fundamental human rights standards and principles, and which may be demanded as such by their beneficiaries, i.e. individuals alone or in association with others, communities, associations and other components of civil society, as well as peoples.

[...]

32. Many documents have since been adopted by international, regional and national bodies to strengthen the notion of the right to the environment and underscore its interdependence with other human rights (the Declaration on Social Progress and Development adopted in General Assembly resolution 2542 (XXIV), dated 11 December 1969 the Charter of Economic Rights and Duties of States; 9/ United Nations environmental programmes, including resolution 421186, dated 11 December 1987, relating to the Environmental Perspective to the Year 2000 and Beyond; 10/ General Assembly resolution 37/7, dated 28 October 1982, proclaiming the World Charter for Nature).

33. The World Charter for Nature proclaims 24 principles of conservation 'by which all human conduct affecting nature is to be guided and judged', with as its basic precept the idea that nature shall be respected and its essential processes shall not be impaired'. Particular attention should be drawn to the following principles, which are directly linked to the rights set out in the international human rights instrument (right to health, to well-being, to an education, to participate in decision-making).

    Principle 11, which concerns in particular the control of activities which might have an impact on nature, assessment of their consequences and environmental impact studies of development projects, and the rehabilitation of degraded areas for purposes in accord with their natural potential and compatible with the well-being of affected populations;

    Principle 15, relating to broad dissemination of knowledge of nature, particularly by ecological education as an integral part of general education;

    Principle 23, which recognizes that 'All persons, in accordance with their national legislation, shall have the opportunity to participate, individually or with others, in the formulation of decisions of direct concern to their environment, and shall have access to means of redress when their environment has suffered damage or degradation';

    Principle 24, pursuant to which each person has a duty to act in accordance with the provisions of the charter and each person acting individually, in association with others or through participation in the political process shall strive to ensure that the objectives and requirements' of the Charter are met.

C. International human rights instrument

34. International human rights instrument contain few specific provisions relating to the environment. The Universal Declaration of Human Rights [sic] economic, social and cultural rights indispensable for his dignity and the free development of his personality'); article 24 (right to rest and leisure); article 25 (right to an adequate standard of living).

(b) *Proclamation of Tehran*

41. Article 18 calls for vigilance concerning scientific discoveries and technological advances which, although they have opened vast prospects for economic, social and cultural progress, may nevertheless endanger the rights and freedoms of individuals.

(c) *International Covenant on Economic, Social and Cultural Rights*

42. Article 1 (right of peoples to self-determination and to freely dispose of their natural wealth and resources), article 7 (a decent living, safe and healthy working conditions, rest and leisure), article 11 (right to an adequate standard of living, and to be free from hunger; programmes to improve methods of production, conservation and distribution of food; disseminating knowledge of principles of nutrition; measures to achieve the most efficient development and utilization of natural resources; equitable distribution of world food supplies), article 12 (right to health; steps to be taken for the healthy development of the child, improvement of all aspects of environmental and industrial hygiene), article 15 (right to enjoy the benefits of scientific progress and its applications).

(d) *International Covenant on Civil and Political Rights*

43. Article 1 (right of peoples to self-determination and to freely dispose of their natural wealth and resources), article 6 (right to life), article 7 (prohibition of cruel, inhuman or degrading treatment or punishment, medical or scientific experimentation without the consent of the person concerned), article 17 (arbitrary or unlawful

interference with privacy or the family) and article 20 (prohibition of propaganda for war).

(e) *International Convention on the Elimination of All Forms of Racial Discrimination*

44. The flagrant discrimination to which marginalized persons, vulnerable groups, minorities and indigenous peoples are subjected vis-à-vis ecological risks, raises sharply the issue of the effective implementation of the basic principle of non-discrimination set out in the convention, and that of the practical implementation of all the provisions of the convention on behalf of disadvantaged individuals and groups (and more particularly article 5 on the right to equal treatment before the tribunals, the right to security of person, political and civil rights, economic, social and cultural rights, the right of access to any place or service intended for use by the general public, and article 6 on the right to effective protection and remedies).

(g) *Convention on the Elimination of All Forms of Discrimination against Women*

45. The observation concerning the Convention referred to above are also valid for this Convention. The Special Rapporteur further wishes to stress

[...]

Chapter II: Right to development, participatory democracy and the environment

A. Some aspects of the problem

1. Indivisibility and interdependence of all human right

47. The close relationship which exists between development – recognized as a human right by several international texts, including the Declaration on the Right to Development adopted by the General Assembly in its resolution 41/128 of 4 December 1986 – and the environment throws into relief the indivisible and interdependent nature of all human rights. The idea of indivisibility has already been emphasized by the Proclamation of Tehran of 13 May 1968, which states in paragraph 13 that:

'Since human rights and fundamental freedoms are indivisible, the full realization of civil and political rights without the enjoyment of economic, social and cultural rights is impossible. The achievement of lasting progress in the implementation of human rights is dependent upon sound and effective national and international policies of economic and social development.'

48. General Assembly resolution 32/130 of 16 December 1977 and the subsequent resolutions on 'Alternative approaches and ways and means within the United Nations system for improving the effective enjoyment of human rights and fundamental freedoms" share the objective of reconciling" different generations of rights and rehabilitating economic, social and cultural rights. This task of reconciliation was to be complete by the Declaration on the Right to Development, which reaffirms in the preamble the principle already embodied in the Universal Declaration of Human Rights of 1948 that:

'everyone is entitled to a social and international order in which the rights and freedoms set forth in that Declaration can be fully realized'.

In article 6 the Declaration on the Right to Development states unequivocally that 'All human rights and fundamental freedoms are indivisible and interdependent' and that they should receive equal attention and urgent consideration. Furthermore, the Declaration passes over neither the internal nor the external factors impeding the realization of the right to development (denial of civil, political, economic, social and cultural rights; inappropriate development policies; unfavourable national and international conditions; need to establish a new international economic order, to realize the right of peoples to self-determination and enable them to exercise their inalienable rights to full sovereignty over all their natural wealth and resources; primary responsibility of States for the creation of national and international conditions favourable to the realization of the right to development, and so on).

49. Underlying the links between the right to development and the right to the environment is the notion of the indivisibility and interdependence of all human rights, whether civil or political, economic, social or cultural. Moreover, it is impossible to separate the claim to the right to a healthy and

[...]

53. The data on the extent of poverty given in the preliminary report (E/CN.4/Sub.2/1991/8) have not basically changed. As can be seen from the World Bank's 'World Development Report 1992', 1 billion people lack an adequate water supply, and about 1.7 billion people do not have adequate sanitation facilities. 13/ UNDP's 'Human Development Report 1993' states that in the developing countries some 800 million people still do not get enough food; nearly 1 billion people – 35 per cent of the adult population – are still illiterate; about one third of the world's total population, or 1.3 billion people, are in absolute poverty; about 17 million people die every year from infectious and parasitic diseases; approximately 95 per cent of the 10–12 million HIV-infected people are in the developing world; each day, 34,000 young children still die from malnutrition and disease; two thirds of illiterates are women; internal conflicts affect some 60 countries, and about 35 million people are refugees or internally displaced; more than 850 million people live in areas that are suffering from desertification. 14/

54. It is impossible to draw up an exhaustive or final balance sheet showing the effect of environmental degradation on human rights

the enjoyment of which is already very much affected by underdevelopment and poverty (intolerable infant mortality and undernourishment; illiteracy; lack of primary health care and of social services; precarious housing; marginalization of the underprivileged strata, or even racism and discrimination; non-participation in the conduct of public affairs and in the country's political, economic and cultural decision-making, and so on). It is easy to see, however, that the poor populations, the underprivileged strata, the minority groups and others are the most affected in that they are more vulnerable to ecological risks and repercussions (absence of legal and material means of protection; lack of access to information; lack of suitable care, etc.). Furthermore poverty, underdevelopment and marginalization reduce the prospects of economic, social and cultural integration or reintegration of the victims. Those victims find themselves in a vicious circle which includes a series of violations of human rights: assaults on life and health; degradation of living conditions and disintegration of the family unit; unemployment; emigration, exodus, resettlement and even forced migrations which lead to further violations of human rights (racism; discrimination; xenophobia; acculturation; violations of dignity and arbitrary detention; refoulement; marginalization; precarious living and housing conditions; prostitution; drugs; street children, etc.).

3. The external factors

55. The structure of international relations, and more particularly the burden of debt and the impact of structural adjustment measures on the least favoured categories, may constitute serious impediments to the achievement of sustainable development.

56. The Brundtland report referred to above had already noted that: 'A mainspring of economic growth is new technology, and while this technology offers the potential for slowing the dangerously rapid consumption of finite resources, it also entails high risks, including new forms of pollution and the introduction to the planet of new variations of life forms that could change evolutionary pathways. Meanwhile, the industries most heavily reliant on environmental resources concept of sustainable and environmentally sound development' which the "Earth Summit", meeting in Rio in 1992, endeavoured to focus by defining an ambitious programme of action, Agenda 21, clarified by a Declaration of 27 principles solemnly adopted on that occasion. The Special

Rapporteur does not intend to revert to the results of this Conference, which she outlined in her earlier reports. 20/ However, she wishes to refer to the features which seem to her to underlie the consensual approach to environmental problems.

64. Reference should be made at this point to the content of the Declaration on International Economic Co-operation adopted by the General Assembly in Way 1990, in particular the 'Revitalization of economic growth and development of the developing countries', which pays ample heed to the environment, thus forging an inseparable link between development and the environment. The Declaration recognizes that 'Economic development must be environmentally sound and sustainable, (para. 16) and notes that the current threat to the environment is the common concern of all. All countries should take effective actions for the protection and enhancement of the environment *in accordance with their respective capacities and responsibilities* and taking into account the specific needs of developing countries. *As the major sources of pollution, the developed countries have the main responsibility for taking appropriate measures urgently*. The economic growth and development of developing countries are essential in order to address problems of the degradation and protection of the environment. *New and additional financial resources* will have to be channelled to developing countries.' (para. 29).

65. One should in this respect bear in mind the premises, defined by the General Assembly in resolution 44/228 of 22 December 1989, premises which, according to the Secretary-General, 'were accepted when the nations of the world called for the United Nations Conference on Environment and Development'. 21/ It will be noted in particular that this resolution stresses that the major cause of the deterioration of the environment is the "pattern of production and consumption, particularly in the industrialized countries' and that other responsibility for containing, reducing and eliminating the global environmental damage must be borne by the countries causing such damage". It recognizes that '*new and additional* financial resources will have to be channelled to developing countries in order to ensure their full participation in global efforts for environmental protection'. It was also decided to examine environmental degradation and the international economic environment *without introducing new forms of conditionality*'. The examination of strategies for national and international action conducive to sustained

and environmentally sound development' should take place "bearing in mind that the incorporation of environmental concerns and considerations in development planning and policies *should not be used to introduce new forms of conditionality in and or in development financing and should not serve as a pretext for creating unjustified barriers to trade"*.

66. The Agenda 21 programme is considered as giving expression to the now accepted principle whereby responsibilities are shared but separate, in accordance with the similarly accepted principle that the polluter pays reaffirmed in Principle 16 of the Declaration of Rio, on the basis of the idea that the polluter should, in principle, bear the cost of pollution', and establishing a global partnership on a new and equitable basis. In this

'Development strategies which have been oriented merely towards economic growth and financial considerations have failed to a large extent to achieve social justice; human rights have been infringed, directly and through the depersonalization of social relations, the breakdown of families and communities, and of social and economic life' (para. 153).

[...]

70. The right to participation has both individual and collective dimensions; it covers economic, social, cultural and political aspects which give full meaning to the concept of democracy. Without going back to the fruitful discussions on this issue, the Special Rapporteur wishes to emphasize the full importance of the concept, of participatory democracy in the context of the environment, without which the concept of sustainable development would be totally without substance.

71. The United Nations Conference on Environment and Development had the merit of stressing the importance of this participation by including it in various solemnly adopted principles (see in particular Principle 10 of the Declaration of Rio on the participation of citizens, Principle 20 on the participation of women, or Principle 22 on the participation of indigenous people and their communities). Moreover, the underlying principle of the implementation of Agenda 21 is the adequate reinforcement of the role which the main groups are required to play. A whole section is devoted to this issue. The Conference was of the opinion that critical to the effective implementation of the

mechanisms agreed to by Governments in all programme areas of Agenda 21 would be the commitment and *genuine involvement* of all social groups, and that one of the fundamental prerequisites for the achievement of sustainable development was broad public participation in *decision-making*. Furthermore, the conference recognized, in the specific context of environment, 'the need for new forms of participation' and 'the need of individuals, groups and organizations to participate in environmental impact assessment procedures and to know about and participate in (pertinent) decisions. 22/

72. The Conference implicitly linked the notion of real participation in the right of access to information by noting that individuals, groups and organizations should have access to information relevant to environment and development held by national authorities, including information on products and activities that have or are likely to have a significant impact on the environment, and information on environmental protection measures'. 23/ The link between participation and information can also be found in Principle 10 of the Declaration of Rio.

73. The Vienna Declaration and Programme of Action, adopted by the World Conference on Human Rights on 25 June 1993, places particular emphasis on participatory democracy and states solemnly that democracy, development and respect for human rights and fundamental freedoms are interdependent and mutually reinforcing. Democracy is based on the freely expressed will of the people to determine their own political economic, social and cultural systems and their full participation in all aspects of their lives.' 24/

[...]

'My people venerate each corner of this land, each shining pine needle, each sandy beach, each wreath of mist in the dark woods, each glade, each humming insect; in the thought and practice of my people, all these things are sacred. The sap rising in the tree carries the memory of the red man.' 26/

78. Echoing Chief Seattle, one Indian leader stated to the working Group on Indigenous Populations at its 1985 session:

'Our principal and fundamental struggle is for the land, our territory and natural resources our defence of the land and natural resources is for the cultural and human survival of our children For us, the first thing is to secure our land, which belongs to us by right, because we are the true owners of the land and natural resources. We indigenous peoples know that without land there can be no education, there can be no health and there can be no life." 27/

79. Experts in the field have been particularly critical of large-scale development schemes in Indian lands, as reflected in the background papers submitted at the United Nations Seminar on the effects of racism and racial discrimination on the social and economic relations between indigenous peoples and States (Geneva, 16–20 January 1989). In one background paper, Prof. Rodolfo Stavenhagen writes:

> 'Much damage has been done to the indigenous peoples through economic development projects The isolated, marginal areas often occupied by indigenous peoples constitute the last great and, until recently, unexploited reserves of natural resources. Neither State planners nor multinational corporations nor international development agencies have hesitated to "incorporate" these areas into the national and international economy. In the process, indigenous peoples have suffered genocide and ethnocide.' 28/

80. Another expert, Prof. Vitit Muntarbhorn, writes:

> '[C]ultural disintegration is compounded by destruction of the ecology and habitat upon which indigenous groups depend for their physical and cultural survival. Deforestation, particularly of rain forests, and pollution introduced by outsiders jeopardize the modus vivendi of indigenous groups. The social nexus binding members of the group to the environment is thus annihilated.' 29/

[...]

81. In part as a reflection on the comments of the experts at the 1989 seminar, the issue of indigenous peoples was addressed at the 1990 Global Consultation on the Realization of the Right to Development. once again, the assessment of the environmental factors of human rights and indigenous peoples was harsh'

> the experience of indigenous peoples and development clearly demonstrated that human rights and development are inseparable, for the abuse of the rights of indigenous peoples is principally a

development issue. Forced development has deprived them of their human rights, in particular the right to life and the right to their own means of their land by unscrupulous acts; article 18 require penalties for land violations; article 19 requires provision of adequate land to enable indigenous peoples to live and increase normally.

85. ILO has a well-developed enforcement process by which indigenous peoples could seek remedies for the violation of the convention. Regrettably, few Governments have ratified Convention No. 169 and there is no public information regarding complaints that are lodged. Additional ratifications will provide increased access to the ILO dispute-resolution mechanisms, including a procedure by which individuals may petition the ILO Governing Body through recognized representative organizations. Under other ILO procedures, organizations may call the matter to the attention of ILO in the form of a representation. Or the ILO Governing Body may open a complaint on its own motion or at the insistence of a delegate to the International Labour Conference. Both representations and complaints are investigated, and the results may be published if the situation is not corrected. 32/

86. The study on racial discrimination, begun by the Special Rapporteur of the Sub-Commission, Mr. Hernan Santa Cruz, in 1965, contained a chapter on indigenous peoples. 33/ The Special Rapporteur's suggestion that the United Nations study the situation of indigenous peoples in a comprehensive fashion led to the appointment in 1971 by the Sub-Commission of Mr. Jose Martinez Cobo to carry out such a study. His report 34/ contains much discussion about indigenous peoples and their land. In 1981, the Sub-Commission proposed the establishment of the Working Group on Indigenous Populations, which met for the first time in 1982. The Working Group has prepared a draft declaration on indigenous rights, which is still under consideration by the working Group. Throughout the drafting period, indigenous land rights and environmental concerns have been the most keenly contested, with indigenous organizations insistent that any formulation of their rights must firmly protect their lands from exploitation and ecological degradation. Their concern is clearly reflected in the 1992 draft as contained in the report of the Working Group on its tenth session, 35/ especially in operative paragraphs 17–20 and 38 which the Special Rapporteur set out in her second progress report. 36/

87. As a further reflection of serious concerns about indigenous peoples, human rights and the environment, in 1992 the United Nations sponsored the United Nations Technical Conference on Practical Experiences in the Realization of Sustainable and Environmentally Sound Self-development of Indigenous Peoples. The report and the background papers 371 provide an analysis of the impact of ecological devastation on indigenous peoples and their struggle to protect their land and its resources, and to develop their economics in an ecologically sustainable fashion that does not jeopardize traditional ways.

88. In her review of cases brought to the Human Rights Committee and to the Inter-American Commission on Human Rights by or on behalf of indigenous peoples, the Special Rapporteur is impressed by the fact that the human rights violations at issue almost always arise as a consequence of land rights violations and environmental degradation and indeed are inseparable from these factors. In her progress report 38/ the Special Rapporteur described Communication No. 16711984 addressed to the Human Rights Committee by Recent Sessions of the Inter-Commission Task Force on Indigenous Peoples of the IUCN World Conservation Union, at which indigenous leaders and others exchanged information and presented case studies on indigenous sustainable development, 48/ are also encouraging developments. The Special Rapporteur is pleased by the increasing co-operation between indigenous peoples and their organizations and environmental organizations which should enhance the abilities of indigenous peoples to preserve their territories from ecological destruction.

93. In spite of some encouraging events, the Special Rapporteur is aware that existing efforts to protect indigenous peoples' rights and their fragile habitat have been inadequate. The situation of indigenous peoples, especially as it relates to human rights and the environment, is at a critical point. No one single solution can hope to address the multifaceted problems. None the less, she is aware that alternatives to large-scale development schemes, with their potentially destructive consequences, exist.

94. These alternatives must be encouraged. Indigenous peoples must genuinely participate in all decision making regarding their lands and resources. The international community, in particular the United Nations and regional monitoring procedures, must respond accordingly.

B. Protection of the environment in periods of armed conflict

95. Montesquieu wrote in *L'esprit des lois*: 'This right of peoples is naturally based on this principle – that the various nations must in peace do one another the greatest good and in war the least evil'. Despite the United Nations Charter's prohibition – in Article 2, paragraph 4 - of the use of force in international relations, war unfortunately remains a constant that fully demonstrates the value of international humanitarian law, a law which imposes rules for the conduct of hostilities, restricts the methods and means of warfare, and protects persons, property and environment liable to be affected in conflicts.

96. The principle of *humanity* and the concept of *proportionality* impose limits on war, the Declaration of St. Petersburg recognizing as early as 1868 that 'the only legitimate object which States should endeavour to accomplish during war is to weaken the military forces of the enemy'.

97. For their part, the Hague Conventions of 18 October 1907 and the regulations relating thereto contain provisions which deal with the protection of the environment, even though this term is not expressly used. In a report submitted to the General Assembly in 1993, 49/ ICRC rightly notes that 'The destruction of property in times of armed conflict is also restricted by customary international law'.

98. The Stockholm Declaration of 1972, apart from enunciating the general duty to protect and improve the environment, expressly states, in Principle 26, that 'Man and his environment must be spared the effects of nuclear weapons and all other means of mass destruction. States must strive to reach prompt agreement, in the relevant international organs, on the elimination and complete destruction of such weapons.

[...]

unnecessary harm. It protects the environment as such and is therefore broader in scope than article 55, which is intended to protect the civilian population from the effects of warfare on the environment. In both cases the following are prohibited: (a) attacks on the environment as such; and (b) making use of the environment as an instrument of warfare'. 51/

103. ICRC considers that, besides article 35, paragraph 3, and article 55, other provisions of Protocol I touch incidently on protection of the environment in armed conflict. In particular, article 56 deals with the danger to the environment resulting from the destruction of dams, dykes or nuclear electrical generating stations. Under the heading 'Protection of objects indispensable to the survival of the civilian population', article 54 prohibits in certain circumstances the destruction of, among other things, agricultural areas or irrigation works. Finally, article 36 obliges the parties to Protocol I to determine whether the acquisition, development or use of a new weapon would be compatible with international law. Of course, the rules on the protection of the environment are to be taken into account during this assessment.

104. Several other legal instruments also deal with protection of the environment in wartime, in particular: the Protocol for the Prohibition of the Use in war of Asphyxiating, Poisonous or Other Gases, and of Bacteriological Methods of Warfare, of 17 June 1925; the convention on the Prohibition of the Development, Production and Stockpiling of Bacteriological (Biological) and Toxin Weapons and on their Destruction, of 10 April 1972; the Convention on the Prohibition of Military or Any other Hostile Use of Environmental Modification Techniques, of 10 December 1976; the Convention on Prohibitions or Restrictions on the Use of Certain Conventional Weapons which may be Deemed to be Excessively Injurious or to have Indiscriminate Effects, of 10 October 1980; the Convention on the Prohibition of the Development, Production, Stockpiling and Use of Chemical Weapons and on their Destruction, of 13 January 1993; the Convention for the Protection of Cultural Property in the event of Armed conflict, of 14 May 1954; and the Convention concerning the Protection of the World Cultural and Natural Heritage, of 23 November 1972.

105. ICRC states that the rules protecting the victims of non-international armed conflict are less well developed than those governing international armed conflict. Article 3 common to the four Geneva Conventions of 1949 does not say anything about protecting the environment during civil wars; it addresses only humanitarian issues in the strictest sense. Protocol II Additional to the Geneva Conventions of 12 August 1949, and relating to the Protection of Victims of Non-International Armed Conflicts, contains no provisions relating explicitly to the environment. However, article 14,

on the protection of objects indispensable to the survival of the civilian population, has a direct impact on warfare and the environment, with its prohibition of attacks on agricultural areas, irrigation works and so on.

106. The protection of the environment in time of armed conflict has come tragically to the fore in the Iran–Iraq conflict, the Gulf war and in the conflict in the former Yugoslavia. Although the ecological consequences of these recent conflicts cannot yet be determined precisely, they have fuelled questions about the content, limits, shortcomings and indeed effectiveness of

[...]

C. The environment and international peace and security

111. The Special Rapporteur commented on the relationship between the environment, human rights, and international peace and security in her note and in her second progress report. 53/ Maintenance of international peace and security is a fundamental purpose of the United Nations and a duty of the organization and its Member States. 54/ The Importance of peace is underscored by its inclusion as a fundamental right in the Universal Declaration of Human Rights, especially its article 28. The Declaration on the Use of Scientific and Technological Progress in the Interests of Peace and for the Benefit of Mankind 55/ and the Declaration on the Right of Peoples to Peace 56/ are especially relevant to the issue of human rights and the environment.

112. The present potential for purposeful or even accidental environmental harm is a serious threat to peace and security, whether during war or in peacetime. Nuclear weapons and biological and chemical substances can eliminate much if not all of life. There are now many methods of altering the climate and destroying essential foodstuffs, and the deprivation that would certainly follow would create social unrest and instability. Population pressures, with or without intentional environmental degradation, will inevitably lead to States vying with each other for resources essential for survival.

113. The International Law Commission recognizes the ominous potential of purposeful environmental destruction and has characterized serious and intentional harm to the environment as a

crime against humanity. In the course of the debates in the Commission, it has been stated that acts with grave consequences to humans and the environment should be considered crimes and that there should be culpability for 'flagrant errors and omissions'. The debates also reflect the growing trend that destruction of the property of an ethnic group should be included in the concept of environmental harm.

114. In the Special Rapporteur's view, acts with substantial environmental and human damage falling short of crimes against humanity can still have a negative impact on international peace and security and are within the scope of the Declaration on the Use of Scientific and Technological Progress in the interests of Peace and for the Benefit of Mankind, the Charter of Economic Rights and Duties of States, and other relevant international instruments. The International Law commission has also been considering this problem in preparing a draft instrument on international liability for injurious consequences arising out of acts not prohibited by international law. 57/

115. The World Health Organization has for its part notified the Economic and social Council that, pursuant to resolution WHA 46.40 adopted by the World Health Assembly on 14 May 1993, the Director-General filed in the Registry of the International Court of Justice a request for an advisory opinion on the following question:

[...]

Chapter IV: Environmental degradation and its impact on vulnerable groups

A. Overview

117. Major environmental crises, such as the 1967 (Torrey Canyon), 1978 (Amoco Cadiz) and 1980 (EKOFIX) oil-spills, the Seveso (1976) and Bhopal (1984) chemical disasters, and the Chernobyl nuclear accident (1986), have highlighted the transnational nature of their impact and their multidimensional repercussions. The state of the environment is nowadays perceived as a world-wide problem that should be addressed globally, in a co-ordinated and coherent manner and through the concerted efforts of the international community. Issues such as the preservation of natural balances, the stability of the ecosystem as a whole, the preservation of natural resources or the very survival of the Earth are urgent because of the scale of environmental damage to the planet and its impact on the individual, on his well-being, and consequently on the enjoyment of fundamental rights, including the right to life.

118. According to the World Commission on Environment and Development (Brundtland Commission), since 1970, when the first Earth Day was celebrated, the world has lost almost 200 million hectares of forest; 11.4 million hectares of tropical forest have disappeared each year; one fifth of arable land has been affected by desertification. The Commission analysed the ecosystems and economic structures of various developed and developing countries. It drew attention to the need to match regulatory measures with planning in order to achieve 'sustainable development' that would make it possible to satisfy the needs of present generations without jeopardizing the opportunities of future generations. The 1992 Earth Summit again highlighted the major threats looming over the planet and the interaction among various phenomena, as is illustrated by the following examples:

1. Climate changes

119. Emissions resulting from human activities increase the atmospheric concentration of gases producing a greenhouse effect. The greenhouse effect will take the form of heating up the planet, probably accompanied by a rise in the level of the sea that might seriously threaten the sea and the climate. The rise in that level in many parts of the world, in particular, islands and low-lying areas, will have an effect on life, land, lifestyles, natural resources, cultural heritage and so on. Apart from the fact that the varying effects of climate on socio-economic systems have always imposed substantial constraints on development, the climate changes expected from the greenhouse effect may render those constraints utterly unbearable (effects on the water cycle and on food production chains; floods and drought; increase in the number, intensity and seriousness of natural disasters). These phenomena, while producing their own adverse effects on the enjoyment of human rights, will also worsen several existing problems and will affect most of all those populations, regions and countries that are particularly vulnerable.

120. In the words of the Ministerial Declaration of the Second World Climate Conference, 'The potential impact of such climate change could pose an environmental threat of an up to now unknown magnitude; and could jeopardize breakdown of the habitual lifestyle of the populations, who in addition live in a state of constant anxiety.' The absence or shortage of reliable information about the induced or delayed effects of such disasters does nothing to reassure those populations. In some instances, where the disasters have occurred in underdeveloped regions or have befallen marginalized population groups, the relief, assistance and allowances extended to the victims fall far short of the requisite minimum standards, to the point where it is possible to detect practices akin to a veritable discrimination that flouts the principles of dignity and equality innate in every human being.

[...]

5. Transboundary transfer of hazardous wastes

125. The transfer of toxic and dangerous products and wastes across frontiers and their dumping also lead to violations of human rights, not

only having regard to the risks incurred by man and his environment but also considering the observed trend to export dangerous substances produced in the North to developing countries, particularly in Africa. These intolerable practices, which impose severe risks on the South, are particularly outrageous in that they transfer problems to particularly vulnerable regions and populations (lack of resources for monitoring and prevention and of appropriate technology; absence of suitable legislation; broken-down sanitation; information that is unreliable, unusable, non-existent or inaccessible).

126. Until the mid-1980s, 80 per cent of the imports and exports of hazardous waste were between developed countries. 61/ In 1988, from 2 to 2.5 million tons of waste were transported among the European member countries of OECD. 62/ It was essentially only after 1986 that the North–South trend emerged. In this connection, Greenpeace has pointed out that between 1986 and 1988 over 6 million tons of hazardous waste were exported from the developed countries to the developing countries and the countries of Eastern Europe, in particular Romania and Hungary. 63/ it also asserted that of the 100 to 300 million tons of waste produced each year by the developed countries, some 50 million were shipped to Africa. 64/

127. While the local capacity for hazardous waste storage and elimination in the developed countries is steadily declining, the volume of waste produced continues to rise. Thus, the European Union is reported to have the capacity to eliminate an estimated 10 million tons of waste while it produces as much as 30 million tons a year. 65/

128. The scandals of 1987 and 1988, In particular the revelation concerning contracts between Western companies and African countries to which the companies concerned paid ridiculously low sums for land on which they could get rid of toxic waste, prompted the developing countries, and especially the countries of Africa 'to react. Within this context, the Council of Ministers of the Organization of African Unity declared, in resolution 1153 (XLVIII) dated 25 May 1988, that such dumping was 'a crime against Africa and the African people'. 66/

129. Similarly, on 7 December 1988, the United Nations General Assembly adopted a resolution condemning the dumping of nuclear and industrial wastes in Africa. 67/]

[...]

1. Women

138. There was good reason why Agenda 21, which was drawn up by the United Nations Conference on Environment and Development, devoted considerable attention to 'Global action for women towards sustainable and equitable development', and proposed a series of objectives for national Governments, together with activities and tangible measures to be undertaken to achieve the full integration of women into the development process and to ensure the effective implementation of their rights. 69/ The Declaration of Rio also notes that 'women have a vital.role to play in environmental management and development. Their full participation is therefore essential to achieve sustainable development' (Principle 20).

139. The decisive role of women in promoting development and preserving the environment is now firmly established. It is recognized that women's organizations have promoted environmental awareness, 70/ and that women play a critical role in the management, use and protection of natural resources and the environment, 71/ and in environmental education.

140. Even if, because of their traditional knowledge, skills and experience, women are no longer regarded as victims of environmental degradation, but as agents that possess essential assets for its preservation, it is still true that in practice they are the first to suffer from environmental degradation and among the last to enjoy the right to a satisfactory environment.

141. The Special Rapporteur notes that discrimination against women regardless of their acknowledged formal rights and the ambitious programmes of action devoted to them, in conjunction with the social inertia and prejudice surrounding the issue of women's emancipation, accounts for the precarious situation of women and the thankless tasks that bring them face to face with the consequences of the deterioration in living, working, housing and other conditions, depriving them of opportunities to enjoy their fundamental rights.

142. In addition, because of delays in the enjoyment of civil, cultural and political rights, it is not possible to ensure effective and genuine

participation by women in public life, and they are thereby prevented from influencing decision-making. Even if a favourable trend is discernible among local communities, in which women are increasingly involved in carrying out development projects, such participation needs to be further encouraged, developed and expanded. Moreover, it does nothing to remedy the fundamental imbalance in participation in public life and political office, from which women are virtually excluded, even in the developed countries. According to UNDP statistics for 1993, women in the developed countries made up 40 per cent of the total labour force, but still held fewer than 10 per cent of parliamentary seats. They held less than 5 per cent of ministerial and other senior posts throughout the world. 72/

143. The Special Rapporteur cannot fail to note a disturbing discrepancy between recognition of the decisive role played by women in promoting sustainable development and the place they occupy in practice. As was noted in a report by the United Nations: 73/

[...]

147. Education and a minimum of prosperity are essential if environmental problems are to be contained and if poor people too are to have a stake in the future. 76/

3. Disabled persons

148. The special Rapporteur wishes to refer to the situation of disabled persons in order to highlight the particular impact of the environment on the enjoyment of their rights as human beings and of their specific rights to enhanced protection which derive from the need to cater for their special requirements.

149. While environmental factors are frequently responsible for disability, the environment in which a disabled person lives is also likely to restrict access to essential care and services, aggravate disabilities, restrict the possibility of enjoying fundamental rights, and even lead to their total denial (right to life, to health, to work, to participation; discrimination, etc.).

150. The Special Rapporteur has discerned a tendency to minimize the problems posed by disabilities, despite the fact that estimates, such

as those of WHO, indicate that over '500 million individuals, i.e. 10 per cent of the world's population, suffer from some form of disability. In addition, 300 million of them live in the developing countries, where they are confronted with the inadequacy of assistance and rehabilitation services. Moreover, according to estimates by ILO, one third of disabled people, i.e. 160 million, are women, and 140 million children. These estimates lead to an unavoidable conclusion: *the impact of the environment* on disabled persons is felt at all stages, at several levels and in varying degrees – upstream as a cause of disability, and downstream by making the possibility of reintegration more difficult. Consequently, throughout their lives, disabled people suffer violations of their rights as individuals, as women or children, as disabled persons – a situation that is exacerbated by poverty.

151. The Special Rapporteur underscores the need for preventive measures to reduce the risk of disability. Non-governmental sources increasingly highlight environmental factors as causes of disability (air and water pollution; armed conflict, chemical weapons and vestiges of war, particularly mines; unhealthy living conditions; inadequate standard of living; natural disasters; technological accidents; nuclear catastrophes; dumping of toxic or hazardous products, etc.).

152. Where natural disasters or man-made accidents are concerned, disabled people are the first victims; they require special assistance which is not always available. This issue deserves special attention, as do the conditions for the reintegration of disabled people into the social, cultural, economic and political life of their country. In this connection, the Special Rapporteur endorses the recommendations contained in the United Nations study *Human rights and disabled persons.* 77/

[....]

disasters include the construction of large dams, Industrial accidents such as chemical explosions and nuclear accidents, improper handling of hazardous wastes and, of course, armed conflict and its consequences.

158. The Special Rapporteur is also concerned by the environmental degradation that often results from the sudden influx of refugee

populations on already stressed lands. This degradation stems from increased demands for food, fuel and other subsistence resources. The Special Rapporteur notes the General Assembly's increasing attention to this net of problems. In resolutions passed during its forty-eighth session, the General Assembly noted the environmental pressures posed by refugees and displaced persons in Central America (res. 48/117), in Azerbaijan (res. 48/114) and in many parts of Africa (res. 48/118).

159. People who flee their homes for environment-related reasons require humanitarian assistance simply to meet their basic survival needs. They do not necessarily seek political asylum or require the kind of international protection implied by the term 'refugee'. Many are displaced within their own countries, yet the scope of the problem may exceed the capacity of their Government and may therefore involve the international community. In this regard, the Special Rapporteur has examined the reports 85/ of Mr Francis Deng , the representative of the Secretary-General on internally displaced persons to the Commission of Human Rights. She hopes the international community will implement the concrete suggestions made by the representative.

160. UNHCR is particularly well placed to facilitate the delivery of essential services to displaced persons in emergency situations, on humanitarian grounds. 86/ The General Assembly affirmed the need to incorporate environmental concerns into the work of the UNHCR. UNHCR has recognized the need to improve understanding of the relationship between migration refugee flows and development and environmental issues. 87/ [...] Settlers and settlements, particularly in countries under foreign domination and in occupied territories, is generally part of a deliberate policy with the aim of changing the demographic structure and the political, cultural, religious and other characteristics of the countries and peoples in question, with the intent to destroy, in whole or in part, a national, ethnic, racial, religious or linguistic group as such, to ensure the domination of one group over another, or to distort the results of a planned self-determination referendum. In all cases, these are illegal practices which run counter to fundamental principles of international law. In some situations, these practices may be regarded an amounting to genocide. 89/

166. The right to development implies, as the Declaration on the Right to Development makes clear, the full realization of the right of peoples to self-determination and to full sovereignty over all their natural

wealth and resources. The pillage of a country's natural resources favoured by relation [sic] of political, economic or other subjection or dependence leads to uncoordinated and extroverted development which, besides keeping the country in a state of chronic underdevelopment, worsens the adverse consequences which that type of development produces on the environment (intensive exploitation of raw materials and products that upsets the ecological balance; wastage of non-renewable energy resources; establishment of polluting and high-risk industries; pauperization of rural areas, etc.).

167. The United Nations General Assembly for its part has regularly reiterated the principle set out in resolution 1803 (XVII) of 14 December 1962 whereby 'The right of peoples and nations to permanent sovereignty over their natural wealth and resources must be exercised in the interest of their national development and of the well-being of the people of the State concerned.' General Assembly resolution 48/46 of 10 December 1993 is worth noting here in connection with the activities of foreign economic and other interests which impede the implementation of the Declaration on the Granting of Independence to colonial countries and Peoples in Territories under colonial domination, in which the General Assembly reaffirms 'the solemn obligation of the administering Powers under the charter of the United Nations to promote the political, economic, social and educational advancement of the inhabitants of the Territories under their administration and *to protect the human and natural resources of those Territories against abuses*' and emphasizes that 'the natural resources are the heritage of the indigenous populations of the colonial and Non-Self-Governing Territories At the same time, the General Assembly expresses its concern about "the activities of those foreign, economic, financial and other interests that exploit" the resources of those Territories. In resolution 48/47 of 10 December 1993, the General Assembly urges the specialized agencies and other organizations of the United Nations system to formulate programmes that will support the sustainable development of small island Non-Self-Governing Territories and adopt measures that will enable those Territories to cope effectively, creatively and sustainably with environmental changes and to mitigate impacts and reduce the threats posed to marine and coastal resources.'

168. It may also be noted that Principle 23 of the Declaration of Rio states that 'The environment and natural resources of people under oppression, domination and occupation shall be protected.']

[...]

fundamental rights of the individual from which, under the International Covenant on Civil and Political Rights of 1966 (art. 4), the European Convention on Human Rights of 1950 and the American Convention on Human Rights (Pact of San José of 1969), no derogation is permitted.

173. The Human Rights Committee considered in its General Comment 6 that the right to life is 'the supreme right from which no derogation is permitted even in time of public emergency which threatens the life of the nation. It is a right which should not be interpreted narrowly the protection of this right requires that States adopt positive measures, such as measures to reduce infant mortality and to increase life expectancy to eliminate malnutrition and epidemics.' 91/

174. According to Professor Galicki, 'The right to life is the most important among all human rights legally guaranteed and protected by contemporary international law. On the other hand, the right to life is the one which is, most of all, connected to and dependent on proper protection of the human environment. It is because this right, like no other, may be directly and dangerously threatened by detrimental environmental measures. The right to life and the quality of life depend directly on positive or negative environmental conditions. Simultaneously, we cannot forget that this is an original right from which all other human rights derive.' 92/

175. As has been noted throughout the foregoing discussion, most assaults on the environment lead to a deterioration in living conditions and constitute risks for survival if not actually accompanied by deaths directly or indirectly caused by these assaults. In the words of Hr. R.G. Ramcharan:

'Threats to the environment or serious environmental hazards may threaten the lives of large groups of people directly; the connection between the right to life and the environment is an obvious one. A discussion of the interrelationship between the two rights should, however, go beyond this [and] may be summarized in the following proposition: 1. There is a strict duty upon states, as well as upon the international community as a whole, to take effective measures to prevent and safeguard against the occurrence of environmental hazards which threaten the lives of human beings. 2.

Every state, as well as the United Nations (UNEP), should establish and operate adequate monitoring and early-warning systems to detect hazards or threats before they actually occur. 3. States which obtain information about the possible emergence of an environmental hazard to life in another State should inform the State at risk or at least alert UNEP on an urgent basis. 4. The right to life, as an imperative norm, takes priority above economic considerations and should, in all circumstances, be accorded priority. 5. States and other responsible entities (corporations or individuals) may be criminally or civilly responsible under international law for causing serious environmental hazards posing grave risks to life. This responsibility is a strict one, and should arise irrespective of whether the act or omission in question is deliberate, reckless or negligent. 6. Adequate avenues of recourse should be provided to individuals and groups at national, regional or international levels, to seek protection against serious environmental hazards to life. The establishment of such avenues of recourse is essential for dealing with such risks before they actually

[...]

181. The International Covenant on Economic, Social and Cultural Rights recognizes that to achieve the full realization of the right to health it is necessary to ensure the improvement of all aspects of environmental and industrial hygiene. As noted by the Special Rapporteur in her 1992 progress report, the implementation of the right to health contained in the 1961 European Social Charter has led the Committee of Independent Experts to take into account measures to prevent, limit or control pollution. 96/

182. Indigenous peoples have alleged in international forums violations of their right to health as a result of environmental destruction. 97/ In one key case, the Inter-American Commission on Human Rights found that the right to health and well-being of indigenous peoples had been violated as a result of the negative environmental effects and dissemination of disease that followed from road construction in the rainforest. 98/

183. International environmental law instruments have frequently referred to the negative effects on health of environmental pollution. Many of these instruments define pollution as the introduction by man of substances or energy into the environment resulting in such

deleterious effects as hazards to human health or which harm/endanger human health. 99/

184. The right to health can be constructively viewed from an environmental perspective in the light of the principles of sustainable development. Under these principles, another facet of the right to health reaches full meaning: as stated by the World Health organization (WHO), 'human health is essential for sustainable development since without health, human beings would not be able to engage in development, combat poverty and care for their environment'. Thus, there is clear interdependence between health and environmental protection. As WHO points out, 'health status is nearly always the best as well as first indicator of environmental degradation.' 100/

185. Although it was already present in the Stockholm Declaration – and particularly well addressed as a sustainable development issue in the report of the United Nations Conference on Environment and Development – it is important to note the significance of health being part of the first principle of the 1992 Rio Declaration and the multiple references to the protection and promotion of health in Agenda 21, particularly in chapter 6, which deals exclusively with human health.

186. The Special Rapporteur welcomes the increased action taken by Governments and United Nations agencies such as FAO, UNEP and WHO, in preparation for and as a result of UNCED, to address environmental problems and their impact on human health. In particular, she notes the significant amount of documentation provided by WHO and appreciates representatives from this organization meeting with her in a special session to discuss a wide variety of matters regarding the relationship between environmental issues and the right to health. The Special Rapporteur would like to acknowledge some recent initiatives of WHO, such as the report of its Commission on Health and the Environment, *Our Planet, Our Health*, 101/ the comprehensive background paper for the Commission on Sustainable Development (CSD) by the Task Manager on Health, the development of programmes on cities and the environment and on health support systems, and the 'Global Strategy for Health and the Environment'. [...] She also commends the Political Statement and Action Programme environmental and health risks, the right of expression and association to facilitate

collective action, and the recognition of the workers, right to refuse to pollute at the workplace.

194. Numerous conventions concluded under the auspices of the International Labour Organisation (ILO) address many different environmental aspects of occupational health and safety. 105/ Vulnerable groups such as children, indigenous peoples, migrant workers and women suffer disproportionately from violations of the right to safe and healthy working conditions. This underlines the necessity of ratifying the international instruments and improving ways and means by which provisions of these instruments can be fully implemented.

F. Right to housing

195. The fundamental right to adequate housing has both a firm basis in international human rights law and a significant environmental dimension. As noted by Mr. Rajindar Sachar, Special Rapporteur on the right to adequate housing, housing rights involve survival, health and environmental conditions in a holistic and interdependent framework and one which transcends the outdated 'four walls and a roof' view of housing. 106/

196. Agenda 21 parallels Mr. Sachar's holistic view of housing rights and sets an objective of achieving adequate shelter, especially for the poor, through an enabling approach to shelter development and improvement that is environmentally sound.

197. The right to adequate housing is enshrined as a basic human right in article 25(1) of the Universal Declaration of Human Rights, and article 11(1) of the International Covenant on Economic, Social and Cultural Rights. Both instruments describe the right to housing as an essential component of the right to an adequate standard of living. The right to housing also appears in many other international, regional and national legal instruments. 107/

198. The Committee on Economic, Social and Cultural Rights, in its General Comment No. 4 (1991) on the right to housing, explains that the right to housing means, among other things, housing not built on polluted sites or in close proximity to pollution sources that threaten the right to health of inhabitants. 108/ The Committee requires that States parties to the International Convention on Economic, Social

and Cultural Rights include in their reports to the committee information on measures concerning environmental planning and health in housing and human settlements. 109/

199. The right to adequate housing also includes the obligation to avoid forced evictions, a practice that constitutes a gross violation of human rights. 110/ [...] Of particular concern is the fact that States often fail to comply with their obligation not to carry out or advocate forced or arbitrary evictions of persons or groups. Forced evictions should take place only when conservation and rehabilitation are not feasible and suitable relocation measures are undertaken. Where forced evictions cannot be avoided, the affected persons have a right to just compensation.

206. United Nations bodies and specialized agencies frequently have emphasized the importance of information in the area of environment. The Declaration of the United Nations Conference on the Human Environment contains reference to the right to information in Principle 19. The 1972 United Nations Educational, Scientific and Cultural Organization Convention for the Protection of the World Cultural and Natural Heritage 116/ requires States to provide the public with information on dangers to the environment. The World Charter for Nature 117/ also contains provisions relating to information, including paragraph 21(a). Principle 10 of the 1992 Rio Declaration on Environment and Development indicates the duty of States to make information 'widely available'.

207. Several regional organizations have also emphasized the need for information regarding the environment. The League of Arab States proclaimed the Arab Declaration on Environment and Development and Future Perspectives 118/ in which the League stresses the right of persons and groups to relevant information, including technical data. In the European Union several directives and recommendations stress the right to information. The EC Directive on Freedom of Access to Information on the Environment 119/ covers the issue most comprehensively. 120/ Regional environmental treaties also emphasize the right to information, including the affirmative duty to disclose or provide information. For example, the Nordic Convention on the Protection of the Environment 121/ requires the States parties to publish relevant information in the newspapers or other forms of public media; the ASEAN Agreement on the Conservation of Nature and Natural Resources 122/ requires the States parties to disclose and disseminate

relevant information. Certain international treaties, such as the Antarctic Protocol on Environmental Protection, 123/ require States to provide environmental information upon request. Other international treaties impose a duty to warn other States of environmental dangers. 124/

208. Within the United Nations system, reporting requirements and increased dissemination of environmental issues can enhance the right to information. Within the United Nations Environment Programme, for instance, performance reports are requested of Governments and organizations. These reports are available to the public. Other branches of the United Nations system are carrying out initiatives to provide relevant and timely information and education regarding the environment. For example, the Department of Public Information has released Status of World Environment in Mexico, Italy and Japan in the local languages, thereby greatly enhancing international dissemination of this important work. 125/ The General Assembly, in its 11 December 1990 resolution 45/76 entitled 'Questions relating to information', directed the Department of Public Information to pay particular attention to both human rights and the environment in its information activities.

209. The right to information is frequently presented as an individual and group right which constitutes an essential attribute of the democratic processes and the principle of popular participation. Indeed, the concept of democratic government as stated in article 21 of the Universal Declaration of Human Rights becomes meaningless unless individuals and groups have access to relevant information on which to base the exercise of the vote or otherwise express the will of the people.

[...]

information regarding pollutants and wastes associated with industrial and agricultural processes. In these circumstances there is a clear duty to disclose.

215. The right to information not only protects individuals and groups, but also Governments themselves. In this light, the Special Rapporteur is aware that in the context of human rights and the environment, the right to information may also be considered a right of States vis-à-vis other States or of States vis-à-vis transnational corporations. In this context a State's access to information would enable it to transmit the information to its residents and to otherwise protect the human rights of those residents. The Special Rapporteur stresses that the right of

States aspect of the right to information is particularly important regarding the issue of toxic waste disposal, the use of nuclear power and disposal of nuclear wastes, and the production or use of toxics because of the human hazards these matters pose.

216. The Special Rapporteur has reviewed information showing that many conflicts have arisen between Governments because Governments of developed countries, transnational enterprises operating from the developed countries or international development banks do not provide full disclosure of potential dangers to human beings or to the environment for contemplated activities. Under these circumstances, individuals and groups have limited recourses because their own Governments may not have the relevant information.

H. Popular participation

217. The right of popular participation in its various forms ranks high in importance for promoting and protecting human rights and the environment. The basic right to popular participation is provided for in article 21 of the Universal Declaration of Human Rights and a number of international instruments. The United Nations system has long recognized the importance of popular participation in the protection of the environment, especially evident in the 1972 Stockholm Declaration, the 1975 United Nations work on popular participation in development 126/ the 1992 Rio Declaration and Agenda 21, and 1993 Vienna Declaration and Programme of Action.

218. The Special Rapporteur stresses that popular participation is closely related to the rights to education and information: without education about the environment and without access to relevant information on issues of concern, popular participation is meaningless.

219. In the United Nations the issue of popular participation became prominent in the context of the right to development. 127/ After the International Seminar on Popular Participation (Ljubljana, 1982), the issue of popular participation has become an essential feature of a wide range of human rights concerns. The General Assembly asked the Commission on Human Rights to address popular participation in a broader context, 128/ reflected in the Commission's work. 129/ Popular participation is a prominent feature of the World Charter for Nature and the Rio Declaration on Environment and Development (see *supra*, chap. II, sect. C).

220. It is important that participation in the environmental context be meaningful – a question of quality of the participation and whether it is

[...]

I. Freedom of association

224. The right to freedom of association forms a crucial element of effective popular participation in matters that relate to the environment and in general. Article 20 of the Universal Declaration of Human Rights and article 21 of the International Covenant on Civil and Political Rights establish freedom of association and assembly as fundamental human rights. In the environmental context these rights encompass the freedom to associate freely and peacefully with others to protect the environment, to protect the rights of others affected by environmental harm, and to take collective action in support of environmental causes.

225. As noted in chapter 29 of Agenda 21, freedom of association has particular relevance in the case of workers. The right to organize plays a critical role in workers' ability to protect and enforce their right to environmental health and safety on the job. outside of the trade union context, the right to association, in conjunction with the right to freedom of expression, is possible for groups of individuals, such as non-governmental organizations, to mobilize the human and financial resources necessary to effectively address environmental problems (see chap. 27 of Agenda 21).

J. Cultural rights

226. The relationship between the deterioration of the environment and the enjoyment of cultural rights has several dimensions, indissolubly linked to the fundamental rights to education, information, freedom of expression, assembly and association, and the right to take part in public life and in decision-making. Cultural rights may equally well be considered from the standpoint of the right to leisure, provided for in a number of international human rights instruments, which leads to the right to the conservation of unique sites constituting the universal heritage.

227. Nearly 20 years ago, the Director-General of UNESCO made the following reflection on the relationship between culture and man's environment: 132/

'The deterioration of the natural environment and, even more, the alienation from this environment of an increasingly large number of people in the industrialized countries are direct and potentially very serious blows to culture itself. What idea can man form of purity unless he initially receives a spontaneous impression of purity from the air he breathes, the river where he bathes, the sky on which he gazes or from all that goes to make up his life at its most instinctive? What secrets can he hear murmured within him if silence without is denied to him? How can he meditate amid tumult? How can he find himself in a continual flux of movement without pattern? And to what discoveries can he direct his steps outside himself, what marvels can he look for in a world where so many animal species are vanishing, where plant life is retreating further and further from our dwellings, and where man is increasingly confronted with the products and the signs of his oppressive presence?'

228. The importance of protecting cultural property and the specific role of UNESCO in this sphere may be recalled at this point. The constitution of

[...]

234. In this context, development models which are extroverted or exclusively growth-oriented, carry the risk of acculturation, or even endangering cultures closely linked to a form of existence of national, ethnic, religious or linguistic minorities or of indigenous peoples. While the Special Rapporteur is aware of the fact that traditional practices which run counter to progress and affect human rights should be eradicated, she also considers that sustainable development only has a real sense in so far as it takes account of the aspirations of the individuals, groups and peoples concerned, and preserves their cultural identity and their means of existence.

[...]

satisfactory environment, entailing corresponding duties towards the State and its institutions and rights and/or obligations for individuals and organs of society. An increasing number of national legislations have developed the framework of laws and regulations needed to ensure the right to a satisfactory environment and have spelt out the substantive content of that right and the ways and means whereby it may be exercised, including remedies to safeguard its effective enjoyment and afford guarantees for its implementation. A few constitutions provide, in the section dealing with human rights and fundamental freedoms, for the right to a healthy environment and the guarantees attaching thereto, including in some cases the right of recourse and petition. Some countries have provided for the punishment of offences against the environment and have introduced into national legislation the principle of compensation for the victims as well as reparation of the damage. There is moreover a trend towards developing and strengthening the means of preventing damage to the environment.

242. At the regional and universal level, recognition of the right to a satisfactory environment as a human right is reflected both in the related normative developments and in the 'environmental' concern that informs the activities of human rights bodies. Although only a few instruments of a binding legal character have established a direct link between the environment and human rights, the regional and international human rights bodies are developing a practice whereby the procedural bases for enforcing the right to a satisfactory environment are becoming more firmly established and the validity of complaints of human rights violations based on ecological considerations is being recognized. These bodies do not dismiss out of hand the idea that ecological factors may hinder the enjoyment of the human rights enshrined in the instruments in their care. On the other hand, those same bodies and more particularly the European Court of Human Rights have, in certain cases, legitimated restrictions on the use of private property in the public interest based on concern for the need to preserve the environment.

243. This review of the activities of human rights bodies and other fields relevant for the study has made it possible to outline the scope of environmental rights. Many human rights are suited to being applied from an ecological perspective, whether those rights are political, civil, social, economic or cultural, and whether they are exercised individually or collectively. The Special Rapporteur has drawn up a list of those rights, albeit a non-exhaustive one and has attempted to assess the effects of the environment or enjoyment of those rights.

244. Her analysis of the ways in which the right to a satisfactory environment relates to other human rights gave the Special Rapporteur occasion to stress the close link existing between that right

and the right to development. The fact in that the affirmation of 'ecological rights' attaching to recognition of the right to a satisfactory environment cannot be understood if we disregard the problems bound up with development both nationally and internationally. It also rests on the indivisibility and interdependence of all human rights.

245. In this context, it is important to bear in mind the consensual aspects which form the basis of the world partnership for sustainable development and serve to reaffirm the principle of the right of peoples to self-determination, hazards. She stresses the need for effective protection of their rights and calls for the rapid adoption of the draft declaration finalized by the Working Group on Indigenous Populations.

251. Conversely, human rights violations in their turn damage the environment. This is true of the right of peoples to self-determination and their right to dispose of their wealth and natural resources, the right to development, to participation, to work and to information, the right of peaceful assembly, freedom of association, freedom of expression, etc.

[...]

252. In the light of the foregoing, the Special Rapporteur is of the view that effective implementation of the right to a satisfactory environment cannot be dissociated from the twinned efforts to preserve the environment and ensure the right to development. Nor can it be achieved without resolute action to ensure the enjoyment of all human rights.

253. in order to give practical expression to the right to a satisfactory environment, there is a need for development strategies that are directed towards the implementation of a substantive part of that right (the right to development, to life, to health, to work, etc.). These must go hand in hand with the promotion of the related procedural aspects (due process, right of association and of assembly, freedom of expression, right of recourse, etc.

254. Implementation of the right to a satisfactory environment calls for commitment and participation on the part of everyone at all levels, beginning with the family unit, where environmental education starts.

It depends on the existence of effective national legal remedies; local administrative or other courts, national institutions and ombudsmen provide guarantees of the protection of this right. The Special Rapporteur notes with satisfaction the development of such recourse guarantees in many countries.

255. The right to a satisfactory environment is also a right to prevention which gives a new dimension to the right to information, education and participation in decision-making. The right to restitution, indemnification, compensation and rehabilitation for victims must also be seen from the angle of the special responsibility that would follow from the absence of preventive measures.

256. The right to a satisfactory environment is also a right to the 'conservation' of nature for the benefit of future generations. This 'futuristic' dimension restores to human rights their original purpose, as embodied in the Charter of the United Nations and the Universal Declaration of Human Rights of 1948. It foreshadows a 'new public order' of human rights which would set acceptable limitations on those rights in the general interest while entailing corresponding duties on the part both of the public authorities and of individuals, associations and other components of civil society.

257. To conclude her study, the Special Rapporteur wishes to cite the argument of Mr. A. Kiss that international law must be based on values, the fundamental values of this century being human rights and the environment. She shares this view and notes that these values are intrinsically bound up with development seen as a world-wide phenomenon resting on various pillars such as

[...]

(e) Human Rights Committee. The Committee could expand its general comment on the right to life in order to include environmental concerns or formulate a general comment defining the links existing between civil and political rights and the environment. Moreover, it should be able, through dealing with complaints, to establish case law that will accommodate environmental concerns;

(f) Working Group on the right to development: environment, debt and development; development, environment and the funding

institutions; participation by the people in activities for development and the environment, structural adjustment programmes, impact on the environment and underprivileged populations and groups;

(g) Working Group entrusted with the preparation of a declaration on the right and responsibility of individuals, groups and organs of society to promote and protect universally recognized human rights and fundamental freedoms. The group could contemplate the inclusion of specific provisions relating to rights and duties in respect of the preservation of the environment;

(h) The working groups, special rapporteurs on thematic questions and country rapporteurs could also, within the areas covered by their mandates, consider the impact of the environment on the enjoyment of human rights and possible measures for correcting situations where rights violations have been observed and help the victims to incorporate them into their rights, particularly with regard to restitution, compensation or rehabilitation.

[...]

260. The interest shown in the impact of the environment on the enjoyment of human rights means that human rights bodies are already in demand and are increasingly being called on to pronounce on the question. In order to avoid disparate practices and to promote the development of an overall, integrated and co-ordinated view in the approach to the various phenomena which will be dealt with in an inevitably sectional way by existing bodies, given their respective areas of competence, it is suggested that:

A co-ordination centre should be set up to deal with the question within the United Nations Centre for Human Rights;

A special rapporteur of the Commission on Human Rights should be appointed with a mandate similar to that generally given to special rapporteurs on thematic questions;

A seminar should be held under the auspices of the Centre for Human Rights to help formulate practical recommendations on the way in which the right to a satisfactory environment could be rationally incorporated into the activities of human rights bodies.

261 In submitting the draft declaration of principles on human rights and the environment contained in the annex to this report to the Sub-Commission on Prevention of Discrimination and Protection of Minorities and the Commission on Human Rights, the Special Rapporteur expresses the hope that the draft will help the United Nations to adopt, in the course of the present United Nations.

[...]

11/ Brundtland Report, 'Our Common Future', UNEP/GC.14/13,

12/ Report of the South Commission, 'The Challenge to the South', 1990, Economica, p. 228.

13/ 'World Development Report 1992', World Bank, Washington 1992, p. 103.

14/ 'Human Development Report 1993', Paris, Economica, data taken from box 1.2, p. 12.

15/ Mohammed Sahnoun, op. cit.

16/ E/CN.4/Sub.2/1992/16, para. 118, p. 32.

17/ E/CN.4/Sub.2/1991/17, pp. 36–50, especially paras. 124–166.

18/ EURODAD, 'Target 92', 1991, p. 16.

19/ 'The realization of the right to development', Consultation, Geneva, 8–12 January 1990, HR/PUB/91/2, 1991, para. 166, p. 48.

20/ See E/CN.4/Sub.2/1992/7/Add.1 and E/CN.4/Sub.2/1993/7.

21/ A/CONF.151/PC/100/Add.l, para. 3.

22/ A/CONF.151/4 (Part III), chap. 23, paras. 23.1 and 23.2.

23/ Ibid.

24/ A/CONF.157.23, Sect. I, para. 8.

25/ E/CN.4/Sub.2/1990/12, para. 33 and note 9; E/CN.4/Sub.2/1991/8, paras. 23–30; E/CN.4/Sub.2/1992/7, paras. 19, 94–95, 99; E/CN.4/Sub.2/1992/7/Add.l;

E/CN.4/Sub.2/1993/7, paras. 29–32, 69, 89–90, 126.

26/ Cited in Mario Ibarra, 'Traditional practices in respect of the sustainable and environmentally sound self-development of Indigenous people' (E/CN.4/Sub.2/ 1992/31/Add.1), para. 94.

27/ J. Uranavi, Statement on behalf of the International Work Group for Indigenous Affairs, 1985.

28/ E/CN.4/1989/22, annex III C, para. 3.

29/ Ibid., annex III A, pp. 27–28.

[...]

46/ Decision of the Third Agrarian Court of the District of Antioquia, Colombia (24 February 1993).

47/ Supreme Court Reports of 31 May 1990.

48/ Reports of a 1994 session in New Mexico, USA, and a 1993 session in Gland, Switzerland, are available from the IUCN World Conservation Union.

49/ See A/481269, sect. II.

50/ Letter DDN/JUR/B9/1405 AAB/VR of 29 December 1989.

51/ Above-mentioned reply to the Special Rapporteur and document DOM/DIRHPG/AAB/RAF entitled 'Protection of the natural environment in time of armed conflict: an overview of the state of international humanitarian law and of the position of the International Committee of the Red Cross', Geneva, 7 August 1991.

52/ See in particular:

Antoine Bouvier, 'La protection de l environment naturel en periode de conflit armé', *Revue internationale de la Croix-Rouge,* No. 792, 1991;

Philippe Antoine, 'Droit international humanitaire et protection de l environnement en cas de conflict armé'; Adams Roberts 'La destruction de l environnement pendant la guerre du Golfe de 1991'; and Antoine Bouvier 'Travaux recents relatifs & la protection de l environnement en periode de conflit armé', *Revue internationale de la Croix-Rouge,* No. 798, 1992;

Ksentini F. Zohra, 'Droit internationale humanitaire et protection des populations, de leurs biens et de l'environnement', *Revue algerienne des relations internationales,* No. 23, 1993.

53/ E/CN.4/Sub.2/1990/12, para. 5, and E/CN.4/Sub.2/1993/7, paras. 113–115.

54/ See in particular the Charter of the United Nations, Articles 1, 2, 55 and 56.

55/ General Assembly resolution 3384 (XXX) of 10 November 1975.

56/ General Assembly resolution 39111 of 12 November 1984.

57/ Work on this topic began in 1978. Mr. Robert Quentin-Baxter was Special Rapporteur from 1978 until 1985. In 1985, Hr. Julio Barboza was appointed Special Rapporteur.

58/ E/1994/16.

[...]

73/ E/CN.6/1990/2, subsequently published under the title Women in Politics and Decision-making in the Late Twentieth Century – A United Nations Study, Martinus Nijhof publishers, 1992.

74/ UNICEF, *The state of the world's children* 1994.

75/ See the reports of the Sub-Commission's Working Group on Contemporary Forms of Slavery.

76/ UNICEF, op. cit. See also: UNICEF and UNEP, 1990: *Children and the environment,* UKEP, Nairobi and UNICEF, New York; UNICEF, 1989: *Children and environment: a UNICEF strategy for sustainable development,* document for the 1989 Executive Board session (E/ICEF/1989/L.6); Report of the symposium 'women and children first', Geneva, 27–30 May 1991, organized under the auspices of UNCED, UNFPA, the Government of Denmark and UNICEF.

77/ Study by Mr. Leandro Despouy, Special Rapporteur of the Sub-Commission, United Nations, 1993 (United Nations publication, Sales No. E.92.XIV).

78/ Extract from a speech given by the Deputy Chairperson of Disabled Peoples' International, Mr. Kalle Konkkola, at the symposium on Environment and Disability, Rio de Janeiro, June 1992.

79/ See E/CN.4/Sub.2/1993/7, paras. 101–106.

80/ The Convention relating to the Status of Refugees, which entered into force on 22 April 1954, defines a refugee as 'one who flees his country of origin due to a well-founded fear of being persecuted for reasons of race, religion, nationality, membership of a particular social group or political opinion'.

81/ The Protocol relating to the Status of Refugees, which entered into force on 4 October 1967, incorporates the Convention definition of refugee without restrictions as to date or geography.

82/ The OAU Convention governing the Specific Aspects of Refugee Problems in Africa of 10 September 1969 states that the term 'refugee' includes 'every person who flees his or her country of origin owing to external aggression, occupation, foreign domination, or events seriously disturbing public order'.

83/ The Cartagena Declaration on Refugees of 22 November 1984 defines refugees as 'persons who have fled their country because their lives, safety or freedom have been threatened by generalized violence, foreign aggression, international conflicts, massive violations of human rights or other circumstances which have disturbed the public order'.

84/ See *The State of the World's Refugees: The Challenge of Protection* UNHCR, Penguin Books, 1993.

[...]

Convention for Cooperation in the Protection and Development of the Marine and Coastal Environment of the West and Central African Region, art. 2 (Abidjan, 1981); United Nations Convention on the Law of the Sea, art. 1 (4) (1982).

100/ See background paper on 'Health, the Environment and Sustainable Development', prepared for the commission on Sustainable Development by the World Health Organization, Task Manager on Health, March 1994, p. 1.

101/ See E/CN.4/Sub.2/1993/7, para. 98.

102/ Conference held in Noordwijk, The Netherlands, 22–23 March 1994. See E/CN.17/1994/12.

103/ See WHO background paper cited at note 95 *supra*.

104 See Asbjorn Eide, *Right to Adequate Food as a Human Right,* Study Series No. 1, United Nations publication, Sales No. E.89.XIV.2, 1989.

105/ Some of the most significant ones are the Chemicals Convention (No. 170, 1990); the Safety and Health in Construction Convention (No. 167, 1988); the Asbestos Convention (No. 162, 1986); Occupational Safety and Health Convention (No. 155, 1981) the Working Environment (Air Pollution, Noise and Vibration) Convention (No. 148, 1977); the Occupational Cancer Convention (No. 139, 1974); and the Benzene Convention (No. 136, 1971).

106/ See E/CN.4/Sub.2/1993/15, section II.

107/ See E/CN.4/Sub.2/1992/15, paras. 62–65.

108/ E/1992/23-E/C.12/1991/4, annex III. The Special Rapporteur on the right to adequate housing shares the Committee's views in this regard. See E/CN.4/Sub.2/1993/15, para. 90.

109/ Revised guidelines regarding the form and contents of reports to be submitted by States Parties under arts. 16 and 17 of the International Covenant on Economic, Social and Cultural Rights (E/1991/23-E/C.12/1990/8, annex IV). The Committee's Guidelines on State reporting and its General Comment No. 4 stand as useful examples of how the United Nations and the international community as a whole might explicate the meaning of other human rights and enhance compliance with those rights.

110/ See EICN.4/Sub.2/1992/15, para. 41; Commission on Human Rights resolution 1993/77 of 10 March 1993; analytical report of the Secretary-General on the practice of forced evictions (E/CN.4/1994/20).

111/ See the reports of the independent expert of the Commission on the right of everyone to own property, Hr. Luis Valencia Rodriguez (EICN.4/1994/19 and Add.1 and E/CN.4/1993/15).

[...]

127/ See, in particular, the United Nations Declaration on Social Progress and Development, General Assembly resolution 2542 (XXIV) of 11 December 1969, calling for Governments to adopt measures for participation of all elements of society in social and economic development schemes.

128/ General Assembly resolution 37/55 of 3 December 1982.

129/ See, for example, E/CN.4/1985/10 and Add.1 and 2; E/CN.4/1991/11.

130/ UNEPZ/Ser.A/9 (1989).

131/ The Special Rapporteur has analysed many cases brought before national courts, European human rights bodies, the Inter-American Commission on Human Rights and United Nations human rights bodies. See E/CN.4/Sub.2/1992/7 and E/CN.4/Sub.2/1993/7.

132/ Report of the Secretary-General: 'The balance which should be established between scientific and technological progress and the intellectual, spiritual, cultural and moral advancement of humanity' (E/CN.4/1199), thirty-second session of the Commission on Human Rights, 1976, p. 37.

133/ Proclaimed by the General Conference of UNESCO at its fortieth session, on 4 November 1966. See 'A Compilation of International Instruments', United Nations, Sales No. E.93.XIV.1, pp. 591–594.

Annex II

[...]

2. All persons have the right to a secure, healthy and ecologically sound environment. This right and other human rights, including civil, cultural, economic, political and social rights, are universal, interdependent and indivisible.

3. All persons shall be free from any form of discrimination in regard to actions and decisions that affect the environment.

4. All persons have the right to an environment adequate to meet equitably the needs of present generations and that does not impair the rights of future generations to meet equitably their needs.

Part II (of the Ksentini Report)

5. All persons have the right to freedom from pollution, environmental degradation and activities that adversely affect the environment, threaten life, health, livelihood, well-being or sustainable development within, across or outside national boundaries.

6. All persons have the right to protection and preservation of the air, soil, water, sea-ice, flora and fauna, and the essential processes and areas necessary to maintain biological diversity and ecosystems.

7. All persons have the right to the highest attainable standard of health free from environmental harm.
8. All persons have the right to safe and healthy food and water adequate to their well-being.

9. All persons have the right to a safe and healthy working environment.

10. All persons have the right to adequate housing, land tenure and living conditions in a secure, healthy and ecologically sound environment.

11. (a) All persons have the right not to be evicted from their homes or land for the purpose of, or as a consequence of, decisions or actions affecting the environment, except in emergencies or due to a compelling purpose benefiting society as a whole and not attainable by other means.

11. (b) All persons have the right to participate effectively in decisions and to negotiate concerning their eviction and the right, if evicted, to timely and adequate restitution, compensation and/or appropriate and sufficient accommodation or land.

12. All persons have the right to timely assistance in the event of natural or technological or other human-caused catastrophes.

13. Everyone has the right to benefit equitably from the conservation and sustainable use of nature and natural resources for cultural, ecological, educational, health, livelihood, recreational, spiritual and other purposes.
This includes ecologically sound access to nature.

Collection and dissemination of information concerning the environment;

Prior assessment and control, licensing, regulation or prohibition of activities and substances potentially harmful to the environment;

Public participation in environmental decision-making;

Effective administrative and judicial remedies and redress for environmental harm or the threat of such harm;

Monitoring, management and equitable sharing of natural resources;

measures to reduce wasteful processes of production and patterns of consumption;

Measures aimed at ensuring that transnational corporations, wherever they operate, carry out their duties of environmental protection, sustainable development and respect for human rights; and

Measures aimed at ensuring that the international organizations and agencies to which they belong observe the rights and duties in this Declaration.

[...]

23. States and all other parties shall avoid using the environment as a means of war or inflicting significant, long-term or widespread harm on the environment, and shall respect international law providing protection for the environment in times of armed conflict and cooperate in its further development.

24. All international organizations and agencies shall observe the rights and duties in this Declaration.

Part V

25. In implementing the rights and duties in this Declaration, special attention shall be given to vulnerable persons and groups.

26. The rights in this Declaration may be subject only to restrictions provided by law and which are necessary to protect public order, health and the fundamental rights and freedoms of others.

27. All persons are entitled to a social and international order in which the rights in this Declaration can be fully realized.

[...]

(b) The lack of timely and relevant information about projects with severe environmental impacts;

(c) The imbalance between the resources available to groups interested in protecting human rights and the environment and the resources available to Governments and/or multinational enterprises;

(d) The human rights and environmental implications of large-scale disasters;

(e) The forced relocation of indigenous peoples and the subsequent ecological ruin of their traditional lands and sacred sites;

(f) The insufficient attention paid by international financial institutions to the special environmental needs of indigenous peoples and other vulnerable groups.

28. Following the Special Rapporteur's recommendation, contained in her 1993 report, that the Centre for Human Rights should convene an expert meeting on human rights and the environment, the Sub-Commission on Prevention of Discrimination and Protection of Minorities, in its resolution 1993/32 of 25 August 1993, invited the Secretary-General to organize such a meeting. Due to serious budgetary problems, the Secretary-General was unable to do so. However, the Sierra Club Legal Defense Fund, in association with the societé suisse pour la protection de l'environnement and the Association mondiale pour l'école instrument de paix, did sponsor the meeting, with the Centre for Human Rights providing the facilities and staff.

29. The Expert Meeting on Human Rights and the environment was held from 15 to 19 May 1994 at Geneva.

[...]

Annex III (of the Ksentini Report)

DEVELOPMENTS IN NATIONAL LEGISLATION AND PRACTICES

A. Summary of Constitutional Provisions

In her two progress reports in 1992 (E/CN.4/Sub.2/1992/7 and Add.1) and in her report of 1993 (E/CN.4/Sub.2/1993/7), the Special Rapporteur noted that many countries had devoted constitutional provisions to the environment. The information reproduced below comprises the data included in the previous reports and those recently communicated to the Special Rapporteur.

1. Afghanistan

The 1990 Constitution proclaims that 'the State shall adopt and implement the necessary measures for the protection of nature, natural wealth and reasonable utilization of natural resources, improvement of the living environment, prevention of pollution of water and air, and the conservation and survival of animals and plants' (chap. II, art. 32).

2. South Africa

The constitution of South Africa, which came into force on 27 April 1994, stipulates that 'Every person shall have the right to an environment which is not detrimental to his or her health or well-being' (sect. 29).

3. Albania

The 1976 Constitution stipulates that 'protection of the land, natural riches, waters and the atmosphere from damage and pollution is a duty of the state, of economic and social organizations and of all citizens' (chap. 1B, art. 20).

4. Algeria

The revised Constitution of 1989 stipulates, in essence, that every citizen has a duty to protect public property and the interests of the national community and to respect the property of others. Under article 17, public property encompasses the various components of the ecosystem (title I, chap. III, art. 63).

5. Germany

It is the responsibility of the legislature to protect the natural bases of man's existence, with due regard for prevention, the 'polluter-pays' principle and cooperation, and to promote uniform ecological conditions of a high standard (text of 1990 supplementing the Basic Law, chap. VII, art. 34).

6. Angola

The 1992 Constitution stipulates that 'the Government of Angola shall seek to protect and preserve the unique environmental heritage of Angola in order to ensure the quality of the human environment for all' (art. IX).

10. Bulgaria

The 1991 Constitution provides that 'Bulgaria shall ensure the protection and conservation of the environment, the sustenance of animals and the maintenance of their diversity, and the rational use of natural resources', and that while 'citizens have the right to a healthy and favourable environment they [also] have an obligation to protect the environment' (chap. II, art. 31).

11. Burkina Faso

The 1991 Constitution provides for 'the right to a healthy environment' and stipulates that 'the protection, defence and promotion of the environment shall be the duty of all' (title I, arts. 30 and 31).

12. Chile

The 1980 Constitution guarantees everyone 'the right to live in an environment free from contamination. It is the duty of the State to watch over the protection of this right and the preservation of the environment' (art.19 (8). An appeal may be lodged to ensure observance of these provisions.

13. China

The 1982 Constitution stipulates that 'the State shall protect and improve the living environment and the ecological environment, and prevent and remedy pollution and other public hazards'. It also ensures the rational use of natural resources and protects rare animals and plants (chap. I, arts. 9 and 26).

14. Colombia

The 1991 Constitution obliges the government authorities and the people to protect the cultural and natural assets of the nation. It establishes a link between public health and protection of the environment (arts. 8, 49, 79).

15. Korea

The 1987 Constitution proclaims that 'All citizens have the right to a healthy and pleasant environment. The State and all citizens shall endeavour to protect the environment' (chap. II, art. 35).

16. Cuba

The amended 1992 Constitution provides, in essence, that the State shall protect the environment and the country's natural resources, over which it shall exercise sovereignty. The State also recognizes the close link between the environment and sustainable economic and social development, which ensures the survival, well-being and security of present and future generations. Citizens also have a duty to contribute to the protection of nature's rich potential (arts. 11(b) and 27).

[...]

25. Equatorial Guinea

The 1982 Constitution stipulates that the State recognizes the right to the protection of health (title VI. chap. II, art. 60).

26. Guyana

The 1980 Constitution obliges every citizen to participate in activities to improve the environment and protect the health of the nation. In addition, the interests of present and future generations are taken into account, and the use of natural resources must be rational (arts. 25 and 36).

27. Haiti

The 1987 Constitution imposes on citizens the civic duty 'to respect and protect the environment'. 'Practices that are liable to disturb the ecological balance are strictly prohibited', as is the importation of 'wastes or residues from foreign sources' (title XI, chap. II, arts. 253 and 258).

28. Honduras

The 1982 Constitution stipulates that 'the State shall maintain a satisfactory environment for the protection of the health of all' (chap.VII, art.145).

29. Hungary

The revised constitution of 1990 'recognizes and enforces the right of everyone to a healthy environment'. Physical and mental health, safety in the workplace and the provision of medical care are further rights recognized by the Constitution (chap. I, sect. 18, and chap. XII, sect. 70/D).

30. India

The 1977 Constitution, as amended in 1985, provides that 'The State shall endeavour to protect and improve the environment and to safeguard the forests and wildlife' and makes it the duty of every citizen 'to protect and improve the natural environment' (part IV, arts. 48 A and 51 A).

31. Islamic Republic of Iran

The 1980 Constitution institutes the protection of the environment in which the present and future generations must live as a public responsibility. Economic or other activities which pollute the environment are prohibited (chap. IV, art. 50).

32. Malta

The 1964 constitution stipulates that 'The state shall safeguard the landscape and the historical and artistic patrimony of the Nation' (chap. II., art. 9).

39. Nigeria

The 1979 Constitution stipulates that 'exploitation of human or natural resources for reasons other than the good of the community shall be prohibited' (chap. II, art. 18).

40. Panama

The 1980 Constitution provides that 'it is a fundamental duty of the State to see to the preservation of ecological conditions and to prevent pollution of the environment and imbalance in ecosystems, with a view to ensuring economic and social development' (chap. VI, art. 110).

41. Papua New Guinea

The 1984 Constitution defines the fourth goal of the State as the conservation of the environment and the rational use of natural resources 'for the benefit of future generations'. In this respect, 'all persons have the basic obligation to protect [the country] and to safeguard the national wealth, resources and environment' (chap. IV).

42. Paraguay

The 1967 Constitution provides that 'The State shall conserve the forestry resources of the country, as well as other renewable natural resources'(chap VI, art. 132)

43. Netherlands

The 1989 Constitution accords priority to any action by the State to promote the 'distribution of wealth', regional planning, and the protection and improvement of the environment (art. 20).

44. Peru

The 1979 Constitution provides that 'Everyone has the right to live in a healthy environment' and that 'It is the obligation of the State to prevent and control environmental pollution'. It also recognizes that natural resources are the patrimony of the nation (chap. II, arts. 118 and 123).

45. Philippines

The 1986 Constitution protects exclusively the country's marine wealth and the rights of its fishermen (art. XII, sects. 2 and 7).

46. Poland

The 1989 Constitution provides that citizens have the right to a natural environment and the duty to protect it (chap. VIII, art. 71).

[...]

54. Sweden

The 1975 Constitution, as amended in 1978, provides that 'it shall be incumbent on the community to guarantee the right to work, housing and education, and to promote social care and security, as well as a favourable living environment' (chap. I, art. 2, para. 2).

55. Taiwan

The 1947 Constitution provides that the State shall foster, *inter alia*, the development of 'water conservancy' and 'public health', and protect the land and assist in its development (chap. XIII, sect. 6, art. 169).

56. Tanzania

The 1984 Constitution calls for guarantees that natural resources will be preserved, developed and used for the benefit of all citizens. It also provides that 'everyone has the responsibility of conserving natural resources' (sect. 2, paras. 9.1 and 27.1).

57. Chad

Under the 1989 Constitution, one of the fundamental responsibilities of the State is 'to preserve the environment and natural resources' (art. 1).

58. Thailand

The 1978 Constitution stipulates that 'The State shall preserve the environmental balance and eliminate pollution, which jeopardizes the health and hygiene of the people', and 'shall have an appropriate demographic policy' (chap. V, arts. 65 and 69).

59. Turkey

The 1982 Constitution stipulates that every person has the right to live in a healthy, balanced environment. It is the duty of the State to protect the environment (chap. VIII, sect. A, art. 56).

60. Vanuatu

The 1980 Constitution stipulates that every person has the duty 'to protect (Vanuatu) and to safeguard the national wealth, resources and the environment in the interests of the present generation and future generations' (title II, chap. II, art. 7).

61. Viet Nam

The 1980 Constitution provides that all the wealth and natural resources of the State are the property of the people and that everyone has the duty to protect and improve the environment (chap. 2, arts. 19, 20 and 36).

'considering the requirements and criteria established under the regulations referred to in section 10 hereof, the Department shall distinguish such factories and workshops that contribute to the pollution of the environment, and shall give the owners or managers thereof notice either to do away with the causes of the pollution within a definite period of time or to discontinue operation (...). In the event that any person concerned should object to such notice he may lodge a complaint with the local court of first instance.'

7. Nepal

Following the United Nations Conference on Environment and Development, the Government of Nepal implemented numerous measures for the protection of the environment. In 1993, the Government adopted the *National Environmental Impact Assessment Guidelines as part of a general policy to promote an integrated approach to the environment and development.

8. Romania

Draft legislation on the protection of the environment provides that the State recognizes the right of everyone to a healthy environment. It sets out a list of measures to be taken by the State to ensure the effective enjoyment of this right.

C. Summary of new domestic cases

For those previously analysed by the Special Rapporteur, please see documents E/CN.4/Sub.2/1992/7 and E/CN.4/Sub.2/1993/7.

1. Canada

In *Regina v. Sparrow*, the Canadian Supreme Court recognized the existence of aboriginal rights and delineated a test to determine whether there had been a 'prima facie' infringement of those rights. The appellant, a member of the Musqueam Band, was charged with fishing with a drift net longer than that permitted by his Band's food fishing licence. The court held that the Constitution Act, 1982 S 35 (1), which recognizes and affirms existing aboriginal rights, requires that any regulation infringing upon indigenous rights must be justified by a valid objective consistent with the Government's fiduciary duty toward the aboriginal peoples. Parties challenging legislation as a prima facie infringement of indigenous rights must show: (i) that the limitation is unreasonable; (ii) that the regulation imposes an undue burden; and (iii) that it denies the holders their preferred means of exercising that right. The Court found the Government's public interest objective to be so vague as to provide no meaningful guidance and so broad as to be unworkable. It allowed the objective of conservation and resource management, however, as consistent with aboriginal beliefs, practices and rights. If on remand it was found that there had been an infringement, indigenous groups would enjoy priority allocation over other commercial and consumer groups after legitimate conservation needs had been met.

For Product Safety Concerns and Information please contact our EU representative GPSR@taylorandfrancis.com Taylor & Francis Verlag GmbH, Kaufingerstraße 24, 80331 München, Germany

Batch number: 10726007

Printed by Printforce, the Netherlands